Adolescence and Individuality

Judith E. Gallatin

Eastern Michigan University

Adolescence and Individuality
A Conceptual Approach to Adolescent Psychology

Harper & Row, Publishers

New York, Evanston, San Francisco, London

Sponsoring Editor: George A. Middendorf
Project Editor: Robert Ginsberg
Designer: Andrea Clark
Production Supervisor: Will C. Jomarrón

Adolescence and Individuality: A Conceptual Approach
to Adolescent Psychology

Library of Congress Cataloging in Publication Data
Gallatin, Judith E   1942-
    Adolescence and individuality.
    1. Adolescent psychology.   I. Title.
[DNLM: 1. Adolescent psychology. 2. Personality.
WS462 G164a]
BF724.G323   1975   155.5   74-17355
ISBN 0-06-042227-0

To my parents and grandparents, who will
no doubt always consider me an adolescent,
and to C., who reserves judgment.

Contents

Acknowledgments

Grateful acknowledgment is hereby made for permission to quote from the following works.

Joseph Adelson. "What Generation Gap?" *New York Times Magazine*, 18 January 1970. Copyright © 1970 by The New York Times Company. Reprinted by permission.

Jeanne Block. "Conceptions of Sex-Role: Some Cross-Cultural and Longitudinal Perspectives." *American Psychologist*, 28 (June 1973): 512-526. Copyright © 1973 by the American Psychological Association. Reprinted by permission.

Henry Borow. "The Development of Occupational Motives and Roles." *Review of Child Development Research*, vol. 2, Lois Wladis Hoffman and Martin L. Hoffman, eds. New York: Russell Sage, 1966. Copyright © 1966 by Russell Sage Foundation, New York.

Elizabeth Douvan and Joseph Adelson. *The Adolescent Experience.* New York: Wiley, 1966. Copyright © 1966 by John Wiley & Sons, Inc. Reprinted by permission of John Wiley & Sons, Inc.

Erik H. Erikson. *Identity: Youth and Crisis.* New York: Norton, 1968. Copyright © 1968 by W. W. Norton & Company, Inc. Reprinted by permission of W. W. Norton & Company, Inc., and Faber and Faber Ltd.

Anna Freud. "Adolescence." *The Psychoanalytic Study of the Child*, 13 (1958).

Anna Freud. "The Ego and Mechanisms of Defense." *The Writings of Anna Freud*, vol. 2. New York: International Universities Press, 1936. Copyright © 1966 by International Universities Press, Inc. By permission of Mark Paterson and International Universities Press, Inc.

G. Stanley Hall. *Adolescence*, vols. 1, 2. New York: Appleton-Century-Crofts, 1904.

Stuart Hauser. "Black and White Identity Development: Aspects and Perspectives." *Journal of Youth and Adolescence*, 1 (1972): 113-130. By permission of Plenum Publishing Corp.

Jerry Jacobs. *Adolescent Suicide*. New York: Wiley, 1971. Copyright © 1971 by John Wiley & Sons, Inc. Reprinted by permission of John Wiley & Sons, Inc.

Alberto Moravia. "Luca." *Two Adolescents*, trans. Angus Davidson. New York: Farrar, Straus & Giroux, 1950. By permission of Farrar, Straus & Giroux, Casa Editrice Valentino Bompiani, and Martin Secker & Warburg Limited.

Daniel Offer. *The Psychological World of the Teenager*. New York: Basic Books, 1969. Copyright © 1969 by Daniel Offer.

F. Paul Pearsall. "Effective Sexual Communication." By permission of the author.

Jean Piaget. *Six Psychological Studies*, David Elkind, ed. New York: Random House, 1967. Reprinted by permission of Random House, Inc., and The University of London Press.

Harry Stack Sullivan. *The Interpersonal Theory of Psychiatry*, Helen Swick Perry and Mary Ladd Gawel, eds. New York: Norton, 1953. Copyright 1953 by The William Alanson White Psychiatric Foundation.

Irving Weiner. *Psychological Disturbance in Adolescence*. New York: Wiley, 1970. Copyright © 1970 by John Wiley & Sons, Inc. Reprinted by permission of John Wiley & Sons, Inc.

Preface

The last thing we discover in writing a book is what to put first.

Blaise Pascal, Pensées

This book was inspired by a casual conversation several years ago. Fresh out of graduate school and assigned to teach the psychology of adolescence, my colleague Carol Guardo and I were commiserating with each other about the lack of an adequate textbook. There simply did not seem to be a book which offered quite what we were looking for. We both wanted a book that would address itself to the significant issues in the field, one that would coordinate theories of adolescence with research on the subject and yet remain down to earth and readable. So we decided to try writing it ourselves. The result, after not quite five years of research, reviewing, and revising, is *Adolescence and Individuality*. When our respective careers separated us by a thousand miles, it became more convenient for me to assume responsibility for writing the text, while Professor Guardo assumed responsibility for preparation of the accompanying book of readings, *The Adolescent as Individual: Issues and Insights*. I remain deeply grateful to Prof. Guardo for her contributions and suggestions in preparation of the text.

My overall objective has been to provide an integrated and coherent account of adolescent development—not exactly an easy task, as the introductory chapter points out. Like much of the rest of psychology, the study of adolescence suffers from a divorce between theory and data. As an additional complication, however, psychologists have found it difficult to agree upon what it is that distinguishes adolescence as a separate developmental stage. Indeed, most of the book is devoted to resolving these two problems.

Chapters 2 to 4 represent an attempt to identify the basic issues in adolescent psychology by comparing three representative theorists: G. Stanley Hall, Anna Freud, and Harry Stack Sullivan. This comparison reveals, first, that all three theorists tend to emphasize the same changes during adolescence (e.g., intellectual growth, increased autonomy, and sexual maturation); second, that although their explanations differ, all three describe adolescence as a period of unusual storm and stress; and third, that none of the three appears to do justice to feminine development.

Feminine development is an issue which proves too annoyingly persistent to be resolved easily, but Chapters 5 and 6 examine "the facts" with respect to the first two points. Chapter 5 reviews the research on intellectual development, moral development, the growth of friendship, and physical maturation during adolescence. Chapter 6 takes up the theme of storm and stress in several of its permutations and ultimately concludes that theory and data do not correspond. Hall, Anna Freud, and Sullivan may all characterize adolescence as a period of great turbulence and turmoil, but research on normal teenagers provides little support for such a view. Furthermore (and this is a particularly sticky dilemma), some psychologists argue that even if adolescence is not conflict-ridden, it *ought* to be, while others counter that teenagers need not undergo great stress and strain in order to become mature and fulfilled adults.

Having uncovered these contradictions, our study seems to have arrived at an impasse. To complicate matters, there are many aspects of normal adolescence (e.g., vocational choice, political development, the growth of self-concept, sex-role learning) and also many "problems of youth" (e.g., drugs, delinquency, suicide, and underachievement) that have yet to be examined. If adolescent psychology is to be approached in an integrated fashion, it is clearly necessary to locate a theory that can resolve the issues and accommodate all these areas. I believe that Erikson's theory comes closest to "filling the bill," and the latter half of the book attempts to examine and apply his work.

In Chapter 7 Erikson's rather intricate theory of personality development is reviewed, and in Chapter 8 his specific contributions to adolescent psychology are discussed. I argue there that Erikson's theory goes a long way toward resolving the problems that have been identified. Instead of depicting adolescence as a period of storm and stress, Erikson refers to it as a period of "normative crisis." In place of the ideal of adolescent turmoil, he substitutes the concept of moratorium. His theory is comprehensive enough to accommodate all the other theories and all the research reviewed in Chapters 2 to 6. And as a final point, his theory also furnishes a convenient framework for discussing a great many aspects of adolescent development, both normal and deviant.

Employing Erikson as a theoretical backdrop, Chapters 9 and 10 take up some of the more commonplace concomitants of adolescent development (e.g., self-concept, vocational choice, political development, sexual identity), and Chapter 11 explores a number of the more troubling problems of youth (e.g., drug use, delinquency, suicide, underachievement, and alienation).

Chapter 12 is devoted to an assessment and a summing up. The point it makes is that although Erikson's theory represents a brilliant contribution to adolescent psychology, his work does suffer from one serious liability—the same one that plagues other theories of adolescent development. That is, it does not, at least in my opinion, do justice to the female adolescent. On balance, the Eriksonian model, like its predecessors, appears to be somewhat "masculine." The book concludes with some tentative recommendations for rectifying this dilemma and with some suggestions for further research.

Being especially sensitive to the problems of feminity, I attempted to "demasculinize" the language of this book. Unfortunately, English does not lend itself very readily to this sort of endeavor, and it became cumbersome to substitute "he or she" and "his or her" every time I would normally have written "he" or "his" (as in the sentence, "Adolescence is the period in which the individual becomes aware of *his* own unique destiny"). Therefore, the feminist in me reluctantly yielded to the stylist. However, in all cases, in which an indefinite "he" or "his" has been employed, I hope the reader will remember that this usage implies "she" and "her" as well.

Numerous colleagues, relatives, and friends have assisted me with *Adolescence and Individuality*. Carol Guardo's help was, needless to say, invaluable. Donald Drummond, Dean of the College of Arts and Sciences at Eastern Michigan University, took a warmly personal interest in the project, as did Bruce Nelson, Vice-President for Instruction at the same university. Joseph Adelson read the earlier chapters and offered some welcome encouragement. Richard Lerner took the time to review and criticize the entire manuscript for me. Barry Fish patiently listened to my harangues and cheerfully loaned me materials, as did Gary Davis, John Knapp, and Peter Benson. My department head, Samuel Karson, did his best to lighten my work load, and Lloyd Johnston of Survey Research Center was kind enough to give me a copy of his excellent book on drug use.

My family, in particular my parents, shared my elation when things were going well and buoyed me up when they were not. And three friends, Berta Mendelsohn, Sally McCracken, and Charles Helppie, all hard-working professionals in their own right, provided me with constructive criticism and much-needed support. I am also especially grateful to George Middendorf and Robert Ginsberg of Harper & Row for their unfailing enthusiasm and consideration.

An uncontrollable habit of thinking and revising at the typewriter made it necessary for me to assume most of the secretarial chores myself on successive versions of the manuscript, but Millicent Hamilton capably came to the rescue while I was working on the final draft and typed part of it for me. Finally, I would like to extend a special vote of thanks to the thousand or so students at Eastern Michigan University who have given me their time and attention as I refined many of the ideas for *Adolescence and Individuality* in the classroom.

JUDITH E. GALLATIN

Adolescence
and Individuality

Introduction

Often . . . this body of his rebelled when he least expected it—
not so much before heavy tasks as for reasons of no importance.
And then Luca was subject to sudden, furious rages during which his
body, already so exhausted, seemed to burn up the little strength
it retained in paroxysms of hatred and revolt. More than anything it
was the dumb, inert resistance of inanimate objects, or rather his own
incapacity to make use of such objects without fatigue or injury
that threw him into these devastating rages. . . . He felt that the
world was hostile to him, and he to the world; he felt he was waging
continuous, nerve-racking warfare against everything around him.

Alberto Moravia, "Luca"

To feel stirring within you the wonderful and melancholy play of
strange forces and to be aware that those you yearn for are blithely
inaccessible to all that moves you—what a pain is this!

Thomas Mann, Tonio Kröger

It was thick in him, the old lust only in a new way; something
besides fighting, striking things, a maddening sexual feeling, a
desire for the universe, a desire to attack and violate it, to make his
reality specific, to establish his presence on earth. He felt no need
to apologize for the bawdy feeling in him. It was not his fault.
He hadn't established the basis of the universe, the manner of life,
the method of remaining sane.

William Saroyan, Seventeen

Our twentieth-century mind seems much preoccupied with adolescence. Writers of various nationalities have professed a peculiar fascination with the period, portraying it as a time of special poignancy and unpredictability. Certainly, the adolescents who emerge from the pages of many a contemporary novel and short story are romantic figures. They are creatures of contradiction. Assailed by changes, they grope toward adulthood and simultaneously experience a pull back toward childhood. They fall in love in an instant and hate with

1

equal suddenness. They sow wild oats and embrace the loftiest ideals with equal fervor.

Nor is it only writers of fiction who are inspired by such images of youthful turmoil. Judging from the amount of national coverage it receives, we may assume that adolescence is a subject that excites great public interest generally. Indeed, it is almost impossible to skim through any of the leading periodicals without encountering an article on the problems of teenage youth or to view an average week of television without being confronted by a piece on drugs, delinquency, or teenage sex—all topics that fall more or less under the heading of "adolescence."

But, turning from literature and the popular media to psychology, from the novel, the documentary, and the psychiatrist's monthly column to the professional journals, we discover a curious paradox. The subject that excites so much interest in the arts and among the lay public draws only the most cursory attention from the academic and research psychologist. Year after year, the authors of the chapter "Developmental Psychology" in the *Annual Review of Psychology* have remarked on the absence of research involving adolescents. The editor of a leading journal in developmental psychology *(McCandless, 1970)* has made a similar observation, noting that studies of the teenage population were underrepresented in his publication. And in a more anecdotal vein, the author of this book vividly recalls the undisguised repugnance a colleague expressed a few years ago at the very thought of teaching adolescent psychology. "I taught that once," he declared. "Never again. There's nothing to teach."

How are we to explain this obvious discrepancy—between the lay public's and the fiction writer's consuming interest in adolescence and what amounts to a neglect of or even downright aversion to the subject among psychologists? Having studied the paradox for a considerable length of time, we believe there are several reasons, some of them having to do with problems that the psychology of adolescence shares with psychology in general, some of them peculiar to the psychology of adolescence itself.

Problems in Common

We receive a broad hint of the common problems of adolescent psychology and psychology in general when we compare the literary portrait of adolescence with the image that emerges from the more traditional textbook. Certainly, the youngster suffers in translation. For, rather than presenting a picture of the adolescent as a whole, the typical textbook breaks him up into segments.[1] There are chapters on physiological changes, emotions, peer-group relations, values, and achievement. Numerous graphs and charts are offered and equally numerous statistics. But the overall result is fragmented and confused. In contrast to the living, breathing adolescent of the novel, short story, and play, the textbook version seems curiously static and lifeless, a loose compendium of assorted facts and generalizations.

Theory Without Data and Data Without Theory

In other words, even the existing research on adolescent psychology lacks coherence. It tends to proceed and to be reviewed piecemeal without regard for any particular conceptual framework, a fate that has befallen research in other areas. The observation of Adelson concerning the study of personality could just as easily be applied to adolescence: "Despite the cant that we continue to preach to our undergraduates to the effect that theory and research are bonded, each inspiriting the other—theory generating data, and data reforming and extending theory—the plain fact is that there are only occasional and erratic articulations between the two" *(1969, p. 218)*. Theorists have tended to develop theories about the young without recourse to experimentation, and researchers have gone about their business compiling data on youth equally oblivious to theory. The overall result has been less than enlightening. We have, on the one hand, a considerable number of untested theories of adolescent development and, on the other, an untidy conglomeration of facts and figures.

Theory and Dehumanization

But merely providing a conceptual framework for the study of adolescence—for instance, by reviewing theories of adolescence and relating the existing research to those theories—will not completely resolve the problem of fragmentation. We could be meticulous about relating data on adolescence to theory and still end up with an image of youth that, though coherent, would be sterile and lifeless. For one of the dilemmas associated with any theory is that in the course of

---

[1] As is explained in the Preface, when "he," "him," or "his" is used in this indeterminate fashion, "she," "her," or "hers" is automatically implied as well.

describing a phenomenon it may merely dissect the phenomenon without making it seem vital or real. Erik Erikson holds forth eloquently on this particular liability in an essay on the psychoanalytic theory of personality development:

> In science, our capacity to think atomistically corresponds to the nature of matter to a high degree and thus leads to the mastery over matter. But when we apply atomistic thinking to man, we break him down into isolated fragments rather than into constituent elements. In fact, when we look at man in the state of pathology, he is already fragmented, so that in psychiatry an atomizing mind may meet a phenomenon of fragmentation and mistake the fragments for atoms. In psychoanalysis we repeat for our own encouragement (and as an argument against others) that human nature can best be studied in a state of partial breakdown, or, at any rate of marked conflict because—so we say—a conflict delineates borderlines and clarifies the forces which collide on these borderlines. As Freud himself put it, we see a crystal's structure only when it cracks. But a crystal, on the one hand, and an organism or personality on the other, differ in the fact that one is inanimate and the other an organic whole which cannot be broken up without a withering of the parts. *(1968, p. 278)*

We shall have more to say about psychoanalytic theory and much more to say about Erikson. Indeed, later on in this book we shall argue that Eriksonian theory provides the most coherent framework for the study of adolescence presently in existence. Here, we would simply like to underscore his warning that the unthinking application of theoretical concepts to human beings may be every bit as dehumanizing as the unsystematic collection of data. Human beings are not merely bundles of statistics. Neither are they merely masses of theoretical concepts. And what is true of human beings in general is true of adolescents in particular. We believe that, just as research on adolescence ought to be related to some sort of theoretical framework, so theoretical concepts themselves ought to be explained and illustrated. Consequently, when we refer to various theories in this book, we shall try to be as nontechnical and "down to earth" as possible.

Problems Apart

But, although we have sketched in the broad outlines of our approach to the study of adolescence, we have still accounted only partially for the lack of attention that adolescence has received. The divorce between theory and data, the dehumanizing effects of theory have not deterred psychologists from other areas similarly afflicted.

Far from it. Research studies on personality, unquestionably a related subject, are currently proliferating at such a rate that it is almost impossible to keep up with them, let alone digest them. And theories of personality development excite far more comment than theories of adolescent development. So we are forced to conclude that there are some special reasons why adolescence has been neglected.

We would like to suggest that these reasons have to do both with the relative youth of the *concept* of adolescence and with the complexities of the adolescent period itself. Or perhaps it is the youth of the concept that makes adolescence *seem* complex. In any case, we can detect an air of bewilderment in the observations of the psychoanalyst Bernfeld, who tackled the subject early in the 1920s:

Adolescence is less well understood from the viewpoint of psychological and sexual development than childhood. One of the reasons for the insufficiency of scientific literature on this period of life is to be found in the *great multiplicity* of phenomena in this age. Adolescence manifests itself in various areas: physiological, psychological, and sociological. Confronted by the enormous variety of individual, social, cultural, historical, and physical differences in the group, one is tempted to question the validity of classifying all these manifestations under the one heading of adolescence. *(Quoted in Spiegel, 1951, p. 6)*

What Bernfeld appears to be suggesting is that so much is happening during adolescence—presumably in comparison with childhood—that it is difficult to keep track of it all.

Adolescence and Psychohistory

But Bernfeld's assessment reflects a view of childhood and adolescence, indeed, of the entire life cycle, that has become prominent only in recent history. And here, in our opinion, is one of the key reasons why the study of adolescence has not yet found favor among psychologists. It is our contention that adolescence has been neglected chiefly because *concepts* like "childhood" and "adolescence" are comparatively new. Childhood, we believe, has received more attention from psychologists, partly because the *idea* of childhood preceded that of adolescence in Western thought and partly because the view of childhood that finally emerged in our own century has made it seem a period of far greater significance than adolescence. A brief review of the history, or more precisely the psychohistory, of both concepts may help to place the study of adolescence in perspective.

The concept of childhood Much as the thought may tax modern credibility, there is evidence that three or four centuries ago Western culture made no particular distinction among childhood, adolescence, and adulthood. To be sure, adults recognized that children are smaller and weaker, but that was about all. And, in fact, paintings executed before the Renaissance portray children as miniature adults rather than as the rounded, cherubic figures we have become accustomed to. The French historian Ariès (*1962*), whose work serves as a source for much of the historical material that we are about to present, has observed that it was common practice among all but the most privileged classes to send children out to work at the tender age of seven (at least it strikes *us* as a tender age). At that point, they either began to learn trades or to assist their parents with farming chores, but they were not protected from the rigors of life as are children of our own era.

Even among those born into wealthy households, Ariès has argued, there was little distinction between the earlier years of an individual's existence and the later ones. It was not unusual for the children of aristocrats and prosperous middle-class citizens to begin schooling at the "precocious" age of four or five and to finish what would be roughly the equivalent of a modern doctoral program at the age of eighteen. But no one took much notice of these youthful prodigies, for, without the distinction between childhood and adulthood, without the notion that there are subjects "too difficult" for children to master, they could not be *recognized* as prodigies.

The closely related idea of segregating children of the same ages in separate grades and teaching them in carefully graduated steps was also foreign to the medieval and early Renaissance mind. A modern observer, brimming over with concepts like "reading readiness" and "programmed learning," would no doubt be appalled if he could somehow magically be transported into a schoolroom of 400 years ago. As learning by rote recitation was the chief method of teaching, the din would probably strike him as intolerable. Then too, though children from wealthy families were likely to start their schooling early, no one objected if a less privileged child found the wherewithal to begin his instruction later. The modern observer would thus be greeted by a motley collection of ages—seven-year-old boys and eighteen-year-old youths all reciting together.

Gradually the concept of childhood as a period of life when the individual should be nurtured and protected but carefully supervised as well began to appear. Ariès's historical analysis remains somewhat vague about the reasons for this change in Western thought, but presumably it had something to do with the changing economic conditions of life. In the sixteenth century a substantial merchant class had begun to arise; it was a segment of society that could *afford* to protect children and to educate them, rather than putting them to work. In this altered climate, the precocious scholars of the Middle Ages and the Renaissance began to disappear; the custom of arranging pupils in grades and keeping various ages apart came to predominate. The idea that the child's mind was somehow different from the adult's mind had begun to take hold. Ariès claims that it remained an upper-class notion for a long time. Well into the nineteenth century, he observes, the lower classes continued to make little distinction between childhood and adulthood, apprenticing their youngsters or sending them off to till the fields at the age of seven or eight, subjecting them to the same legal penalties as adults, marrying them off in their early teens. It was necessary for more children to survive infancy and for the ranks of the middle class to grow before the concept could become firmly established.

The French philosopher Montaigne, inventor of the modern essay and ahead of his time in many respects, apparently had a glimmering of the concept of childhood nearly 400 years ago, for he exhorted adults to teach children only what they were ready to learn:

> Our tutors never stop bawling into our ears as though they were pouring water into a funnel; and our task is only to repeat what has been told us. I should like the tutor to correct this practice, and right from the start, according to the capacity of the mind he has in hand, to begin putting it through its paces, making it taste things, choose them, and discern them by itself; sometimes clearing the way for him, sometimes letting him clear his own way. I don't want him to think and talk alone. I want him to listen to his pupil speaking in his turn. . . . *The authority of those who teach is often an obstacle to those who want to learn.*
> It is good that he should have his pupil trot before him, to judge the child's pace and how much he must stoop to match his strength. For lack of this proportion we spoil everything; and to be able to hit it right and to go along evenly in it is one of the hardest tasks that I know: it is the achievement of a lofty and very strong soul to know how to come down to a childish gait and to guide it. *(Frame, 1957, p. 110)*

But despite his almost modern "sense of proportion" and despite his very clear recognition of the difference between the child's mind and the adult's, Montaigne in many ways retained the medieval view of childhood. The same man who advised pacing the little scholar according to his capacity to learn also expressed sentiments about his own children that might offend our twentieth-century sensibilities.

However advanced ideas regarding education may have been, Montaigne observed with what sounds suspiciously like distaste: "I cannot entertain that passion which makes people hug infants that are hardly born yet, having neither movement in the soul nor recognizable shape to the body by which they can make themselves lovable. And I have not willingly suffered them to be brought near me"—this in an essay entitled "On the Affection of Fathers for Their Children." And he was capable of viewing the deaths of his own progeny with a kind of philosophical resignation that would strike most of us as callous: "I have lost two or three children in their infancy, not without regret, but without great sorrow" (Ariès, 1962, p. 39). Of course, in an era when a child who survived infancy was a greater rarity than one who died, such detachment may have been more understandable.

Nonetheless, if even one of the most advanced thinkers of the sixteenth century could adopt this less than affectionate tone in speaking of children, it is not surprising that the modern concept began to take firm hold a full 200 years later, in the eighteenth century. It was, in fact, another leading philosopher, this time a Swiss, who pointed out what remains perhaps the crucial distinction between childhood and adulthood. The child, argued Jean Jacques Rousseau, differs from the adult in being unable to reason, incapable that is, of thinking in abstractions. He can learn, to be sure, and he can remember, but before the age of twelve or so, he is very much a prisoner of his senses, limited in thought to what he can actually see or manipulate. Actually, Rousseau distinguished several stages in the progression from infancy to what he called the "age of reason," and as the reader will see in a later chapter, his account is astonishingly similar to that of a twentieth-century Swiss philosopher, Jean Piaget.

Early in life, declared Rousseau,

when memory and imagination are still inactive, the child attends only to what actually affects his senses. . . . He wants to touch and handle everything. Put no obstacle in the way of his restless movements. He learns to feel heat, cold, hardness, softness, weight, and comes to judge the size and shape of bodies and all their sensory qualities by looking at them, fingering them, listening to them, above all by comparing sight and touch. (Boyd, 1955, p. 46)

Infancy gradually comes to an end as the child acquires the ability to speak, but his thinking remains for a considerable time rather narrowly focused:

Before the age of reason the child receives images but not ideas. The difference between them is that images are simply the exact pictures of sense-given objects, whereas ideas are notions of the objects determined by their relations. An image may exist by itself in the imagining mind, but every idea presupposes other ideas. . . .

That is why I say that children being incapable of judgment have no true memory. They retain sounds, shapes, sensations, but rarely ideas, and still more rarely their relations. It may be objected that they learn some of the elements of geometry, but really that only shows that so far from being able to reason for themselves they cannot even recollect the reasoning of others. For if you follow these little geometricians in their lesson you will find that all they have recollected is the exact picture of the figure and the words of the demonstration. The least new question upsets them and so does any change of figure. Their knowledge is all sensation; nothing has got through to the understanding. *(Boyd, 1955, pp. 46–47)*

This second stage of childhood, marked by the ability to use language but the inability to reason in anything like an adult sense, is finally superseded by a stage that ushers in the beginnings of true rationality. At twelve or thirteen, the child becomes capable of understanding the concepts that will ultimately allow him to take his place in the adult world: both the laws of nature and the laws of society.

By outlining these stages of development—and clearly distinguishing the thinking of the child from the thinking of the adult—Rousseau helped to cement the concept of childhood once and for all in Western culture. Nonetheless, Ariès claims, the concept was not widely recognized for more than a century. Only the wealthy were much interested in educating (and economically solvent enough to educate) their offspring. Consequently they remained the only people to concern themselves very much with differences between the child's intellect and the adult's. For the son of a farmer, carpenter, or blacksmith, who was likely to be put to work as soon as he was physically able, the whole question was irrelevant. Indeed, according to Ariès, the concept of childhood has become universal—accepted for the most part throughout all classes in Western society—only in the past 100 years. The idea that young human beings have qualities that make it necessary for them to be brought up apart from the workaday world and kept in school up to a certain age is thus of surprisingly recent vintage. (Those readers who remain somewhat skeptical might look at Upton Sinclair's novel *The Jungle*, an exposé of the meat-packing industry written in 1906, which contains some horrifying descriptions of seven and eight year olds forced to work a brutal twelve-hour day.)

The elusive concept of adolescence   What is even more significant for our purposes is that the concept of adolescence—as a stage intervening between childhood and adulthood—apparently developed even later in history. We catch a hint of it in Rousseau's suggestion that the age of reason begins with the early teens, but although Rousseau advised continuing the youngster's education up through the teens and postponing marriage until the mid-twenties, his description of adolescence was much less complex than the one we cited earlier, the rather bewildering account advanced by Bernfeld. And there is in Rousseau little of the turmoil and romance associated with the contemporary portrait. To be sure, he noted at one point that at twelve or thirteen "the sex passions, the most violent and terrible of all, have not yet awakened" *(Boyd, 1955, p. 70)*, but he did not enlarge upon this theme. Rousseau also suggested that during this long span, between the dawn of the age of reason and the proper age for marrying, the youth ought gradually to find his place in society, but he did not seem to think there is anything especially problematic about this task.

In fact, the intellectual historian Ariès, who has so painstakingly traced the growth of the concept of childhood, argues that the concept of adolescence as a period of storm and stress, a period more complex than childhood, did not appear before the late eighteenth century and did not take hold in any very broad sense before the twentieth. Even more intriguingly, in startling contrast to the pages and pages he devotes to childhood, the methodical Ariès himself has little more to say about the history of the concept of adolescence. He observes that the practice of extending schooling through the teens (but again, only for the privileged youngster) helped to differentiate this newly recognized stage of life both from childhood and from adulthood, but he notes as well that even after the practice had become fairly well established, childhood and adolescence continued to be confounded. "Inside the school world, the adolescent was separated from the adult and confused with the child, with whom he shared the humiliation of corporal punishment . . ." *(Ariès, 1962, p. 262)*. Only as the armies of the eighteenth century began to try to attract "glorious youths" to their ranks, Ariès insists, did anything like the modern notion of adolescence begin to emerge, and then only in a rudimentary way:

> This notion of adolescence was to bring about a major transformation of education: the pedagogues henceforth attributed a moral value to uniform and discipline. The correlation of the adolescent and the soldier in school resulted in an emphasis on characteristics such as toughness and virility which had hitherto been neglected and which henceforth were valued for themselves. A new concept had appeared, though as yet in embryonic form, a concept distinct from that of childhood: the concept of adolescence. *(1962, p. 268)*

Indeed, judging from the sparseness of his remarks concerning adolescence, we might gather that for Ariès the concept is still embryonic. In any case, he dismisses the subject with this tantalizing final observation:

If economic or social circumstances bring about a relaxation of family control, childhood and youth may escape from the isolation in which they are enclosed by a tradition going back to at least the eighteenth century; *that is probably what is happening today, with childhood losing some of its special characteristics in favour of a new age group: adolescence. (1962, p. 285, italics added)*

Although this type of "psychohistorical analysis" is itself relatively new (and somewhat controversial, we may add), an increasing number of psychologists appear to agree with Ariès that the developmental period called adolescence is largely an "invention" of modern industrial society. Bakan *(1971)*, Demos and Demos *(1969)*, Keniston *(1968)*, Musgrove *(1965)*, and Muuss *(1971)* all argue that the concept is intimately bound up with the existence of child-labor laws and a mass educational system—both of which keep the majority of young people out of the work force and economically dependent upon their parents until relatively late in their teens. Keniston in particular insists that the legal and social changes that have made adolescence possible are themselves the results of modern affluence. "Only," he remarks, "when a society produces enough to liberate young men and women between the ages of twelve and eighteen from labor can it demand that they continue their educations and allow them to continue their psychological development" *(Keniston, 1968, p. 244)*. He goes on to point out that only in the past thirty or forty years has Western society become prosperous enough to accord very many youngsters this prerogative.

In short, the same sort of changes that allowed childhood to become a more or less universal experience in Western culture have, in Keniston's opinion, caused the human life cycle to be differentiated into yet another stage, a period of transition between childhood and adulthood. Just as the rise of the middle class following the Renaissance is supposed to have made it possible for increasingly large numbers of children to be kept out of the work force and educated, the unprecedented prosperity of the twentieth century has allegedly permitted large numbers of youngsters in their teens to *remain* unemployed and "to continue with their psychological development." Not that the experience of adolescence is necessarily as nearly universal as is the experience of childhood. It is probably reasonable to wonder if, even today, a ghetto youth who is forced to drop out of school and support his family experiences a "modern" adolescence.

But even if we assume that the ghetto youth is the exception rather than the rule, Keniston's assertions bring us squarely back to the question with which we began this chapter, albeit slightly re-phrased. What *is* the modern concept of adolescence? What sort of psychological development is supposed to occur during the teenage years? And if the concept of adolescence is relatively new to the Western world, how does the fact that it *is* relatively new help to explain the present, rather disorganized state of adolescent psychology?

The Modern Concept of Adolescence: Confusions and Complexities

Although it is difficult to put such suppositions to the test scientifically, we would like to suggest that the comparative "new-ness" of the concept is responsible in a number of ways for the confusion that surrounds the psychology of adolescence. Let us re-turn to the colleague who complained that there was "nothing to teach." What could he have meant? We suspect that he was com-menting on the difficulty of distinguishing between *childhood* and adolescence, and, in a sense, he had a point. If we cannot differen-tiate between the two, if nothing distinctive occurs during adoles-cence, there is indeed "nothing to teach." And the trouble is that it *is* difficult to specify what the experience of adolescence contributes to the human life cycle.

Since Rousseau, we have gradually come to regard the child not as an adult in miniature but as a potential adult. The human infant is considered to begin life as fundamentally irrational, illogical, de-pendent, and uncontrolled. And childhood has thus come to be regarded as a period of life in which the rudimentary skills of adult-hood are acquired: walking, talking, self-discipline. We have also come to agree with Rousseau that with the "dawn of reason" child-hood ends and adolescence begins. But, as the adolescent has already acquired one of the key requisites of adulthood (the capacity for abstract thought) at this point, it is still not clear what *else* he is supposed to experience. If the child already possesses the rudi-ments of adulthood by the time he reaches his teens, just what is supposed to occur during adolescence? There *is* one obvious physical change as well, namely the attainment of the capacity to reproduce. But this biological event usually takes place quite early in the teens, and, if anything, it is generally regarded (as is the attainment of reason) as marking the beginning, rather than the end, of adoles-cence. What *else* is to occur between puberty and full-fledged adult-hood, supposedly almost a decade away? The youngster can already talk, walk, reason, and distinguish right from wrong. Why is adolescence necessary?

A good many psychologists have apparently asked themselves the same question without arriving at a very satisfactory answer. This failure is, we suspect, one of the chief reasons that the study of childhood tends to overshadow the study of adolescence. Childhood has come to be viewed as the really critical period of human existence, the "formative years" when all the traits that distinguish our species from the rest of the animal kingdom become manifest. Adolescence by comparison appears, if not uneventful, at least less well defined—hence the intense interest in the earlier period and the comparative neglect of the later one.

It is not surprising, therefore, that those psychologists intrepid enough to undertake the study of adolescence seem rather like the educators of the eighteenth century—confused about the distinction between childhood and adolescence. The more traditional textbook illustrates in graphic fashion the results of such confusion. Earlier we argued that textbooks ordinarily fragment the adolescent, assigning a chapter each to topics like physical development, social development, achievement, values, and intellectual growth—never quite managing to produce a really coherent picture. As a matter of fact, this format is precisely the one used in most textbooks on *child* development, and although we may argue that even for this subject it is not the ideal approach, somehow it seems to work much better. Because we have come to view the child as relatively unformed and amorphous, there is a certain logic to identifying all the key events of childhood (motor development, language acquisition, moral development, and so forth) and treating each in a separate chapter. But the same approach applied to the study of adolescence is ultimately rather unsatisfying, perhaps because, with the exception of puberty, all the "key events" have already taken place, and the chapter-by-chapter rendition simply appears to be "more of the same."

In any case, the confusion between childhood and adolescence becomes even more apparent when we examine a definition of adolescence by the author of a well-known textbook:

Adolescence is both a way of life and a span of time in the physical and psychological development of an individual. It represents a period of growth and change in nearly all aspects of the child's physical, mental, social, and emotional life. It is a time of new experiences, new responsibilities, and new relationships with adults as well as peers. *(Horrocks, 1955, p. 218)*

We are back to the bewilderment of Bernfeld, but the reason for his mystification has become clearer. Despite the implication that a great deal happens during adolescence, there is nothing in the definition we have just cited to distinguish adolescence from childhood. Childhood is also marked by physical, mental, social, and emotional changes, as well as "new experiences, new responsibilities, and new relationships with adults as well as peers." So for that matter is adulthood. Merely ticking off the categories of experience will not tell us what is special about adolescence, for these categories do not change a great deal between birth and death. What *does* change is the quality of experience. The adolescent does not react to the world (nor does it react to him) in quite the same way that a child does.

What is the essential difference? Although we intend to devote most of this book to answering that question, we may begin to sketch in the outlines here. Within the past ten or twenty years there have been an increasing number of attempts to specify what is distinctive about adolescence. Friedenberg, for instance, has defined it as "the period during which a young person learns who he is, and what he really feels. It is the time during which he differentiates himself from his culture, though on the culture's terms" *(1959, p. 29)*. Upon analysis, this definition too turns out to be somewhat vague. What does it mean for the youngster to "learn who he is" or "what he really feels"? Just what is involved in "differentiating himself from his culture"? But we do have here the germ of an important concept. Implicit in Friedenberg's definition is the idea that during adolescence the youngster acquires the ability to adopt a perspective on his own life experience that is quite foreign to the child. As we have seen, childhood has come to be characterized as a period in which certain basic skills emerge, but these skills are more or less the same for everyone. Although child-rearing practices may vary considerably from one society to another, all societies have to make sure that their children learn to walk, talk, and develop degrees of social control. These skills are the critical and fundamental attributes of man.

However, when Friedenberg speaks of the adolescent's "differentiating himself from his culture," he is describing an event that is qualitatively different. What he seems to suggest is the dawning awareness of what might be called a "sense of individuality," an awareness that can occur only at the beginning of Rousseau's "age of reason." We may paraphrase Friedenberg and propose that what the young person is supposed to learn during adolescence is not so much "who he is" but *what sort* of "who" he is—and also what he can expect out of life as a result. This concept of adolescence appears to be gaining ground at the present time in psychology, and it resembles to some extent the image of adolescence that is currently so popular both among writers of fiction and in the news media—the notion that the teenage years represent a romantic and turbulent search for "selfhood."

Erikson's definition of adolescence   Now just what is involved in this search, and how is it markedly different from anything that occurs during childhood? Let us return to Erikson for the beginnings of an answer. Erikson, whose definition of adolescence is rather more elaborate than that of Friedenberg, speaks of acquiring a sense of personal identity during the interval that marks the end of childhood and precedes the attainment of adulthood. But this acquisition is no easy task, for, as Erikson observes:

> Young people must become whole people in their own right, and this during a developmental stage characterized by a diversity of changes in physical growth, genital maturation, and social awareness. The wholeness to be achieved at this stage I have called a *sense of inner identity*. The young person, in order to experience wholeness, must feel a progressive continuity between that which he has come to be during the long years of childhood and that which he promises to become in the anticipated future; between that which he conceives himself to be and that which he perceives others to see in him and to expect of him. Individually speaking, identity includes, but is more than, the sum of all the successive identifications of those earlier years when the child wanted to be, and was often forced to become, like the people he depended on. Identity is a unique product, which now meets a crisis to be solved only in new identifications with age mates and with leader figures outside the family.   *(1968, p. 87)*

What Erikson appears to be saying is that during adolescence the youngster somehow manages to assemble what he has learned about himself during childhood. During childhood he has mastered certain skills, perhaps begun to develop certain talents, started to acquire certain traits. But before the "age of reason," before he can begin to view himself with a degree of objectivity, he cannot decide precisely what to *do* with them, how to fit them together so that he will be able to have some sort of meaningful existence during adulthood. By the beginning of adolescence, the child has acquired the tools of adulthood. During adolescence, Erikson seems to suggest, he learns how to use them.

Furthermore, Erikson maintains that the sense of personal identity that each youngster ultimately fashions for himself is *unique*. It depends upon such contingencies as the abilities he has been born with, the opportunities he has had to develop those abilities, the emotional experiences he has undergone, the kind of parents he has had, and the culture in which he has spent his childhood—which is no doubt why Erikson stipulates that formulating a sense of identity "necessitates in different individuals and in different societies, great variations in the duration, in the intensity, and in the ritualization of adolescence" (1959, p. 119). The intelligent, articulate son of a banker or professor may have far more opportunity (and leisure) to engage in a romantic search for selfhood than the poverty-stricken and less gifted son of an unskilled laborer. Similarly, a child brought up in the rigid caste system of India will most likely acquire a view of himself during adolescence that is quite different from that of an American youngster. (We should add at this point that because of our own background and because most of the research to which we have access has been undertaken in this country, we shall be concentrating on the American teenager in this book.)

A Prospectus

To sum up, the modern concept of adolescence—the concept that begins to emerge in the writings of Friedenberg and has been further articulated by Erikson—emphasizes such elements as the integration of past experience, the development of a sense of individuality, and growing awareness of personal destiny. If this definition of adolescence represents, in fact, a reasonable approximation to reality, if what is supposed to occur during adolescence is some sort of decisive integration, we can see once more why the more traditional textbook is generally less than enlightening. Simply cataloguing the events of adolescence does not tell us how they are interrelated and integrated. We need to know not only what intellectual, social, emotional, and biological changes occur but also what impact each may have on all the others. Furthermore, by emphasizing what is common to all adolescents and concentrating on the experiences of the "typical teenager," the more traditional textbook obscures the really critical development of adolescence: the development of a sense of individuality or, as Erikson puts it, of a sense of inner identity.

In our view, Eriksonian theory provides the best "conceptual umbrella" for the study of adolescence. More than any other theory in existence it manages to do justice to the complexities of adolescent psychology. But in order to appreciate Erikson's contributions, it is useful to know something about the major theories of adolescent development that preceded his and to consider the issues that become apparent when we compare these theories. What we have attempted in this chapter is a brief history of the concept of adolescence. What we propose to do in the next three chapters is to trace the history of adolescent psychology.

REFERENCES

ADELSON, J. Personality. *Annual Review of Psychology*, 1969, **20**, 217–252.

ARIÈS, R. *Centuries of Childhood.* New York: Knopf, 1962.

BAKAN, D. Adolescence in America: From Idea to Social Fact. *Daedalus*, 1971, **100**, 979–995.

BERNFELD, S. Über eine typische Form der Männlichen Pubertät. *Imago*, 1923, **9**, 169–188.

BOYD, W. *The* Emile *of Jean Jacques Rousseau.* New York: Bureau of Publications, Columbia University, 1955.

DEMOS, J., and DEMOS, V. Adolescence in Historical Perspective. *Journal of Marriage and the Family*, 1969, **31**, 632–638.

ERIKSON, E. Identity and the Life Cycle. *Psychological Issues*, 1959, **1**, 1–171.

ERIKSON, E. *Identity: Youth and Crisis.* New York: Norton, 1968.

FRAME, D. M. *The Complete Essays of Montaigne.* Stanford: Stanford University Press, 1957.

FRIEDENBERG, E. *The Vanishing Adolescent.* New York: Dell, 1959.

HORROCKS, J. E. What is Adolescence? *Education*, 1955, **76**, 218–221.

KENISTON, K. *Young Radicals.* New York: Harcourt Brace Jovanovich, 1968.

McCANDLESS, B. Editorial. *Developmental Psychology*, 1970, **2**, 1–4.

MUSGROVE, F. *Youth and the Social Order.* Bloomington: Indiana University Press, 1965.

MUUSS, R. Adolescent Development and the Secular Trend. In R. Muuss (Ed.), *Adolescent Behavior and Society: A Book of Readings.* New York: Random House, 1971. Pp. 51–64.

SPIEGEL, L. A Review of Contributions to a Psychoanalytic Theory of Adolescence (1951). In M. Gold & E. Douvan (Eds.), *Adolescent Psychology.* Boston: Allyn & Bacon, 1969.

Adolescence and Developmental Psychology: Contributions of G. Stanley Hall

In all probability, whatever it is that makes the adolescent a baffling entity is closely related to whatever it is that makes human beings in general rather mysterious. As Shakespeare's Hamlet exclaims: "What a piece of work is man! How noble in reason! How infinite in faculty! In form and moving how express and admirable! In action how like an angel! In apprehension how like a god! The beauty of the world! The paragon of animals!" (*Hamlet*, Act II, scene ii).

The psychology of adolescence is actually a specialty within the area of developmental psychology, and the essential task of developmental psychology is to explain how man manages to become what he is, to chart his progress from the helpless infant to that "paragon of animals," the fully grown adult. With all of developmental psychology as a backdrop, the question that confronts the student of adolescent psychology is how the span of years he has chosen to examine—the decade, give or take a few years, that follows puberty and precedes young adulthood—contributes to making man what he is. So far, as we have already noted, psychologists have lacked a coherent answer.

The Basic Assumptions of Psychology

Yet, upon pondering the basic task of developmental psychology in general, it becomes clear that there are some definite assumptions underlying our inquiry. The distinguished personality theorists Clyde Kluckhohn and Henry A. Murray strike at the very heart of the matter in their observation that:

> Every man is in certain respects
> a. like all other men
> b. like some other men
> c. like no other man. *(1948, p. 35)*

In order to have a science of psychology at all, we have to assume that every member of the human species has some features in common with every other member. This assumption is, in fact, basic to the very meaning of the word "species." If human beings did not share certain qualities as a group, if each man, in effect, spoke his own language, our task as psychologists would be hopeless. As human beings, we are all born, mature, and die. We are all susceptible to injury and have certain fundamental needs. And, as a species, we all possess those characteristics that led even the melancholy Hamlet to marvel and that are enumerated more prosaically by Kluckhohn and Murray: "an erect posture, hands that grasp, three-dimensional and color vision, and a nervous system that permits elaborate speech and learning processes of the highest order" *(p. 36)*.

Similarly, acknowledging the principle that every man is like *some* other men, psychologists have found it necessary to subdivide the great mass of humanity into various groups, the members of each group sharing qualities that distinguish them from members of other groups. Whatever the current trend toward unisex fashions, women have qualities that allow them to be distinguished from men, the British differ as a group from the French, the rich from the poor, children from adults, and so on. (Indeed, in this book, we are obviously making the assumption that "adolescents" differ sufficiently from both "children" and "adults" to merit being studied separately.)

And finally, granting the characteristics that every human being shares with every other human being, granting the features that members of various groups hold in common, we must still admit that every man is somehow unique. In many respects each human being is like *no* other. Even genetically indistinguishable identical twins raised in the same surroundings by the same set of parents do not develop completely identical personalities.

The great challenge to developmental psychology is to reconcile these three principles—to do justice to all the similarities between human beings, as members both of the human race and of various groups, without doing violence to the differences. And, as a specific area of developmental psychology, the psychology of adolescence shares this challenge. Perhaps the chief reason that this specialty has languished has been an overemphasis on similarities, otherwise known as "norms," and not enough attention to differences, to the infinite variety of the adolescent experience. Somehow in outlining what are supposed to be "typical experiences" for all adolescents— physical growth, achieving autonomy from parents, developing the capacity for adult love, preparing for occupations—we have permitted the image of adolescence itself to become fragmented. Which leads us to the next question: Taking account of the fundamental task of adolescent psychology, how are we to proceed? How are we to do justice to adolescents in general without doing violence to them in particular?

The Necessity for Theory

In their recent book entitled *Child Development and Personality*, Mussen, Conger, and Kagan remark that "American psychology, including child psychology, has been traditionally and stubbornly empirical. The great stress of modern developmental psychology, and its greatest scientific strength, has been objective observation, description, and measurement" *(1969, p. 15)*. In our opinion, this great strength also exposes a certain weakness. Thanks to the "stubbornly empirical" tradition of American psychology, a considerable body of data on teenagers—on their growth patterns, their sexual development, their social habits—already exists. No doubt much of this information is useful, but, unfortunately, little of it has been related to any particular theory of adolescence. Like characters in search of an author, these facts beg for some sort of conceptual framework, some scheme of organization, which, as we indicated earlier, is the purpose of theory. Just what does a theory allow us to do that mere data collection does not? The psychoanalytic scholar David Rapoport expresses it very well: "Many features of observables can be counted, rated, and measured, but the observables themselves cannot tell us which features and what method of counting or measuring them will reveal the relationship between them and the explanatory concepts: only theory can do that" *(1960, p. 36)*.

Although the value of research should not be underestimated, collecting facts about adolescence will not, in and of itself, produce a coherent psychology of adolescence. What is needed in addition is a theoretical framework to tie the facts together and indicate as well which facts are missing. Only in this way can we avoid the sterility and confusion of the traditional approach, which assigns each aspect of adolescence its separate chapter and summarizes the research findings in encyclopedic fashion. Needless to say, what we propose is no easy task, but we have as a kind of compass in this endeavor the Eriksonian concept of adolescence, the notion that adolescence involves some sort of decisive integration of past experience, the development of a sense of individuality, and growing awareness of personal destiny. Indeed, rephrasing Erikson's definition a bit to incorporate the three basic assumptions of psychology, we might say that during adolescence the individual learns that he is in certain respects:

a. like all other men
b. like some other men
c. like no other man.

We ourselves came to favor Erikson's orientation after reviewing and comparing a number of other theories of adolescent development, and it is these steps that we propose to retrace in this and the next two chapters. In this way we can begin to identify some of the complexities of adolescent development, proceed to review pertinent research, and, ultimately, use Erikson's theory to effect a kind of grand synthesis.

Theories of Adolescence

The approach we have adopted entails looking at adolescence and evaluating its significance in terms of the entire human life cycle. The three theorists we have chosen to review, G. Stanley Hall, Anna Freud, and Harry Stack Sullivan, have examined adolescence from a similar perspective, attempting to relate it both to earlier and to later periods of development. But there are other reasons for selecting these theorists as well. In discussing Hall, we shall elaborate on the historical theme introduced in Chapter 1, for his theory, formulated almost seventy years ago, has had a hitherto unsuspected impact upon our contemporary image of adolescence. Similarly, a comparison of Anna Freud, who represents the orthodox psychoanalytic point of view, and of Sullivan, who broke away from psychoanalysis to formulate his own "interpersonal" theory, will serve to highlight some of the most salient issues in adolescent psychology.

Obviously, our plan of attack is not the only possible one. Devotees of the social-learning school, for instance, may wonder why we have not included it as a "representative" theory of adolescent development—particularly in view of its widespread popularity among psychologists. As a matter of fact, we do think that social-learning theory has something to contribute to the study of adolescence, and in subsequent chapters we shall discuss it more specifically.

We should also point out that two well-known specialists in adolescent psychology have actually made very liberal use of social-learning principles in their own textbooks *(Horrocks, 1969; McCandless, 1970)*. However, and here we reveal our bias, these attempts strike us as somewhat forced and artificial. Our aim is to place adolescence in context within the rest of the human life cycle and to discover what is unique about the period. But this objective seems to us incompatible with a strict social-learning orientation. Indeed, because it tends to analyze all behavior in terms of "stimulus-response" connections, social-learning theory purposely *avoids* making any distinction between one period of development and another. We are thus compelled to agree with a recent critic of the school *(Bowers, 1973)*. By itself, social-learning theory constitutes too simplistic an approach to human development. It is best used, this critic has argued, in combination with other points of view—which is precisely how we intend to use it.

Developmental Theory: Basic Assumptions

In addition to the assumptions that underlie the study of psychology, any theory of human development must make two additional assumptions. First, any developmental theory has to assume that there is a certain order or pattern to human growth. If there were no such coherence to existence, if life were completely chaotic, it could not be studied. Second, because it is impossible to examine every single event in an individual's life, developmental theorists must exercise a certain selectivity and assume that some events are more significant than others. Keeping these two basic assumptions in mind, we confront a number of important questions, all of them very much interrelated:

a. What is the *nature* of the pattern of human development? Does development proceed by fits and starts or is it a smooth, continuous process?

b. Just what *are* the significant events in the human life cycle?

c. What *causes* these significant events? Or, putting it another way, what principles govern human behavior?

d. Taking all of the preceding questions into account, what is the relationship between events at one point in the human life cycle and events at another point? Are occurrences early in development more important than later ones? Does what happens early in the life cycle place such a decisive stamp on the human character that later events can have relatively little impact, or can character be significantly altered later in life?

As might be expected, different theorists give different answers to these fundamental questions. The three we have chosen to review here *do* agree about the overall pattern of human development. All three envision it as uneven and variable, proceeding by leaps and bounds during certain periods of life, slackening and tapering off during other periods—hence divided into distinct phases. All three, for instance, view adolescence as a particularly stormy and tempestuous phase of life—in contrast to the supposedly quiescent period of late childhood that precedes it.[1] They also concur to some extent on what are alleged to be the key events of adolescence: the attainment of sexual maturity, the growth of intelligence, widening of social horizons, and increasing autonomy from parents. However, they disagree considerably on what *causes* the developmental dislocations of adolescence and fail to reach a consensus on the overall significance of the period. Does the purported[2] turbulence of adolescence result from the emergence of new responsibilities and conflicts or from the reappearance of old conflicts that must now be settled once and for all? Are events earlier in childhood so decisive as to render adolescence a relatively inconsequential phase of life, or can the direction of the personality be altered significantly during this period? These questions should be kept in mind during the review that follows.

[1] Although this perspective may seem to the reader to be such a natural way of viewing development that any other is unimaginable, we should like to point out that there are, in fact, others. The very influential researcher Arnold Gesell pictures human growth as a regular and orderly process. He believes that whatever discontinuities occur are determined not so much by what *phase* of life the individual has entered as by what *year* of life he has attained. Whether in early childhood, middle childhood, or adolescence, development during the even-numbered years (two, eight, fourteen) is supposed to be relatively harmonious, development during the odd-numbered years comparatively uneven and unsettling.

[2] We use the words "alleged" and "purported" here intentionally. In Chapter 6 we shall examine the notion that the popular view of adolescence as a period of storm and stress is, in fact, a myth.

G. Stanley Hall: The Historical Perspective

G. Stanley Hall is widely praised as one of the great pioneers in American psychology. His two-volume, 1300-page study of adolescence, published in 1904 (and entitled, appropriately enough, *Adolescence*), is often described as "monumental." At the same time, for one so well known, his works are probably among the least read, having been dismissed long ago as "badly out of date" and "irrelevant." Any one who has actually tried to digest Hall's *Adolescence* can readily suggest at least one reason for this comparative neglect. It is in many ways a difficult work, at times repetitious, at times disorganized, and at times simply obscure. Edward Thorndike, himself something of a pioneer in psychology, reviewed it soon after publication and was undoubtedly justified in commenting:

The general make-up and style . . . of the book are such, it must be confessed, as to trouble even an enthusiastic reader. The richness of the summaries of fact and opinion does not atone for the failure to state clearly the probable answer to the main problem. At times irrelevant details blur the issue. Torrents of rhetorical enthusiasm over youth, love, genetic psychology and other matters will irritate the scientific student and probably will befuddle the "general reader." One has to gyrate about from whales to vital statistics, to the lives of saints, to Jacksonian epilepsy, to the Hopi dancers until one prays for a range of knowledge equal to . . . Hall's to empower him to see the unity and organization of the book or any chapter in it. *(Thorndike, 1904, p. 224)*

In addition to presenting these organizational and stylistic difficulties, Hall appears to have fallen victim to what we might call, for lack of a more elegant scientific label, the "baby-with-the-bath-water phenomenon." Because one of the principles he proposed for explaining human development was discredited, his work as a whole was discredited. Coming to intellectual maturity during the late nineteenth century, Hall was much influenced by Darwin's theory of evolution and developed an extension of this theory to explain the unfolding of the human life cycle. Just as the human species as a whole appears to have evolved from lower forms of life (an ape-like creature, a monkey-like creature, and so forth, down to a probable one-celled amoeba-like creature), Hall suggested that various stages of life between infancy and adulthood mirrored various stages in the evolutionary history of mankind. In infancy, for instance, the child was supposed to resemble a very primitive ancestor of the human race that had existed countless centuries before, in middle childhood, a more advanced but still prehistoric version of humanity. In fact, claimed Hall, it was more than a matter of mere resemblance. The evolutionary history of the human race as a whole *determined* the way in which any individual would develop. It was a pattern stamped into the very tissues of the human organism and must unfold according to a fixed and unalterable sequence. For reasons that will become clear later on, this view of human development was dismissed soon after it was first proposed, and a great many of Hall's other observations followed it into oblivion.

No matter how justified various criticisms of his work may have been, it is unfortunate that *Adolescence* has been ignored to such an extent. A review of the two-volume study convinced us that Hall had contributed much more to the psychology of adolescence than has generally been acknowledged. Judging from the amount of attention Hall has received in a number of recent articles and books *(Conger, 1973; Grinder, 1969, 1973; McCullers, 1969)*, we are not alone in this view. For it was Hall, with his cataloguer's eye and empirical bent, who first sketched in the basic dimensions of the adolescent experience. It was Hall, influenced perhaps by the German romantic tradition he had come into contact with in his studies abroad, who was the first psychologist to characterize adolescence as a period of storm and stress. In formulating the theory of recapitulation, Hall also pointed up the necessity of uncovering the principles that govern human growth. And finally, in linking adolescence with the development of individuality, Hall was actually far ahead of his time.

Hall's Theory of Adolescent Development

Recapitulation: The Fundamental Assumption

We have observed that any developmental theory, in addition to describing a pattern in human growth, usually also concerns itself with what *determines* this pattern. What is it that transforms the helpless, speechless infant into an independent, articulate adult over the course of a couple of decades? Is it largely a matter of inborn characteristics, properties of the living organism that cause it to develop along certain lines regardless of what happens to it, or is it owing principally to outside forces, actual experiences the organism has once it enters the world? This question represents, of course, the well-known "nature versus nurture" controversy, which has raged throughout the history of psychology. Indeed, it raged long before psychology was recognized as a separate discipline. Almost three centuries ago, the English philosopher John Locke came down strongly on the side of nurture when he suggested that the human infant was a tabula rasa, a blank slate that could take on virtually any characteristic depending on what the world chose to write upon it. Hall, on the other hand, reflecting the scientific climate of his times, was more inclined to throw in his lot with nature. In his view, the outside environment was relatively unimportant in determining the course of human development, at least until adolescence. The progression between infancy and puberty was supposed to be fixed and obedient to certain biological laws.

The influence of Haeckel and Rousseau   We remarked earlier that Hall applied Darwin's theory of evolution to explain the unfolding of the human life cycle. Actually there were a couple of intermediate steps. Although prior to Darwin there was already a vague awareness that the way in which the human being (and many other organisms, for that matter) developed in the womb roughly paralleled the way in which the human species had developed over countless eons, it was only after the publication of Darwin's discoveries that the connection was stated explicitly *(Grinder, 1967)*. The nineteenth-century biologist Ernst Haeckel, himself responsible for disseminating many of Darwin's ideas, formulated what he believed to be the fundamental law of development. He hypothesized that ontogeny—the sequence of growth that an individual organism follows in the womb and before birth—is a brief repetition of phylogeny—the sequence of development that the organism's ancestors and forerunners followed during evolution. It was as if, Haeckel suggested, the organism must briefly repeat its own evolutionary history in the interval between conception and birth. The fact that the human embryo, for instance, exhibits gill slits, rather than lungs, when only a few weeks old was taken as an indication that human beings had evolved from some sort of fish-like creature countless millions of years before.

Hall applied to *postnatal* development the same principle that Haeckel had employed to describe prenatal development. He theorized that during the years between infancy and sexual maturity the child was also repeating the history of the species—but not the entire history. This postnatal recapitulation was more circumscribed and condensed. Rather than reflecting the entire sweep of evolution, childhood was supposed to proceed in stages, each of which mirrored a primitive stage of the human species. Very early childhood might correspond, Hall speculated, to a monkey-like ancestor of the human race that had reached sexual maturity around the age of six. The years between eight and twelve allegedly represented a reenactment of a more advanced, but still prehistoric form of mankind, possibly a species that had managed to survive by hunting and fishing. Indeed, the passion that many nine- and ten-year-old boys exhibit for outdoor sports and fights was cited as evidence *(Hall, 1904, I, 44)*.

But Haeckel and Darwin were not the only theorists who exerted influence on Hall. A close examination of his work reveals the impact of Rousseau's thinking as well. In fact, as Grinder *(1967)* has observed, Hall's formulations represented an ingenious amalgam of the thinking of Darwin, Haeckel, and Rousseau. In distinguishing between the child's mentality and the adult's, Rousseau had also implied that childhood was somehow more primitive in character than adulthood, that during infancy and before the advent of spoken language the child responded to the world much as an animal might, and that during later childhood he was roughly the intellectual equivalent of a savage. In applying his observations to education, the Swiss philosopher underscored the supposedly primitive elements of childhood more explicitly. Since the youngster was incapable of grasping the principles of geometry or the meaning of abstractions like "justice" and "freedom" before the "dawn of reason" in adolescence, why not let him indulge his "savage instincts" during childhood? What sense did it make to cram his head full of ideas that he could not understand anyway?

That Hall was well acquainted with Rousseau's recommendations is apparent in the following excerpt from the preface of *Adolescence*:

Rousseau would leave the prepubescent years to nature and to these primal hereditary impulsions and allow the fundamental traits of savagery their fling till twelve. Biological psychology finds many and cogent reasons to confirm this view if only a proper environment could be provided. The child revels in savagery, and if its tribal, predatory, hunting, fishing, fighting, roving, idle playing proclivities could be indulged in the country and under conditions that now, alas! seem hopelessly ideal, they could conceivably be so organized and directed as to be far more truly humanistic and liberal than all that the best modern school can provide. *(1904, I, x.)*

Rousseau's influence is even more apparent in Hall's characterization of adolescence, and here *our* characterization of Hall as a theorist who threw in his lot with heredity in the age-old debate over heredity versus environment requires some qualification. Hall definitely thought that development during *childhood* was a kind of passive unfolding ordained by nature. However, with the approach of puberty, development was supposed to become more plastic and fluid. Although still under the thumb of nature as far as his sexual development was concerned, the adolescent was allegedly far more sensitive than the child to "outside influences," far more capable of being molded by them. Now was the time, Hall declared, for educators to step in and offer guidance. The reader may catch echoes here of Rousseau's insistence that only during adolescence did the child become capable of reasoning like an adult—and was, hence, truly educable.

Despite the fact that Hall was drawing upon a well-established philosophical tradition, the supposed shift between heredity and environment might seem to represent an inconsistency in his thinking. However, it probably made perfect sense to the theorist himself. We of the twentieth century are so inured to rapid change and "progress" that we are inclined to take them for granted. We are used to hearing and to reading that modern technology has created a speedily changing world, a rate of progress so accelerated that the human race can scarcely keep pace with it. We tend to forget that this particular view of human history is itself relatively recent. The man of science in Hall's time found himself confronted by what must have seemed a remarkable phenomenon. Whereas Darwin's theory of evolution indicated that it had taken *millions* of years for the human species to emerge, nineteenth-century archeological studies were beginning to suggest that man had proceeded from a level of savagery not far above the animals to a highly complex and civilized existence in only a few *thousand* years. What could account for civilization itself?

Adolescence and evolution   Although he never went so far as to formulate the actual mechanisms involved, Hall believed that the explanation for civilization was somehow bound up with the changes that occurred during adolescence. He observed that the comparatively steady rate of growth during childhood seemed vastly accelerated. And paralleling this rapid physical spurt at adolescence, there was an increase in sensibility, a heightening of all capacities.

The earlier stages of development, determined as they were by inborn forces, tended to reflect "what man has in common with the animals," but the later stages, Hall declared, "raise him above them and make him most distinctively human . . ." *(1904, I, 39)*. In addition to acquiring the ability to reproduce during adolescence, the individual rather abruptly became aware of all the institutions that would hereafter shape his adult life: religion, economic forces, morality, politics. His intellectual powers increased, making him more amenable to schooling. And anticipating adult love and the responsibilities of marriage, he became capable of developing passionate attachments to individuals of the opposite sex.

Adolescence, then, according to Hall, was a particularly vital period in furthering nature's evolutionary scheme for mankind. It had a kind of dual significance. On the one hand, it represented the recapitulation of a stage of human history midway between the primitive and civilized. On the other hand, because the adolescent was becoming sensitive to the great institutions of the culture in which he resided, he would ultimately contribute to *changing* those institutions. In the opening chapter of *Adolescence* Hall remarked: "Thus the augmented individuality of adolescence is developed in the interest of the species for the sake of which sex itself originally arose, and to serve which art, science, and religion came into being, together with all the institutions which the powers acquired at this age have since created" *(1904, I, 44)*.

And later on, elaborating on this theme, he offered the following rationale for linking the adolescent's budding sense of individuality with the continuing progress of civilization:

This is germane to a state of nature when the child no longer needs parental protection but, in primitive life and warm countries, breaks away and shifts for himself. Hitherto he has been the center in his environment, has been fed, sheltered, and taught, and with all the flush of morning, and springtide hopes, goes out to maintain subsistence, and ultimately to become the center of another family; all this before the longer apprenticeship to life which civilization has enforced was known. It is the time for large views and plans; life problems now press upon him; ambition and self-affirmation are never of such high selective value. His ego must be magnified and all in the new environment subordinated to it. Strife and labor, intensified and prolonged are imperative. It is now or never, the impulsiveness of youth can not wait and its ambition is never so exorbitant. Now, instead of head hunting, winning a new name, wrestling alone with spirits or other of the drastic initiations of savages, the civilized and more sedentary youth must vent his intensification of personal feelings in dreams of greatness—and who has not at this season been prince, millionaire, hero, walked with the great of earth or heaven, in reverie? Perhaps the very repressions of modern life have given added color and range to the ideal. The youth's powers are now tested, and who knows, but he may become the greatest among men? *(1904, I, 315–316)*

Adolescence would supply the life blood to sustain society in its march toward progress. It was, given the adolescent's increased sensitivity, flexibility, and awareness, a kind of second birth. "In some respects," remarked Hall, "early adolescence is thus the infancy of man's higher nature, when he receives from the great all-mother his last capital of energy and evolutionary momentum" *(1904, II, 71)*. To be sure, Rousseau had also, more than a century before, described this period as a kind of rebirth, but Rousseau had never gone so far as to declare:

. . . for those prophetic souls interested in the future of our race and desirous of advancing it, the field of adolescence is the quarry in which they must seek to find both goals and means. If such a higher stage is ever added to our race, it will not be by increments at any later plateau of adult life, but it will come by increased development of the adolescent stage, which is the bud of promise for the race. *(Hall, 1904, I, 50)*

In the light of the growing interest in adolescence at the present time, Hall's pronouncements of 70 years ago have a strikingly contemporary ring, but curiously, as Grinder has recently observed *(1967)*, the implications of such views were never fully appreciated in his own time.

Hall's Portrait of Adolescence

This oversight appears all the more curious when we examine Hall's description of the adolescent experience in detail, for it is similar in many respects to modern descriptions. Indeed, glancing at the table of contents for his two-volume study, we begin to suspect all the more that his influence on adolescent psychology has been greater than is commonly acknowledged. Although a few of the chapter headings seem faintly antiquated, most of them—"Growth in Height and Weight," "Sexual Development," "Adolescent Love," "Social Instincts and Institutions," "Intellectual Development and Education," "Juvenile Faults, Immoralities, and Crimes," "Diseases of Body and Mind"—are more than a little reminiscent of many current textbooks. Whatever other changes have occurred in psychology over the past 70 years, the dimensions of the adolescent experience—at least as far as psychologists are concerned—seem to have altered only slightly. True, a contemporary reader may find Hall's moralizing about the supposed evils of masturbation somewhat amusing, particularly in view of Kinsey and his colleagues' revelation *(1948)* that it is almost universal among boys and quite widespread among girls. But allowing for the changes in sexual attitudes that have occurred since Hall, there are many passages in *Adolescence* that could be lifted verbatim and ascribed to a present-day psychologist without anyone's being the wiser. We offer as an illustration an excerpt that draws a comparison between childhood and adolescence:

At dawning adolescence this old unity and harmony with nature is broken up; the child is driven from his paradise and must enter upon a long viaticum of ascent, must conquer a higher kingdom of man for himself, break out a new sphere and evolve a more modern story to his psycho-physical nature. Because his environment is to be far more complex, the combinations are less stable, the ascent less easy and secure; there is more danger that the youth in his upward progress, under the influence of this "excelsior" motive, will backslide in one or several of the many ways possible. New dangers threaten on all sides. It is the most critical stage of life, because failure to mount almost always means retrogression, degeneracy, or fall. One may be in all respects better or worse, but can never be the same. The old level is left forever. Perhaps the myth of Adam and Eden describes this epoch. The consciousness of childhood is molted, and a new, larger, better consciousness must be developed, or increased exposure and vulnerability will bring deterioration. *(1904, II, 71–72)*

Indeed, a pair of well-known contemporary psychologists have adopted much the same theme:

The metaphor commonly chosen for the discussion of adolescent development has the bridge as its central image. The child at this period is pictured between two worlds, closer to childhood, but with his back turned to it, facing the adult status that lies ahead, on the other side of the adolescent pass. The conception is clear, simple and apt in some ways. But we would suggest that the adolescent's relationship to these two worlds is not simple and unidirectional. There is a great deal of wavering, backtracking, and even simultaneous movement in both directions (as though the youngster were trying to encompass the whole transitional span by widening his step, avoiding complete commitment to either side). In addition to these complexities of pace, we would add another condition about the child's relation to the future adulthood which makes the meta-phor even less descriptive. The fact is that adulthood is not just a prospect that the child sees ahead of him. It is also a crucial component of his activities and life as he makes the adolescent transition. *(Douvan & Adelson, 1966, p. 22)*

Hall was perhaps the first psychologist to characterize adoles-cence as a period of great complexity—a "betwixt and between" stage of human development yet one that could have a particularly decisive impact on adult personality. Unfortunately, as has already been observed, he was unable to do justice to his own conception. In attempting to describe what he envisioned as the intricacies of the period, he apparently encountered the same kind of organizational difficulties that have confounded students of adolescence ever since. Like many who succeeded him, Hall ended up describing the in-dividual pieces of the puzzle, but not how they fitted together. In fact, to provide a coherent account of Hall's theory, we actually have to impose a scheme of organization, to group his myriad observations under a few general headings. Nonetheless, we believe his work may be discussed under roughly three major topics: the dimensions of the adolescent experience, the larger societal context in which adolescent development occurs, and the problem of sex differences.

The Dimensions of the Adolescent Experience

Biological changes   In view of the profound influence the theory of evolution exerted on Hall's thinking, it is scarcely surprising that he began his study of adolescent psychology with a series of chapters on physical growth. As indicated, Hall believed that with the advent of puberty there was a sudden acceleration of growth, and he took this spurt as a key bit of evidence for his claim that adolescence was a period of special significance. Considering the vast array of data that Hall cited to back up his description of "the adolescent growth spurt," it is apparent that he was influenced not only by Darwin's theory but by Darwin's *method* as well. For every observation about the physical development of the pubescent youngster, literally pages and pages of statistics and graphs are offered in support. Like a biologist meticulously counting up the various species of plants and animals he has encountered on a remote island, Hall carefully documented his assertions, the following passage being a typical example of his particular brand of scholarship:

N. V. Zak, e.g., measured the height and chest girths of 1,434 pupils of Moscow Real-schools and 2,811 from classical *gymnasia.* He finds that height decreases during the day slightly at eleven, much more at fourteen, and less at eighteen while weight increases also most at fourteen. At every age these boys are markedly taller than peasant boys. The pubertal increment of growth in height at from thirteen to fourteen is more rapid than that of English, Swedish, or Boston boys, but the decline of rate from sixteen on is most marked yet with a tendency to resume growth at twenty-one. *(1904, I, 8–10)*

Confronted with this sort of statistical barrage, we cease to wonder where the encyclopedic style of the modern textbook originated. (We shall cover some of the same ground, though less exhaustively, in Chapter 5.)

Sexual development   Hall used the term "saltatory"—from the Latin *saltare*, meaning "to leap"—to describe the rate of development during adolescence. It is an apt term for the burst of growth which was supposed to herald the approach of puberty. And very likely influenced by the revelations of psychoanalysis, which were just beginning to have an impact in this time,[3] Hall did not shrink from describing the other key development that inevitably accompanied the adolescent's great leap forward. Supposedly dormant all through childhood, the sexual impulses, given a powerful push by nature, suddenly awoke, and the youngster was abruptly flooded by feelings he had never known before. In fact, Hall believed sexuality to be such a potent force that he declared at one point: "Many crimes and immoralities of early adolescence are from a blind impulse on which consciousness does not act at all. In the psychic evolution of the sexual impulse there is often at first a period of general perturbation before the brain reacts on the sex organs" (1904, I, 284). And a little farther on he remarked, "In normal adolescence, if entirely uninstructed, the evolution of this function begins as something entirely new in the experience of the individual, but so strong that it will more or less dominate the life" (1904, I, 285). Once an individual had acquired the ability to reproduce and had begun to experience all the desires that usually accompany the appearance of this particular capacity, his existence would never be the same.

However, although he was modern enough to give an unequivocal account of the adolescent's sexual awakening, Hall was also something of a Victorian moralist. Interspersed with his factual account of what took place at puberty are numerous warnings about the dangers of sexual excess. As noted, even ordinary masturbation, now thought to be exceedingly common among adolescent males, was denounced as a great evil.

Hall's grounds for this attack were rather vague, and he admitted that many of the supposed consequences of indulging in "the secret vice" were, in fact, mythical. Masturbation did not, he declared, cause insanity—contrary to popular belief. On the other hand, he claimed, apparently with great conviction:

Growth, especially in the moral and intellectual regions, is dwarfed and stunted. There are early physical signs of decrepitude and senescence. Gray hairs, and especially baldness, a stooping and enfeebled gait, the impulsive and narrow egoism which always goes with overindulgence, marks of early caducity which may crop out in retina, in cochlea, in the muscular or nervous system, in the stomach—all the troubles ascribed to this cause are distinctly senescent in their nature. Life has been lived out

---

[3] Ironically, though the emergence of psychoanalysis was to be partially responsible for the decline of Hall's own theory, he was a great admirer of Sigmund Freud and arranged for Freud's only lecture tour in the United States.

with abandon: its energies have been overdrawn, and its wheels have run down like the mainspring of a clock the regulator of which has been lost, so that the term "fast" has a profound biological significance. *(1904, I, 444)*

As products of a more permissive society, we may find Hall's exhortations amusing, but there is a theme underlying them that is very much alive in our modern conception of adolescence.

The emotional dimension We are speaking of the notion of storm and stress. Once acquainted with Hall's warnings about the imperiousness of adolescent sexuality, we do not need much imagination to conclude that he considered it responsible for making adolescence a period of emotional turbulence and instability. To be sure, there was a positive side to his view. With the emergence of sexual feelings, the nervous system generally became more sensitive and responsive. The senses of hearing, sight, and touch were all supposedly heightened. The capacity to love and love deeply began to develop. For this was the period of sudden romantic attachments (which cooled just as suddenly) and passionate friendships.

But this increased reactivity—a sign of the transition taking place between man's lower nature and his higher capabilities—could take its toll. Even the normal adolescent purportedly became susceptible to abrupt shifts in mood, full of high spirits one moment and sunk in despair the next. Actual abnormalities and aberrations, Hall asserted, also became increasingly common. He cited figures to show that the rate of insanity multiplied during adolescence—as did the rate of delinquency. (Not surprisingly, he remained enough of a Darwinian to suggest that those youngsters who actually succumbed either to crime or to mental disease were probably victims of some "hereditary taint.") Indeed, taking both the developing capacity for tender emotions and the notion of storm and stress into account, the portrait of adolescence that emerges most persistently from Hall's work is one fraught with polarities and contradictions:

Perhaps at no time of life can goodness be so exotically pure and true, virtue so spotless, and good works spring from such a depth of goodwill, which, since Kant, is often made the source of all real morality. Conscience, though not new-born, now can first begin to play a leading role. It awakens with a longing hunger and thirst for righteousness, prompts to highest aspiration and resolve. Benevolence and love to all persons and all being is fresh from its original source, and there are hearty good wishes for the general and special weal of others and ingenuity in anticipating and gratifying their desires, so that for brief periods youths and maidens sometimes seem too good for this earth.

But we need have no fear. From the same soil in which these budding virtues spring and bloom so delicately arise rank weeds; physical appetites are grossly indulged naively, even though they may sometimes seem almost bestial; propensities to lie break out, perhaps irresistibly, for a time. Anger slips its leash and wreaks havoc. Some petty and perhaps undreamed meanness surprises the onlooker. The common constraints of society are ruptured, or there are spasms of profanity; perhaps a sudden night of debauch, before knowledge had put up proper defenses; perhaps some lapse from virtue, which seems almost irretrievable, but which in fact should never be so readily pardoned and forgotten. The forces of sin and those of virtue never struggle so hotly for possession of the youthful soul. *(1904, II, 82–83)*

Being as interested in instructing the young as he was in studying them, Hall believed that this sort of duality, the adolescent's tendency to embrace extremes and his unpredictability, presented educational institutions, essentially the guardians of civilized society, with one of their greatest challenges. That such excesses occurred impressed upon Hall

in an unmistakable way the subhuman origin of human nature. Many of these are given us in great abundance at adolescence, and the problem of moral and religious education is whether we can thoroughly civilize these barbaric and bestial proclivities and bring them into the harmony and unity of the completed character. *(1904, I, 297)*

We catch here, in an equally unmistakable way, an echo of the theme of recapitulation. The relationship between the adolescent and adult society was, for Hall, very similar to the relationship between a primitive tribe and a group of colonists. The tribe might possess all the rudiments and tools of civilization, but without outside assistance and intervention it would never be able to attain civilization.

The cognitive dimension Fortunately for mankind, the adolescent did possess a formidable tool, one that, properly shaped and directed, would allow him to rise far above his animal ancestors. Endorsing the idea that Rousseau had advanced almost 150 years before and accommodating it to evolutionary theory, Hall observed that the birth of intellect accompanied the birth of sexuality. Whereas childhood was a period for acquiring the basics, for rote memorization and drill, only during adolescence did the youngster truly acquire the capacity to *reason*. Again, Hall pointed to the parallel between the development of the individual and the evolutionary history of the species. Just as the ability to reason appeared relatively late in the developmental cycle, so man's superior powers of cognition were thought to be among the last to have evolved.

With the dawn of these new capacities, the adolescent was able to push beyond the narrow confines of the child's world. Unlike the child, naïve, easily duped, and inclined to be rather superstitious, the adolescent was supposed to demonstrate the beginnings of adult skepticism, that singularly human ability to view a situation from more than one perspective. The child tended to live from day to day, forever in the present, with little awareness of the events that had preceded his arrival on earth and equally little awareness of his own future. During adolescence a true sense of time—an appreciation of history and an ability to visualize the future—began to develop. So too did the ability to employ certain logical principles. Hall cited a number of studies—long since fallen into obscurity—to support his observations, the following being a typical example:

Shaw spoke and immediately wrote on the blackboard names of things, requiring the pupil to write at once as rapidly as possible whatever the term suggested to his mind. In studying these returns, it was found that the younger child's interest was self-centered in individual and particular acts, while older children recognized general or universal use. *(1904, II, 486)*

It was intellectual skills like these that would ultimately enable the adolescent to take his place in civilized society. Indeed, these were the very skills upon which society depended, which brings us to another facet of Hall's portrait of adolescence.

The moral and social dimension   Not only did the growth of his own intellect permit the youngster to think more like an adult; it also enabled him to *act* more like an adult—or at least to comprehend the principles that were supposed to govern adult behavior. Even the older child, according to Hall, remained something of a savage as far as morality was concerned. The adolescent, by contrast, had a much firmer and more mature grasp of society's rules and regulations. Quoting another researcher, Hall observed that "with the dawn of adolescence at the age of twelve or shortly after comes the recognition of a larger life, a life to be lived in common with others, and with this recognition the desire to sustain the social code made for the common welfare" *(1904, II, 394)*.

What did this social code entail? A firmer grasp of societal rules and regulations was a part of it, but so was a new feeling for humanity. Hall took note of these humane sentiments in summarizing a study that must have predated Piaget's explorations of moral judgment *(1932)* by a good 30 or 40 years:[4]

---

[4] We shall review Piaget's work on cognitive development during adolescence in Chapter 5.

From one thousand boys and girls of each age from six to sixteen who answered the question as to what should be done to a girl with a new box of paints who beautified the parlor chairs with them with a wish to please her mother, the following conclusion was drawn. Most of the younger children would whip the girl, but from fourteen on the number declines very rapidly. Few of the young children suggest explaining why it was wrong, while at twelve, one hundred and eighty-one, and at sixteen, seven hundred and fifty-one would explain. The motive of the younger children in punishment is revenge; with the older ones that of preventing a repetition of the act comes in; and higher and later comes the purpose of reform. With age comes also a marked distinction between the act and its motive and a sense of the girl's ignorance. Only the older children would suggest extracting a promise not to offend again. Thus with puberty comes a change of view-point from judging actions by results to judging by motives, and only the older ones see that wrong can be done if there are no bad consequences. *(1904, II, 393–394)*

Religious development This finer grasp of moral principles was supposed to bring the adolescent several steps nearer than the child to the assumption of adult responsibilities. Although Hall himself does not make the connection explicit, the development of moral sensibilities was presumably associated closely with the growth of religious feeling during adolescence. (In any case, the chapters entitled "Adolescent Psychology of Conversion" and "Social Instincts and Institutions" are presented back to back in Volume II of *Adolescence.*) Clearly a devout man himself, Hall regarded religion, with its universal principles of human dignity and its emphasis on selflessness, as yet one more evidence of man's higher nature. Consequently, it was logical for the pubescent youngster, who was, it ought to be stressed once more, supposedly reliving the evolution of his race, to develop an interest in religion. Hall declared that the largest number of religious conversions occurred during adolescence and gave this rationale:

In its most fundamental sense, conversion is a natural, normal, universal and necessary process at the stage when life pivots over from an autocentric (self-centered) to an heterocentric (other-centered) basis. Childhood must be selfish in the sense that it must be fed, sheltered, clothed, taught, and the currents of its environment set toward and not from it. Again, infancy is generic and abounds in rudimentary physical and psychic traits common to many forms of higher animal as well as of human life. In the adolescent infancy of the soul a similar totalizing tendency appears on a higher plane. Youth seeks to know, get, feel all that is highest, greatest, and best in man's estate, circumnutating in wide sweeps before it finds the right object upon which to climb. *(1904, II, 301–302)*

It might be useful to note at this point how firmly entrenched the concept of childhood—as a period of helpless dependency and vulnerability—had become in Hall's early twentieth-century mind. Even more noteworthy are his strenuous attempts to differentiate the concept of adolescence from that of childhood. Indeed, in speaking of the "totalizing tendency" of the adolescent, Hall touched once again upon a theme that we have already observed in his work, a theme that was to be taken up in many forms and variations by other researchers. Although intellectual, moral, and religious development during adolescence were eventually to provide a counterweight to all that was bestial in man's nature, even in pursuing these loftier interests the youngster might end up embracing extremes. The new sense of morality could be transformed into a naïve idealism. Religious devotion could become an almost cruel kind of self-sacrifice, as Hall demonstrated by citing the lives of saints, many of whom had begun to lead lives of utter self-denial in early adolescence. And newly aware of his own powers of reason, a youth might strain them trying to solve problems that were, in the final analysis, insoluble. In short, the image of adolescence as an era of intensity and excess is one that recurs persistently in Hall's account.

The Large Societal Context: Critiques
of American Culture

With this picture of the teenager—unpredictable, contradictory, containing both the best and worst features of mankind—before Hall, it is not surprising that substantial portions of *Adolescence* are given over to impassioned critiques of the American educational system and, at times, to American society in general. Having come under the influence both of Rousseau's educational philosophy and of Darwin's theory of evolution, Hall's motto for the education of children could pretty well be summed up as "Nature is right." Because all the former experiences of the human species had somehow been stamped into his very tissues, the child was going to recapitulate the history of his race no matter what anyone else did. The stages between infancy were fixed and unalterable. Consequently—and here Hall's essential sympathy with Rousseau showed through very plainly—it made no sense to appeal to reason in educating a ten-year-old. He was still at too primitive a stage in his development to be capable of logic. The best course for educators was to make sure he got plenty of exercise out of doors (so that he could effectively live out all those primitive and savage tendencies) and to subject him to rote drill within the classroom.

The education of the adolescent was quite another matter, in Hall's view. Newly arrived at the age of rationality, far more flexible than the child, yet still given to excesses and extremes, he required more delicate and imaginative handling. And this, declared Hall, was rarely what he actually received. Too often, Hall claimed, returning to the topic in chapter after chapter, the methods appropriate to childhood were simply continued during adolescence. Like many a modern educator, Hall accused the American school system of being stifling and dehumanizing:

Everywhere the mechanical and formal triumph over content and substance, the letter over the spirit, the intellect over morals, lesson setting and hearing over real teaching, the technical over the essential, information over education, marks over edification, and method over matter. We coquet with children's likes and dislikes and cannot teach duty or the spirit of obedience. In no civilized land is teaching so unprofessional or school boards at such a low level of incompetence. Nowhere are the great traditions of the race so neglected, the high school so oblivious of either the nature or the needs, or both, of the adolescent stage of life. *(1904, I, xvii)*

Clearly, Hall was a firm believer in the necessity of intellectual discipline, but not a discipline that is imposed for its own sake. Rather than setting the curriculum before the adolescent arbitrarily, in unrelated bits and pieces, the teacher should, he declared, capitalize on the youngster's growing ability to conceptualize and show him the *principles* that underlay what he was supposed to learn. Rather than droning at his pupils, the teacher should make every effort to involve them directly, using diagrams and charts, employing a conversational tone, asking provocative questions, and in general trying to stimulate discussion.

For all his liberalism, however, Hall was in many ways something of an academic conservative. As he encouraged the teacher to challenge his pupils, virtually in the same breath he advised him to "address his efforts more to the upper and less to the lower half of his class" *(1904, II, 530)*. Hall was also bitterly critical of high schools for trying to prepare all their students for a university education. Such education was a privilege, he declared, that should be reserved for the very best minds. He was equally impassioned in his attack on the notion that college constituted some sort of preparation for life, hardly a view that would endear him to many present-day educators:

Another related surd that has acquired great vogue and wrought only mischief is that fitting for college is essentially the same as fitting for life. Indeed, life, it is said, is preparing for an examination. The lawyer crams for his cases; the doctor for his critical trials; the business man for crises. Life itself is an examination. Therefore, that state of man where he is fitting for college is really the best school for life. This involves the colossal assumption that the college has so adjusted itself to the demands of the world as it now is, that the old maxim—*non vitae sed scholae discimus* (we teach school rather than life)—presents an antithesis which no longer exists, and the schools and teachers that complain that they must fit for college rather than fit for life are nonsuited. . . . Life is not coaching nor cramming, and very few of its tests consist in getting up subjects and writing them. . . . *(1904, II, 512–513)*

In a scholarly and informative paper, Grinder and Strickland (1963) provide a possible explanation for this strain of élitism in Hall. Himself educated in both the United States and Germany, Hall appears to have acquired a certain sympathy for the European system of higher education, which was then and remains today more selective than the American system. (Roughly 5 percent of all German youth goes on to college, compared with close to 50 percent who enroll after high school in this country.) Such a system fitted in best with his own views on evolution. The human race had progressed to where it was—to the very pinnacle of the animal kingdom—because it had managed to develop all sorts of ingenious capacities for withstanding the rigors of nature. Therefore the most efficient way to ensure the continued advance of mankind (and Hall firmly believed that the human race was still evolving) was to select the most intelligent young people and educate them.

Perhaps it was also the memory of a more leisurely and less mechanized life in Europe that prompted Hall to extend his criticisms of the American educational system to American society in general. Although industrialization was providing man with the most comfortable existence he had ever known, it might ultimately strip him of his humanity:

We are conquering nature, achieving a magnificent material civilization, leading the world in the applications though not in the creations of science, coming to lead in energy and intense industrial and other activities; our vast and complex business organization that has long since outgrown the comprehension of professional economists, absorbs ever more and earlier the best talent and muscle of youth and now dominates health, time, society, politics, and lawgiving, and sets new and ever more pervading fashions in manners, morals, education, and religion; but we are progressively forgetting that for the complete apprenticeship to life, youth needs repose, leisure, art, legends, romance, idealization, and in a word, humanism. *(1904, I, xvi–xvii)*

Hence, long before the current concern over pollution and the recent spate of articles deploring the deteriorating quality of American life,

Hall was raising serious doubts about whether the United States was furnishing its youth with the best of all possible worlds. Judging from the number of educators and critics who have echoed him since (among them Erik Erikson, on whose theory we shall focus later), these misgivings were quite prophetic. At any rate, it seems to have been difficult for Hall to study adolescence without making forays into social criticism, a tendency much in evidence among contemporary students of adolescence.

The Problem of the Female Adolescent

Before concluding this review of Hall's work and examining the reasons for his decline, there is a final aspect of his theory to be discussed. Although we have already mentioned sexual development, we have not yet touched upon sex *differences*. Psychologists generally concur that the development of the female adolescent cannot simply be equated with that of the male adolescent. Judging from the chapters Hall devotes to menstruation and to adolescent girls and their education, the distinction between male and female was drawn even more sharply in his time. Indeed, as contemporary as other parts of *Adolescence* may sound, these particular chapters seem positively antiquated—which should serve as a reminder of how rapidly the status of women has changed over the past 70 years.

Hall's pronouncements on the education of women and their proper role in society would scarcely have won him much support from present-day Women's Liberation and Planned Parenthood organizations. As might have been expected in one who stressed the biological destiny of the human race to such an extent, Hall considered reproduction to be the female's most important function. In order to safeguard their child-bearing capabilities, girls who had begun to menstruate were to be treated with exquisite care. For some years following their first period, it was probably better for them not to work. Nor should they be taught anything that was too taxing intellectually. In fact, although he did not favor keeping women in a state of utter ignorance and did advise teaching them at least the basics of reading, writing, and arithmetic, Hall was not enthusiastic about sending large numbers of them to college. (Of course, since Hall was not enthusiastic about sending large numbers of men to college either, it would be wise not to make too much of this particular view.) He also expressed opposition to the idea of coeducation, which was currently coming into vogue in the United States, claiming that educating boys and girls together would prove too distracting for both parties.

It was probably much less male chauvinism than honest concern for the future of the human race that prompted most of Hall's suggestions with regard to the female adolescent. Not dreaming of the medical advances that were to reduce infant mortality rates drastically, he observed that it was necessary for each woman to bear an average of six children merely to keep the population stable (!). Hence his declaration that "in any ideal community the greatest possible number of women must be devoted to maternity and marriage" *(1904, II, 576)*. All the evidence at his disposal indicated a certain antagonism between attaining a high level of education and producing a large number of children. Not only were the female university graduates of Hall's day unlikely to marry, but even if they did so, they exhibited a distressing lack of fertility, averaging less than a child apiece. Perhaps, he speculated, "any organ like the brain or reproductive parts, if overworked may draw upon the vigor of the others" *(1904, II, 573)*, for male graduates were little more prolific than females. In any case, woman's place was clearly in the home.

As may be imagined—and these passages make fascinating reading for those who are interested in the contemporary Women's Liberation movement—Hall was quite critical of the new spirit of feminism just beginning to make its presence felt in the early 1900s. Nature had not intended women to be like men, and tampering with their biological destiny might imperil the entire human race:

. . . woman's body and soul are made for maternity and she can never find true repose for either without it. The more we know of the contents of the young woman's mind the more clearly we see that everything conscious and unconscious in it points to this as the true goal of the way of life. Even if she does not realize it, her whole nature demands first of all children to love, who depend on her for care, and perhaps a little less, a man whom she heartily respects and trusts to strengthen and perhaps protect her in discharging this function. *(1904, II, 610)*

Ironically, much as he might have offended present-day supporters of women's rights, Hall was probably something of a radical in his own times. Always mindful of woman's reproductive role, he encouraged girls to take pride in their periods, rather than regarding them as nuisances or irksome burdens. Indeed, he even went so far as to assign the female of the species a major, if somewhat indirect, role in bringing about civilization. In a bit of anthropological speculation that is, interestingly enough, almost the opposite of one recently advanced by Morris *(1969)*, Hall suggested that women had played an important part in domesticating men. Naturally more delicate and fastidious, they had probably been inclined to select the gentler representatives of the male sex for mates and had thereby passed on this more agreeable temperament to their offspring.[5] And however dubious Hall may have been about allowing women to attend college, he was not about to urge them to become "dumb Doras" either. If anything, he was opposed to this time-honored feminine type:

The caricatured maidens "as beautiful as an angel but as silly as a goose," who come from the kitchen to the husband's study to ask how much is two times two, and are told it is four for a man and three for a woman, and go back with a happy, "Thank you, my dear"; those who love to be called baby, and appeal to instincts half parental in their lovers and husbands; those who find all the sphere they desire in a doll's house . . . and are content to be men's pets; whose ideal is the clinging vine, and who take no interest in the field where their husbands struggle, will perhaps soon survive only as a diminishing remainder.   *(1904, II, 612)*

In other words, although it was unnecessary and even undesirable for an adolescent girl to aspire to be her eventual husband's intellectual equal, it might be nice for her to be capable of carrying on an intelligent conversation with him.

As further evidence of what were probably liberal views in his time, Hall also urged women to fashion a unique role for themselves in society rather than competing with men:

Now that woman has by general consent attained the right to the best that man has, she must seek a training that fits her own nature as well or better. So long as she strives to be manlike she will be inferior and a pinchbeck imitation, but she must develop a new sphere that shall be like the rich field of the cloth of gold for the best instincts of her nature. *(1904, II, 617)*

We have presented Hall's views on femininity not only for their historical interest. In his recognition of sex differences and his suggestion that girls differed psychologically, as well as physically, from boys, Hall introduced a problem into the study of adolescence that was to perplex psychologists from that time forward. As will become apparent, one of the key dilemmas for students of adolescent psychology is to devise a theory that will do as well by the female youngster as it does by the male.

[5] On the other hand, Morris argues in *The Naked Ape (1969)* that the reason women have their characteristic physical shape can be attributed to men. Back in the mists of prehistory, this was the shape our male ancestors were supposed to have found most erotically stimulating.

The Decline and Fall of Hall's Theory

On balance, despite many of his observations that are clearly out of date, we are impressed by how contemporary much of Hall's theory sounds. His characterization of adolescence as a period of storm and stress corresponds surprisingly well to the prevailing image of the teenage years. Judging from the number of current textbooks that employ a similar format for describing the adolescent experience, he appears to have identified the key dimensions in his two-volume study. Furthermore, in emphasizing the importance of adolescence as a period of human development, Hall was actually ahead of his time. He depicted adolescence as a phase in which various elements of the personality are integrated and a sense of individuality emerges. He also hinted that in conjunction with these developments the adolescent begins to become aware of his own uniquely personal destiny: "In adolescence, individuation is suddenly augmented and begins to sense its limits and its gradual subordination to the race which the Fates prescribe" *(1904, II, 58)*. Later on, we shall show that Hall actually anticipated the contemporary theorist Erik Erikson in assigning this sort of significance to the period. Why, then, did his theory fall into obscurity? Why is he so often given lip service as the "father of adolescent psychology" but so seldom read?

We alluded to some of the probable reasons earlier, suggesting that Hall was a victim of what we facetiously called the "baby-with-the-bath-water phenomenon." It may be useful to remember at this point that all human development between birth and maturity was, according to Hall's theory, governed by the principle of recapitulation. Infancy, early childhood, middle childhood, and adolescence were all purportedly brief reenactments of prior stages in the history of the human species. But soon after it was introduced, the theory of recapitulation was attacked and thoroughly discredited. Thorndike, who was himself to exercise a profound influence on American psychology, demonstrated in a devastating analysis that the analogy simply did not hold. A two-year-old child, argued Thorndike, had already surpassed *all* previous stages of mankind—monkey-like, ape-like, Neanderthal, what have you. Furthermore, was there any evidence to show that the course of development during infancy actually corresponded to the evolution of civilization? No, replied Thorndike: "Reaching for objects, holding them, putting them in the mouth, sitting up, standing erect, fighting, and sex instincts, whose dates of appearance in individual development are fairly well known, come in nothing like the order and at nothing like the dates of racial development" *(Grinder, 1967, p. 242)*. The theory was, in short, untenable, and consequently, scarcely a decade after it had been proposed, it was discarded. As part of the theory of recapitulation, Hall's theory of adolescence was put to rest as well, carrying with it, in our opinion, a great many potentially valuable insights to an untimely scientific grave.

In addition, as we have already indicated, Thorndike was justified in faulting Hall for a conspicuous lack of organization. His pages and pages of research citations, his excursions into moralizing and philosophizing, his lack of structure—all make for difficult reading. Douvan and Gold *(1966)* have commented in a recent article that, although Hall may have identified many of the basic *categories* of the adolescent experience (sexual development, physical growth, moral development, changes in intellect), he did not try to show how they might interact, how the numerous facets of adolescence might be fitted together into a coherent whole. It was probably not so much, as Douvan and Gold have suggested, a matter of Hall's being "supremely atheoretical," for, as we have seen he continually attempted to relate his observations to the theory of evolution. It was more, we suspect, because the theory itself was inadequate—lacking in concepts that would indicate *how* all the changes that occurred during the adolescent years were to be related. Actually, the changes that Hall described were in large part aspects of what we would call "psychological" or "personality" development today. Basically biological in orientation, the theory of evolution simply did not concern itself with this sort of development and therefore lacked principles that would explain it. Thus, recalling Rapoport whom we quoted at the beginning of this chapter, it was probably inevitable that Hall ended up merely describing "the observables" without being able to relate them. (We might add that a great many other students of adolescent psychology have apparently labored under the same handicap.)

Indeed, with personality theory still in its infancy during the early 1900s, it is difficult to see how Hall could have done otherwise. Perhaps the ultimate reason that Hall has been neglected for the past 70 years is, as Douvan and Gold intimate, a matter of "historical accident." It is always something of a mystery why one theory triumphs and another goes underground—or vanishes altogether. Certainly, the history of science is filled with examples of ideas that were advanced too early in the day to win wide acceptance. When Galileo, for instance, declared that the earth circled the sun rather than itself comprising the center of the universe, he was denounced as a heretic and forced to recant publicly. Presumably, the people who lived in the seventeenth century were not yet willing to have their planet, the very center of their own existence, reduced to a role of such utter insignificance. Similarly, psychologists of the early twentieth century may not have been ready, in fact, may not have been *equipped* to assign much importance to the teenage years of the human life cycle. Other intellectual advances had to occur before insights like Hall's could be appreciated.

One of these developments becomes apparent when we return briefly to Hall's comparison of *childhood* and adolescence. In retrospect, he appears to have *over*estimated the significance of adolescence. Because of his commitment to evolutionary theory and Rosseau's educational philosophy, Hall was inclined to view the course of childhood as fixed by nature. The psychologists who succeeded him reacted almost violently against this notion and emphasized instead the malleable and impressionable character of childhood. In a celebrated study, a colleague of Thorndike's, J. B. Watson, taught an infant to fear white-colored objects by frightening the little boy while he played in the presence of a white rabbit. If tiny infants were so amenable to outside influences, Watson declared, perhaps *all* human development was dependent on environment rather than heredity. In any case, young children were clearly far more accessible to education, far more capable of being molded by adults than Hall had thought. Consequently, under the influence of Thorndike and Watson, representatives of the new "learning theory" and "behaviorism," American psychologists turned their attention to early childhood, and adolescence disappeared from view.

Because of the appearance of another school of psychology, much the same thing occurred in Europe; nevertheless, earlier than its American competitor, this same school was eventually to take up the study of adolescence—which brings us to our next theory.

REFERENCES

BOWERS, K. S. Situationism in Psychology: An Analysis and a Critique. *Psychological Review*, 1973, **80**, 307–336.

CONGER, J. *Adolescence and Youth: Psychological Development in a Changing World*. New York: Harper & Row, 1973.

DOUVAN, E., & ADELSON, J. *The Adolescent Experience*. New York: Wiley, 1966.

DOUVAN, E., & GOLD, M. Modal Patterns in American Adolescence. In L. W. Hoffman & M. L. Hoffman (Eds.), *Review of Child Development Research*. Vol. II. New York: Russell Sage, 1966.

GRINDER, R. *Adolescence*. New York: Wiley, 1973.

GRINDER, R. The Concept of Adolescence in the Genetic Psychology of G. Stanley Hall. *Child Development*, 1969, **40**, 355–369.

GRINDER, R. *A History of Genetic Psychology.* New York: Wiley, 1967.

GRINDER, R., & STRICKLAND, C. G. Stanley Hall and the Social Significance of Adolescence. *Teacher's College Record*, 1963, **44**, 390–399.

HALL, G. S. *Adolescence.* New York: Appleton, 1904. 2 vols.

HORROCKS, J. E. *The Psychology of Adolescence.* (3rd ed.) Boston: Houghton Mifflin, 1969.

KINSEY, A., POMEROY, W., & MARTIN, C. *Sexual Behavior in the Human Male.* Philadelphia: Saunders, 1948.

KLUCKHOHN, C., & MURRAY, H. Personality Formation: The Determinants. In C. Kluckhohn & H. Murray (Eds.), *Personality in Nature, Society, and Culture.* New York: Knopf, 1948.

McCANDLESS, B. R. *Adolescents: Behavior and Development.* New York: Holt, Rinehart & Winston, 1970.

McCULLERS, J. G. Stanley Hall's Conception of Mental Development and Some Indications of its Influence on Developmental Psychology. *American Psychologist*, 1969, **24**, 1109–1114.

MORRIS, D. *The Naked Ape.* New York: Dell, 1969.

MUSSEN, P., CONGER, J., & KAGAN, J. *Child Development and Personality.* (4th ed.) New York: Harper & Row, 1974.

PIAGET, J. *The Moral Judgment of the Child.* London: Routledge & Kegan Paul, 1932.

RAPOPORT, D. The Structure of Psychoanalytic Theory: A Systematic Attempt. *Psychological Issues*, 1960, **6**, 1–157.

THORNDIKE, E. L. The Newest Psychology. *Educational Review*, 1904, **28**, 217–227.

Anna Freud's Theory of Adolescence: The Principle of Recapitulation Transformed

As her name suggests, Anna Freud is the daughter of Sigmund Freud, the Viennese psychiatrist who was himself the founder of psychoanalysis. Indeed, in order to understand her theory of adolescence, it is necessary to be acquainted with the contributions of the senior Freud as well. Like many of his American colleagues, Sigmund Freud (1856–1938) was inclined to ignore adolescence—though for rather different reasons. Whereas Hall believed that personality begins to acquire a decisive stamp only at puberty, Freud came to regard early childhood as the crucial period, principally on the basis of his work with the emotionally disturbed. In the course of determining what had gone wrong with his patients, Freud concluded that their disorders were ultimately the result of events that had occurred during the first five years of life.

In a theory formulated during the early 1900s (at roughly the same time that Hall was compiling his magnum opus on adolescence), Freud gave an account of human development that placed far more emphasis on childhood than Hall had. The child was not, Freud observed, completely impervious to outside influences. Though biology was a powerful source in determining his makeup, he was not simply a slave to his genes. If anything, the child was more plastic and impressionable than the adolescent—at least during the very earliest years of his existence. It was not the years following puberty that dictated what form an adult's personality would take. According to Freud, the decisive experiences had occurred long before the adolescent had attained sexual maturity. Hence, during the first 30 or so years of its history, psychoanalysis discounted the importance of adolescence and concentrated instead on infancy. Except for a few scattered papers, it was not until 1936 that Anna Freud, by then a psychoanalyst herself, noted this oversight and neatly summarized the reasons for it. The explanation, she declared, was obvious:

Psychoanalysis does not share the view that the sexual life of human beings begins at puberty. According to our theory, the sexual life has two starting points. It begins for the first time in the first year of life. It is in the early infantile sexual period and not at puberty that the crucial steps in development are taken, the important pregenital phases of sexual organization are passed through, the different component instincts are developed and brought into action and the normality or abnormality of the individual, his capacity or incapacity for love, are determined. We expect to derive from our study of this early period the knowledge of the origin and development of sexuality for which academic psychology seeks in its study of puberty. Puberty is merely one of the phases in the development of the human life. *(1936, p. 139)*

It should be abundantly clear that according to psychoanalysis, not only did the really significant events of life occur in early childhood but also that those events had something to do with sexuality. Unlike "academic psychologists" (and very likely Hall could have been included among them), psychoanalytic thinkers did not believe that the sexual instincts lay dormant all through childhood only to spring to the fore during adolescence. Quite the contrary, according to psychoanalysis, these drives originated in infancy, and if they were too severely thwarted at this time, the individual could become emotionally crippled, that is, neurotic, in adulthood. Here, in our view, is the fundamental difference between Hall's theory of human development and Sigmund Freud's. For Hall, the unfolding of the human life cycle was governed, at least up until adolescence, by a vague evolutionary principle he chose to call "recapitulation." For Freud, sexuality was the guiding force in life, the ultimate source of all human energy.

This difference becomes all the more intriguing when we actually examine the psychoanalytic description of adolescence. Although written some 30 years after the publication of Hall's two-volume study and with a growing awareness that adolescence had assumed the status of a "stepchild" in psychoanalysis, Anna Freud's portrayal is remarkably similar to Hall's. Again, the pubescent years are characterized as a time of opposites and extremes:

Adolescents are excessively egoistic, regarding themselves as the center of the universe and the sole object of interest, and yet at no time in later life are they capable of so much self-sacrifice and devotion. They form the most passionate love-relations, only to break them off as abruptly as they began them. On the one hand, they throw themselves enthusiastically into the life of the community and, on the other, they have an overpowering longing for solitude. They oscillate between blind submission to some self-chosen leader and defiant rebellion against any and every authority. They are selfish and materially minded and at the same time full of lofty idealism. They are ascetic but will suddenly plunge into instinctual indulgence of the most primitive character. At times their behavior to other people is rough and inconsiderate, yet they themselves are extremely touchy. Their moods veer between light-hearted optimism and the blackest pessimism. Sometimes they will work with indefatigable enthusiasm and at other times they are sluggish and apathetic. *(1936, pp. 137–138)*

Clearly, there is no quarrel between Anna Freud and Hall about the overall *description* of adolescence. We find many of the same features in Anna Freud's account that we encountered in Hall's: the romantic intensity, the storm and stress, the contradictions, the extremes of good and bad. What turns out to be at issue, however, is the *cause* of this rather dramatic upheaval. In fact, though he may have been meticulous about delineating various aspects of adolescent turmoil, Hall was somewhat remiss when it came to suggesting a cause. Presumably it had something to do with his thesis that adolescence represented a transitional stage of human history and hence was a neither-here-nor-there period of development. Presumably, it also had something to do with the sudden eruption of sexual feelings, which, Hall claimed, could temporarily disable the brain.

The Freudian Explanation of Adolescent Upheaval

Psychoanalysis offers a much more specific hypothesis, one that implicates sexuality far more directly in the adolescent upheaval. Interestingly enough, upon examining it closely, we again find that it involves the principle of recapitulation, although in a different version. The drama of adolescence, psychoanalytic theory asserts, is due to the reappearance at puberty of sexual conflicts that have occurred much earlier, during the first five or six years of life. What is recapitulated is not part of the genetic history of mankind but part of the *individual's* own past.

Obviously, if adolescent turmoil is the result of certain critical experiences during infancy, we need to know something about the nature of those experiences and *why* they are repeated in order to understand what produces such turmoil. In other words, in order to understand the psychoanalytic explanation of adolescence, it is necessary to be acquainted with the psychoanalytic theory of childhood, otherwise known as "infantile sexuality."

Just what are the key events of childhood and why, according to psychoanalytic theory, do they exert such a profound influence on all subsequent development? Many of us, having grown up in a culture in which psychoanalytic concepts are widely accepted, are scarcely inclined even to wonder about the answer to this question. We take it for granted that the early years of life are the "formative ones" and that if people find themselves in emotional difficulties during adulthood it must all be due to "something that happened in their childhood." Yet, as ideas go, the notion that *childhood* rather than adolescence is the decisive period for personality development, that early experience is somehow more crucial than later experience, is not an old one. Certainly, Hall, writing less than a century ago, did not subscribe to it, and the idea came as something of a surprise to the man who first proposed it, Sigmund Freud. In fact, he almost discarded it.

As a psychiatrist practicing during the late 1800s in Vienna, Freud was, in effect, wandering in a kind of scientific neverland. The cause of mental illness was still a mystery, and many of the emotional disorders of the day took particularly perplexing forms. People would complain, for instance, about not being able to walk when there was nothing demonstrably wrong with their legs or of not being able to hear or see when no medical ailment could be detected. From his studies with the French physician J. M. Charcot *(Jones, 1953)*,[1] Freud learned that many of these baffling symptoms could be removed under hypnosis. A patient had only to be put into a hypnotic trance and told that he would be able to walk, see, hear, or do whatever he was currently unable to do, and voilà!, he would be able to do them. Clearly, these peculiar symptoms were produced by "something in the mind," some mysterious force that no one could yet fathom. Unfortunately, Charcot's discovery that they could be removed under hypnosis only partially resolved the enigma. For as soon as his patients were brought out of their trance, these strange ailments returned, rendering them just as blind, deaf, or lame as ever. The exact nature of the psychological forces that had induced such disorders remained a mystery, one that was to be unraveled only by Freud.

[1] The following account of the discovery of infantile sexuality is adapted from the biography of Sigmund Freud by Ernest Jones *(1953)*.

In the course of searching for a method to treat this odd sort of malady, which bore the psychiatric label *hysteria*, Freud discovered that a patient sometimes obtained relief from his symptoms if he could recall the circumstances under which they had first appeared. (Actually, Freud became aware of this technique through a senior colleague of his, Josef Breuer. It was Breuer who had first used the so-called cathartic method successfully.) Following this lead, Freud found that the patient, while talking about his symptoms, often dredged up childhood memories that seemed somehow related to his illness. One type of memory recurred with suspicious regularity, although Freud was dumbfounded when he encountered it initially. At the time, he was treating a group of female patients. Sooner or later, with almost monotonous uniformity, each remembered a dismaying but similar event. At a certain point in her treatment, each claimed to have been seduced by an adult male—all too frequently her father. At first the shocked and appalled Freud, whose moral standards were apparently quite as stringent as those of G. Stanley Hall *(Jones, 1953)*, was inclined to accept these memories at face value, and he spent many unhappy hours shaking his head over the hypocrisy of the Victorian society in which he lived. Freud even went so far as to publish a paper citing childhood seduction as the cause of hysteria.

Gradually, however, the truth began to dawn upon him. Although they had not intended to, Freud realized, his patients had been deceiving him. It was simply too much of a coincidence that all had been seduced at the tender age of four or five. What they were recalling, Freud concluded, with considerable embarrassment and chagrin at having been taken in, were childhood *fantasies*.

Plagued by a sense of his own short-sightedness and gullibility, Freud almost threw over his practice at this point. But it is perhaps a mark of his genius that he reconsidered and eventually recognized that he had made an astounding discovery instead. Although the concept of childhood as a period of helplessness and dependency had taken fairly firm hold in the late 1880s, the prevailing image was one of innocence and purity. True, Rousseau had likened the child to a savage, but it was a "noble savage" he had in mind, a creature basically good and uncorrupted by the worldly civilization in which he resided. However, Freud reasoned, if his patients had childhood fantasies of being seduced, even if those seductions had never occurred, that must mean that children were capable of experiencing sexual feelings. They were not, as most Victorian adults supposed, totally innocent of such matters until puberty. Sexuality did not spring up suddenly full blown at adolescence. It originated in infancy, and judging from the role it seemed to play in bringing about the neurotic miseries of his patients, Freud concluded that it was the key force in life. Bit by bit, drawing upon his experiences with patients, his observations of children, and his own penetrating self-analysis, Freud formulated a theory of personality development that emphasized a series of events in early childhood—the same events that another psychoanalytic theorist, his daughter Anna Freud, was later to claim were responsible for much of the storm and stress of adolescence.

The Theory of Infantile Sexuality

Because of this hypothesized relationship between experiences during early childhood and adolescent turmoil, we propose to review the psychoanalytic theory of infantile sexuality in some detail. It turns out, as a matter of fact, to be a rather intricate theory. Being the sort of painstaking intellectual craftsman that he was, Freud was never entirely satisfied with his account of personality development. (His biographer, Ernest Jones, reports that he was actively engaged in revising it virtually until the day he died.) The set of ideas that instructors of introductory psychology present as "orthodox Freudian theory" is thus really an amalgam of three interlocking theoretical systems: an account of what are considered the three most significant developmental stages (the theory of infantile sexuality), an account of how the personality fits together (the structural theory), and an account of how the mind functions (the topographical theory). In the following review we shall present concepts from each of the three theories and show how they are interrelated.[2]

Structural Aspects: The Id and the Ego

Despite the fact that Freud's theory concentrates much more intensely than that of Hall on the events of early childhood and assigns to those events a much more critical role in personality development, the two theories do seem to share a fundamental assumption about human growth. Earlier we noted Hall's belief, adapted from both Rousseau and Darwin, that the initial stages of development reveal "what man has in common with the animals"; a similar theme pervades psychoanalytic theory. Ironically, it was the elaboration of this theme that led Freud to a view of childhood

[2] Our review of psychoanalytic theory owes much to Brenner's primer (1955) on the subject.

almost diametrically opposed to that of Hall, a view that also incurred the wrath of Freud's Victorian critics.

It would not do, Freud claimed, simply to let the child unfold as he might with little attention to his education. For far from being a helpless innocent, spotless and untarnished as yet by vice, the newborn human being as Freud pictured him was a creature seething with imperious desires and demands. Helpless he might be, but not innocent, at least not in the conventional sense of the word. Filled with cravings that he wanted satisfied immediately, there was nothing especially pure or noble about him. In fact, Freud declared, the infant's personality (if it could even be described as that) consisted of little *but* these drives. Perhaps in an attempt to reflect the impersonal and relentless quality of these drives, Freud referred to them in a kind of theoretical shorthand as the *id* (Latin for "it"). The id was the reservoir of basic biological impulses that the infant brought with him into the world, and, as such, it was the ultimate source of all human energy. In fact, Freud was eventually to claim that all of human existence centered around the struggle between this "animal side" of man's nature and his more civilized inclinations *(1930)*.

In his original state, the infant was not well equipped to tolerate much delay in satisfying his wants. He was, as Freud put it, a slave to the *pleasure principle*, demanding instantaneous gratification of any need that happened to arise. (This notion is, of course, nothing new to anyone who has ever had the experience of keeping a very young baby waiting for a feeding.) But he was also subject to what must seem a cruel paradox. Although something of a tyrant in insisting upon the immediate gratification of his desires, the infant was powerless to do anything about himself and totally dependent upon others to do *for* him. Inevitably, because it was impossible for these others to anticipate his needs perfectly in advance and to respond to them, he experienced considerable frustration. This frustration, Freud reasoned, was so painful and produced such overwhelming feelings of helplessness and anxiety that soon after birth another structure of the personality began to arise, a structure that could exert some control over the unruly id and thus could begin to spare the infant some of the misery of having his wishes thwarted.

Again, in a kind of theoretical shorthand, Freud called this new agency the *ego* (Latin for "I") and designated it the "rational part of the personality." The ego was supposed to consist of a set of functions that human beings perform to keep themselves more or less in contact with reality: accurately perceiving any events that happen to be taking place, remembering what has occurred in the past, thinking logically, acting appropriately, and so forth. Obviously,

as far as the infant was concerned, these skills were quite rudimentary. At two or three months, he might have progressed to the
stage at which, instead of screaming uncontrollably until he was fed
no matter what anyone else did to distract him, he would stop crying
as soon as he caught sight of his mother warming the bottle. But
he was scarcely capable of any great feats of logic. It would take
years of interacting with the world—literally bumping up against it—
before he would develop anything resembling an adult ego, before
he would be capable, that is, of speaking in coherent sentences,
reasoning in abstractions, remembering past events and anticipating
future ones, and generally conducting himself like a civilized human
being. Even so, such was the imperiousness of the id, so little did the
basic nature of man's drives change from infancy to adulthood, that
it was possible throughout life for the id to overrule the ego and to
substitute its pleasure principle once again for the ego's reality
principle. (In fact, as we shall soon see, this domination of the id
was thought to pose a very distinct danger at puberty.)

The ego's relation to the id, Freud has explained, is fundamentally
one of a rider to his horse. There was little question which was the
more reasonable and sensible of the two, but it was always possible,
if the rider became unduly preoccupied or inattentive, for the horse
to win the upper hand. Loss of control remained perpetually a threat,
even though the child was eventually to acquire another agency to
assist the ego in its dealings with the id. But we shall discuss this
other structure of the personality, the *superego*, after introducing
some additional concepts from the theory of infantile sexuality.

The Developmental Aspect

So far, although we have identified the id as a "reservoir of
drives," we have not described these drives very specifically. Upon
examining them, we also learn a good deal about the *sequence* of
human development prescribed by psychoanalytic theory. Like Hall,
Freud divided the human life cycle into distinct phases, but rather
than considering them brief recapitulations of earlier stages in man's
evolutionary history, Freud believed that each was marked by the
emergence of a different aspect of human sexuality. In fact, during
the three very earliest phases of the life cycle, lasting a total of five
or six years, the three main components of sexuality, which would
later be integrated in adulthood, were all supposed to appear
separately. Each drive had its period of ascendance and then yielded
to another. But what force underlay this orderly progression? What
determined it?

In answering this question we uncover another similarity between Hall and Freud. Although Freud and Hall divided the human life cycle quite differently and although Freud considered early experience to be much more significant, they held rather similar views about what *caused* the human life cycle to unfold as it did. It was basically a matter of biology: There was simply something built into the human constitution that dictated the order in which various sexual drives would become manifest.

The oral phase   During the very first period of life, lasting roughly eighteen months, the energies of the id (which Freud called the *libido)* were concentrated on activities that involved the mouth. But the infant's interest in his mouth went beyond mere feeding. Even when he was not taking in nourishment, Freud pointed out, the infant was likely to be using it for sucking—on his thumb, his blanket, his toys, literally anything within his grasp. Hence Freud labeled this period the *oral phase.*

But we have still not made the connection between these early oral concerns and adult sexuality. As it turns out, Freud's view of sexual activity was more comprehensive than the rather narrow conception prevalent in his time. In describing the link between the oral phase and adult sexuality, Freud noted that the mouth *did* after all, possess a certain erotic significance, and he suggested that the infant's interest in sucking was part and parcel of the same drive that revealed itself in adulthood in the form of kissing and other related pursuits. (It was this sort of observation, incidentally, that aroused so much opposition among his Victorian critics.) Furthermore, because the earliest period of infancy is also the period of greatest vulnerability and helplessness, Freud suggested that there might be a link as well between feelings of dependency in adulthood and those experienced during the oral period. In fact, the term "oral" in psychoanalytic parlance is often synonymous with "dependent."

The anal phase   In the normal course of events, the infant, after having invested his id energies, or libido, chiefly in his mouth, became equally concerned with another area of his body, the anal region. This shift was not, in Freud's view, solely a biological development. To a certain extent, the infant was likely to have experiences that would frustrate his attempts to pursue his oral pleasures. He was likely to be weaned somewhere in the second year of life, if not before. His passionate interest in sucking was likely to have met with some disapproval (even in our modern era, there are still a good many parents who are anxious to discourage thumb sucking)— as would his inclination to put foreign objects in his mouth. However, even with all these pressures to weaken his orality, Freud still regarded the infant's growing preoccupation with the anal portion of his body as largely biological in origin. There was, according to Freud, something built into the child that made him become especially interested in his own toilet functions around the age of a year and a half or so.

Once again, Freud was meticulous about pointing out the connection between the youngster's anal concerns and adult sexuality, although in this case it was probably more readily apparent. Because of their proximity in the body, Freud theorized, there is probably always some link between excremental functions and sexual ones. In his own day it is possible the equation between the two was even more marked, for middle-class Victorians tended to regard sexual behavior with much the same disapproval reserved for toilet functions—as dirty and unmentionable. Then too, Freud remarked, the anal region could become an erotic zone in its own right. It sometimes figured prominently, he noted, in homosexual relations.

In any case, the infant was eventually to find his anal pleasures even more sharply curtailed than his oral ones had been. Inevitably, in an attempt to equip him for polite society and to free themselves from the diaper pail, his parents would begin to toilet-train him. Since these efforts to interfere with his anal activities made no particular sense to the child (it would be a long time before he acquired the ego skills that would permit him to consider the matter from his parents' point of view), a good deal of hostility was likely to develop on both sides. Although, in the end, the child generally yielded and learned to control both his bowels and his bladder, he could, during the actual training process, create plenty of difficulty for his parents by remaining passively resistant and stubborn. Indeed, if the exchange between parent and child became unusually acrimonious during this stage, the infant might develop into a permanently stubborn and resistant individual, an "anal" personality. Similarly, if the parents overemphasized the importance of being clean, neat, and well regulated during this period, they might well produce the sort of person who would be excessively concerned with neatness and order in adulthood. In fact, the experience of severe conflict during *any* of the three psychosexual phases could leave a very definite imprint upon the adult personality.

The phallic phase   Following the anal phase, by about the end of the third year of life, the child was propelled into the last phase of infantile sexuality, the phallic, or Oedipal, period. At this juncture, his libido, concentrated during the previous stage on the anal region, became centered instead upon the genitals. The little boy, in effect, became aware of his penis, discovered that it could give him pleasure, and consequently came to value this part of his anatomy very highly. The little girl was supposed to make a corresponding, though somewhat less dramatic discovery—that she too had a sexual organ, the clitoris, which, when stimulated, would bring her pleasure. Certain extremely important consequences were to follow from this awakening of phallic sexuality, although, as we shall see, Freud believed that they were far more clear-cut for the little boy than for the little girl.

As a result of his developing sexual awareness, Freud maintained, the little boy began to experience feelings for his mother, perhaps only vague feelings yet unmistakably akin to those he would later experience in adulthood when attracted to a woman. True, Freud admitted (1924), he might have only the foggiest idea of what sexual intercourse was like, but his desire to have his mother all to himself became evident nonetheless—as did a feeling of hostility for his father, who was his most serious rival. To lend credence to his account of this emotional tangle, aptly designated the "Oedipus complex" (after the Greek king who unwittingly murdered his father and married his own mother), Freud observed that by the time he was three, the little boy was likely to have acquired a strong affectionate bond with the woman who had been caring for him. Thus, it was natural for this relationship to develop sexual overtones—at least from the little boy's point of view—once his id energies became invested in his genitals.

Such a situation could not long endure. The little boy's Oedipal wishes concerning his mother and his desire for exclusive possession of her were even more impossible to fulfill than were the wishes for oral and anal gratification he had entertained and learned to subdue earlier in life. It soon became obvious that his mother was not about to give his father up, nor did his father exhibit much enthusiasm for surrendering *his* claims. Indeed, the little boy began to worry about having something far less pleasant happen to him.

In an attempt to demonstrate how the child's mind worked during this early period, Freud suggested that the little boy began forming dark suspicions about his father that had no basis in reality. Because *he* would have liked to eliminate his father—even adopting, perhaps, the rather drastic solution of murdering him—the child assumed that his father harbored similar feelings for him. In fact, Freud claimed, the little boy became obsessed with the thought that his father would inflict a very specific and terrible revenge upon him if he persisted in his desires. He conceived the fear that his father would deprive him of the very organ he had come to prize, his penis.

Obviously, his fear was highly irrational (although in Freud's day when small boys were discouraged from masturbating by threats of having either the penis or the offending hand removed it may have seemed more plausible). Only a demented father would ever have contemplated such a punishment for his son. However, in early childhood, between the ages of three and five, the child's ego was still too weak to distinguish reality from fantasy very reliably. To wish to do something was almost the equivalent of doing it. To fear something was almost equivalent to having it occur. Hence the castration complex he had developed forced the little boy to resolve the Oedipus complex—with far-reaching consequences, Freud maintained, for the structure of his personality.

A Return to the Structural Theory: The Emergence of the Superego

Clearly the male child could not remain forever in the complicated emotional tangle he had gotten himself into, ardently desiring his mother yet dreading the worst from his father. Besides, triumphing over his father and actually replacing him at his mother's side would be almost as disastrous as losing out to his father and being permanently maimed. To win, he would somehow have to put his rival out of the way, and since, during the first five years of his life the little boy had presumably developed some affection for his father, along with his feelings of hatred, the loss of his father would be a painful one. This ambivalence toward his father, the Oedipus complex, the castration complex—some way of resolving them had to be found.

The solution, Freud theorized, ultimately added a new structure to the personality, an agency that would ally itself with the ego to ensure that the powerful impulses emanating from the id would be controlled forever. For the way in which the little boy resolved the Oedipus complex—with all its passion, conflict, and dread—was to *identify* with his father, to become like him. It may be difficult to comprehend how identifying with his rival might allow the male child to extricate himself from the Oedipus complex, but Freud proposed several advantages. First of all, recalling the popular maxim, "If you can't lick 'em, join 'em," it was a means of disarming the father. It was as if, by trying to imitate his parent, the little boy were saying to him: "Look, you have nothing to fear from me. I am not really your enemy. The truth of the matter is that I want to be like you. So you needn't punish me for anything." Second, by identifying with his father, the child could retain the hope—however vain and foredoomed to disappointment—that he might some day resemble his father so closely that his mother actually *would* prefer him. Finally, and perhaps most important, in the course of identifying with his father, the little boy acquired a superego.

As the English translation of this term implies (it means roughly "over-I"), the superego is the moral aspect of the personality, which "watches over" the ego, making sure that the individual does not transgress against society—or at least making him feel guilty if he does. What was the connection between the child's identification with his parent and the formation of the superego? In the course of striving to become like his father, Freud explained, the little boy adopted his father's values and standards. Once internalized, these values and standards became the little boy's own—much as if he had acquired an internal parent or guardian. Thus equipped, the child could assume some responsibility for controlling his impulses —oral and anal, as well as Oedipal, ones. Before internalizing this "voice of conscience," he had been compelled to rely on his parents to keep him from doing wrong. (Anyone who has had much contact with children knows how much more trustworthy five-year-olds are than two-year-olds in refraining from doing what they have been told not to. According to psychoanalytic theory, the difference could be explained by the presence of a superego in the five-year-old and the absence of one in the two-year-old.)

The Topographical Theory

Even with the Oedipus complex resolved and the superego in residence, however, we are still faced with the question of where all the objectionable impulses and horrifying fantasies had *gone*. It was most unlikely that they had merely vanished. The answer is contained in the so-called topographical theory, Freud's account of how the mind functions.

It may be remembered that Freud first discovered the Oedipus complex in the course of treating his patients. Contrary to what Hollywood versions of psychoanalysis might lead us to believe, their fantasies of childhood seduction were not recalled immediately but appeared only after many hours of pouring out their feelings and associations. Freud's work with Charcot—who had demonstrated that hysterical symptoms could be removed under hypnosis—had already convinced him that the mind functioned on various levels, that an individual could be aware of something in a deeply submerged portion of his mind and totally unaware of it at a more superficial level. His work with neurotic patients, who recalled their early childhood fantasies only after laborious hours of therapy, confirmed his suspicions about how the mind functioned.

Evidently, he surmised, there were vast regions of the mind, storehouses of old memories and images, which remained inaccessible to the individual in his ordinary waking state. These thoughts had been disposed of because they were, for the most part, dangerous, that is, morally unacceptable. Such had been the fate of the little boy's Oedipus complex, and indeed, it was to be the fate thereafter of any id impulse that the superego objected to. The ego, the rational part of the personality that was supposed to control the functions of perceiving, remembering, and thinking, as well as any voluntary physical activity, would refuse to become *conscious* of it, and the impulse would remain in some *unconscious* region of the mind.

Freud called this whole process of keeping unacceptable impulses, fantasies, memories, and associations out of consciousness *repression*, and considered it one of the simplest techniques the ego could employ for defending itself against the id. There were other, more complicated strategies the ego could rally in its defense. An individual could, for instance, admit into consciousness only an aversion for something he unconsciously desired (a maneuver Freud termed "reaction formation"). But Freud emphasized that the defense always represented a compromise the ego had worked out between the superego and the id. The impulse that was being barred from consciousness would reveal itself in some disguised way. The girl who had repressed an awareness of her own sexuality might unwittingly become provocative, the perennial innocent who somehow (she was never quite sure how) managed to find herself in one compromising situation after another with members of the opposite sex. The citizen who expressed concern about the presence of pornography in his community and appointed himself a one-man censorship committee would have to view the very material he ostensibly abhorred. As will be seen shortly when we take up the psychoanalytic account of adolescence, the ego could develop even more elaborate tactics for controlling the id.

Feminine Psychology Revisited

But before continuing with the psychoanalytic theory of personality development, we would like to comment on a problem encountered previously, in our discussion of Hall: the problem of feminine psychology. So far we have given a detailed description of the little boy's progress through the first five years of life, but not the little girl's—and with good reason. Though Freud considered the oral and anal phases to be essentially the same for both sexes, he readily admitted that there were various theoretical difficulties with the feminine version of the Oedipus complex. In fact, after pondering this particular dilemma for a number of decades, Freud was moved to comment rather drily, "We have, after all, long given up any expectation of a neat parallelism between male and female sexual development" *(1931, p. 253)*.

The issue was basically one of motivation. Like the little boy, the little girl had by the age of three formed a strong attachment to her mother. What was to impel her to become interested in her *father*? And once interested in him, what produced the impetus for her to give him up once more and identify with her mother?

Freud formulated the concept of "penis envy" to account for the little girl's Oedipus complex, but he was never very satisfied with the results. Sometime during her early childhood, he hypothesized, the little girl was supposed to become aware of the anatomical difference between the sexes, of the fact that the male child has a penis and she does not. The shock of this discovery and the resulting feelings of inferiority, were sufficient to turn her against her mother. It was her mother, after all, who had given birth to her, and hence it was her mother who must be responsible for her genital defects. Thereafter, the little girl was supposed to turn to her father, presumably in the hope that *he* would supply the penis the mother had been unable or unwilling to. But when this hope inevitably met with disappointment, the female child resolved her version of the Oedipus complex by resuming a more cordial relationship with her mother, identifying with her, and comforting herself with the thought that though she might never possess a penis, she might, on the other hand, be able to bear her father a child some day.

Freud acknowledged that this account might well pose more questions than it actually answered. Clearly, the little girl could not continue to entertain the fantasy of one day giving birth to her father's child forever. As a matter of fact, Freud remarks vaguely and almost in passing, "the Oedipus Complex is later gradually abandoned because this wish is never fulfilled" *(1924, p. 275)*, but this only introduces another problem. If the female child's Oedipus complex was relinquished only gradually, what consequences would this process have for the feminine superego? The male superego purportedly gained much of its force from the little boy's fear that he would be castrated for refusing to banish his desires for his mother and to identify with his father. Obviously, it was impossible for the little girl to be motivated by such anxieties. Would this impossibility not weaken her identification with her mother and hence the kind of superego she was able to internalize? Would she not, then, develop a less rigorous moral code than the little boy?

Freud, in fact, drew precisely this conclusion, although somewhat tentatively and hesitantly:

> I cannot escape the notion (though I hesitate to give it expression) that for women the level of what is ethically normal is different from what it is in men. Their superego is never so inexorable, so impersonal, so independent of its emotional origins as we require it to be in men. Character traits which critics of every epoch have brought up against women—that they show less sense of justice than men, that they are more often influenced in their judgments by feelings of affection or hostility—all these would be amply accounted for by the modification in the formation of their superego which we have already inferred. *(1925, pp. 196–197)*

Though present-day feminists might take exception to Freud's characterization, the problem is inescapable: how to construct a theory of personality development, and hence of adolescence as well, that will accommodate both the female and the male.

Latency: The Quiet Interlude

The problem of sex differences will be explored at several other points in this book. In the meantime, we propose to return to the more general subject of development and to examine the period which was supposed to intervene between the resolution of the Oedipus complex (at age five or six) and the approach of puberty (at age twelve or thirteen). Although Freud may have believed that early childhood played a much more significant role in determining the course of human existence than did Hall, he seems to have been about as interested in chronicling the events of later childhood, that is, he largely ignored the period. This span of years allegedly represented a time of relative quiescence. The troubling sexual urges of the earlier stages had been forced underground, ostensibly leaving the youngster free to continue his advance toward civilized adulthood.

However, the precise changes which figured in this advance were not described in great detail. During latency the child was supposed to develop a stronger superego (i.e., a set of moral standards that made him less dependent on adult authorities for judgments of right and wrong). But with the main theater of life, sexuality, temporarily darkened and deserted, there was little of importance to review.

It was not that Freud believed that the child's impulses grew less imperious during this comparatively placid interlude between infancy and adolescence. Only the child's capacity to *contain* the promptings of his own id changed. Or, as Anna Freud put it, echoing her father in delineating the psychoanalytic point of view, "The immutability of the id is matched by the mutability of the ego" *(1936, p. 141)*. The drives of the id constituted a primitive, unreasoning core that could not be altered. The only hope for humanity, the only attribute which would raise man above the animals and permit him better control over his drives was his own rationality, and it was hence this "ego-aspect" of the personality that had to be strengthened during childhood.

Even so, Freud likened the id to a river that has been dammed up. Given a powerful enough shock, the dam that held this reservoir in check could develop cracks and fractures, threatening to overwhelm the individual with a flood of unruly drives. Freud's dealings with his patients had convinced him that all neurotic symptoms represented a desperate attempt to keep id impulses in check. The woman who suffered from hysterical paralysis was afraid her legs might carry her into forbidden territory; the hysterically deaf man refused to hear his own "unspeakable" wishes.

But not only those who had found the stresses of existence too arduous to withstand bore witness to the enduring strength of man's basic drives. There were periods in the life cycle of every normal individual, according to psychoanalysis, when the impulses so decisively repressed at the end of the phallic phase could again threaten to break loose and to overpower the ego. Having demolished the Victorian concept of childhood innocence, Sigmund Freud demonstrated little interest in describing these later periods, but Anna Freud, to whom we now turn, was instrumental in promoting the view that adolescence was one of them. The legendary turbulence of the pubescent years, she declared, could be attributed to the fact that in adolescence "a relatively strong id confronts a relatively weak ego" *(1936, p. 140)*.

Variations on the Theme of Recapitulation:
The Psychoanalytic Theory of Adolescence

As different as its account of childhood may be, the psychoanalytic portrait of adolescence is, as already noted, similar to Hall's in many respects. Psychoanalysis also portrays the adolescent as tempest-tossed and contradictory, as exhibiting both the best and worst sides of human nature. It is the *interpretation* of all this fabled storm and stress that differs. To be sure, recapitulation has something to do with it, but it is a different sort of recapitulation. The turbulence of adolescence, Anna Freud suggests, is a reflection not of an earlier, transitional stage in human evolution, but of earlier phases in the individual's own history. The conflicts of infantile sexuality, particularly Oedipal conflicts, return in full force. It is as if the id, lying dormant and subdued for a number of years during latency, has suddenly acquired a new power to press its claims.

Although Anna Freud does not explore this point in much detail, we gather that the id's newfound vitality is basically a matter of biology. The hormonal and physiological changes that bring about puberty also increase the strength of the sexual drives. In the brief preadolescent period just preceding the actual appearance of puberty, *all* the old psychosexual conflicts allegedly return in full force. Recalling the oral conflicts of the very earliest phase of infancy, the youngster alternates, declares Miss Freud, between clinging dependence and exaggerated independence, as if he sometimes felt as helpless as a baby and at other times needed to reassure himself that he was not. Mirroring the anality of the second stage of early childhood, he might at the same time become excessively messy, or less often, excessively neat. Finally, reflecting his previous Oedipal conflicts, he might become exceedingly curious about sex and yet exhibit great embarrassment and prudery about it as well. At puberty, the picture abruptly becomes less mixed; sexual concerns begin to take up center stage, but supposedly there are always overtones of the earlier phases as well.

The Difference Between Adolescence
and Early Infancy

As already noted, because of its ostensible resemblance to early childhood, psychoanalytic thinkers were disinclined to examine the developmental problems of adolescence. If the neurotic problems of *adulthood* could inevitably be traced back to the psychosexual discords of infancy, was not the study of adolescence, itself merely a recapitulation of infantile sexuality, unnecessary? Certainly, this view prevailed in orthodox psychoanalytic circles until 1936, when Anna Freud published a set of papers now firmly established as a classic in the field. (Indeed, Miss Freud observes in one of her more recent papers on the subject [*1958*] that it is still the predominant view.) No matter how much the teenage youngster's conflicts may seem to resemble those of the five-year-old, she remarked, there *are* differences. Neither the struggle the adolescent wages with his own impulses nor his strategies for defending himself against those impulses are quite the same.

Internal conflict versus external restraint   Taking up the first point, Freud noted that although the temptations of the thirteen-year-old and the five-year-old might be very similar, the setting in which they took place had altered in the meantime. In the interim between the Oedipal period and puberty, the youngster had acquired what might be called a "character structure":

> The ego of the early infantile period was undeveloped and indeterminate, impressionable and plastic under the influence of the id; in the prepubertal period, on the contrary, it is rigid and firmly consolidated. It already knows its own mind. The infantile ego was capable of suddenly revolting against the outside world and of allying itself with the id to obtain instinctual gratification, but, if the ego of the adolescent does this, it becomes involved in conflicts with the superego. Its firmly established relations to the id on the one hand and the superego on the other—that which we call character—makes the ego unyielding. It can know but one wish: to preserve the character developed during the latency period, to re-establish the former relation between its own forces and those of the id, and to reply to the greater urgency of the instinctual demands with redoubled efforts to defend itself.   *(1936, pp. 146–147)*

The conflicts of early childhood had occurred, and in large part had been resolved, because of "external influences," such as disapproving parents. These conflicts might reappear in adolescence and the same "external influences" might still be present, but there was now an added internal dimension. The small child curbed his impulses largely out of the fear of suffering at the hands of adult authorities if he did not. This motive persisted to some extent even after the Oedipus complex had been resolved and the superego had taken up residence, for the long years of the latency period were necessary to enable the superego to become a strong "inner voice of conscience." By the time the youngster had reached puberty, however, the superego had become quite "firmly consolidated," and the ego had become equally determined to obey *its* commands rather than the importunities of the id. Consequently, the turmoil the adolescent experienced—the same turmoil that had so impressed G. Stanley Hall—was due principally to his own feelings of guilt about the host of forbidden desires which the onset of puberty had abruptly triggered. Although well aware that his parents would disapprove of him should he yield to temptation, Anna Freud maintained that he was more concerned about the loss of his own self-esteem.

The eventual outcome of the entire adolescent ordeal would depend upon the type of equilibrium the individual's ego could manage to reestablish—between the moral prohibitions of the superego and the promptings of the id. This equilibrium in turn depended upon a number of other variables. There was, first of all, the actual strength of the id-impulses themselves, which was "conditioned by the physiological process at puberty." In other words, one adolescent, simply by virtue of the type of constitution he had inherited, might experience much stronger sexual urges than another—and consequently have a much more difficult time controlling them. Second, there was the "character formed during the latency period" to take into account. Did the adolescent have the sort of rigid ego that could not tolerate any type of gratification whatsoever? Was he generally rather self-indulgent? Or had he generally steered a middle course between the id and superego? Presumably, this characterological factor would also help to determine his sexual adjustment during adulthood. And finally, "the nature and efficacy of the defence-mechanisms at the ego's command" should be considered. Did the adolescent habitually handle his id-impulses by barring them from consciousness altogether (i.e., by repressing them)? Or did he have a more sophisticated armamentarium of defenses at his disposal—such as finding a socially acceptable substitute for whatever forbidden wish was troubling him? Could he, for instance, write a poem about some grand passion he had acquired rather than attempting to satisfy it directly? In general, the more the primitive sexual energies could be diverted into "socially useful" channels, the happier the eventual outcome of the adolescent ordeal.

The possible extreme resolutions of this youthful struggle—total inhibition or uncontrolled self-indulgence—were relatively easy to envision. Anna Freud noted:

> Either the id, now grown strong, may overcome the ego, in which case no trace will be left of the previous character of the individual, and the entrance into adult life will be marked by a riot of uninhibited gratification of instinct. Or the ego may be victorious, in which case the character of the individual during the latency period will declare itself for good and all. When this happens, the id impulses of the adolescent are confined within the narrow limits prescribed for the instinctual life of the child. (1936, pp. 149–150)

Between these two extremes—complete self-indulgence in adulthood versus utter self-denial—there was a vast range of possibilities. In any case, *some* sort of sexual adjustment had to be effected during adolescence. But since the factors that determined this adjustment were largely a matter of prior experience (what sort of physical constitution the individual had been born with, what sort of defenses he had learned to employ, and so forth), adolescence was merely a kind of battleground. It could play only a secondary role in shaping the adult personality.

Special Features of the Adolescent Struggle: Defensive Maneuvers

To be sure, the internal conflicts were so intense that some very special maneuvers were required. These defensive strategies represented, in fact, the second way in which adolescence differed from early childhood, according to Anna Freud. Seeking to control the sudden "surge of libido," the youngster often adopted strategies that had been virtually unknown in infancy. In describing these distinctive maneuvers, Freud pointed to some of the same features of adolescence that Hall singled out for comment, but once again her interpretation was different.

Asceticism Like Hall, who demonstrated such an interest in the lives of the saints, Anna Freud observed that some adolescents passed through periods of self-denial, defending their austerities with a zeal that was almost monastic:

Young people who pass through the kind of ascetic phase which I have in mind seem to fear the quantity rather than the quality of their instincts. They mistrust enjoyment in general and so their safest policy appears to be simply to counter more urgent desires with more stringent prohibitions. Every time the instinct says, "I will," the ego retorts, "Thou shalt not," much after the manner of strict parents in the early training of little children. This adolescent mistrust of instinct has a dangerous tendency to spread; it may begin with instinctual wishes proper and extend to the most ordinary physical needs. We have all met young people who severely renounced any impulses which savoured of sexuality and who avoided the society of those their own age, declined to join in any entertainment, and, in true puritanical fashion, refused to have anything to do with the theater, music or dancing. We can understand that there is a connection between the forgoing of pretty and attractive clothes and the prohibition of sexuality. But we begin to be disquieted when the renunciation is extended to things which are harmless and necessary, as, for instance, when a young person denies himself the most ordinary protection against cold, mortifies the flesh in every possible way, and exposes his health to unnecessary risks, when he not only gives up particular kinds of oral enjoyment but 'on principle' reduces his daily food to a minimum, when, from having enjoyed long nights of sound sleep, he forces himself to get up early, when he is reluctant to laugh or smile, or when, in extreme cases, he defers defecation and urination as long as possible, on the grounds that one ought not immediately to give way to all one's physical needs. *(1936, pp. 154–155)*

But although Hall had done little more than observe this rigidly moralistic behavior during adolescence, Anna Freud, as the reader may already have gathered, had a ready explanation: The biological rearrangements associated with puberty tended to make the id even more importunate than it had been in infancy, and this sudden surge of impulse required some unusual countermeasures. Ordinary defense mechanisms would no longer suffice. Because the id had temporarily grown so powerful, *any* form of gratification had somehow become suspect.

But how did such wholesale self-denial differ from the more conventional defense mechanisms? It may be recalled that ordinary defenses are supposed to be *compromise* formations. The ego essentially works out a means of satisfying both the id and the superego to some extent without completely satisfying either. In the case of adolescent asceticism, Anna Freud maintained, there was no such accommodation. Because of the dread of being overwhelmed by his own impulses, the adolescent took the extreme course of giving up all pleasures for a time—but fortunately, only for a time. For most youngsters who employed this stringent defensive maneuver (and Freud seems to imply that not all youngsters make use of it), periods of restraint were followed, inevitably, by periods of abandon, "the adolescent suddenly indulging in everything which he had previously held to be prohibited and disregarding any sort of external restrictions" *(Freud, 1936, p. 156)*.

Nonetheless, despite the difference between Anna Freud's interpretation of adolescent "religiosity" and Hall's, in a passage that has gone largely unnoticed—perhaps because it appears almost as an afterthought—Miss Freud reveals that psychoanalysis and recapitulation theory may be a great deal closer than anyone has previously suspected. There is, she hypothesizes, a deeper and more fundamental significance to adolescent asceticism. The youngster's dread of his own impulses is not solely a matter of social training, not solely a result of having been punished for giving way to temptation during infancy. Social pressure, of course, constitutes an important element in the production of a civilized human being, but it is possible that this sort of influence merely capitalizes on something inborn, the result of human evolution. Perhaps the antagonism between ego and id is, in part, a biological phenomenon—or so Freud appears to imply:

> Long ago the analytical study of neuroses suggested that there is in human nature a disposition to repudiate certain instincts, in particular the sexual instincts, indiscriminately and independently of individual experience. This disposition appears to be a phylogenetic inheritance, *a kind of deposit accumulated from acts of repression practiced by many generations and merely continued, not initiated by individuals.* (1936, p. 157, italics added)

In other words, after thousands of years of repressing his sexual drives, man had actually developed an inborn predisposition for self-control. The violent asceticism of some adolescents—this strange need to deny themselves all pleasure—was an indication of a "phylogenetic inheritance." It was something that had mysteriously been stamped into the genes.

This little-noticed hypothesis of Anna Freud's seems strikingly similar to Hall's concept of recapitulation, to his assertion, that is, that adolescence represents a brief repetition of an earlier period of human evolution, midway between savagery and civilization. When Erikson's theory is discussed later on (in Chapters 7 and 8), it will become clear that this type of evolutionary theme is a persistent one as far as interpretations of adolescence are concerned.

Intellectualization   In the meantime, there are other aspects of Anna Freud's theory to be explored. It may be remembered that Hall had been particularly struck by the growth of the capacity to reason during adolescence. Freud too comments on this phenomenon, but here the similarity between the two theorists is more apparent than real. For Hall, these newfound powers of intellect constituted further evidence that the youngster was entering the transition between primitive modes of thinking and civilized ones. For Freud, they were chiefly the outward sign of a new and unusual defensive strategy, a new means of controlling impulses. To be sure, the adolescent often performed intellectual feats which were nothing short of remarkable:

> The range of these abstract interests and of the problems which these young people try to solve is very wide. They will argue the case for free love or marriage and the family life, a free-lance existence or the adoption of a profession, roving or settling down, or discuss philosophical problems such as religion or free thought, or different political theories, such as revolution *versus* submission to authority, or friendship itself in all of

its forms. If, as sometimes happens in analysis, we receive a faithful report of the conversations of young people or if—as has been done by many of those who make a study of puberty—we examine the diaries and jottings of adolescents, we are not only amazed at the wide and unfettered sweep of their thought but impressed by the degree of empathy and understanding manifested, by their apparent superiority to more mature thinkers, and sometimes even by the wisdom which they display in their handling of the most difficult problems. *(1936, pp. 159–160)*

However, closer examination revealed that these flourishes of intelligence were in reality serving the interests of defense. The very issues the adolescent had suddenly become so fond of debating merely represented, according to Anna Freud, opposing sides of his own inner conflict, disguised and raised to a lofty intellectual plane: "Once more, the point at issue is how to relate the instinctual side of human nature to the rest of life, how to decide between putting sexual impulses into practice and renouncing them, between liberty and restraint, between revolt against and submission to authority" *(1936, p. 161)*. By casting his own internal struggle in the form of an abstract argument, the adolescent could manage to gain some distance from it. Rather than having, say, to face his renewed feelings of hostility for his father, the youngster could content himself with denouncing the "tyranny of all authority."

Hence, the fact that adolescents in general seemed brighter than younger children was essentially owing to the enormous surge of libido at puberty. Intellectualization joined asceticism as one of the special maneuvers in the adolescent's defensive repertoire, and rather like a forest ranger who becomes more sharp-sighted when he hears that there might be a fire in the area, his ego, responding to the increased "instinctual pressure," expanded its powers of rationality. Freud actually went so far as to suggest that sexuality in one form or another played a highly significant role in motivating *all* intellectual curiosity:

Hitherto the decline in intelligence of little children at the beginning of the latency period has been explained in another way. In early childhood their brilliant intellectual achievements are closely connected with their inquiries into the mysteries of sex and, when this subject becomes taboo, the prohibition and inhibition extends to other fields of thought. No surprise has been felt at the fact that, with the rekindling of sexuality in the prepubertal period, i.e., with the breakdown of the sexual repression of early childhood, the subject's intellectual capacities revive in all their old strength.

This is the ordinary explanation, to which we may now add a second.

It may be that in the latency period children not only *dare* not indulge in abstract thought: they may have no need to do so. Infancy and puberty are periods of instinctual danger and the "intelligence" which characterizes them serves at least in part to assist the subject to surmount that danger. In latency and adult life, on the other hand, the ego is relatively strong and can without detriment to the individual relax its efforts to intellectualize the instinctual process. *(1936, p. 164)*

Adolescent love: a new form of identification   In addition to asceticism and intellectualization, there was a third phenomenon which commanded Anna Freud's attention, and once more it was one that the encyclopedic G. Stanley Hall had also discussed. Adolescence was the season of passionate friendships and equally passionate crushes. But as all-consuming as these relationships and (often unrequited) romances were, they had a tendency to be short-lived. Despite his capacity for devotion, the adolescent was supposed to be, on the whole, rather fickle, swearing undying allegiance to a friend one week, ignoring him the next—at least so it appeared to both theorists. Hall had attributed both this growing capacity for devotion and the accompanying flightiness to the adolescent's generally increased sensitivity, which purportedly was manifested, it may be remembered, in a heightened sense of hearing, sight, and smell. But for Anna Freud the explanation for this new and unstable interest in people outside the immediate family once again involved the notions of conflict and defense.

The youngster's disinclination to have much to do with his parents, the fabled "youthful rebellion," occurred in Anna Freud's estimation, not because the adolescent's widening circle of acquaintances made his parents seem old-fashioned or unduly restrictive, but because the resurgence of infantile sexuality made it dangerous to remain emotionally attached to them. At puberty, all the old Oedipal wishes reawakened—all the more dangerous because they could now be acted upon in earnest. As in early childhood, the youth was compelled to fight off an attraction for his mother and resolve conflicting feelings of hatred, fear, and love for his father. The safest course was to withdraw from both parents, living like a stranger in his own house. But having given up the "love objects" who had meant so much to him for such a large portion of his life, the adolescent was left with an emotional void. The impassioned attachments he formed to those his own age, the crushes he conceived, the episodes of hero worship for certain adults—all represented attempts to fill it.

The very transience of these relationships was an indication of their defensive character. In fact, Anna Freud declared, the adolescent was behaving much as he had done during early childhood:

The psychic situation in this and similar phases of puberty may be described very simply. These passionate and evanescent love fixations are not object relations at all, in the sense in which we use the term in speaking of adults. They are identifications of the most primitive kind, such as we meet with in our study of early infantile development, before any object love exists. Thus the fickleness characteristic of puberty does not indicate any inner change in the love or convictions of the individual but rather a loss of personality in consequence of a change in identification. *(1936, p. 169)*

Once again the parallel between events occurring in adolescence and much earlier experiences is highlighted—and the earlier experiences assigned a greater significance in determining the ultimate direction of the adult personality.

The Overall Significance of Adolescence

We might gather from the foregoing discussion that psychoanalysis is inclined to discount the importance of adolescence altogether, but this would be something of an exaggeration. While Anna Freud concedes a lesser role to adolescence in shaping human destiny than did Hall, she does not advocate that the period be totally disregarded. Indeed, in her more recent work *(1958)* she declares that the alleged storm and stress of puberty constitute an essential part of human growth. Psychoanalysis might still regard the early years of childhood as the more truly formative ones—and hence still look upon adolescence as a kind of "stepchild"—but the upheaval that accompanies the reawakening of sexuality is, in Freud's opinion, entirely necessary, and even desirable. Only by undergoing a certain amount of turmoil, she claims, can the individual enter upon a genuinely mature adulthood:

There is . . . the ever recurrent question whether the adolescent upheaval is welcome and beneficial as such, whether it is necessary, and more than that, inevitable. On this point, psychoanalytic opinion is decisive and unanimous. The people in the child's family and school, who assess his state on the basis of behavior, may deplore the adolescent upset which, to them, spells the loss of valuable qualities, of character stability, and of social adaptation. As analysts who assess personalities from the structural point of view, we think otherwise. We know that the character structure of the child at the end of the latency period represents the out-come of long drawn-out conflicts between id and ego forces. The inner balance achieved, although characteristic for each individual and precious to him, is preliminary only and precarious. It does not allow for the quantitative increase in drive activity, nor for the changes of drive quality which are both inseparable from puberty. Consequently, it has to be abandoned to allow adult sexuality to be integrated into the individual's personality. The so-called adolescent upheavals are no more than external indications that such internal adjustments are in progress. *(1958, p. 264)*

Though secondary in importance to infancy, the period of adolescence does not *solely* mirror the conflicts of early childhood. The first five years of life may place a decisive stamp on human character, but the upheavals of adolescence represent attempts to adjust this character structure to the more complex demands of adult sexuality.

For a theory that comes to rather similar conclusions via quite a different route, we turn next to Harry Stack Sullivan.

REFERENCES

BRENNER, C. *An Elementary Textbook of Psychoanalysis.* New York: International Universities, 1955.

FREUD, A. Adolescence. *Psychoanalytic Study of the Child,* 1958, **13,** 255–278.

FREUD, A. *The Writings of Anna Freud.* Vol. II. *The Ego and the Mechanisms of Defense.* (Rev. ed., 1936) New York: International Universities, 1966.

FREUD, S. *Civilization and its Discontents.* (1930) New York: Norton, 1961.

FREUD, S. Female Sexuality. (1931) *Collected Papers.* Vol. V. London: Hogarth, 1952. Pp. 252–272.

FREUD, S. The Passing of the Oedipus Complex. (1924) *Collected Papers.* Vol. II. London: Hogarth, 1950. Pp. 269–276.

FREUD, S. Some Psychological Consequences of the Anatomical Distinction Between the Sexes. (1925) *Collected Papers.* Vol. V. London: Hogarth, 1952. Pp. 186–197.

JONES, E. *The Life and Work of Sigmund Freud.* Vol. I. New York: Basic Books, 1953.

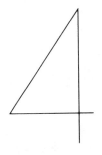

A Third View
of Adolescence:
Sullivan's
Theory

One of our aims in reviewing both Hall's and Anna Freud's theories was to establish a kind of historical perspective on the psychology of adolescence. So far we have uncovered an interesting assortment of similarities and differences between the two. Both theorists characterize what occurs during adolescence as a "recapitulation," but because Hall believed that the adolescent was reliving a stage in human evolution midway between savagery and civilization, he assigned the period a crucial significance in shaping the adult personality. Since she regarded it essentially as a repetition of the events of early childhood, Freud, on the other hand, relegated adolescence to a lesser role.

Similarly, both theorists portray adolescence as a period of storm and stress, a stage in which both the best and worst sides of human nature are simultaneously revealed. But Hall, insofar as he attempted to explain the turmoil of adolescence, considered this upset merely as further proof that a momentous transition between some lower form of human life and a higher one was taking place, while Anna Freud attributed this same turmoil to the resurgence of infantile sexuality.

Finally, although Hall and Anna Freud seem to agree substantially on the key developments during adolescence—the growth of intellect, increasing religiosity and moralism, the appearance of attachments to people outside the family—they offer different interpretations. Actually Hall did little more than catalogue the changes that were supposed to make an appearance at the onset of puberty, regarding them all, presumably, as a product of the adolescent's "heightened sensitivity." Freud, by contrast, claimed that these changes were the result of strategies the adolescent was employing to defend himself against impulses that had been abruptly strengthened at puberty.

Nonetheless, in addition to whatever other features they may have in common and transcending their differences, there is one fundamental assumption that underlies both the "Hallian" and psychoanalytic points of view. Both theories are inclined to award biology the largest share in determining the sequence and course of human development, particularly early development. For Hall, the various stages the child passed through, up to and including adolescence, were evidence of a great evolutionary principle at work. For psychoanalysis, the oral, anal, and phallic phases were, by implication, the result of a force which resided in the human genes, automatically playing itself out between infancy and the age of six. Indeed, for psychoanalysis, biology, in the form of sexual impulses, remains the prime mover even in adulthood.

The third theory to be presented, though not denying the importance of biology, tends to place it in the background and hence gives still a different account of adolescence. Both Hall and the psychoanalytic thinkers who succeeded him appear to have been especially fascinated by the primitive and animalistic sides of human nature. Harry Stack Sullivan (1892–1949), however, gives greater emphasis to whatever it is that renders the human species *unique*. When we recall our discussion at the beginning of Chapter 2 on the assumptions psychology must make in order to study human development at all, Sullivan's position seems unequivocal:

> Excluding the outcomes of heredity or developmental disasters to which the term, idiot, is correctly applied, the individual differences in the inborn endowment of human animals are relatively unimportant in comparison with the differences of the human animal from any other species of animal—however spectacular the differences between humans may seem against the background of life histories in any particular cultural area. *(1953b, p. 21)*

And what were the similarities among human beings that distinguished them from all other species? Basically, Sullivan claimed, they had to do not so much with the gratification of certain biological impulses, for these impulses (and our colleagues in learning theory might remind us of this as well) are common to other animals also.

They had much more to do with the satisfaction of what Sullivan called "interpersonal needs," needs for security and emotional support that come into being with the first breath of life and become increasingly elaborate throughout the course of development. Man is the only animal who can communicate in a very complex way with others of his own species (i.e., in spoken sentences, written words, and intricate symbols), and he is also the only animal who *needs* to communicate in this fashion.

In stressing the interpersonal dimension of human existence, Sullivan, who was originally trained in the psychoanalytic tradition but broke away from it, was reacting against a particular strain in Freudian theory. This strain is hinted at in Anna Freud's pronouncement that "the immutability of the id is matched by the mutability of the ego." As noted earlier, one of the tenets of psychoanalysis is that the basic human drives change very little throughout life—only the capacity to handle them changes. Consequently, man's existence is viewed pretty much as an internal struggle, a constant and by no means always successful battle to keep the primitive forces inside him at bay. No matter what degree of civilization man achieves, there is always a primitive part of him waiting for its chance to be released. Since psychoanalysis focuses its attention on this infantile core that all of us supposedly retain no matter what pinnacles of age or wisdom we may attain, it tends to impart a somewhat "reductionistic" account of personality development. Problems that crop up later in life are generally assumed to reflect and hence are reduced to problems that occurred much earlier. The adolescent's growing autonomy from his parents, his withdrawal from them, and his tendency to turn increasingly to those outside the family circle, are seen, for instance, not as signs of maturation, of branching out, but as defenses against the "return of the repressed." The emotional coolness with which the youngster regards his parents purportedly represents a defense against the resurgence of his old Oedipal feelings.

Sullivan, by contrast, views human development less as an internal struggle and more as a matter of achieving certain crucial relationships with other people, or, as he puts it, "securing certain interpersonal needs." In order for an individual to succeed in becoming a normal, civilized human being, his relationships with others must become increasingly complex and differentiated between infancy and adulthood. If the psychoanalytic model of development is almost a geologic one—picturing the formation of personality as similar to the formation of the earth's crust, with layer piled on successive layer—then perhaps the appropriate analogy for Sullivan's theory would be a mosaic. Personality begins as a small, almost shapeless fragment, and gradually other parts are added to form a coherent and integrated whole. (At the risk of carrying the metaphor too far, we could say that according to the psychoanalytic account, the danger the individual must continually face throughout his lifetime is like that of an eruption or earthquake, whereas for Sullivan it is more a matter of not being able to fit the pieces together properly.)

In Sullivan's view, the fixative necessary to hold the design in place is interpersonal intimacy:

> It begins in infancy with an integrating tendency that we know only by inference from pathological material later, but which we nonetheless accept unhesitatingly—*a need for contact with the living.* And its next great increment is a *need for tenderness*—for protective care delicately adjusted to immediate situations. This need continues into childhood. But in childhood a *need for adult participation* is added—that is, a need for the interest and participation of significant adults in the child's play. This activity takes the form of expressive play necessary to provide the child with equipment for showing what he feels, in manual play necessary for the coordination of the very delicate and intricate relationships of vision and prehensile hands, and so on, and in verbal play, which is the basis of all the enormously important acquisitions to personality which are reflected by verbal behavior and abstract thought. All of these activities become more pleasure-giving to the child because of the adult's participation. By the juvenile era, there is added the *need for compeers*, as indispensable models for one's learning by trial and error; and this is then followed by a *need for acceptance* which is perhaps known to most of you by its reverse, the fear of ostracism, fear of being excluded from the accepted and significant group. And added to all these important integrating tendencies, there comes in preadolescence the need for *intimate exchange*, for friendship, or for—in its high refinement—the love of another person, with its enormous facilitation of consensual validation, of action patterns, of valuational judgments, and so on. This becomes, in early adolescence, the same need for intimacy, friendship, acceptance, intimate exchange, and in its more refined form, the *need for a loving relationship, with a member of the other sex.* Now this is the great structure which is finally consolidated, made meaningful, as the need for intimacy as it characterizes late adolescence and the rest of life. *(1953b, pp. 290–291, italics added)*

In the Sullivanian scheme of things, what begins in infancy as a global and diffuse need for security, a need that can initially be satisfied by any responsive and mothering adult who happens to be handy, becomes increasingly refined, until at maturity it is fulfilled by one's mate and a few close friends. What was once amorphous and uncritical has grown increasingly differentiated and selective.

Clearly this interpretation of human development—which emphasizes interpersonal needs rather than libido as the driving force in life—is quite different from the psychoanalytic account. Gone are the psychosexual stages and the distinctions between conscious and unconscious. In their place is an "interpersonal setting" in which an entity that Sullivan terms the "self-system" matures.

Infancy, Anxiety, and the Beginnings of the Self-System

Indisputably, there is one assumption Sullivan holds in common with orthodox psychoanalytic theory. Like psychoanalysis, his account of what motivates human behavior involves the concept of tension reduction. Certain needs, that is, are assumed to arise within the individual, and these impel him to engage in various activities until some means of satisfaction or relief can be located. However, in the psychoanalytic version of this particular principle, it is the need for sexual gratification that provides the key to all human motivation, whereas, for Sullivan it is essentially the *need to be free of anxiety.*[1]

Not that psychoanalytic theory denies the importance of anxiety. Far from it. As we noted earlier, Sigmund Freud speculated that the infant learned to channel his impulses because of his anxiety about being overwhelmed by them. But there is a difference in emphasis. For Freud the id impulses were primary. They were always seen as the "prime movers" in human affairs even though it was anxiety which caused them to be brought under control. Though Sullivan is, as we shall see, less specific than Freud about the origins of anxiety, he assigns the concept a more central role in his theory.

What the tiny infant seeks in his first steps toward formulating a sense of self, a sense of the kind of person he is, is relief from an "uncanny feeling of dread" that is likely to beset him soon after birth. This feeling, Sullivan insists, can only be evoked by other people (probably, as far as the infant is concerned, by his parents) and, accordingly, can only be alleviated by them. Sullivan is actually somewhat vague about the precise origins of anxiety but suggests that it is somehow communicated by the mother to her child. Sooner or later, presumably, the mother is upset by some turn of events

---

[1] Oddly enough, although Sullivan was inclined to give greater weight to later development than psychoanalytic theorists generally do, he was especially effective in treating patients whom he believed had suffered damaging experiences very early in life. He maintained that these individuals—who had become profoundly disturbed or "psychotic" in adulthood—had been subject to such devastating anxiety in infancy that it had become impossible for them to build up a coherent self-image.

while caring for her infant, and in a mysterious, nonverbal way transmits this feeling to him.

At first, because it is difficult for the infant to coordinate his experiences, he is only dimly aware that there is a difference between situations in which he feels anxious and those in which he feels secure. Perhaps it has to do with something as subtle as the way in which his mother holds him when she herself is feeling anxious versus the way in which she holds him when she is feeling nurturant. Nonetheless, the child becomes strongly motivated to avoid situations which produce anxiety and to maintain those in which he feels secure. Since his security depends upon how the people who are caring for him react to him, he begins attempting to encourage reactions that will make him feel good about himself—and trying to inhibit, suppress, and otherwise keep from view those aspects of himself that arouse anxiety. Sullivan terms these efforts "security operations." (The student of learning theory will no doubt detect a certain similarity between "security operations" and "conditioned responses.")

Naturally, during what Sullivan describes as *infancy*, the child's capacity for bringing about desired states and avoiding undesirable ones is rather limited. The unusual dependency into which human beings are born, more extreme and long-lasting than that of practically any other species, puts them quite literally at the tender mercies of their caretakers during the early years of life. However, even during his first two years, the infant learns that certain actions on his part (and these vary with the kind of parents he has) result in the dreaded feeling of anxiety, and they tend to be dropped from his active repertoire.

Sullivan suggests, for example, that for some unfortunate children, any sort of behavior associated with sexuality falls under this taboo very early in infancy—long before the Oedipus complex would even have had a chance to develop. He offers the following somewhat fanciful case of a still small baby and an anxiously puritanical mother:

We take him in the cradle, and here we see him, after the fashion of all his predecessors, actively and pleasantly engaged in the exercise of such ability as he has discovered. He will perhaps not have kicked a slat out of the cradle, but he will certainly have poked all the slats of the cradle, he will have felt of nearly everything, including a great deal of himself, he may have put a good deal of himself in his mouth, or tried to, but in this business of exercising newly elaborated motor systems and gradually clarifying sensory feel, he will almost inevitably, since we make it a "him," have fallen upon a small protuberance in the groin, and in doing this he will have found it handy. It is suited to manipulation. It is astonishingly well located geometrically. A slight curve in the elbow puts it well within reach of the already nimble fingers.

So far nothing of any moment has occurred. But we will now have, let us say, the mother—fathers usually keep fairly far from the nursery— we will have the mother encounter this discovery in the infant and we will make her a person who has been forced to organize the self on the basis of our more rigid puritanic tradition.

Under these circumstances, although in ordinary circumstances she is not wholly unaware of this anatomical peculiarity of the male, in her own infant she will feel that Satan is in the very near vicinity, that here is a manifestation of the bestial nature of man in the very act of erupting in her infant, and she will want to do something about it. She will wish to save this infant. Lord knows what awful visions unroll before her eyes as she witnesses this; but anyway the infant is badly upset by empathy, undergoes various somatic disturbances, and experiences what amounts to an acute and severe discomfort. *(1953a, pp. 59–60)*

Though the infant's memory is none too retentive at this stage in his life, and though the mother may have to resort to the expedient of putting mittens on him or tying his hands, it does not take him terribly long to make the connection between a profound feeling of anxiety and his habit of trying to get at his genitals. Once he does associate the two, the habit is likely to be broken—so decisively that he experiences discomfort and consequently blots out aware-ness of *anything* associated with sexuality for a long time to come. This is admittedly only a hypothetical case, but it illustrates the way in which Sullivan believes the self-system is built up. While they may not have to undergo experiences as traumatic as those of the child described, sooner or later most children learn that there are certain aspects of themselves—sensations, thoughts, fantasies—that must be ignored if they are not to be afflicted with anxiety.

Childhood

During infancy the child continues to build up his self-system in a somewhat haphazard fashion. Though Sullivan admits that he can only guess at what the infantile mind must be like, he assumes that the child has only rather primitive ways of organizing the impres-sions at his disposal during this stage. Hence, the child's ability to see the world as the adults who care for him see it is limited. Probably, Sullivan suggests, he has his own set of private symbols for conceptualizing most of what is going on around him—he can think, in Sullivanian terms, only in the *parataxic* mode. But as he learns to speak, the infant acquires a tool that will enable him to form a perception of the world that corresponds much more closely to that of his parents. He becomes aware of the labels that his culture has agreed to place upon various objects and events. He learns, for instance, that the black, furry animal with the long tail and the inordinate fondness for lapping milk is called a "cat." He also learns to connect a picture in his story book—flat and two-dimensional—with this same label. (Still later, as we shall see, he begins to make the same sort of connection between his visual memory of this furry creature and some arbitrary marks on a piece of paper, otherwise known as the letters "c," "a," "t," which make up the word "cat.")

The acquisition of language has an enormous impact upon the formation of the self-system according to Sullivan. For by learning the labels for objects and events employed by adults, the child becomes far more capable of understanding and being understood. Rather than flailing about and screaming if he wants something, for instance, he can simply ask for it. It also becomes possible for him to organize and classify his own experiences in the way everyone else does, or as Sullivan puts it, to *validate* them *consensually*. By learning the terms that society has agreed to apply to certain feelings, for instance, he comprehends what it is to feel "happy," to feel "sad," and most important of all, to feel "anxious."

In the process of coming to view the world as adults view it (Sullivan refers to this as thinking in the *syntaxic* as opposed to the more primitive *parataxic* mode), the child also becomes aware of the labels these adults reserve for *him*, aware that they see him as one type of person in one situation and quite a different type of person in another. When they approve of the sort of person he is, they are inclined to employ the labels "good," "obedient," "clever," "pretty," "nice," and so forth. When they disapprove of him, he is more likely to hear the terms "noisy," "naughty," "mean," "stupid," and "ugly" applied to his person.

Since disapproval is likely to provoke the anxiety he dreads so much, the child is apt to concentrate on becoming what the adults surrounding him approve of, but whether or not he does, he is, in any case, gradually forming an impression of himself. It takes a long time for this impression to acquire much clarity or stability, for all during childhood (a span Sullivan designates as roughly the years between two and six) the youngster tends to revert to the *parataxic* mode of thought—for example, by making up his *own* words for objects. Nonetheless, the process of building up the self-system is well under way.

There are, of course, as the child soon discovers, certain experiences and phenomena that adults are loath to identify—although they manage to make it clear that the child is not to refer to such occurrences in their presences. Because he cannot compare his own perceptions of such events with those of other people, because he cannot "validate" them "consensually," the child never learns to make much sense of these events. At best, they remain a part of his private—or parataxic—world, thoughts and fantasies that he keeps strictly to himself. At worst, because of the anxiety they evoke in others and consequently in himself, they are denied access to consciousness altogether. Although Sullivan does not employ the term "repression," what he has described is clearly similar to the psychoanalytic concept, and, as must be evident, he believes, as do orthodox Freudians, that in our culture the kinds of experiences the child is encouraged to exclude from awareness have to do with sexuality.

The Juvenile Era

Having delineated some of the fundamental principles and features of Sullivan's theory, it is now appropriate to ask how his perspective affects his account of adolescent development. In particular, how does his belief that the need for security, rather than "discharge of libido" or "recapitulation," is the governing force in life influence his description of the pubescent youngster? Actually, we receive an important clue to the answer from Sullivan's description of the years *between* what he calls "childhood" and "early adolescence."

It may be remembered that psychoanalytic theory tends to discount the importance, not only of adolescence, but of the entire period that intervenes between the resolution of the Oedipus complex and puberty as well, of what is described as the "latency period." Anna Freud characterizes these years as a time of consolidation—of strengthening the ego's control over the id, of keeping the repressed impulses of infancy in check—and hence devotes even less attention to them than she does to adolescence. Sullivan, on the other hand, considers this supposedly tranquil portion of the human life cycle to be a period of considerable significance and divides it into two distinct phases: the juvenile era and preadolescence. Thus, in addition to dispensing with certain psychoanalytic concepts, Sullivan takes a different position on an issue that has been implicit in much of our discussion so far, that of the importance of early versus later experience. Because the development of personality, in Sullivan's opinion, reflects an ever-widening and increasingly differentiated pattern of relationships—rather like a network or a mosaic—the events of the first few years of life need not exert such an all-powerful influence. To be sure, if they are disastrous, they may, but they need not.

It is not that Sullivan *dismisses* infancy, as did Hall, and assigns to later experience a greater part in determining what direction the adult personality will take. Rather, he argues that, important as the events of early infancy are, there is the possibility of significant growth—or deterioration—later on: "Although the structure of the self-system is such that its development in general is rather powerfully directed along the lines it has already taken, it is much more subject to influence through new experience, either fortunate or unfortunate, at each of the developmental thresholds" *(1953b, p. 247)*.

To quite an extent, Sullivan believes, our adult personalities reflect the way in which we were treated during infancy and early childhood. The labels we were taught to apply to our experiences then—including experiences that supposedly reflected how charming, clever, stupid, or ugly we were—have a way, he maintains, of remaining with us. But they can be altered somewhat—for good or ill—by our relationships with people other than those who took responsibility for us during infancy. It is at the beginning of each new phase of development (i.e., at each "developmental threshold") that these other people—at times friends, at times teachers, and at times lovers—enter our lives.

In general, perhaps to differentiate his own position the more clearly from psychoanalysis, Sullivan tends to emphasize the corrective aspects of later experience. In striking contrast to Anna Freud, he pictures the juvenile era, lasting roughly from the age of six to the age of ten or eleven, not as a period of relative quiet but as a very eventful span of years. The tasks the child faces as a result of moving out beyond the confines of the family home and into the public school system are portrayed as far more complicated, the opportunities for encountering perceptions of the world different from his own considerably greater:

At this stage—if only because the juvenile has just come from the home situation and his previous experience has been with older and younger siblings, or with really imaginary playmates—there is a truly rather shocking insensitivity to feelings of personal worth in others. Thus the school years are a time when a degree of crudeness in interpersonal relations, very rarely paralleled in later life, is the rule. But, in spite of this, *the opportunity which is laid before the young juvenile for catching on to how other people are looked upon by authority figures and by each other is an exceedingly important part of the educative process, even though it is one to which no particular attention is conventionally given.* A great deal of this educative experience, which tends to correct idiosyncrasies of past socialization, is never discussed as such. Ten, fifteen, or twenty years after one has left the juvenile era, the experience is extraordinarily inaccessible to ready recall, if, for instance, one is undergoing an intensive study of personality.

The rate of growth of personality through all these earlier phases is truly amazing. We realize this more and more as we begin to analyse the enormous number of rather exquisite judgments which one uses in directing one's life in an incoherent culture among people with many specific limitations and individual abilities and liabilities. And the amount of education for life that comes from the juvenile era is immensely important. The juvenile can see what other juveniles are doing—either getting away with, or being reproved for—and can notice differences between people he had never conceived of, *because previously he had nothing whatever on which to base an idea of something different from his own experience. (1953b, p. 230, italics added)*

The impressions the child has formed, both of the world and of himself, may be jarred considerably once it is necessary for him to interact with adults other than his own parents and with children other than his own siblings. Far more than in his own rather narrowly circumscribed household, the school child becomes aware that he lives in a community populated with a great many different types of individuals. It is a community that requires both a good deal of "competition" with others and a good deal of "cooperation" with them. Basically, the youngster is expanding his store of categories available for organizing and sorting out his own experiences. The fund of labels, the concepts he has already mastered at home, may be greatly modified or expanded—both on the playground and in the schoolroom. And in the course of reacting to various people—teachers, policemen, his schoolmates, the bully who sets upon him on his way home—and being reacted to, he forms an increasingly differentiated perception of what he himself is like, a more refined self-image.

If he is fortunate, Sullivan theorizes, the child also begins to develop skills which will enable him to "get ahead" in life. In fact, in contrast to the way in which Anna Freud describes the so-called latency period, Sullivan portrays the juvenile era as one of considerable intellectual growth. This is, in all probability, because he does not try to derive all mental development from sexual curiosity. Anna Freud suggests that the repression of infantile sexuality exerts a kind of dampening effect on the child's mind, an effect that is not overcome until the onset of puberty threatens the old defenses. Sullivan, on the other hand, appears to view intellectual development as a kind of steady progression between infancy and adulthood. Although he remains somewhat indefinite about the precise way in which such skills are acquired, he observes that as a result of all the educative forces brought to bear on the child (both inside and outside the classroom), he gradually develops the capacity to monitor his own thinking in some highly significant ways. These skills, which begin to manifest themselves during the juvenile era, are particularly apparent—or are made conspicuous by their absence —in situations that call for some kind of public performance:

> An almost inevitable outcome of the most fortunate kind of juvenile experience is the appearance of what I call *supervisory patterns* in the already very complex system of processes and personifications that make up the self-system. These supervisory patterns amount in certain instances to subpersonalities—that is, they are "really" imaginary people who are always with one.
>
> Perhaps I can make my point by mentioning three of these supervisory patterns that everyone knows most intimately from very prolonged personal experience. When you have to teach, lecture in public, as I am doing, or do any talking in which it's quite important that the other fellow learns something from you, or thinks that you're wonderful, even if obscure, you have as a supervisory pattern a personality whom I might call your *hearer*. Your hearer is strikingly competent in judging the relevancy of what you are saying. This hearer patiently listens to all your harangues in public and sees that the grammar is stuck together and that things that are too opaque are discussed further. In other words, it is really as if a supplementary, or a subordinate, personality worked like thunder to put your thoughts together into some semblance of the English language. . . .
>
> All of you, whether or not you have a diligent hearer, have now long had, as a supervisory pattern, the *spectator*. The spectator diligently pays attention to what you show to others, and do with others; he warns you when it isn't quite cricket, or it's too revealing, or one thing and another; and he hurriedly adds fog or camouflage to make up for any careless breach. And if any of you write seriously, or even write detective stories, you have another supervisory pattern of this kind—your *reader*. (1953b, pp. 239–240)

As they are incorporated, these supervisory patterns presumably enable the child to perform far more "intelligently" at ten than he did at six, but there is also a less felicitous side. In the course of acquiring a grasp of the kinds of behavior his culture considers appropriate, the child may lose access to some of his own rich but private fantasy life. There is the danger that if his ideas do not fit the categories of thought or language provided for them by his teachers, classmates, and family, they will be eliminated from awareness: "The effect of the juvenile era is, literally, to make it hard to recall what went on in childhood unless it turns out to be perfectly appropriate and easily modified to meet the strenuous attempt by the society to teach the young to talk, to read, and to 'act right' " (1953b, p. 233). And here Sullivan touches upon the basic dilemma of education—how to impose discipline on thinking and to enable people to communicate with each other without stifling their individual creativity.[2]

Along the same lines, he notes that another of the less desirable outcomes of training the child's mind may be the formation of stereotypes, those arbitrary classifications of other people which the child adopts without much reflection but tends to resist giving up. Sullivan explains this sort of unthinking tenacity as being basically a matter of efficiency; that is, as part of the child's strategy for coping with an increasingly complex world that demands a great many judgments and decisions:

Since there is so much to be done in this era and so much pressure on the juvenile to take over any successful patterns for doing it, in our type of school society at least, one of the conspicuous outcomes is that a great many juveniles arrive at preadolescence with quite rigid stereotypes about all sorts of classes and conditions of mankind. (1953b, p. 238)

One of the most universal stereotypes concerns members of the opposite sex. Few juveniles, Sullivan notes, are able to prevent themselves from absorbing rather crude notions of what girls and boys respectively are supposed to be like—which may help to explain the animosity and distance that prevails between the sexes at this age. According to Sullivan, learning to lump members of any group together, with little or no regard for individual differences, is unfortunate because such stereotypes tend to be incorporated into the child's self-system, as part of the way he views both the world and himself. He learns who he is, after all, by comparing himself with others. And, it should be recalled, once the self-system has taken a particular course, it is likely to maintain that course simply for purposes of preserving the individual's self-esteem.

However, if the child is able to navigate the more perilous straits of the juvenile era with relative success and to emerge without undue anxiety about "talking, reading, and acting right" or an excess cargo of stereotypes, he should enter the second phase between childhood and puberty—preadolescence—with what we

[2] Another theorist who has been influenced by the Sullivanian school, Schachtel, makes a similar point in a very interesting book on creativity. See Metamorphosis (1959), especially the chapter "On Memory and Childhood Amnesia."

term a budding sense of personal destiny. Sullivan himself refers to his concept as "orientation in living." He remarks:

> The juvenile actually has an opportunity to undergo a great deal of social experience, in contrast to the child, who cannot have any orientation in living in the larger world. To the extent that the juvenile knows, or could easily be led to know, what needs motivate his relations with others, and under what circumstances these needs—whether they be for prestige or for anything else—are appropriate and relatively apt to get by without damage to self-respect, to this extent the person has gotten a great deal out of his first great plunge into socialization. If this comes off successfully, he inevitably has established some things which he can really call his values, from the pursuit of which he will not be deflected by other things that come along and might be obtained; in other words, a striking aspect of good orientation in living is the extent to which foresight governs the handling of intercurrent opportunities. *(1953b, p. 244)*

G. Stanley Hall, of course, made note of a similar development, but he believed that it occurred *during* adolescence rather than before. The issue will become even more complicated later on when we take up Erikson's theory. Nonetheless, according to Sullivan, having taken his first "big plunge" into the extended community outside his home, the child is ready for another—the comparatively painless encounter that is supposed to occur during the phase that just precedes adolescence.

Preadolescence

Sullivan describes a relatively brief "preadolescent" stage between the juvenile era and puberty which also stands in rather sharp contrast to the psychoanalytic account. (As will be recalled, psychoanalysis would consider this period as part of latency.) If the juvenile era is characterized by a broadening of social relationships, preadolescence is a time of deepening relationships. Having moved decisively outside the confines of his family and having learned something about the various kinds of people there are in the world, the child begins to focus his attention on a relatively small circle of friends and, ideally, on one individual in particular, his chum. The need for interpersonal security that has gradually expanded to include a need for playmates his own age is further refined into what Sullivan designates as the *need for intimacy*. Though Sullivan again remains somewhat indefinite about what causes the youngster to develop these longings for someone of the same sex and roughly the same age, he maintains that these relationships may have a great beneficial and corrective influence, perhaps even overcoming earlier traumatic experiences:

Because one draws so close to another, because one is newly capable of seeing oneself through the other's eyes, the preadolescent phase of personality development is especially significant in correcting autistic, fantastic ideas about the self or others. I would like to stress—at the risk of using superlatives which sometimes gets very tedious—that development of this phase of personality is of incredible importance in saving a good many rather seriously handicapped people from otherwise inevitable serious mental disorder. (1953b, p. 248)

In other words, even if an individual's childhood has been unrelentingly miserable, his personality can still be salvaged, in Sullivan's opinion, if he can manage to find a close friend during preadolescence. The revelation that *someone* considers him attractive and worthwhile may counteract the low opinion of himself that certain significant others (most likely his parents) may have encouraged him to form. This conclusion is not, obviously, quite the one that we would be inclined to draw from psychoanalysis—which tends pretty much to discount the entire span of years between early childhood and adolescence (and even adolescence itself). When Anna Freud, for example, actually does touch upon the subject of friendship, she speaks only of *adolescent* friendships, and even these friendships are described as mere primitive substitutes for attachments the adolescent has abruptly been forced to discard—his relationships with his parents.

According to Sullivan, on the other hand, even if the child has not totally withdrawn from his parents, long before he reaches adolescence he has already grown away from them to some extent and has become part of a wider society beyond the home. And just as the child's interpersonal relationships take on a more differentiated quality during preadolescence, so does his standing in the adult community. When not completely preoccupied with his chum, the preadolescent, Sullivan asserts, tends to spend his remaining free time with a gang. The way that adults react to this gang gives him a foretaste of what his eventual position in the social hierarchy may be:

. . . the gang as a whole finds that it has a relationship to the larger social organization, the community, and that it is assessed by the community. Community acceptance of the gang is likely to depend on whether or not the gang is antisocial, and it may also depend on how widely representative the gang is. (1953b, p. 257)

Furthermore, the organization of the gang itself is to some extent a mirror of the larger society:

Within the gang, experience in social organization is reflected in how closely integrated the gang is, how stable its leadership is, and how many leaders for different things there are. Sometimes there are preadolescent gangs in which you would find, if you made a careful study, that the members maintain subordination to a number of different leaders, each for different circumstances, which is really pretty refined social organization in miniature. *(1953b, p. 257)*

But if the Sullivanian account of the years preceding adolescence differs quite radically from the psychoanalytic version, there is at least one common theme. Although Sullivan's description of the juvenile era does not convey the same aura of tranquillity as the psychoanalytic account of latency, his description of the preadolescent era does. Sullivan views this brief period—when the child's self-centeredness has purportedly begun to dissolve and he reaches out to another human being with an emotion very much like love—as one unparalleled in the human life cycle for its peace and comfort: "I believe that for a great majority of our people, preadolescence is the nearest they come to untroubled human life—that from then on the stresses of life distort them to inferior caricatures of what they might have been" *(1953a, p. 56)*. And a good many of the stresses which follow find their origin in adolescence.

Early Adolescence

In order to render Sullivan's interpretation of adolescence intelligible, it has been necessary to review briefly his account of the years preceding adolescence. Generally, excepting his assertion that the preadolescent stage is the least troubled in human existence, Sullivan's description of childhood is quite different from Anna Freud's. Interestingly enough, when we turn to his portrait of adolescence, many of the same features highlighted by both Hall and Freud are apparent once more, though once again, as in our comparison of Hall and Freud, the interpretation is quite different.

Like Hall and Anna Freud, Sullivan regards adolescence as a period of storm and stress (the early part of it, at least, since he distinguishes between early and late adolescence). But just as Hall and Freud each had his or her own views concerning the precise cause of this youthful turmoil, so too does Sullivan. For Hall, adolescence was tumultuous because it represented a stage that was ambiguous in an evolutionary sense—midway between the primitive and the civilized. For Anna Freud it was more a matter of the "return of the repressed," the resurgence of infantile sexuality. But for Sullivan, adolescence is tempestuous, neither because it recapitulates a transitional stage in human history nor because it recalls the conflicts of an earlier period in childhood, but because it presents a number of new and perplexing challenges—challenges, Sullivan believes, which Western culture does very little to facilitate.

Like Anna Freud, Sullivan singles out puberty as the culprit, but more because it stirs up feelings that the youngster has *never* experienced before than because it weakens his defenses against previous conflicts. Sullivan, of course, was perfectly well aware that children were capable of being stimulated sexually and equally well aware that if they actively sought out such stimulation, they were likely to be much frowned upon and discouraged. But he was not inclined to attribute great significance to infantile sexuality.

There is, he insisted, a profound difference between the infant who accidentally discovers a particular portion of his anatomy and the pubescent youngster who has had his first wet dream. The infant is not capable, in any differentiated sense, of sexual desire, of directing his feelings in any very coherent way toward another individual. The adolescent, on the other hand, is, and he is also rather abruptly endowed with another capacity allegedly beyond the competence of the younger child, the ability to experience orgasm. As a result of the physiological changes taking place within his body, the adolescent develops a new interpersonal need, the need for what Sullivan calls "lustful satisfaction." This need must be integrated with the other great interpersonal need, which up to this point has been the governing force in the child's life, the need for security, or as Sullivan describes it, the need to be free of anxiety. Unfortunately, the sort of integration required is not easily attained, at least not, according to Sullivan in a culture like ours, a culture that tends, first of all, to treat sexuality as something to be screened out of awareness and, second, to impose a long waiting period between the time the youngster first experiences lust and the time he may legitimately satisfy it. The stage is thus set for all sorts of "collisions between needs," and it is these collisions that make adolescence problematic.

There is the sheer incongruity of it all to contend with. As Sullivan observes in his characteristically blunt way: ". . . there is a rather abrupt change, relatively unparalleled in development, by which a zone of interaction with the environment which had been concerned with excreting waste becomes newly and rapidly significant as a zone of interaction in physical interpersonal intimacy"

(1953b, p. 263). "Unparalleled" is probably the key word, emphasizing what is unique about the period of adolescence rather than what is redundant. Having long regarded his genitals as unclean, and perhaps even dangerous, the pubescent youngster is faced with the prospect of having them play a critical part in his attempts to establish intimacy with another human being. He is driven by his own newly emerging sexual needs toward physical contact, but to achieve a relationship that is both physically and emotionally intimate may prove a singularly difficult undertaking. Even without involving anyone else, simply overcoming his own long-standing anxieties about sexuality may turn out to be traumatic enough for the adolescent youth.

Writing in an era that was considerably more permissive than G. Stanley Hall's, Sullivan observes that even though *science* no longer regards masturbation as a great evil, it may still be a source of anguish for the uninformed teenager:

These sundry collisions that come along at this stage may be the principal motives for preadolescents or very early adolescents getting into "homosexual" play with some remarkable variations. But a much more common outcome of these various collisions—these difficulties in developing activity to suit one's needs—is the breaking out of a great deal of autosexual behavior, in which one satisfies one's own lust as best one can; this behavior appears because of the way in which preadolescent society breaks up, and because of the various inhibitions which have been inculcated on the subject of freedom regarding the genitals. Now this activity, commonly called masturbation, has in general been rather severely condemned in every culture that generally imposes marked restrictions on freedom of sexual development. That's very neat, you see; it means that adolescence is going to be hell whatever you do, unless you have wonderful preparation for being different from everyone else—in which case you may get into trouble for being different. *(1953b, p. 270)*

The same sort of cultural disapproval may make initial overtures toward the opposite sex even more uncomfortable. As noted, the early adolescent has been spending most of his time with members of his own sex—his chum and his gang. Now, suddenly, he is expected to achieve the same degree of intimacy with a member of the opposite sex. As Sullivan puts it, he must transfer his affections from someone *like* himself (the Sullivanian term for this type of relationship is *isophilic*) to someone of a completely different sex, quite unlike himself (a *heterophilic* relationship). Or rather, he is expected to begin fumbling in this direction, since marriage, the only culturally approved form of such intimacy, is still a remote prospect. But by this time, the youngster is likely to be encumbered, in addition to all his anxieties about sexuality, with a whole host of stereotypes about the opposite sex he absorbed way back in the juvenile era.

To complicate matters even further, his parents, who may have managed to remain in the background while he was quietly playing with his chum and running with his gang, may now suddenly make some strenuous attempts to discourage his interest in the opposite sex:

> One of the most potent instruments used in this particular is ridicule; many an adolescent has been ridiculed practically into very severe anxiety by parents who just do not want him to become, as they think of it, an adult interested in such things as sex, which may get him diseased or what not, or may result in marriage and his leaving home. *(1953b, p. 268)*

Sullivan does not mean to imply that such familial opposition is necessarily the rule, but the example does serve to point up some of the intricacies of integrating sexuality with other crucial needs in life. No wonder that he describes preadolescence as a kind of calm before the storm and declares, rather pessimistically, it would seem: "The number of wretched experiences connected with adolescents' first heterosexual attempts is legion, and the experiences are sometimes very expensive to further maturation of the personality" *(1953b, p. 271)*.

Again we gain the impression that Sullivan explains much of the flailing around that is supposed to occur during adolescence—the heights and depths, the grand passions and the fickleness—not so much as the result of *internal* conflicts, as Anna Freud does, but as the result of *interpersonal* difficulties. The anxieties connected with sexuality are "internal," but they create problems for the adolescent only as they affect his relationships with others. Anna Freud undoubtedly also recognizes this interpersonal dimension, for she too observes that one of the key tasks of adolescence is to integrate adult sexuality into the personality *(1958, p. 264; see also Chapter 3)*, but she does not, like Sullivan, go into detail on this point, nor does she trace the implications.

Late Adolescence

Interestingly enough, though Sullivan pays a great deal of attention to the biological, social, and emotional aspects (indeed, he considers them interrelated and inseparable), he mentions the intellectual gains of adolescence only in passing—and then only as a feature of late adolescence. Perhaps, having established the juvenile era as a period of extensive mental growth, he considers subsequent expansion of the intellect a foregone conclusion—and hence unworthy of further comment. Or perhaps he regards the interpersonal dilemmas of early adolescence as so all-consuming as to overshadow any other developments. In any case, it is only after the stresses of adolescence have been discussed in detail that Sullivan returns to the subject of intellectual growth.

Assuming the adolescent has managed to fit sexuality into his life without any undue dislocations (no mean task in Western culture, according to Sullivan), he should spend his last years before assuming full adulthood becoming what is referred to colloquially as a "well-rounded" individual. As Sullivan puts it: "Late adolescence extends from the patterning of preferred genital activity through unnumbered educative and educative steps to the establishment of a fully human or mature repertory of interpersonal relations, as permitted by available opportunity, personal and cultural" (1953b, p. 297). In the absence of any specific age range, we assume that this is a description of the late teens and early twenties.

Far from ignoring the possible intellectual changes and educational aspects of late adolescence, Sullivan concentrates on them almost exclusively. Presumably, once the individual has settled upon his own "pattern of preferred genital activity" (which generally—but not always—involves establishing some sort of intimate relationship with a member of the opposite sex), he can turn his mind to other matters. Sullivan points out, for instance, what an enlightening experience college can be for the sizable number of late adolescents who attend it:

Insofar as the long stretch of late adolescence is successful, there is a great growth of experience in the syntaxic mode. Consider, for example, a person from a fairly well-knit community and a pretty good home, who has fortunately achieved a patterning of his genital behavior. If he then goes to a university, he is given several years of truly extraordinary opportunity to observe his fellows, to hear about people in various parts of the world, to discuss what has been presented and observed, to find out, on this basis, what in his past experience is inadequately grasped, and what is a natural springboard to grasping the new. In other words, for the fortunate the educational opportunity provided by living at a university is very great. (1953b, pp. 298–299)

Late adolescence is probably more reminiscent of the juvenile era and preadolescence than any of the other developmental phases —except that during these preadolescent phases the youngster was only beginning to become aware of the extended community outside his immediate family, whereas during late adolescence he learns to find his place in that community. The school-age child, whom the educational system is bent upon teaching to "talk, read, and act right," is gradually introduced to the basic skills he will need for communicating in a civilized society. During late adolescence, in Sullivan's view, a person learns how to make far more effective use of these tools. "In other words, in late adolescence, one refines relatively personally-limited experience into the consensually dependable, which is much less limited" (1953b, p. 299).

But one need not, Sullivan observes, go to college to be "integrated into society." The youth who takes a factory job after high school also receives an education, albeit one less formal than he might obtain at a university:

Some of those whose opportunities are great are potentially able to integrate literally with the world society—to be at home in the world. Those who are working as apprentices in machine shops, for example, have, needless to say, vastly less opportunity in terms of geographical and cultural scope. But still they are now, from the viewpoint of society, going concerns in every way—provided with franchise, expected to pay income tax, and the like. In general, late adolescents are adults in the eyes of the law, and have all the benefits and handicaps thereunto appertaining. (1953b, pp. 299–300)

Ideally, the expansion of the mind, and hence the personality, that marks the end of adolescence is something that "goes on and on," continuing indefinitely throughout the individual's life cycle. The differentiation of social relationships—all the way from the infant's global need for tenderness to the young adult's much more specific affection for a few friends and his mate to the older person's more abstract tolerance and "love for humanity"—has no fixed limit. However, Sullivan observes, with more than a trace of pessimism, the need to be free of anxiety prevents "a great many" people from realizing their potential. The rigidity and closed-mindedness that shut out the uncertainties of life effectively also close the door to many experiences and relationships.

The Problem of Feminine Development

We cannot conclude our review of Sullivan's theory without noting that he too acknowledges the existence of sex differences in development—and rather candidly admits that he has little to say about them. As may already have become apparent, there is a distinctly masculine cast to Sullivan's account of adolescence, a circumstance that has to do with the nature of his clinical practice.

Apparently, he treated a larger number of male patients than female, and since, like Sigmund Freud, he based much of his theory of personality development on his experiences with patients, he was inclined to believe that his formulations applied better to men than to women—particularly his ideas about adolescence.

In addition to his lack of expertise, Sullivan's neglect of the girl's development seems to be tied in with his view that it is "more complicated" and rather more mysterious than the boy's. Perhaps the only time he singles out the female adolescent for special notice is when he observes, with all his usual irony, that her sexual maturation does not coincide particularly well with the male adolescent's:

> I believe that according to conventional statistical experience, women undergo the puberty change somewhat in advance of men; in a great many instances, this leads to a peculiar sort of stutter in the developmental progress between the boys and the girls in an age community so that by the time most of the boys have gotten really around to interest in girls, most of the girls are already fairly well wound up in their problems about boys. From the standpoint of personality development, it would be convenient if these things were timed slightly better; but I suppose that in the beginning when everything was arranged—I've never had any private information on the subject, by the way—procreation was fully as important as a feeling of self-esteem is now in a highly developed civilization. And so women get ready for procreation quite early: in fact one of the important problems in adolescence is how to avoid the accident of procreation. (1953b, p. 266)

As an interesting historical footnote, G. Stanley Hall was also aware of this same "developmental stutter," but had a rather different explanation. Admitting some degree of puzzlement over the fact that women achieve biological maturity earlier than men, he suggested that it might represent nature's way of ensuring the well-being of the species. Perhaps, he argued, it was a protection against premature impregnation. If women achieved puberty a year or two in advance of males the same age and also experienced the growth spurt thought to be associated with puberty earlier, this would render them, for a short time, taller and stronger than their male age-mates. Thus equipped, they would be in a better position to repel any undesired sexual overtures, and by the time they were ready for procreation they would be a little older, a little more robust, and hence a little more likely to bear healthy children.

Whether this particular—and still baffling—feature of feminine development reflects a mechanism to ensure the "survival of the fittest" or simply represents a whim of the Creator, the problem of feminine development remains, and with it, as we have indicated, the question of whether there is a theory of adolescence which can do justice both to boys and to girls.

Overview

Three different theories of adolescence have been presented, each of which presents a similar portrait of the adolescent. Hall, Anna Freud, and Sullivan all regard adolescence as a period of turmoil. Although the actual emphasis may vary from one theorist to another, all three describe more or less the same features of the adolescent experience: the physiological changes of puberty, the heightening of intellect, the branching out of social relationships. The major differences, in our opinion, have to do with interpretation. Hall, the first psychologist to undertake a detailed analysis of adolescence, regarded the alleged storm and stress of the period as evidence that some momentous "recapitulation" of human history was underway. Anna Freud, whose father, Sigmund Freud, profoundly influenced the modern view of childhood, explains adolescent turmoil in terms of the "resurgence" of infantile sexuality. And Sullivan, who reacted against the "reductionistic" tendencies of orthodox psychoanalysis to some extent, attributes the same storm and stress to difficulties in integrating lust with other interpersonal needs.

As far as the developmental significance of adolescence is concerned, Hall assigns it a major part in determining the adult personality; Freud views it, by and large, as a period of decidedly secondary importance; and Sullivan falls somewhere in between, pointing up the immense impact of early childhood experience, but viewing adolescence as a period of considerable import as well. These theories present us with certain "observables" and raise, when we compare them, certain issues. At this juncture, it is legitimate to ask just what the facts *are* and how the issues may be resolved—and these are the questions we propose to take up next.

REFERENCES

FREUD, A. Adolescence. *Psychoanalytic Study of the Child*, 1958, **13**, 255–278.
SCHACHTEL, E. *Metamorphosis*. New York: Basic Books, 1959.
SULLIVAN, H. S. *Conceptions of Modern Psychiatry*. New York: Norton, 1953a.
SULLIVAN, H. S. *The Interpersonal Theory of Psychiatry*. New York: Norton, 1953b.

Adolescents: They Act and Look More Like Adults than Children—But Somehow They Aren't Adults

We have observed that although our three representative theorists disagree about what *causes* adolescents to be the way they are, their overall characterization is quite similar. The picture of adolescence that emerges from the writings of all three is a distinctly romantic one, filled with conflict, turmoil, restlessness, and self-searching. To put the matter simply, Hall, Anna Freud, and Sullivan seem to agree that adolescence as a stage of life differs from both childhood and adulthood, and they would all probably concur in the following proposition: Adolescents *act* more like adults than children (i.e., they reason more like adults, have themselves under better control, and are more independent), adolescents *look* more like adults than children (i.e., they are larger than children and visibly closer to sexual maturity), yet somehow they are *not* adults (i.e., they are supposed to be more impulsive than adults, less consistent, less "settled"). At this point, having laid some of the theoretical groundwork, it is appropriate to ask what the facts are. What does research indicate about the key developments of adolescence? What kind of accommodation between theory and data can we begin to achieve?

These questions, of course, bring us back to a dilemma that we explored earlier: the difficulty of coordinating theoretical formulations with empirical findings. As we observed in Chapter 1, psychology in general and adolescent psychology in particular are plagued by a split between theory and data. Harry Stack Sullivan and Anna Freud, for instance, were clinicians and derived their accounts of adolescent development almost solely from their work with patients. On the other hand, psychologists who have actually done research on adolescence have paid little attention, by and large, to any particular theory, preferring simply to correlate one variable with another. A survey of the research literature reveals a great many studies of the purely empirical variety—"Parent-Child Relations and Father Identification among Adolescent Boys," "Family Relations of Bright High-Achieving and Under-Achieving High School Boys," "Developmental Maturity as a Determinant in Prestige of Adolescent Girls," and so forth. Consequently, we have decided to be selective rather than exhaustive in this chapter and the next. Rather than assigning each area of adolescent development a separate chapter and attempting to list every conceivable finding, we shall review the comparatively small body of studies that pertain to the issues we have already identified.[1]

Adolescents Act More Like Adults:
The Growth of Intellect

As noted earlier, the notion that there are significant changes in intellectual capacity during adolescence dates all the way back to the eighteenth-century philosopher Jean Jacques Rousseau. Upon entering his teens, Rousseau asserted, the youngster acquires the capacity to comprehend abstract ideas and relationships, rather than being confined in his thinking to concrete images. This theme has appeared persistently in our comparison of Hall, Anna Freud, and Sullivan as well. All three theorists acknowledge—either explicitly or implicitly—that adolescents are capable of greater intellectual feats than younger children.

But although all three recognized cognitive development as one of the most important facets of adolescent development, we can be reasonably sure that there are two points on which they would disagree. Most likely they would disagree about whatever it is that *accounts for* the adolescent's increased powers of intellect, and they would probably not be in perfect agreement about the overall *course* of cognitive growth either, that is, they would disagree about whether

[1] For a more encyclopedic approach, the reader is referred to Conger *(1973)*, Grinder *(1973)*, and Horrocks *(1969)*.

the ability to reason in abstractions appears abruptly at the beginning of adolescence or whether it is a skill that develops gradually throughout the course of childhood.

As for whatever it is that causes the mind to unfold, Hall would, in all probability, employ a purely biological or "evolutionary" explanation and invoke the principle of recapitulation. The adolescent can reason on a higher plane than the child, Hall would probably argue, because he has now entered a phase that corresponds to a more advanced stage of human evolution than does childhood.

Anna Freud would undoubtedly give credit to the defense mechanism of intellectualization instead. The advent of puberty, according to psychoanalytic theory, brings all the old instinctual wishes of early childhood to the fore once more, and Freud would claim that as a consequence the adolescent must adopt some extraordinary measures to prevent himself from succumbing. One way in which he can gain distance from his conflicts is to cast them in the form of abstract debates. The adolescent finds it much easier, Freud would insist, to engage in philosophical speculations about free will and submission to authority than to recognize that his superego is pulling him in one direction and his id in another. As a kind of inevitable by-product of all this intellectualization, so the psychoanalytic explanation goes, the adolescent appears brighter than the younger child.

How Sullivan would account for the increased mental capacities of the adolescent is a bit more problematic. As may be recalled, he discusses the cognitive gains of the juvenile era and late adolescence but for the most part refrains from commenting on the subject in his description of early adolescence. However, we might guess that he would point to social interaction as the chief influence on intellectual growth during adolescence or, indeed, during any other period of life. According to Sullivan, the human mind evolves as it does because of the child's myriad encounters with other people. Consequently, he would probably claim that by virtue of contacts with parents, siblings, peers, teachers, and assorted others, the child is forced to accommodate himself to various points of view. He learns, as a result of all this communication and confrontation, what labels his culture assigns to experience, and ultimately he becomes capable of reasoning like an adult.

The second issue—whether the capacity to comprehend abstract ideas appears abruptly or matures gradually—can be dealt with more succinctly. Hall and Freud both assert in no uncertain terms that it is a sudden development. Both characterize the preadolescent child as rather constricted and dull, and both apparently believe that the dawn of reason coincides more or less with the advent of puberty.

Though Sullivan's position must again be inferred, we think it fairly safe to assume that he would disagree with Hall and Freud. Sullivan appears to believe that the human mind unfolds rather slowly and steadily, constantly adding to its store of concepts and categories. Therefore, he would probably argue that the early adolescent's ability to work with abstractions represents a logical extension of development that has occurred earlier, principally in the juvenile and pre-adolescent eras, and in all likelihood he would claim that the adolescent's conceptual skills emerge gradually rather than abruptly.

The Facts of Cognitive Growth

But what are "the facts"? There seems to be little doubt that adolescents are indeed "brighter" than younger children, an observation we can verify by consulting several studies (Boyne & Clark, 1959; Jones & Conrad, 1933; Wechsler, 1958) which have compared the performance of adolescents and younger children on standardized I.Q. tests. These tests are usually composed of a battery of set tasks: arithmetic problems, vocabulary items, information questions, proverbs, and so forth. In general, the number of items that a child can master within any particular section of the test rises steadily with age, leveling off after late adolescence.

However, when we turn to the question of whatever it is that causes adolescents to appear more intelligent than younger children, that is, whether this change may be attributed to biological maturation, intellectualization, or social interaction, the answer becomes considerably more elusive. Although it is possible to evaluate a child's performance on an I.Q. test with a fair degree of accuracy, it is much more difficult to ascertain what has determined his performance. Just how are "biological maturation" or "social interaction" to be measured? And even if some kind of measurement could be devised, it would still be extremely difficult to assess and weigh the impact of such forces on the development of intelligence.

The difficulties are chiefly methodological. Imagine that a researcher wanted to trace the effects of "social interaction" on intelligence. He would have to select a population of infants, assign them to various groups, and see to it that each group was raised with differing degrees of "social interaction" (assuming, of course, that he could find an adequate measure of this particular factor). In addition, he would have to make sure that he had controlled all the other possible variables that might affect intelligence: hereditary endowment, biological maturation, nutrition, illness, and so forth.

Obviously, the practical and ethical impediments to conducting such an "experiment" would be insurmountable.

To be sure, there are studies that point to the importance of what we rather vaguely call the "social environment." Spitz's data on "hospitalism" *(1945, 1946)* indicate that children who are raised in institutions and deprived of meaningful contact with other human beings are likely to suffer severe retardation. But Spitz's work has been criticized by a number of other researchers *(Casler, 1961; Yarrow, 1961)* precisely because he did not control for numerous other factors that could have affected the development of these institutionalized children.

How Intelligence Matures: Piaget's Theory
of Mental Development

Nonetheless, even though we cannot yet furnish a definitive answer to the question of *why* intelligence matures as it does, there is a good deal to be said about *how* it matures. Among researchers who have sought to trace the course of cognitive growth, the Swiss theorist Jean Piaget has probably been the most influential.

The result of over 40 years of intensive study, his work on intelligence is currently having a profound impact on both research and education. In its broadest outlines, Piagetian theory recalls once more the observation of Rousseau (who, as noted earlier, was also Swiss). Like Rousseau, Piaget asserts that in childhood thought is dominated by images, by what the child can actually see and touch, whereas in adolescence the capacity to comprehend abstract ideas becomes manifest. But he has gone far beyond Rousseau in tracing the implications of this general principle. Rousseau merely set down what he had observed without employing any particular conceptual framework. (Indeed, in the eighteenth century there was none available.) Piaget, on the other hand, has devised a highly elaborate theoretical system to describe the way in which human thought matures.

Basically, he assumes that in the span of years between infancy and the beginning of adolescence, the child acquires the ability to perform certain *logical operations*. There is, Piaget contends, an inherent similarity between the kind of thinking many adolescents are capable of engaging in and the system of philosophical principles we call "logic." He also assumes, and here he resembles the personality theorists we have reviewed in the preceding chapters, that the child's progress from infantile thought to adult ideation occurs in several well-defined stages. In Piaget's view, there is a very definite, indeed, an invariant, pattern to cognitive development. Although the mathematical complexities of Piagetian theory are beyond the scope of this book (see Flavell [1963] for a more detailed account), the stages designated by the theory can be discussed in a comparatively straightforward manner.

The Four Piagetian Stages

As we have observed, what sets the adolescent apart from the younger child is his ability to transcend what he can actually perceive, to move beyond concrete objects to ideas and concepts. According to Piaget, the transition from the primitive mentality of infancy to the essentially mature ideation of adolescence occurs in four distinct steps: the sensorimotor stage, the intuitive (or preoperational) stage, the stage of concrete operations, and the stage of formal operations.

The sensorimotor stage   Precisely because the infant cannot tell us what is going on "inside his head," we have to infer what his thinking is like, and here Piaget's careful studies have proved to be invaluable. Although the parallel has not to our knowledge been pointed up before, Piaget's vision of what early intellectual functioning is like corresponds in many respects to Sullivan's. Both theorists characterize the infant's relationship to the world, even from the first moment of birth, as fundamentally *interactive.* Both assert that the child constantly receives sense impressions of what is going on around him and that he is constantly responding to and being molded by those impressions. Perhaps the chief difference is that Sullivan is concerned primarily with the child's relationships with other *people*, while Piaget tends to concentrate more on the child's relationships with *objects*, to his physical rather than his social environment.

In Piaget's terminology, the infant continuously *assimilates* information about the physical world through various sensory channels (seeing, feeling, touching, hearing) and gradually *accommodates* himself to what he has taken in through these channels. By means of these twin processes, the child begins to build up a repertoire of perceptual skills and responses which Piaget calls *schemas*. The very first schemas are little more than primitive reflexes—for example, the infant's initial and almost accidental attempts to place his thumb in his mouth. But as these reflexes are exercised and the child undergoes more and more stimulation, his skills and responses become increasingly refined.

Precisely because assimilation and accommodation are complementary (i.e., they occur continuously and exert a mutual influence on each other) it has always been difficult to discern in practice where one ends and the other begins. However, the following exposition (furnished by one of Piaget's most distinguished students, John Flavell) should help to clarify the relationship between the two:

An infant comes in contact for the first time with a ring suspended from a string. He makes a series of exploratory accommodations: he looks at it, touches it, causes it to swing back and forth, grasps it, and so on. These accommodatory acts do not take place *in vacuo*; through past interactions with various other objects the child already possesses assimilatory structures (schemas) which set in motion and direct those accommodations. Piaget would say that the ring is assimilated to the concepts of touching, moving, seeing, etc., concepts which are already part of the child's cognitive organization. The child's actions with respect to the ring are at once accommodations of these concepts or structures to the reality contours of the ring and assimilations of this new object to those concepts. *(Flavell, 1963, p. 51)*

In this way, the child acquires, arduously but steadily, certain notions of constancy that adults are very much inclined to take for granted. He learns, for instance, that an object removed from his field of vision does not simply cease to exist. Simultaneously, he develops certain capabilities: the ability to search for an object that has been hidden from him, the ability to coordinate what he has heard or felt with what he has seen, and so forth.

But during this initial sensorimotor stage, the infant's capacity to perform intellectual tasks is seriously limited. The kinds of problems he can solve tend to be restricted to those that can be acted out bodily. In the following experiment with his eighteen-month-old daughter, Piaget captures in a particularly vivid way the concrete quality of sensorimotor thought. He has carried out two previous experiments with the little girl, employing two props, a matchbox with a sliding cover and a watch chain. In the first experiment, he has placed the watch chain in the match box and left the cover wide open so that the child can simply turn the box over and shake the chain free. In the second, he has placed the chain in the box, closed the cover, but left sufficient space for the baby to extricate the chain merely by inserting her index finger. Now he is ready for a third:

Here begins the experiment which we want to emphasize. I put the chain back into the box and reduce the opening to 3 mm. It is understood that Lucienne is not aware of the functioning of the opening and has not seen me prepare the experiment. She only possesses two preceding schemata: turning the box over to empty it of its contents, and sliding her finger into the slit to make the chain come out. It is of course this last procedure that she tries first: she puts her finger into the slit to make the chain come out and gropes to reach the chain, but fails completely. A pause follows during which Lucienne manifests a very curious reaction bearing witness not only to the fact that she tries to think out the situation and to represent to herself through mental combination the operations to be performed, but also to the role played by imitation in the genesis of representations. Lucienne mimics the widening of the slit. She looks at the slit with great attention: then, several times in succession she opens and shuts her mouth, at first slightly, then wider and wider! Apparently Lucienne understands the existence of a cavity subjacent to the slit and wishes to enlarge that cavity. The attempt at representation which she thus furnishes is expressed plastically, that is to say, *due to the inability to think out the situation in words or clear visual images she uses a simple motor indication as a "signifier" or symbol.* . . . Soon after this phase of plastic reflection, Lucienne unhesitatingly puts her finger in the slit, and instead of trying as before to reach the chain, she pulls so as to enlarge the opening. She succeeds and grasps the chain. *(Piaget, 1952, pp. 337–338)*

Indisputably, Lucienne's strategy for solving the puzzle is an ingenious one. (Sullivan might very well describe it as a particularly interesting example of parataxic thinking.) But it is cumbersome and time-consuming. An adult can imagine only vaguely (and with no little trepidation) what it might be like to approach all problems in this manner, without the benefit of verbal concepts. Hence, the next stage of mental development, the stage in which the child acquires the ability to speak, represents a very major advance.

The intuitive stage   What Piaget terms the intuitive stage falls roughly between the age of two, the age at which most children usually begin to speak, and seven, the age at which formal schooling traditionally commences. Again the resemblance to Sullivan is marked, for Sullivan also points to the emergence of language as an extremely significant developmental landmark. When Piaget explains *why* he considers speech such an important advance, the degree of correspondence between the two theorists becomes even more striking.

   Like Sullivan, Piaget observes that once the child is capable of using words, "the possibility of verbal exchange with other persons arises" *(1967, p. 17)*, and verbal communication is a far more efficient means of discourse than the "body language" of the sensorimotor period. Then too, the advent of language heralds the "internalization of words (i.e., the appearance of thought itself sup-ported by a system of signs") *(1967, p. 17)*. So not only is the child increasingly able to exchange ideas, but even in the absence of other people he can begin to organize his own experiences and catalogue them. (Sullivan would, of course, call this the appearance of the *syntaxic mode* of thought.) But most importantly, perhaps, the acquisition of language permits "the internalization of action as such, which from now on, rather than being purely perceptual and motor, as it has been heretofore, can represent itself intuitively by means of pictures and 'mental experiments' " *(1967, p. 17)*. In other words, the ability to think in verbal concepts gives the child a much greater degree of flexibility than he enjoyed during the sensorimotor period. His existence becomes less a matter of trial and error and more one of anticipation and forethought. When faced with a problem, he need not, like Lucienne with her matchbox and watch chain, "act out" all the possible solutions. Once he is capable of verbal thought, the child can begin to imagine various strategies and can select the most likely from a range of possibilities.

Beyond the more immediate consequences, the acquisition of language has broad social implications. As Piaget observes, "language is, in effect, the vehicle for concepts and ideas that belong to everyone, and it reinforces individual thinking with a vast system of collective concepts. The child becomes immersed in these con-cepts as soon as he masters words" *(1967, p. 22)*. Speech takes the child a giant step in the direction of becoming a civilized human being. And once again, Piaget's observation brings Sullivan to mind. When Piaget speaks of enhancing individual thinking with a vast array of "collective concepts," he sounds almost as if he were re-ferring to Sullivan's notion of "consensual validation." Consensual validation, it may be recalled, is the process by which an individual clarifies his own experience—essentially by comparing it with that of others. Thus both Piaget and Sullivan appear to believe that language constitutes an indispensable instrument for such clarification.

Nonetheless, although speech furnishes the child with a power-ful conceptual tool, the kind of thinking he exhibits during the intui-tive stage contains its own peculiar set of limitations. Whereas the problem-solving ability of the infant is restricted to what he can act out bodily, the two-to-seven-year-old child tends to be constrained by what he can actually *see*. Though he is now capable of com-municating with adults, he is still unable to grasp certain concepts. And when he attempts to discover the solution to a problem, it is by *intuition* rather than by reason. Piaget illustrates this distinction with the following examples:

Present the subject with six or eight blue discs aligned with small spaces between them and ask him to pick out the same number of red discs from a pile at hand. At four to five years, on the average, children will construct an arrangement of red discs of exactly the same length as the blue discs but without bothering about the number of elements nor about making each red disc correspond to each blue one. Here we see an example of a primitive form of intuition which consists of evaluating quantity merely by the space it occupies, i.e., by the global perceptual qualities of the whole collection that is envisaged, without regard to its constituent relationships. Between five and six years, by contrast, there is a much more interesting reaction. The child matches a red disc with each blue one and concludes that the correspondence of each element results in the equality of the two series. However, if we move out the discs at the extreme ends of the red series so that they are no longer exactly underneath the blue ones but a little to one side, the child, who saw that nothing was added or subtracted, believes that the two series are no longer equivalent and contends that the longer series contains "more discs." *(1967, pp. 30–31)*

During this intuitive stage, the child knows roughly what is meant by the *words* "the same as" or "more than," but he does not understand the *concepts.* His actual thinking is subject to what Piaget terms "the primacy of perception." If a row of discs *looks* at a glance as if it contains the same number as another row, it is judged to be "equal" even if it is not. The concept of "equal" (in the sense of containing the same number of elements) is still somewhat confused. However, during the phase that follows the intuitive stage, the child's intellect begins to break the hold that perception has exercised over it.

The stage of concrete operations   The stage of concrete operations spans the ages of approximately seven to eleven or twelve. Once again, Piaget's description of this particular period is reminiscent of Sullivan. Like Sullivan, Piaget notes that with the commencement of formal schooling—which also throws the child into contact with a wide variety of other children and adults—the child's intellectual horizons are broadened considerably. Indeed, Piaget's account of how logical thought evolves brings to mind Sullivan's description of the juvenile phase. Like Sullivan, Piaget emphasizes the school-age child's increased ability to "take the other person's point of view" and his increased capacity to order his thoughts:

Instead of the impulsive behavior of the small child, accompanied by unquestioned beliefs and intellectual egocentricity, the child of seven or eight thinks before acting and thus begins to conquer the difficult process of reflection. Reflection is nothing other than internal deliberation, that is to say, a discussion which is conducted with oneself just as it might be conducted with real interlocutors or opponents. . . . The important point is that . . . the child of seven years begins to be liberated from his social and intellectual egocentricity and becomes capable of new coordinations which will be of the utmost importance in the development of intelligence and affectivity. With respect to intelligence, we are now dealing with the beginnings of the construction of logic itself. Logic constitutes the system of relationships which permit the coordination of points of view corresponding to different individuals, as well as those which correspond to successive precepts of the same individual. *(1967, pp. 40–41)*

In his dealings with other people—playmates, older children, parents, teachers—the school child must learn to relinquish some of his self-centered concentration on his own wants and needs, his "egocentrism" as Piaget calls it. This gradual "decentering" has a formidable impact on the child's intellect. For as he acquires the ability to appreciate other points of view, he also becomes much less bound by his perceptions. During the stage of concrete operations, the child is markedly less likely to be misled by the "look of things" than he was during the intuitive stage. He can, in effect, stand to one side of a task and reflect upon it, a maneuver quite foreign to the youngster who is still solving problems by intuition. In the experiment with the discs described above, the five or six year old concludes that there are more red discs than blue discs simply because the line of red discs is *longer.* The seven or eight year old is capable of recognizing that if the *number* of discs in each line is the same, it makes no difference if one line is longer than the other. Even while looking at the two uneven lines he can rearrange them "in his head" so that they correspond once more. In short, he has begun to comprehend that some of the actions that can be performed on objects are *reversible*, and he no longer confuses the concepts of length and equality.

However, as the term "concrete operations" may suggest, there is still an element of "concretism" or "egocentrism" to the child's thinking during this period. Confronted with a task, the seven year old is far more flexible than the five year old, but he is still not capable of systematically ticking off *all* the possible solutions. Another experiment of Piaget's (described in Inhelder & Piaget, *1958, pp. 108–109)* serves to illustrate the limitations of concrete operational thought:

The child is presented with four flasks (numbered "1," "2," "3," and "4"), each of which contains a "colorless, odorless" liquid. The four flasks are thus "perceptually identical." Flask 1 contains sulphuric acid; flask 2, water; flask 3, oxygenated water (hydrogen peroxide); and flask 4, thiosulphate.

The experimenter also introduces an eye dropper (which is referred to as "g") containing a fifth substance, potassium iodide. When potassium iodide (g) is mixed with sulphuric acid (1) and hydrogen peroxide (3), a yellow color results. If thiosulphate is in turn added to this combination of liquids (1 + 3 + g), it will bleach the entire mixture out. In front of the child, the experimenter takes two beakers which have been prepared in advance, one containing a mixture of sulphuric acid (1) and hydrogen peroxide (3), and the other containing plain water (2). He adds several drops of potassium iodide (g) to each, producing a yellow color in the beaker containing liquids 1 and 3 and getting no reaction at all, of course, in the beaker containing liquid 2 (plain water). The child is then shown the flasks numbered "1," "2," "3," and "4," given the eye dropper (g) and asked to produce the yellow color himself, using the flasks in any manner he wishes.

A seven year old typically attacks this problem in what seems to be a systematic manner, but he quickly becomes stymied:[2]

(The subject) tries 4 × g, then 2 × g, and 3 × g: "*I think I did everything . . . I tried them all.*" "What else could you have done?"—We give him the glasses again: he repeats 1 × g, etc. "You took each bottle separately. What else could you have done?"—"*Take two bottles at the same time.*" (He tries 1 × 4 × g, then 2× 3 × g, thus failing to cross over between the two sets of bottles, for example, 1 × 2, 1 × 3, 2 × 4, and 3 × 4). When we suggest that he add others, he puts 1 × g in the glass already containing 2 × 3 which results in the appearance of the color: "Try to make the color again." "*Do I put in two or three?*" (He tries with 2 × 4 × g, then adds 3, then tries it with 1 × 4 × 2 × g). "*No, I don't remember any more.*" *(Inhelder & Piaget, 1958, p. 111)*

At the beginning, there is a certain logic and order to this seven year old's performance. He does proceed spontaneously to *pair* the substance in the eye dropper with the substance in each bottle separately. But it takes a prod from the examiner to induce him to mix *three* liquids together, and even when he hits upon the solution to the puzzle by chance, he cannot reproduce it. As soon as his initial strategy has failed, his behavior becomes increasingly random and disorganized. The sheer number of possible solutions has apparently befuddled him.

The stage of formal operations   Only during the stage that succeeds that of concrete operations, can the youngster finally free himself from the "primacy of perception" and begin to reason more or less like an adult. According to Piaget, the stage of formal opera-

---

[2] In the account of the experiment the expressions "4 × g," "2 × g," and so forth, are used as shorthand for "liquid 4 with substance g," "liquid 2 with substance g," and so forth.

tions commences around the age of twelve and reaches its peak around the age of fifteen. At this point in mid-adolescence, the individual has purportedly acquired all the basic conceptual tools necessary to carry him through his adult life. Not that his intellect will function in the same way at thirty that it did at fifteen, but there are, in Piaget's view, no further major advances. Indeed, once a person has become capable of formal thought, no major advance is *possible*. This type of mental activity represents the highest form of human ideation.

But what are the characteristics of this type of thinking? How does the adolescent's ability to comprehend formal relationships set him apart from the younger child? If we take a look at the way in which a thirteen year old approaches the problem with the flasks, the difference quickly becomes evident:

> "*You have to try with all the bottles. I'll begin with the one at the end* (from 1 to 4 with g). *It doesn't work any more. Maybe you have to mix them.*" (He tries 1 × 2 × g; 2 × 4 × g; with the two preceding combinations this gives six two-by-two combinations systematically). "*It doesn't work. It only works with (1 × 3 × g).*" "Yes, and what about 2 and 4?" "*2 and 4 don't make any color together. They are negative. Perhaps you could add 4 in 1 × 3 × g to see if it would cancel out the color*" (he does this). "*Liquid 4 cancels it all. You'd have to see if 2 has the same influence* (he tries it). *No, so 2 and 4 are not alike, for 4 acts on 1 × 3 and 2 does not.*" "What is there in 2 and 4?" "*In 4 certainly water. No the opposite, in 2 certainly water since it doesn't act on the liquids; that makes things clearer.*" "And if I were to tell you that 4 is water?" "*If this liquid 4 is water, when you put it with 1 × 3 it wouldn't completely prevent the yellow from forming. It isn't water. It's something harmful?*" *(Inhelder & Piaget, 1958, p. 117)*

What is striking about this adolescent's performance (especially when compared with the seven year old's) is the extent to which it recalls that of a scientist in his laboratory. He approaches the task before him with a distinct hypothesis and proceeds to test it in an orderly and consistent fashion, drawing conclusions from the way in which each trial solution turns out. He is also capable of deducing critical information about the nature of the substances he is dealing with and casts his deductions in the form of what is called a *propositional statement*: "If this liquid 4 is water, *(then) when* you put it with 1 × 3, it wouldn't completely prevent the yellow from forming. It isn't water." He is, in short, employing what Piaget refers to as the *hypothetico-deductive* mode of reasoning. Rather than mechanically pairing various bottles, as the seven year old does, the thirteen year old rapidly envisions *all* the possible combinations (including mixing three liquids together) and sets out to discover which is the correct one. He begins, as did the seven year old, with combinations of two but quickly shifts to combinations of three. All in all, the adolescent is able to envision many more sides to the problem than the younger child, and his approach is consequently far more flexible and far less confused.

The emergence of formal thought has wider ramifications as well. The adolescent's capacity to comprehend abstract ideas, to imagine possibilities other than those that are visibly present, permits him to put the finishing touches on his own personality. Unlike the younger child, who must, for the most part, parrot back the beliefs of people who are "older and wiser" than himself, the adolescent can begin to formulate his own values and his own "philosophy of life." He is capable of constructing what Piaget describes as a "personal system":

> Personality formation begins in middle to late childhood (eight to twelve years) with the autonomous organization of rules and values, and the affirmation of will with respect to the regulation and hierarchical organization of moral tendencies. But there is more to the person than these factors alone. These factors are integrated with the self into a unique system to which all the separate parts are subordinated. There is then a "personal" system in the dual sense that it is peculiar to a given individual and implies autonomous coordination. *Now this personal system cannot be constructed prior to adolescence, because it presupposes the formal thought and reflexive constructions we have just discussed.* . . . One might say that personality exists as soon as a "life plan" (*Lebensplan*), which is both a source of discipline for the will and an instrument of cooperation, is formed. But this life plan presupposes the intervention of thought and free reflection, which is why it is not elaborated until certain intellectual conditions, such as the attainment of formal or hypothetico-deductive thought, are fulfilled. *(1967, pp. 65–66)*

Hence, once again, in the thinking of Piaget as in that of G. Stanley Hall, we find a link between adolescence and the notion of individuality.

Is formal thought universal? However, it is only a short step from "individuality" to "individual differences"—and a dilemma. That an adolescent is capable of thinking for himself and reasoning "like an adult" does not mean that he has necessarily reached the pinnacle of his powers—or that he ever will. By the age of fifteen he may have acquired the basic "mental equipment" of an adult, but what happens to this equipment depends on a number of factors: what sort of educational opportunities he has, how much intellectual curiosity he has, what sort of occupation he enters, and so forth. Indeed, in recent years Piaget *(1972)* and others have found it necessary to clarify the relationship between such "environmental influences" and formal thought.

Although various researchers *(Elkind, 1966; Flavell, 1963; Peel, 1960)* have confirmed that normal children do in fact pass through the first three Piagetian phases—sensorimotor, intuitive, and concrete operational—in precisely the order described, the formal stage has proven to be more elusive and problematic. Dulit *(1972)*, for instance, discovered that the percentage of subjects attaining this level of thinking varied according to the kind of population under consideration (e.g., "younger adolescent" versus "older adolescent") *and* the type of task employed. A mere 10 percent of the "younger adolescents" (mean age fourteen) in his study were able to devise a truly formal solution to the "liquids experiment" (the same experiment that is outlined above). Among a group of older adolescents (ages 16–17) the proportion rose to only 28 percent. And even among a group of older, *gifted* adolescents attending a special high school for prospective science majors, the figure was only 62 percent. (A group of "average" adults, aged 20 to 55, scored a sorry 25 percent.) Thus Dulit suggests that a kind of critical "branching" or "tracking" may occur at adolescence. It is probable, he surmises, that the youngster with special aptitudes, educational opportunities, and training will attain the formal level of thinking far more readily than the less gifted and privileged adolescent. (And even among the most talented and highly educated group, formal thought is apparently not universal.)

Similarly, Dulit speculates that the comparative absence of formal thought among "average" adults may reflect "societal demands"—or the lack of them. The majority of adults, he notes, are not in occupations that *require* much formal thought. "By contrast," he points out, "the 'demand' for concrete-level functioning (conservation of number, conservation of mass and volume, serial ordering, correspondence) is very considerable in modern society, even in 'everyday life' " *(1972, p. 300)*. Hence most adults remain relatively "concrete" in their thinking.

Although Piaget does not emphasize the role of cultural training to quite the extent that Dulit does, he too has recently *(1972)* admitted that it can have a marked impact on intellectual functioning —particularly the capacity for formal thought. The student of law and the student of physics, he observes, may both possess the ability to think in formal terms, but each will display this ability in rather different situations. Therefore, though he insists that all normal people develop the *potential* for formal thought at some point during adolescence, he concludes that "they reach this stage in different areas according to their aptitudes and their professional specializations" and that "the way in which these formal structures are used ... is not necessarily the same in all cases" *(1972, p. 10)*.

A Return to Basic Issues

This discussion of formal thought brings to mind two issues introduced earlier. Before embarking upon a summary of Piaget's theory, we raised the question of whether the human mind comes to maturity abruptly or gradually, and we also asked what causes the human intellect to develop as it does. In Piaget's opinion, the first issue can be settled decisively. The appearance of formal thought (assuming, of course, that it appears at all) is not, he claims, a sudden development. Rather, it is a logical extension of skills the child has acquired during earlier stages:

> The eruption of this new kind of thinking, in the form of general ideas and abstract constructions, is actually much less sudden than it would seem. It develops in relatively continuous fashion from the concrete thinking of middle childhood. The turning point occurs at about the age of twelve, after which there is rapid progress in the direction of free reflection no longer directly attached to external reality. *(1967, p. 61)*

Hence, here too, Piaget's position seems to lend more support to Sullivan than to either Hall or Anna Freud, both of whom argued that the adolescent's ability to comprehend abstract ideas becomes manifest rather suddenly.

Piaget is somewhat less emphatic about the second issue (i.e., what *causes* the human mind to develop as it does). Generally, he has been more inclined to describe intellectual functioning than to explain it, and in view of the difficulties involved in arriving at a definitive answer, such reticence is not surprising.

When Piaget does turn his attention to the subject of causation, two themes stand out. His explanation is based, first, on a "tension-reduction" model, and in this respect he resembles both Anna Freud and Sullivan, whose systems also revolve around the principle of tension reduction. For Anna Freud, the primary motive in life is to maintain a certain minimal level of gratification, to strike an acceptable balance between id, ego, and superego. For Sullivan, the need to maintain a certain level of security is the prime mover. In Piaget's system, the principle of tension reduction appears as "the need to maintain equilibrium." This need, he claims, is characteristic of all living organisms and applies just as well to the unfolding of the human intellect as to any other kind of growth:

The psychological development that starts at birth and terminates in adulthood is comparable to organic growth. Like the latter, it consists essentially of activity directed toward a relatively stable level character- ized by the completion of the growth process and organ maturity, so that mental life can be conceived as evolving toward a final form of equilibrium represented by the adult mind. *(1967, p. 3)*

The infant experiences, we might infer, a kind of primitive equilib- rium at birth, but it does not take the world long to upset it, with noises, lights, tactile sensations, and the like. From this point onward, the individual embarks on a never-ending cycle of reestablishing equilibrium, having it disturbed once more, establishing a new equilibrium and having *it* disturbed, and so on. (This is, of course, where the complementary processes of assimilation and accom- modation enter the picture.)

And, as we have already seen, in addition to "equilibrium seek- ing" (or *equilibration*, as it is called), Piaget also assigns an im- portant role to social interaction. (Indeed, we have commented on the resemblance between Piaget and Sullivan in this regard.) Without this second factor, without day-to-day contacts and collisions with other people, Piaget appears to believe that no child would ever develop the capacity for *either* concrete operational or formal thought:

One quality stands out in the thinking of the young child: he con- stantly makes assertions without trying to support them with facts. This lack of attempts at proof stems from the character of the child's social behavior at this age, i.e., from his egocentricity conceived as a lack of differentiation between his own point of view and that of others. *It is only vis à vis others that we are led to seek evidence for our statements. We always believe ourselves without further ado until we learn to consider the objections of others and to internalize such discussions in the form of reflection.* (1967, p. 29, italics added)

Presumably it is also only vis à vis others that the child develops some degree of self-control and an appreciation of right and wrong— which leads us to our next topic.

Moral Development

In addition to agreeing that adolescents seem "smarter" than children, Hall, Anna Freud, and Sullivan would probably all credit adolescents with greater self-discipline, however erratically such self-discipline might be displayed. The adolescent who emerges from all three theoretical accounts is better equipped to decide matters of conscience for himself than is the child. Hall attributes this heightening of moral sensibilities to the rise of rather vaguely described "social feelings." Anna Freud would no doubt adduce "consolidation of the superego" as the critical factor. Having resolved the Oedipus complex by identifying with his parents (purportedly around the age of five or six), the child is supposed to spend the next seven or eight years internalizing the moral strictures he has thereby acquired. The result, according to psychoanalytic theory, is a more or less autonomous superego. And although Sullivan does not discuss moral development per se, his explanation would very likely correspond roughly to that of the social-learning theorists. He would probably assert that in the course of learning what society considers appropriate behavior, the adolescent also manages to fashion a set of values for himself. Indeed, Sullivan implies in his discussion of the concept of orientation in living that if nothing goes seriously amiss in the socialization process, these values have already begun to appear near the end of the juvenile era.

Moral Judgment Versus Moral Behavior

In surveying the facts, we quickly discover that it is useful to make a distinction between moral reasoning and moral behavior. It would be logical to assume that the two would go together and that the adolescent's sturdier conscience and finer grasp of moral principles would permit him to behave in a more exemplary fashion than the child. However, *most* of the existing research reveals that the truth is not so convenient. St. Paul lamented, "The good which I want to do, I fail to do," and as we shall see, this adage captures with a fair degree of accuracy the relationship between moral knowledge and moral actions.[3]

Moral Judgment

Separating the two aspects of moral development, we find research on the growth of moral judgment to be relatively straight-

---

[3] Our three representative theorists appear to be quite aware of the possible discrepancy between the adolescent's values and his actual behavior. Although they emphasize the adolescent's increased autonomy, Hall, Anna Freud, and Sullivan all characterize adolescence as a period of increased impulsiveness, of wavering back and forth between extremes of propriety and unruliness, of idealistic altruism and excessive selfishness. We shall examine some of these less salutary aspects of moral development in the next chapter, which is devoted to a discussion of storm and stress.

forward and clear-cut. Although a number of researchers explored the area early in the twentieth century,[4] once again it is Piaget who has conducted the most influential study *(1932)* and provided the impetus for a host of other investigators. Piaget interviewed a group of children between the ages of seven and thirteen, questioning them about a variety of moral dilemmas. As might be imagined, he interprets his findings employing much the same frame of reference as he does for his other work in cognitive development.

Piaget claims that just as the child's thinking gradually shifts from concrete to formal, his orientation toward other people changes slowly from egocentric to sociocentric. During the early years, he is inclined to be absolutist and authoritarian about all questions concerning right and wrong. When Piaget asks a six year old if the rules to a game of marbles may ever be altered, he is met with a categorical "no." His father and grandfather played it this way, the six year old replies, and therefore the rules are sacred. A twelve or thirteen year old, on the other hand, is likely to answer that "of course" the rules may be changed if all players are amenable, thereby demonstrating an implicit understanding of the concept that rules, rather than being synonymous with the Ten Commandments, are the result of mutual agreement.

Similarly, if a six year old is told the story of a little boy who has accidentally dropped a sweet roll in the lake, he is likely to respond: "That's too bad. But it's his own fault for being so clumsy. He shouldn't get another." An adolescent is inclined, by contrast, to take a more compassionate view, pointing to the culprit's tender age and recommending that he receive another treat. According to Piaget, the younger child is governed by a rather primitive form of retributive justice. For him, a "punishment" implies a crime, and losing a roll in the lake is clearly a punishment in his eyes. He is incapable of taking extenuating circumstances into account. The adolescent, however, is supposed to make moral judgments on the basis of what Piaget calls *equity*, assigning punishments in accordance with the transgressor's ability to take responsibility for his crime. In short, the adolescent is thought to employ the same sort of hypothetico-deductive approach in reasoning out moral dilemmas that he does in solving intellectual puzzles. Rather than being tied to concrete facts and a narrow range of possibilities like the younger child ("There is a punishment, therefore there must be a crime"), he is able to think in terms of the potential and envision a much wider range of alternatives ("There is an unfortunate event; someone may or may not be to blame").

[4] See our discussion of this topic on pp. 36–37 of Chapter 2.

Other Research on Moral Development

As in the case of his work on intellectual development, Piaget's research on moral development has been corroborated by a substantial number of other investigators *(Boehm & Nass, 1962; Caruso, 1943; Janis, 1961; Johnson, 1962; Lerner, 1937; MacRae, 1954).* Having surveyed this body of data, Lawrence Kohlberg *(1964)*, himself one of the most prominent researchers in the area, has summarized those aspects of Piaget's theory that appear to have been borne out. Kohlberg claims that adolescents from a variety of countries and cultural settings have been shown to differ from younger children on six different dimensions of moral reasoning.

First of all (and this feature of adolescent thinking is also cited by G. Stanley Hall), teenagers are much more likely to take account of *intentions* in judging the seriousness of a transgression. Younger children are apt to base their appraisals on the amount of physical damage done. For example, a six year old is likely to say that a child who broke five cups while helping his mother set the table is more culpable than a boy who broke one cup in the course of stealing some jam. For the thirteen year old, it is just the reverse. Second, the adolescent is more likely to display a kind of *relativism* in his determinations of right and wrong, for instance, condoning a poor man's theft of a loaf of bread in order to feed his starving family. The younger child is likely to declare that stealing is wrong no matter what the circumstances. Third, adolescents are better able to keep in mind what Kohlberg terms *independence of sanctions* than are younger children. A very young child is likely to declare that a person has done something wrong simply if he is disciplined, no matter how mistaken or unjust the punishment might be. The older child recognizes that good deeds may sometimes go unrewarded—or even meet with what looks like punishment. Similarly, adolescents are less likely to retain *naturalistic views of misfortune.* If a six year old is told that a bridge collapsed under someone just after the person stole a few apples, he is likely to regard the catastrophe as actual retribution for the theft. The thirteen year old inclines much less toward superstition and more typically greets such occurrences with remarks like, "Well, the bridge didn't know the person had stolen, after all!" In addition, the teenager has a finer appreciation of *reciprocity* than the younger child. Asked, "What would the Golden Rule say to do if a boy came up and hit you?" a six year old not uncommonly replies, "Hit him back," thus substituting a tit-for-tat morality for the time-honored ethical precept. Thirteen year olds are more likely to interpret the Golden Rule as "Putting yourself in someone else's place." And finally, with increasing age, notions of *restitution and reform* begin to come to the fore. Young children are prone to advocate severe punishments for even relatively minor crimes (shooting people if they are caught shoplifting, for instance). Adolescents are more inclined to suggest that offenders be rehabilitated, that some attempt be made to understand their motives for committing crimes, that they be reeducated, and so forth.

Though these six dimensions of moral judgment appear to be more or less universal and show up in a wide variety of different countries and cultures, Kohlberg *(1964; Kohlberg & Kramer, 1969)* observes that there are several aspects of Piaget's general theory of moral development that are either in error or in need of further refinement. For instance, Piaget claims that one of the major reasons that the child acquires such notions as reciprocity and intentionality is that he is required to interact with other children. The social encounters that occur in the classroom and on the playground allegedly force him into an awareness of other people's feelings and motives. Piaget goes on to assert *(1932)* that another result of all this social interaction is a shift in allegiance from more traditional authorities (parents, teachers, and the like) to the child's own peers. A twelve year old, Piaget declares, will advocate telling a lie to protect a friend—even though he knows that lying violates the established order of the day. However, Kohlberg contends that other researchers (himself included) have *not* uncovered the same shift in loyalties. On the contrary, Kohlberg claims that, when asked to choose between conventional morality and what might be termed the "law of the gang," most adolescents come down on the side of convention.[5]

Furthermore, Kohlberg contends, Piaget did not carry his analysis of moral development far enough into adolescence. The oldest children in Piaget's original study were only thirteen, and anyone who peruses it is left with the impression that moral development is, for all intents and purposes, complete by this age. By age thirteen, Piaget seems to imply, the child has managed to incorporate the basic tenets and precepts of the society in which he resides. However, despite the controversies that have recently arisen concerning his work *(Keniston, 1970; Simpson, in press)*, Kohlberg's own research would seem to indicate that there can be significant transformation in moral reasoning throughout the course of adolescence and even up into young adulthood.

---

[5] We shall have more to say on this particular issue when we take up the topic of adolescent rebellion in Chapter 6.

Kohlberg's stages of moral development   Kohlberg distinguishes three levels of moral judgment and subdivides each of these levels into two stages. During the first stage (stage 1) of what Kohlberg labels the *premoral* or *preconventional* period, the child makes his determinations of right and wrong solely in terms of the overt physical consequences: how much damage was done, whether or not someone was punished, and so forth. In the second stage (stage 2) of this period, a kind of "naïve instrumental hedonism" begins to appear. The child does recognize concepts like "equal sharing" and "fair play," but he interprets them in a completely pragmatic way. He seems to believe that people follow the rules and treat one another well because they can "get something" out of it. Hence, reciprocity at this stage "is a matter of 'you scratch my back and I'll scratch yours'" *(Kohlberg & Kramer, 1969, p. 100).*

This premoral phase typically takes up the years between seven and eleven or twelve. By early adolescence, most youngsters have attained the level of *conventional* morality. During the first conventional stage (stage 3), a kind of "good boy–nice girl" morality predominates. That which is moral is judged to be that which pleases or is approved of by others—and also that which is directed toward helping others. At this stage, the first references to intention become apparent as well (i.e., the youngster is likely to remark that another person "means well" when he describes a particular piece of behavior). In the second conventional stage (stage 4), the adolescent is able to move beyond mere social desirability and begins to recognize a genuine moral order. It is at this point that appeals to authority —the law, the state, a Supreme Being—start to emerge. What is right, as Kohlberg and Kramer put it, "consists of doing one's duty, showing respect for authority and maintaining the given social order for its own sake" *(1969, p. 100).*

Up to this point in Kohlberg's account, there is no serious departure from Piaget. Indeed, Piaget describes essentially the same progression in moral judgment (although employing somewhat different terminology) between childhood and early adolescence. However, Kohlberg goes on to delineate two additional stages at what he terms the *postconventional, autonomous,* or *principled* level. When the adolescent reaches the first stage of this level (stage 5)— and he does not do so, customarily, until the end of high school— his respect for "law and order" is replaced by a kind of "social contract" orientation. He recognizes the necessity of having a legal code, but he becomes sensitive as well to the rights of the individual. The moral order is viewed as a body of rules agreed upon by the people in a particular society for the purpose of guaranteeing their individual and collective interests. It is not (as in the previous stage) something that has been handed down from on high, nor is it something that can never be altered. And finally, during the second postconventional stage (stage 6), which may or may not be attained by early adulthood, the young person formulates an abstract moral code of his own.[6] At this stage, according to Kohlberg, the individual employs "self-chosen ethical principles," ones which can be applied consistently and universally, in arriving at moral judgments. As examples, Kohlberg and Kramer list the "universal principles of *justice* of the *reciprocity* and *equality* of *human rights* and of respect for the dignity of human beings as *individual persons*" *(1969, p. 101)*.

It will probably be helpful at this point to offer some illustrations, and we therefore turn to the following set of excerpts from Kohlberg's own research. All the subjects had been asked to resolve a life-and-death situation:

Stage 1: No differentiation between moral value of life and its physical or social status value.

Tommy, age ten (Why should the druggist give the drug to the dying woman when her husband couldn't pay for it?): "If someone important is in a plane and is allergic to heights and the stewardess won't give him medicine because she's only got enough for one and she's got a sick one, a friend, in back, they'd probably put the stewardess in a lady's jail because she didn't help the important one."

Stage 2: The value of a human life is seen as instrumental to the satisfaction of the needs of its possessor or of other persons. Decision to save life is relative to, or to be made by, its possessor.

Tommy, age thirteen (Should the doctor "mercy kill" a fatally ill woman requesting death because of her pain?): "Maybe it would be good to put her out of her pain, she'd be better off that way. But the husband wouldn't want it, it's not like an animal. If a pet dies you can get along without it— it isn't something you really need. Well, you can get a new wife, but it's not really the same."

Stage 3: The value of a human life is based on the empathy and affection of family members and others toward its possessor.

Tommy, age sixteen (Same question): "It might be best for her, but her husband—it's a human life—not like an animal, it just doesn't have the same relationship that a human being does to a family. You can become attached to a dog, but nothing like a human you know."

Stage 4: Life is conceived as sacred in terms of its place in a categorical moral or religious order of rights and duties.

Jim, age sixteen (Same question): "I don't know. In one way, it's murder, it's not a right or privilege of man to decide who shall live and

---

[6] There is a hint of this type of development during adolescence in Piaget's remarks about the formulation of a "personal system," but Kohlberg's investigation of the phenomenon is both more systematic and more detailed.

who shall die. God put life into everybody on earth and you're taking away something from that person that came directly from God, and you're destroying something that is very sacred, it's in a way part of God and it's almost destroying a part of God when you kill a person. There's something of God in everyone."

Stage 5: Life is valued both in terms of its relation to community welfare and in terms of being a universal human right.

Jim, age twenty (Same question): "Given the ethics of the doctor who has taken the responsibility to save human life—from that point of view he probably shouldn't but there is another side, there are more and more people in the medical profession who are thinking it is a hardship on everyone, the person, the family, when you know they are going to die. When a person is kept alive by an artificial lung or kidney it's more like being a vegetable than being a human who is alive. If it's her own choice I think there are certain rights and certain privileges that go along with being a human being. I am a human being and have certain desires for life and I think everybody else does too. You have a world of which you are the center, and everybody else does too and in that sense we're all equal."

Stage 6: Belief in the sacredness of human life as representing a universal human value of respect for the individual.

Jim, age twenty-four (Should the husband steal the drug to save his wife? How about for someone he just knows?): "Yes. A human life takes precedence over any other moral or legal value, whoever it is. A human life has inherent value whether or not it is valued by a particular individual."

(Why is that?): "The inherent worth of the individual human being is the central value in a set of values where the principles of justice and love are normative for all human relationships." *(Adapted from Kohlberg & Kramer, 1969, pp. 101–102)*

Other Issues Concerning Moral Judgment

However, in addition to providing evidence that an individual's moral sensibilities can continue to evolve throughout adolescence, Kohlberg's research raises a number of other important issues, two of which should be familiar by now.

Norms   There is, first, the question of norms. Kohlberg reports *(Kohlberg & Kramer, 1969; Kohlberg & Gilligan, 1971)* that most of the adolescents he has studied have managed to reach stage 3 or stage 4, the stages of conventional morality. However, only a minority (roughly 30 percent) progress *beyond* this level to either of the so-called postconventional stages. Furthermore, there are indications that cultural setting has some impact on the development of moral judgment. Kohlberg's original research was performed on middle class *American* youngsters. When he collected data in less industrialized parts of the world (e.g., in Mexico and rural Turkey), he discovered that although the overall progression from stage 1 to stage 6 was much the same, only 4 percent of the subjects had attained the postconventional level by age seventeen.

Indeed, Kohlberg has recently been the object of some rather harsh—and probably justifiable—criticism for his failure to take such cultural differences into account *(Simpson, in press)*. Whether intentionally or unconsciously, Kohlberg implies that "stage 5" or "stage 6" morality is somehow more "exemplary" and "on a higher plane" than "stage 3" or "stage 4" morality. Thus he is in effect suggesting that cultures in which "postconventional" morality is largely absent are "less advanced" and represent a "lower level of development." But this conclusion in itself, Simpson observes, involves a value judgment—and one that is perhaps both debatable and arbitrary.

In a thoughtful article on Kohlberg's research, Keniston makes much the same point. An individual can reach the postconventional stage, he notes, and yet adopt a philosophy that is inherently "immoral": "There are at least a few whom we know from personal experience or from history who seem truly postconventional in moral reasoning but whose genuine adherence to the highest moral values is *not* matched by compassion, sympathy, capacity for love and empathy" *(p. 444)*. He cites as a chilling example the German teenagers who embraced fascism and became "Hitler Youth" during World War II.

Sex differences   Kohlberg's work also confronts us once more with the related and ubiquitous problem of sex differences. Citing the findings of a number of other researchers *(Haan, Smith, & Block, 1968; Turiel, 1969)*, Kohlberg asserts that stage 3 of the conventional level tends to be "terminal" for girls. Fewer girls than boys, he claims, proceed to any of the higher stages. In other words, women purportedly are more inclined to retain a "good boy–nice girl" orientation to questions of right and wrong than are men. It is social desirability (being agreeable, doing what is approved, taking care not to hurt people's feelings) rather than principle (law and order, duty, justice, human dignity) that is supposed to underlie their moral judgments—at least to a greater extent than is true with men.

Douvan and Adelson *(1966)*, to whom we shall be referring frequently, furnish some additional, though more impressionistic, support for this alleged sex difference. After interviewing a large sample of "typical" adolescents (more than 3000), they concluded that their female subjects were less "internalized" and "autono-mous" than their male subjects. To be sure, the girls were more conforming than the boys and reported fewer conflicts with their parents, but they did not seem to be fashioning a personal creed. Though the boys appeared to have more difficulty controlling their impulses (they expressed more fears about keeping themselves out of trouble, admitted more often to have broken rules, and so forth), they also seemed to be more actively engaged in formulating their own standards of conduct rather than simply adopting their parents' values wholesale.

Hence, however much present-day proponents of Women's Liberation might object, there does seem to be at least some em-pirical support for Sigmund Freud's assertion that conscience is less highly developed in women than it is in men (see Chapter 3, p. 63). Nonetheless, if this observation is pushed very far, another paradox quickly becomes evident. Women may be less "autonomous" morally, but they are also "better behaved"—less likely to engage in delinquency during adolescence and far less likely to commit crimes of violence *(Short, 1966)*. How can we account for this apparent discrepancy between moral judgment and moral behavior?

Some of the researchers we have just cited *(Douvan & Adelson, 1966; Kohlberg & Kramer, 1969)* invoke a kind of "social learning" explanation and suggest that it may be a matter of the way in which the feminine role is defined. Generally, girls are expected to be more "conforming" and "conventional," and they are not encouraged to become "analytical" or to "think for themselves" to the extent that boys are. Hence, they become "good" without necessarily becoming independent as well. Providing additional support for this hypothesis, the sociologist Mirra Komarovsky *(1950)* observes that women are expected to be more responsive to other people's feelings than men are and that they are allowed less freedom than men in making their own decisions.

As might be imagined, we shall have much more to say about the entire subject of sex differences. The fact that they crop up in this context serves only to highlight yet another issue with respect to moral development: the discrepancy between values and behavior.

Moral Behavior

Although not all adolescents progress at the same rate and al-though relatively few of them achieve the rarified heights of Kohl-berg's stage 6, there is little question that, taken as a group, they can decide questions of right and wrong in a more enlightened manner than younger children. Nonetheless, as we have already seen, the relationship between moral judgment and moral behavior, at least in the case of girls, is not completely clear-cut. As it turns out, what is true for girls seems to be true of adolescents in general.

Despite the fact that a majority of adolescents achieve the conventional level of moral reasoning, relatively few grow up to become pillars of the community. In their study of adolescent character, for example, Havighurst and Taba *(1949)* concluded that only a minority of their subjects could be described as behaving in a morally autonomous fashion. In this pioneering investigation, the researchers amassed a large amount of information on a sample of teenagers living in a typical midwestern town. Employing a wide variety of techniques—ratings from teachers, evaluations by peers, personality inventories, projective tests—they identified five distinct character types: self-directive, adaptive, submissive, defiant, and unadjusted. Although the first three types of teenagers enjoyed high character ratings (i.e., they were judged to be law-abiding, considerate, and generally well-behaved), only the self-directive group appeared to have evolved an autonomous moral code—and they represented a rather modest 21 percent of the total sample. The submissive and adaptive types, though outwardly conforming, seemed simply to have *absorbed* their values, their "good behavior" being more a function of habit or a desire for social approval than of conscious choice. And the unadjusted and defiant types, of course, could not even be described as well behaved. To complicate matters still further, Havighurst and Taba found it impossible to assign any label at all to a substantial portion of their sample—about a third of the adolescents studied.

Another well-known piece of research conducted by Hartshorne and May *(1928–1930)* revealed, somewhat to the disillusionment of the experimenters, that children do *not* necessarily become more honest and trustworthy as they approach adolescence. In a series of studies, school children were observed in the classroom carrying out a variety of tasks that they had been told were tests. They were given ample opportunity to cheat—and many of them did. But what is most significant is that fourteen year olds were every bit as likely to avail themselves of such opportunities as eleven year olds.

However, lest we conclude that there is no relationship whatsoever between age and moral behavior, Kohlberg comes to the rescue with some additional and interesting data *(1966; Kohlberg & Kramer, 1969)*. In reviewing the Hartshorne and May research, Kohlberg and Kramer *(1969)* insist that the picture may not have been as bleak as it appeared. Though the *overall* amount of cheating remained constant, some children apparently became consistently more honest and others consistently more dishonest with increasing age. Furthermore, Kohlberg (1966) claims that some as yet unpublished research does uncover a relationship between level of moral reasoning and moral behavior, after all. A study of school children (Krebs, 1967) determined that those reasoning at the lower levels of Kohlberg's scale were far more likely to cheat when given the chance than were those who had attained the higher levels. Whether or not these results will be corroborated by other researchers remains to be seen, and it might be well to view them, at least for the present, with a certain degree of skepticism.

All in all, perhaps the most definitive conclusion we can draw about moral development is that adolescence seems to usher in the great variety of character styles associated with *adulthood*. Certainly, there is considerable evidence that teenagers as a group resolve moral dilemmas in a more sophisticated manner than younger children—and that older teenagers are, by and large, more sophisticated than younger teenagers. However, there are also evidently some sex differences in moral judgment, and only a small proportion of all adolescents appear to develop a highly differentiated moral code. Nor is the teenager's increased comprehension of moral issues necessarily translated into more exemplary behavior —although there is some very tentative indication of a relationship between the kind of values a teenager espouses and his conduct.

Social Development

A discussion of moral development brings us close to another facet of the adolescent experience, that of social development. In addition to crediting teenagers with greater moral autonomy, the three representative theorists we have reviewed have all characterized adolescents as more independent in another respect. Hall, Anna Freud, and Sullivan all describe the adolescent as cutting some of his ties to his parents and establishing bonds of affection with those of his own age—the celebrated shift from parent to peer. Just as in the case of moral development, however, we can assume that they would disagree about the precise details of this transition.

Being more of a cataloguer than a personality theorist, Hall merely notes that it does occur. Anna Freud, on the other hand, describes friendships as a kind of stopgap maneuver. With the resurgence of Oedipal feelings at puberty, the adolescent's parents purportedly become "dangerous objects" once again, and it is necessary to achieve some distance from them. But this retreat from his family creates an emotional void which the adolescent is supposed to try to fill with a series of passionate (and short-lived) friendships. By contrast, Sullivan depicts the growth of friendship as a gradual progression, and he also assigns to it a much more significant role in personality formation than either of the other two theorists. If a child does *not* form close relationships with other children, Sullivan asserts, his capacity for intimacy later in life may be seriously hampered. As is apparent from his discussion of the "chum relationship," Sullivan believes that this capacity for intimacy ought to begin to develop *before* adolescence, during the preadolescent era.

Research on Social Development: Friendship

Turning once more to "the facts," we discover that there is actually not a great deal of information on the development of social relationships during adolescence. As was true of intellectual development, however, the existing data would seem to lend more support to Sullivan than to Anna Freud—at least as far as American and Australian adolescents are concerned. If children are asked to imagine how their classmates in school view them and the self-ratings are compared with the actual ratings, the disparity between the two sets becomes smaller and smaller with increasing age *(Ausubel, Schiff, & Gasser, 1952; De Jung & Gardner, 1962)*. Between the ages of nine and seventeen, the youngster apparently becomes capable of judging how he appears to others with greater and greater accuracy, a finding that would tend to suggest that social awareness does indeed develop gradually.

There is also little evidence that adolescents use friendships to fill a profound emotional void *or* that these friendships are transient, erratic affairs. One of the best-known set of studies on the subject *(Horrocks & Buker, 1951; Horrocks & Thompson, 1946; Thompson & Horrocks, 1947)* indicates that during adolescence friendships are, if anything, more stable than in childhood. In this particular series of investigations, the subjects, ranging in age from 11 to 18, were asked to name their three best friends. Two weeks later the question was repeated and the choices compared. The older the subject, the more likely he was to have retained the same three best friends, a finding that does not lend much credence to Anna Freud's assertion that adolescents are fickle in their affections. Furthermore, there *is* some support for Sullivan's contention that friendship provides a mirror for the self and a testing ground for attitudes and values. In a study of a small midwestern town (by now also something of a classic),

Hollingshead (1949) discovered that high school students tended to select their friends on the basis of common interests and social background.

Of course, Sullivan claims that friendship takes on this reciprocal quality during *preadolescence* because of the child's emerging need for intimacy and subsequent search for a chum. He also suggests that his observations might apply better to male than to female children. Ironically, the type of relationship he describes turns out to be more characteristic of adolescents than of preadolescents and more prevalent among girls than boys. In their national survey of youngsters between the ages of 11 and 18, Douvan and Adelson (1966) discovered that preadolescents and early adolescents of both sexes were much less interested in the personal qualities of their friends than in the opportunity to share activities with them. In this study, one of the few intensive pieces of research to be conducted with normal adolescents, the subjects were interviewed individually. When girls between the ages of 11 and 13[7] were asked what a friend ought to be like, the following composite appeared:

. . . the early adolescent mentions fewer qualities than older girls do. More important, the qualities she does mention are fairly superficial ones. For example, she wants a friend to be amiable, easy to get along with, cooperative, and fair. The friend ought not to be a crab, grouchy, mean, selfish, or a show-off.
What we miss in this surfeit of adjectives is the sense that a friendship can be emotionally relevant. The girl alludes to those surface qualities of the other that promote or hinder the swift and easy flow of activity. In this respect, the friendship is not yet relational. One wants a partner who is neither demanding nor disagreeable, whose personality will not get in the way of activity. (1966, pp. 186–187)

With older adolescent girls, however, Douvan and Adelson observed something approaching the intimacy that Sullivan ascribes to preadolescent chums. Both in middle and late adolescence, girls defined their friendships in terms of virtues like loyalty, the ability to keep confidences, emotional support, and common interests. The researchers concluded that these older subjects were much more capable of establishing a *relationship* with another person, of truly sharing experiences and being responsive to their friends.

Significantly, there was no comparable development among the boys (who were principally between the ages of 14 and 16) in the survey. In fact, Douvan and Adelson note:

[7] Because of funding and design limitations, the researchers were unable to obtain a sample of boys between the ages of 11 and 13.

When we ask the boys the criteria they use for choosing a friend, and ask about the sources of a boy's popularity, they name rather concrete qualities. Their answers bear a striking resemblance to those given by the preadolescent girl. They believe a friend ought to be amiable and coopera- tive, and in general demand little in the way of genuine interaction. They want the friend to be able to control impulses and here they particularly have aggression in mind. They also mention excessive hostility ("he's mean, a bully, picks fights") as a major source of unpopularity. Apart from exercising a degree of control, the friend is seen as having few obligations in the relationship. Boys at this age do not emphasize, as girls do, the affective elements in friendship. They make no demands for closeness, mutual understanding, or emotional support. . . . All in all, the boys show little concern with the relational aspects of friendship. Friendship for them, as for the youngest group of girls, involves a tie to a congenial companion, with whom one shares a common interest in reality oriented activities. *(1966, pp. 195–196)*

Confronted with this disparity between boys and girls and with the fact that, even among girls, truly intimate friendships do not seem to develop before midadolescence, we begin to wonder if Sullivan's portrayal of the "chum relationship" is not somewhat romanticized. It is possible, of course, that the boys in the Douvan and Adelson study were not able to convey feelings of deep attach- ment to the interviewer (who was, after all, a stranger). However, in the absence of more detailed information on either sex, we are inclined to conclude that though Sullivan's description of friendship during childhood and adolescence appears to be more accurate than Anna Freud's, his account does not completely do justice to "the facts" either.

Dating

On the other hand, if we turn our attention from the *quality* of friendship during childhood and adolescence and examine the overall sequence of social development instead, Sullivan's formulations prove to be surprisingly precise. As may be recalled, Sullivan de- scribes the chum relationship as an example of *isophilic object choice* (i.e., seeking out an intimate of the same sex on the part of the preadolescent). With the appearance of the lust dynamism in early adolescence, a shift from isophilic to what Sullivan terms *heterophilic object choice* is supposed to occur. Having achieved a degree of intimacy with a member of the same sex and having been confronted for the first time with full-blown sexual feelings, the youngster allegedly begins to move in the direction of establishing a close relationship with someone of the opposite sex. For a variety of reasons, this effort is viewed as a rather perilous enterprise. Stereotypes about the opposite sex acquired during childhood, difficulties in integrating lust with intimacy, and parental misgivings all, Sullivan asserts, make the transition anything but smooth. In any case, the shift from isophilic to heterophilic intimacy is supposed to take a number of years and not to be completed (even if all goes well) much before late adolescence.

Upon consulting one of the best research studies on the subject, we discover a pattern of social development very similar to the one outlined by Sullivan. In his survey of Australian adolescents (whom we must assume to be sufficiently comparable to American adolescents) Dunphy (1963) observed that at the age of twelve or thirteen his subjects were indeed still carrying out most of their social activities in unisexual cliques and gangs. At this point there was very little mixing between the sexes. Gradually, however, these unisexual groups would begin to interact, although nothing as "daring" as actual dating would take place. Then the more prestigious members of each group would begin to date, and eventually to organize themselves into heterosexual cliques (i.e., mixed groups). For a while these mixed cliques would interact with each other, forming what Dunphy termed the "fully developed crowd." With the approach of late adolescence, however, the crowd would begin to disintegrate and a new set of cliques would begin to appear. These consisted generally of couples who were either going steady or engaged. Presumably, these young men and women had achieved some degree of "heterophilic intimacy," but judging from all they had passed through, we might conclude that it was no mean accomplishment. To be sure, Dunphy points out that the adolescents he studied varied a good deal, with one group of girls being socially isolated at the comparatively advanced age of sixteen and another, rather precocious, clique actively dating at fourteen. Nonetheless, it seems clear that boys and girls do not typically manage to establish close relationships with each other overnight, and there are a number of other researchers who lend support to Dunphy's findings (see Figure 1).

In a review of the literature on teenage dating, Burchinal (1964) cites several studies (Breed, 1956; Christensen, 1952, 1958; Crist, 1953; Williams, 1949), all of which indicate that a substantial number of adolescents express something less than wild enthusiasm about their initial encounters with the opposite sex. In fact, in one of these studies (Williams, 1949), fully one third of a sample of high school students declared that they considered themselves "failures" in dating—and also (not surprisingly) that dating was not a pleasurable

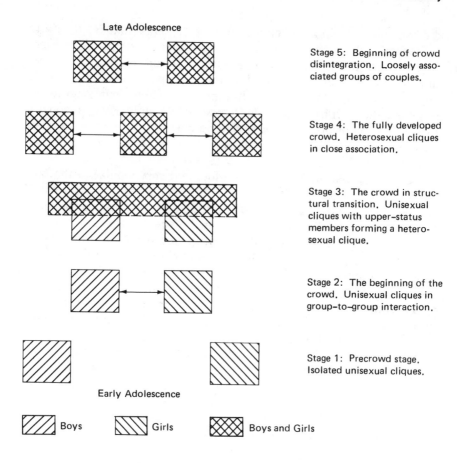

Figure 1. Stages of development in adolescence. (From Dexter C. Dunphy, "The Social Structure of Urban Adolescent Peer Groups," *Sociometry*, **26** (1963), p. 236.)

experience. Similarly, Douvan and Adelson *(1966)* report that the adolescents in their sample appeared to enter into dating quite timidly and tentatively, with the girls not achieving an appreciable degree of self-confidence about the whole matter until the age of seventeen or eighteen. And an intensive study of 73 "normal" adolescent boys by Offer *(1969)* comes to much the same conclusion. When queried about his relationships with girls, a typical high school sophomore replied, "I stay away from girls because I am too young, and we don't understand each other" *(p. 81)*. All in all, adolescents seem to ease themselves into the sort of emotional intimacy that precedes (or that is *assumed* to precede) marriage in a rather gingerly fashion.

Adolescents Look More Like Adults:
A Brief Account of Physical Development

We have examined some of the ways in which adolescents are supposed to *act* more like adults than children do. One of the incontrovertible facts of human development is that they *look* more like adults than children do, and no account of adolescent psychology can be complete without a brief discussion of this fact. Actually, adolescents appear to be more "grown-up" than children in two important respects. In terms of sheer physical bulk, they are on the average taller and larger. For the most part, they also look much more like sexually mature adults than children do.

Although all three of our representative theorists concerned themselves quite explicitly with adolescent sexuality, only Hall paid much attention to the more prosaic subject of physical development. As noted, he characterized human growth as being "saltatory" in nature, that is, proceeding in fits and starts and becoming especially explosive at puberty. The facts, such as they are, partially bear him out. The British physiologist Tanner *(1962)* observes that in *general* the child's physical development follows a smooth and regular course with no abrupt bursts or lags. However, in the couple of years which precede puberty, the child does indeed undergo a "growth spurt" and begin to shoot up at a rate unmatched in any other period of his life. After this celebrated spurt, which lasts approximately two years, the rate of growth again slackens until the youngster reaches his adult height, typically in midadolescence for girls and late adolescence for boys.

We use the word "typically" with a certain degree of caution, for as Tanner points out, there is enormous variation in individual growth patterns. On the *average*, the sudden burst associated with adolescence occurs between the ages of 12½ to 15 in boys and about two years earlier in girls, but it can occur earlier or considerably later. It is also interesting to note that though girls mature physically at an earlier age than boys (the reader may recall that both Hall and Sullivan were well aware of this fact), there is as yet no satisfactory explanation for the disparity.

Indeed, Tanner observes that the entire physiology of growth is something of a mystery. It is apparently controlled by an area in the basal part of the brain called the *hypothalamus*. This area secretes hormones that stimulate the *pituitary*, a gland that lies just beneath the base of the brain. Once stimulated, the pituitary in turn releases a growth hormone, and it is this substance that determines the rate at which a child matures. If, for instance, the pituitary runs wild and produces too much of the growth hormone, the unhappy result may be a giant; too little, and the equally unhappy result may be a dwarf. Before adolescence, the pituitary secretes its hormones in a comparatively steady and regular fashion. However, with the approach of adolescence, some mechanism within the brain presumably causes the hypothalamus to step up its production of hormones. This change sets in motion a rather complex set of chemical transformations and the ultimate outcome (via the pituitary) is the "adolescent growth spurt."

Sexual Development

But the general increase in height that marks the beginning of adolescence is a relatively minor part of the story. There is another change that is of far greater significance to the student of adolescent psychology. What we have in mind is the unavoidable fact of puberty. Perhaps the most potentially troublesome way in which adolescents resemble adults is that they can *reproduce* like adults, and it is the emergence of this particular capacity which is supposed to create much of the "storm and stress" traditionally associated with the teenage years. Indeed, although our three theorists would disagree about precisely what causes such adolescent turmoil, they would very likely concur that in general it has something to do with puberty.

The issue of storm and stress, in our opinion, is sufficiently complex to merit a separate chapter. What we propose to do here is to outline briefly the changes that accompany sexual development during adolescence.

Once embarked upon this task, we encounter yet another variation of a by-now familiar theme. Although most people talk about puberty as if it were some clearly defined event, almost as if it could be circled on the calendar, there is apparently no single criterion for determining precisely when it has occurred. One of the leading developmental psychologists, David Ausubel, insists that the best one can do is point to a combination of changes:

The choice of an adequate criterion of sexual maturity in determining the age of pubescence is in many ways a pseudo-problem. First pubescence by definition refers to a *constellation* of typical bodily changes associated with sexual maturation and not to any particular change. The choice of reproductive capacity as the most crucial representative of the physical changes which take place is purely arbitrary, and is hardly defensible on either biological or behavioral grounds. Second, each of the component bodily changes occurs over a period of time rather than all at once. Hence, when the physical phenomena of pubescence are considered as a whole, it is meaningless to conceive of a definite *age* at puberty. It is more reasonable to think of an *interval* of several years embracing a series of changes that are initiated in characteristic sequence and progress to completion at different rates of development. *(1954, p. 93)*

In other words, what we call puberty is a particular pattern of growth rather than a single event. As in the case of the "growth spurt," it is initiated by the hypothalamus. The actual sequence goes something like this: The hypothalamus secretes a "tropic" hormone which in turn stimulates the pituitary gland. The pituitary gland then proceeds to release hormones which stimulate the adrenal glands, tiny bits of tissue which are located on top of the kidneys. *These* glands secrete hormones which in turn affect the reproductive organs—the testes in boys and the ovaries in girls. At the end of this rather involved chain of events, the reproductive organs themselves begin to secrete hormones which at long last bring about the constellation of changes known as "puberty."

In boys these hormonal secretions typically trigger the following visible (and audible) transformations. According to Tanner *(1962)*, the testicles first begin to increase in size and there may be a slight accompanying growth of pubic hair. About a year later, the general growth spurt commences, and because the testicles have now started to secrete the male sex hormone, the boy's penis also begins to enlarge, gradually reaching its adult size. Then underarm (axillary) hair and facial hair begin to appear. Concurrently, about the time the growth spurt has gotten underway, the boy's voice box or larynx starts to enlarge, and about the time his reproductive organs are fully developed, his voice begins to deepen. Somewhere in the midst of all these alterations, the boy's testes become capable of producing mature sperm and he experiences his first ejaculation. (The exact timing of this event varies considerably from individual to individual, but according to Kinsey, *1948*, the vast majority of male adolescents have had it occur by age 15.) And accompanying it are the various changes that mark the development of the masculine physique—the broadening of the shoulders, the narrowing of the waist, and so forth.

In girls, once the ovaries have started to enlarge, the first visible sign of puberty is the growth of the breasts, a process that usually begins before the teens and takes several years to complete. After this, pubic hair begins to appear. At some point in the general sequence of events, the growth spurt has begun to occur, and about the time it has passed its peak (typically around the age of 13 or so) one of the most dramatic events associated with puberty takes place: The girl has her first menstrual period. The physiology of menstruation is exceedingly complex (and still not too well understood), but with the appearance of the menarche the girl has acquired the capacity to reproduce—or will acquire it shortly. Actually, in most girls a "sterile phase" lasting approximately a year follows the first period. The girl may continue to menstruate (although it is not unusual for her to be markedly irregular), but she is incapable of becoming pregnant. Why this occurs is yet another mystery of feminine physiology, but it is suspected that early in adolescence the ovaries are simply not capable of producing mature ova. We might mention as well that gradually during her teens the girl's body takes on the familiar hour-glass (or in some cases, pear-shaped) contours of womanhood—her bosom fills out, her hips widen, and her waist narrows.

Particularly noteworthy, we think, is the fact that most boys and girls attain sexual maturity by their midteens but that relatively few of them exercise their newly developed ability to reproduce at this age. Which brings us back to the proposition advanced at the beginning of this chapter: Adolescents differ from children in *acting* more like adults in some respects and *looking* more like adults, but somehow they are *not* adults. All three of our theorists appear to believe that this curious discrepancy is tied in with sexual development. The adolescent is pictured as having all the impulses and many of the virtues of the adult, and the clash between impulse and virtue is supposed to create a great deal of storm and stress. In the next chapter, we shall examine the question of how stormy and stressful adolescence actually is.

REFERENCES

AUSUBEL, D. *Theory and Problems of Adolescent Development.* New York: Grune & Stratton, 1954.

AUSUBEL, D. P., SCHIFF, H. M., & GASSER, E. B. A Preliminary Study of Developmental Trends in Socioempathy: Accuracy of Perception of Own and Other's Sociometric Status. *Child Development*, 1952, **23**, 111–128.

BOEHM, L., & NASS, M. L. Social Class Differences in Conscience Development. *Child Development*, 1962, **33**, 565–575.

BOYNE, A. W., & CLARK, J. R. Secular Change in the Intelligence of 11-year-old Aberdeen School Children. *Human Biology*, 1959, **31**, 325–333.

BREED, W. Sex, Class, and Socialization in Dating. *Marriage and Family Living*, 1956, **18**, 137–144.

BURCHINAL, L. G. The Premarital Dyad of Love Involvement. In H. T. Christensen (Ed.), *Handbook of Marriage and the Family.* Chicago: Rand McNally, 1964.

CARUSO, I. H. La notion de responsabilité et du justice immanente chez l'enfant. *Archives de Psychologie*, 1943, **29**, (Whole No. 114).

CASLER, L. Maternal Deprivation: A Critical Review of the Literature. *Monographs of the Society for Research in Child Development*, 1961, No. 26.

CHRISTENSEN, H. T. Dating Behavior as Evaluated by High School Students. *American Journal of Sociology*, 1952, **57**, 580–586.

CHRISTENSEN, H. T. *Marriage Analysis: Foundations for Successful Family Life.* (2nd ed.) New York: Ronald, 1958.

CONGER, J. *Adolescence and Youth: Psychological Development in a Changing World*. New York: Harper & Row, 1973.

CRIST, J. R. High School Dating as a Behavior System. *Marriage and Family Living*, 1953, **15**, 23–28.

DE JUNG, J. E., & GARDNER, E. F. The Accuracy of Self-Role Perception: A Developmental Study. *Journal of Experimental Education*, 1962, **31**, 27–41.

DOUVAN, E., & ADELSON, J. *The Adolescent Experience*. New York: Wiley, 1966.

DULIT, E. Adolescent Thinking à la Piaget: The Formal Stage. *Journal of Youth and Adolescence*, 1972, **1**, 281–301.

DUNPHY, D. C. The Social Structure of Adolescent Peer Groups. *Sociometry*, 1963, **26**, 230–246.

ELKIND, D. Conceptual Orientation Shifts in Children and Adolescents. *Child Development*, 1966, **37**, 493–498.

FLAVELL, J. *The Developmental Psychology of Jean Piaget*. New York: Van Nostrand Reinhold, 1963.

GRINDER, R. *Adolescence*. New York: Wiley, 1973.

HAAN, N., SMITH, M. B., & BLOCK, J. Moral Reasoning of Young Adults: Political and Social Behavior, Family Background, and Personality Correlates. *Journal of Personality and Social Psychology*, 1968, **10**, 183–201.

HARTSHORNE, H., & MAY, M. A. *Studies in the Nature of Moral Character*. New York: Macmillan, 1928–1930. (3 vols.)

HAVIGHURST, R. J., & TABA, H. *Adolescent Character and Personality*. New York: Wiley, 1949.

HOLLINGSHEAD, A. B. *Elmtown's Youth*. New York: Wiley, 1949.

HORROCKS, J. E. *The Psychology of Adolescence*. (3rd ed.) Boston: Houghton Mifflin, 1969.

HORROCKS, J. E., & BUKER, M. E. A Study of Friendship Fluctuation of Preadolescents. *Journal of Genetic Psychology*, 1951, **78**, 131–144.

HORROCKS, J. E., & THOMPSON, G. G. A Study of Friendship Fluctuations of Rural Boys and Girls. *Journal of Genetic Psychology*, 1946, **69**, 189–198.

INHELDER, B., & PIAGET, J. *The Growth of Logical Thinking from Childhood to Adolescence*. New York: Basic Books, 1958.

JANIS, M. The Development of Moral Judgment in Preschool Children. Yale University Child Study Center, 1961.

JOHNSON, R. A Study of Children's Moral Judgments. *Child Development*, 1962, **33**, 327–354.

JONES, H. E., & CONRAD, H. S. The Growth and Decline of Intelligence. *Genetic Psychology Monographs*, 1933, **13**, 223–298.

KENISTON, K. Student Activism, Moral Development, and Morality. (1970) In Dorothy Rogers (Ed.), *Issues in Adolescent Psychology*. (2nd ed.) New York: Appleton, 1972.

KINSEY, A. C., POMEROY, W. B., & MARTIN, C. E. *Sexual Behavior in the Human Male*. Philadelphia: Saunders, 1948.

KOHLBERG, L. The Development of Moral Character. In M. L. Hoffman and L. W. Hoffman (Eds.), *Review of Child Development Research*, Vol. I. New York: Russell Sage, 1964.

KOHLBERG, L. Moral Education in the Schools: A Developmental View. *The School Review*, 1966, **74**, 1–29.

KOHLBERG, L., & GILLIGAN, C. The Adolescent as a Philosopher: The Discovery of Self in a Post-Conventional World. *Daedalus*, 1971, **100**, 1051–1086.

KOHLBERG, L., & KRAMER, R. Continuities and Discontinuities in Childhood and Adult Moral Development. *Human Development*, 1969, **12**, 93–120.

KOMAROVSKY, M. Functional Analysis of Sex Roles. *American Sociological Review*, 1950, **4**, 508–516.

KREBS, R. Some Relations Between Moral Judgment, Attention, and Resistance to Temptation. Unpublished doctoral dissertation, University of Chicago, 1967.

LERNER, E. Perspectives in Moral Reasoning. *American Journal of Sociology*, 1937, **43**, 249–269.

MACRAE, R. A Test of Piaget's Theories of Moral Development. *Journal of Abnormal and Social Psychology*, 1954, **49**, 14–18.

OFFER, D. *The Psychological World of the Teenager.* New York: Basic Books, 1969.

PEEL, E. A. *The Pupil's Thinking.* London: Oldbourne, 1960.

PIAGET, J. Intellectual Evolution from Adolescence to Adulthood. *Human Development*, 1972, **15**, 1–12.

PIAGET, J. *The Moral Judgment of the Child.* London: Routledge & Kegan Paul, 1932.

PIAGET, J. *The Origins of Intelligence in Children.* New York: International Universities, 1952.

PIAGET, J. *Six Psychological Studies.* New York: Random House, 1967.

SHORT, J. F. Juvenile Delinquency: The Socio-Cultural Context. In L. W. Hoffman and M. L. Hoffman (Eds.), *Review of Child Development Research*, Vol. II. New York: Russell Sage, 1966.

SIMPSON, E. L. Moral Development Research: A Case Study of Scientific Cultural Bias. *Human Development*, in press.

SPITZ, R. Hospitalism: A Follow-up Report on Investigation Described in Volume I, 1945. *Psychoanalytic Study of the Child*, 1946, **2**, 113–117.

SPITZ, R. Hospitalism: An inquiry into the Genesis of Psychiatric Conditions in Early Childhood. *Psychoanalytic Study of the Child*, 1945, **1**, 53–74.

TANNER, J. M. *Growth at Adolescence.* Oxford: Blackwell, 1962.

THOMPSON, G. G., & HORROCKS, J. E. A Study of Friendship Fluctuations of Urban Boys and Girls. *Journal of Genetic Psychology*, 1947, **70**, 53–63.

TURIEL, E. Developmental Processes in the Child's Moral Thinking. In P. Mussen, J. Langer, & M. Covington (Eds.), *New Directions in Developmental Psychology.* New York: Rinehart, 1969.

WECHSLER, D. *The Measurement and Appraisal of Adult Intelligence.* (4th ed.). Baltimore: Williams & Wilkins, 1958.

WILLIAMS, M. J. Personal and Family Problems of High School Youth and Their Bearing of Family Education Needs. *Social Forces*, 1949, **27**, 279–295.

YARROW, L. J. Maternal Deprivation: Toward an Empirical and Conceptual Reevaluation. *Psychological Bulletin*, 1961, **58**, 459–490.

But Somehow
They Aren't Adults:
The Issue of
Storm and Stress

*The thing that irritated him most was that the hunger of his
senses should so easily overthrow his desire for liberation
and death. At that time the two cats that belonged to
the house, a male and a female, had entered upon their love
period. This had happened before but Luca, apart from
watching them with amusement, had paid little attention. Now,
after what had happened between him and the governess,
he seemed to recognize himself in the male and her in
the female. . . . All those comings and goings between his
own room and the sitting room, those contacts, that
invention of pretexts that would lead to contacts—what
were they but the mutual pursuit of two animals mysteriously
troubled by desire? With this difference, however, that
the two cats could not rebel against nature because they
consisted of nothing but nature; whereas he resented this
obedience as an act of humiliating passivity, and the force
which imposed it as a tyranny.*

Alberto Moravia, "Luca"

As we have pointed out, sexuality is assigned a very prominent role
in bringing about the fabled storm and stress of adolescence. Our
three representative theorists, Hall, Anna Freud, and Sullivan, all
portray the awakening (or in Freud's case the *re*awakening) of
sexual desire as an event of almost cataclysmic proportions. Hall,
of course, believed that the forces unleashed by puberty were likely
to overwhelm the adolescent completely, making him a prime
candidate for delinquency and debauchery. Although more restrained,
Freud holds, on the whole, very similar views. Coming as it does
after the alleged lull of the latency period, the resurgence of infantile
sexuality during adolescence is supposed to produce a great deal
of conflict and turbulence. This view is, in fact, essentially the psychoanalytic position on the issue of storm and stress. Other practi-

tioners *(Blos, 1962; Josselyn, 1952; Spiegel, 1951)* have consistently underscored the link between sexuality and turmoil during adolescence.

What we find most interesting is that Sullivan, who has divorced himself from the psychoanalytic camp on so many other matters, also believes that sexual drives can wreak havoc during adolescence. Indeed, he is so pessimistic about the youngster's initial forays into this forbidden realm that he offers the following rather startling advice:

> In the olden days when I was distinctly more reckless than now, I thought that a good many of the people I saw as mental patients would have been luckier in their adolescence had they carried on their preliminary sexual experimentation with a good-natured prostitute—that is, this would have been fortunate in comparison to what actually happened to them. Not that I regard prostitutes as highly developed personalities of the other sex; but if they happen to be in the business of living off their participation in genital sport and are friendly, they at least will know a good deal about the problems in this field that earlier adolescents encounter, and will treat them with sympathy, understanding, and encouragement. *(1953, p. 271)*

However, instead of seeking out a friendly and supportive prostitute for their first encounter, many youths, Sullivan suggests, end up with people who are intolerant of any sexual blundering or inexperience. Thus, the stage is set for disaster:

> If there has been a lively lustful fantasy and little or no overt behavior with respect to the genitals . . . then it is almost certain that on the verge of actual genital contact, precocious orgasm will occur in the man; and this precocious orgasm suddenly wipes out the integration and just leaves two people in a practically meaningless situation although they had previously made immense sense to each other. Such an occurrence reflects very severely on the self-esteem of the man concerned and thereby initiates a still more unfortunate process which is apt to appear as impotence. The recollection of so disastrous an occurrence, which has been in terms of anxiety pretty costly, is quite apt to result in either of two outcomes: there may be an overweening conviction that that's the way it's going to go, that one just hasn't any "virility," that one's manhood is deficient; or there may be frantic attempts to prove otherwise, which, if they were kept up long enough, would work. Unless there has been some genital activity, or unless the woman is quite expert in reducing the anxiety of the male, or even his sexual excitement, this precocious orgasm is very apt to be a man's introduction to heterosexual life. *(1953, pp. 271–272)*

Though it is difficult to tell how much Sullivan's views were colored by his experience with severely disturbed adults, he creates the distinct impression that sexual adventures during adolescence are at best uncomfortable and at worst frankly traumatic, at least as far as the male adolescent is concerned. But is this actually the case?

Sexual Behavior During Adolescence

Once again, we are confronted by certain methodological problems in attempting to ascertain "the facts." Just as there are experiments that the student of intellectual development cannot ethically perform, there are certain questions that the student of sexual behavior finds it difficult to ask—particularly of teenagers. Sexual matters are generally considered "private" or "embarrassing" —so much so, that some specialists maintain that they are not even a proper subject for investigation. Edgar Friedenberg, for instance, declares: "In my experience adolescents rarely discuss sex with adults unless adults insist on it. Even though sexuality is central to adolescents it would have demeaned my subjects if I had tried to engage them in a discussion of it" (1965, p. 126). Nonetheless, there are a few studies that can provide us with some enlightenment. Perhaps the best known and most comprehensive of these is the so-called Kinsey Report (1948; Kinsey, Pomeroy, Martin, & Gebhard, 1953). Kinsey, a zoologist who apparently had very little of Friedenberg's reticence (Pomeroy, 1972), handled some of the ethical problems involved in "sex research" by employing adult volunteers. The subjects, who numbered approximately 16,000 in all and came from every conceivable walk of life, were questioned in detail about their sexual experiences: at what age they had become aware of sex, when orgasm had first occurred and under what circumstances, whether or not they had ever been involved in any homosexual activity, what their main sources of "sexual outlet" were, and so forth.

Sexual Behavior Prior to Adolescence: The Issues of Infantile Sexuality and Latency

Kinsey's data definitely lend support to the psychoanalytic contention that sexual awareness begins in infancy (rather than in adolescence, as Hall had assumed), for he and his colleagues cite reports of small children being observed in various masturbatory activities. Indeed, although such children are probably rather unusual, there is even some evidence that infants can experience orgasm. Demonstrating his passion for detail, Kinsey cites the observations of a young mother (who had obviously had some clinical training) on her three-year-old little girl:

> Lying face down on the bed, with her knees drawn up, she started rhythmic pelvic thrusts, about one second or less apart. The thrusts were primarily pelvic, with the legs tensed in a fixed position. . . . There was marked concentration and intense breathing with abrupt jerks as orgasm approached. She was completely oblivious to everything during these later stages of activity. *(Kinsey et al., 1953, pp. 104–105)*

However, if Kinsey's findings corroborate the Freudian concept of infantile sexuality, they provide *no* support for one that is closely related: There is no evidence that sexual interest wanes after the age of five or six, only to emerge full blown once again at puberty. In other words, there does not seem to be a period of latency. If anything, Kinsey reports, sexual interest *increases* during the very phase when it is supposed to lie dormant. Though a certain percentage of his subjects recalled masturbating or playing sexual games with friends before the age of seven (roughly 20 percent for boys and 12 percent for girls), a larger percentage claimed that they had first engaged in sexual activities between the ages of eight and thirteen (roughly 50 percent of the boys and 36 percent of the girls). For the most part these activities did not involve anything more startling than masturbation or exhibitionism (of which the childhood game of "Doctor" is a familiar variant). And, interestingly enough, any sexual play was much more likely to take place with a child of the same sex than one of the opposite sex, a finding that supports Sullivan's notion of isophilic object choice.

Orgasm, the Teenager, and the Recurring Problem of Sex Differences

Though a small proportion of children apparently develop the capacity to experience orgasm before puberty, much more typically this capacity does not appear until sometime in the teens. Indeed, for *boys* the ability to achieve a sexual climax (i.e., to ejaculate) is one of the hallmarks of puberty. This is not the case for girls, and here we encounter one of the anomalies of human sexuality, one that has probably been responsible for more than its share of human misery. In males, what we might call reproductive maturity and sexual maturity are virtually indistinguishable. As soon as a boy becomes capable of ejaculating, he also becomes capable of fathering a child. There is no corresponding relationship in girls. The arrival of the first menstrual period does not automatically signal the ability to experience orgasm. In contrast to the boy, a girl may be *biologically* mature for years before she achieves her first sexual climax. In fact, a woman may raise an entire family without *ever* having an orgasm, something which would be most unlikely for a man.

The key to the whole paradox has to do with differences in what is termed "sexual responsiveness." A man cannot usually impregnate a woman without first having become sexually aroused, but a woman can become very pregnant indeed without having enjoyed the slightest twinge of sexual desire. There is at present no completely satisfying explanation for this discrepancy. According to one line of argument, girls are simply born with less imperious drives than boys and consequently take longer to become fully responsive. Conversely, there is another school that points to the double standard and "sexual repression" as the culprits. The proponents of this particular view argue that boys and girls are born with equally strong drives but that because the culture sets stricter standards of conduct for girls, they tend to repress their instincts to a greater extent than boys—hence the difference in the ability to achieve orgasm. And finally, there are psychologists (one of the most prominent being Judith Bardwick in a recent book on feminine psychology, *1971*) who claim that *both* nature and nurture are responsible for this male-female difference. Girls, they contend, are less capable of sexual arousal than boys from birth *and* they are encouraged to go *on* being less responsive—at least until they have entered into a legally sanctioned sexual relationship (i.e., by getting married).

Sex Differences in Sexual Activity

Whatever the source of this particular sex difference, it is very much in evidence throughout adolescence. Kinsey *(Kinsey et al., 1948)* concludes from his data that a boy is likely to experience his first ejaculation (most commonly as a result of masturbation) sometime between the ages of eleven and fifteen. In any case, this span of years accounted for over 90 percent of the males in his study. The corresponding figures for girls *(Kinsey et al., 1953)* are startlingly lower. Only 23 percent of the female subjects in Kinsey's investigation reported having experienced orgasm by the age of fifteen. Indeed, it was not until the age of twenty-nine that the incidence ran as high as 90 percent. And there is probably reason to doubt even these figures. Bardwick *(1971)* observes that women some-times have difficulty determining whether or not they have ever had a climax.

As might be expected, adolescent boys also tend to be a good deal more active sexually than adolescent girls. Kinsey infers, for instance, that masturbation is almost universal among boys but that it is by no means as common among girls. Only about 60 percent of the women in his study reported ever having masturbated, and they were a far more variable group than men. While masturbation tends to become a more or less regular activity for the adolescent male—neither something that he engages in compulsively nor something that he shuns—girls who avail themselves of this outlet do not assume any particular pattern. Of the female subjects who reported having masturbated during adolescence, some recalled doing so only once or twice a year while others claimed frequencies of ten to twenty times a week.

And what is true of masturbation is true of most of the other typical sexual outlets during adolescence. Whether the activity involves erotic dreams, homosexual contacts, petting, or premarital intercourse, boys tend to engage in it more frequently than girls and with less variability.

Socioeconomic Differences and the Issue
of Sexual Upheaval

Of course, male-female differences in sexuality are not the only ones worth noting. There are socioeconomic variations as well. A consideration of these variations, along with sex differences, brings us face to face once more with the issue to which this chapter is devoted: Is the entrance into full-blown sexuality traumatic for most adolescents? Certainly it does not seem to be for the lower-class male. By the age of fifteen, Kinsey discovered, nearly half of the lower-class males in his sample had engaged in intercourse. He concludes: "They have nothing like the strong (higher-level) tabu against premarital intercourse, and, on the contrary, accept it as a natural and inevitable and as a desirable thing. Lower-level tabus are more often turned against an avoidance of intercourse and against any substitution for simple and direct coitus" *(Kinsey et al., 1948, p. 379)*.

Among the middle- and upper-class males one finds, to be sure, a greater degree of reticence. Only 10 percent of them reported having engaged in intercourse by the age of fifteen. (Offer reports a similar percentage in his study of "normal" upper-middle-class adolescent boys, *1969*.) But they nonetheless indulged in a considerable variety of substitute activities, most prominently masturbation and petting, without any apparent ill effects.

Since Kinsey was more interested in the activities themselves than in any accompanying emotional turmoil, it *is* somewhat difficult to ascertain from his data whether the adolescent male's burgeoning sexual drives are a source of intense psychic conflict. Other researchers who have addressed the issue more directly, however, have concluded that the portrait of adolescence as a period of sexual storm and stress has been overdone. Offer reports that his "normal" subjects exhibited a degree of embarrassment when weighing the merits and disadvantages of premarital intercourse (most of them expressed the view that it was "all right" but not until after graduation from high school). But they also readily admitted masturbating and denied that this activity created any special problems for them. Similarly, although Douvan and Adelson *(1966)* did not include any explicit questions on sex in their survey of typical adolescents, they surmise from semiprojective data that sexuality was not a source of great turmoil during adolescence.

So much for the lower-, middle-, and upper-class male teenager. What about their female counterparts? We note, first of all, that Kinsey did *not* discover large socioeconomic variations among his female subjects. Whether they came from high-status or low-status homes, women tended to report that they had been less sexually active than men during adolescence and that they had experienced more difficulty attaining orgasm.

Feminine inhibitions   The picture that emerges for the female adolescent, whatever social class she belongs to, is more one of inhibition and repression of, rather than overt conflict over, sexuality. This impression is strengthened by a few studies that have attempted to trace the growth of sexual fantasies during adolescence. Employing the Thematic Apperception Test, a projective test that requires subjects to tell stories about a series of standardized drawings, Sanford *(1943)* discovered an *increase* in sexual fantasies for male adolescents but a *decrease* for females. In a study comparing high school girls, college girls, and adult women, Tooley *(1966)* obtained similar results. She also used the T.A.T. and found that high school females avoided telling stories that were explicitly sexual in content to a greater extent than the older female subjects. And finally, Powell *(1955)* had 448 males and females, aged 10 to 30, give their associations to a list of words. The list was designed to tap various areas of possible conflict: religion, vocational outlook, heterosexual relations, and so forth. The researcher compared the amounts of time it took subjects to give associations to the "stimulus" words to the times it took them to respond to a list of supposedly "neutral" words, reasoning that it would take subjects longer to respond to words that represented areas of conflict. He discovered that with the onset of adolescence, *both* boys and girls appeared to become slightly more anxious about sexuality, but that the increase for girls was larger than that for boys. Although in the absence of any clear-cut data we must be cautious in drawing conclusions, we suspect that a good many adolescent girls prevent sexual drives from becoming a source of storm and stress simply by not permitting themselves to become aware of them. (And, as we mentioned earlier, girls may have less powerful drives to cope with as well.)

Anxieties concerning sex   Can we conclude, then, that sex is a completely conflict-free area for most adolescents? Not quite. Powell's study seems to indicate that teenagers are, at the very least, a bit "nervous" about such drives, and there are additional data that lend support to his. Shipman *(1968)*, for instance, observed a marked increase in "sexual worries" during adolescence. The pre-pubescent youngsters in his sample, he reports, were relatively unconcerned about masturbation, petting, pregnancy, and venereal disease. However, a majority of post pubescent youngsters (78 percent of the girls in a sample of 261 and 71 percent of the males in a sample of 108) eventually admitted to some degree of preoccupation with at least one of these matters. Offer *(1972)* obtained similar results from eight different samples of teenagers over a period of years (1962–1970). However, unlike Shipman, he concluded that sexual anxieties were at their peak during early adolescence (ages 13–14) and on the decline during late adolescence (ages 17–18). Of course, Shipman had his subjects simply check off areas of possible concern while Offer required his to register their agreement or disagreement with various statements ("thinking or talking about sex frightens me"; "sexual experiences give me pleasure"), so that this disparity may reflect differences in methodology. In any case, though neither researcher found evidence of any wholesale emotional upheaval, both identified sex as an area of considerable concern during adolescence.

Adolescent Sexuality and Sex Education

Many of those who have studied adolescent sexuality imply that improved sex education programs might help to dispel even the moderate anxieties which exist. In a departure from his usual objectivity, Kinsey delivers the following denunciation of the school system in particular and of womanhood in general:

> For the mass of unmarried boys, intercourse still provides the chief sexual activity. This means that the majority of males in the sexually most potential and most active period of their lives have to accept clandestine or illegal outlets. . . . The situation is complicated by the fact that the average adolescent girl gets along well enough with a fifth as much sexual activity as the adolescent boy, and the frequency of outlet of the female in her twenties and early thirties is still below that of the average adolescent male. As mothers, as school teachers, and as voting citizens, women are primarily responsible for the care of these boys; and to a large degree, they are the ones who control the moral codes, schedules for sex education, campaigns for law enforcement and programs for combatting what is called juvenile delinquency. It is obviously impossible for a majority of these women to understand the problem that the boy faces in being constantly aroused and regularly involved in his normal biological reactions. *(Kinsey et al., 1948, p. 223)*

Douvan and Adelson *(1966)* are less inclined to hold either the schools or "matriarchal society" responsible for the adolescent's ignorance concerning sexual matters. Instead they suggest that his lack of sophistication stems from a kind of tacit conspiracy between the youngster and his own parents. The whole topic of sexuality is sufficiently "taboo" to keep it from coming up explicitly within the family. Everyone prefers to talk around it, with the following rather predictable result:

> Because there is so much covertness in this arrangement, and thus so much ambiguity, all parties are likely to feel far more tension than they need to. The parents uneasy lest the children go too far, the youngsters imagining themselves to be more wicked and defiant than they actually are, and the observer believing there to be more conflict in sexual codes than is actually the case. *(1966, p. 82)*

Shipman *(1968)* confirms this general impression with some hard facts. Only a tiny percentage (8 percent in all) of the adolescents in his study received any accurate information about intercourse, conception, and birth from their parents. Most of the rest were forced to rely on books. And Bandura and Walters *(1959)* have actually recorded some parental misgivings for posterity. These researchers compared a small sample (26 in all) of "aggressive" and rather poorly adjusted adolescent males with a group of "normal" controls, carrying out extensive interviews with their parents in the process. Though the parents of the aggressive boys appeared to be slightly more "permissive" about sexual matters, the prevailing attitude was one of disapproval and repression. Fathers and mothers alike—but in particular mothers—declared that their youngsters were "too young" for any kind of sexual experimentation, that such activity ought to be forsworn until marriage, that premature indulgence might lead to illegitimate pregnancies and venereal disease, and so forth.

Hence, it is not surprising that, when given the opportunity, teenagers themselves complain about the absence of sexual instruction. Offer *(1969)* reports that his "typical" adolescent boys expressed considerable dissatisfaction about this particular gap in their education, claiming that everyone—parents, teachers, coaches, and Sunday school instructors—had been remiss. Indeed, Offer quotes at length from an interview with one youth who had managed to sum it up for all the rest:

In sixth grade the athletic director showed us a movie about mating; the birds and bees movie. The athletic director was giggling just like the rest of us. When the movie was over, he asked if anyone had any questions. One boy asked a question concerning girls. The class roared and that was the end of that. Later my mother told my father to tell me about girls. He took me aside and said: "You know all about girls, don't you?" I said, "Sure, Dad," and that was the end of that. In church they told us that we would get sex education in school. No one really told us anything. *Everyone was passing the buck.* (1969, pp. 87–88)

All in all, the claim that sexual feelings provoke great conflict during adolescence appears to be exaggerated. But there is little doubt that teenagers worry about and are embarrassed by sex—and apparently so are adults.

Other Variations on the Theme of Storm and Stress

Sexual conflicts and turmoil are, we should add, only part of the traditional portrait of adolescence. The mere mention of the teenage years brings to mind phrases like "adolescent rebellion," "generation gap," and "domination of the peer group." With the onset of puberty, the youngster is supposed to begin experiencing (in addition to all the unaccustomed sexual feelings) a growing sense of alienation from his parents—from all adult authority, in fact. If his previous relationship with his parents was harmonious, now, abruptly, all is supposed to be altered. Where he previously respected their judgment, the adolescent now allegedly challenges his parents on even the most trivial matters. Increasingly, his views clash with theirs, and increasingly he turns to those his own age in an effort to provide himself with moral support for his revolt.

We have already suggested that the image of adolescence as a period of great sexual turbulence requires some modification. What sort of evidence is there to support the contention that it is a period of emotional storm and stress and general rebelliousness? As it turns out there is not, at least in our opinion, a great deal. Though our three representative theorists, and a great many journalists and novelists as well, all subscribe to the proposition that "adolescence is hell," the facts do not seem to bear them out.

One of the first to puncture the myth of storm and stress was the anthropologist Margaret Mead *(1928)*. She did not deny that *American* teenagers might suffer all manner of agonies. Indeed, she assumed that they did. What she disputed was the assumption that adolescence was *universally* a period of storm and stress. There were cultures, Mead contended, where the transition from childhood to adulthood was accomplished without any sign of crisis or disruption. Her own study of Samoan girls prompted the following observations:

With the exception of a few cases . . . adolescence represented no period of crisis or stress, but was instead an orderly developing of a set of slowly maturing interests and activities. The girls' minds were perplexed by no conflicts, troubled by no philosophical inquiries, beset by no remote ambitions. To live as a girl with many lovers as long as possible and then to marry in one's own village and have many children, these were uniform and satisfying ambitions. *(1928, p. 120)*

Why were these adolescents from a primitive culture spared the torments of their American counterparts? Mead believed that it had to do with the absence of sexual taboos in Samoan society, an absence that she claimed contrasted markedly with the general repressiveness of American society. In Samoa, she noted, adolescents were not confronted by any restraints or prohibitions. Sexual expression was accepted openly as a part of life and teenagers were not expected to abstain. Hence, with a major source of emotional conflict removed, adolescence in Samoa was typically rather placid.

Other researchers have subsequently gone even farther than Mead and raised the question of whether, even for American youngsters, adolescence is necessarily a period of storm and stress. To be sure, there are undoubtedly some youngsters who find it a difficult stage. The figures on delinquency and adolescent suicide are unequivocal. Beginning with the teens, more and more young people (a disproportionate number of them from deprived backgrounds) run afoul of the law *(Short, 1966)*. Similarly, the rather gloomy statistics on the subject show a sharp increase in suicides and suicide attempts during adolescence *(Jacobs, 1971; Weiner, 1970)*. However, it is hazardous to generalize from an unfortunate fraction to the population as a whole. When we turn to the great mass of adolescents, "storm and stress" begins to look more and more like a myth and less and less like reality. Let us examine various parts of the myth one by one.

Adolescent Rebellion

As noted, rebellion is supposed to be one of the chief ingredients of adolescent turmoil. With the onset of puberty, the youngster's relations with his parents purportedly become strained. He begins to question their judgment, to quibble with their values. In fact, his sense of revolt may become so intense that he ends up challenging *all* authority. The student activism of the late 1960s and early 1970s has been cited by a number of writers as an example of this sort of indiscriminate defiance *(Aldridge, 1970; Feuer, 1969)*. However, this rather romantic characterization receives only limited support in fact.

Two studies we have mentioned previously *(Douvan & Adelson, 1966; Offer, 1969)* do report an increase in disagreements between teenagers and their parents during adolescence. But the largest number of disputes occurred during the early teens and centered on relatively mundane matters: what hours to be in, what clothes to wear, how big an allowance to ask for, and so forth. Few of the subjects in either study reported being at odds with their parents as far as basic values were concerned. On the contrary, most adolescents professed to share their parents' ideals and declared themselves quite content with their families. They did not, on the whole, complain of overly harsh discipline or undue restrictions. Nor did they believe themselves to be excluded from family decisions. In short, it was a rare teenager who described his parents as "old fogies." And, as might have been expected, girls reported an even more harmonious and tranquil home life than did boys. Indeed, Douvan and Adelson express surprise at the extent to which adolescent girls, far from actively rebelling, seem to identify with their parents:

We had originally believed that adolescent girls would be actively interested in distinguishing between their own standards and their parents' dicta; and we imagined we would find evidences, however covert, of a struggle between child and parents as this process developed. But we find few signs of rebellion or conflict. The girls largely feel their parents' rules to be fair, right, or lenient. Only a quarter of them state *any* reservations, however mild, about their parents' rules, and only 5 per cent consider them to be unjust or severe. About half the girls in the sample tell us that they have some part in setting the rules at home; and we find, to our great surprise, that whether or not she participates in rule-setting has no effect on the girl's feelings about parental rules. Those who have rules made for them are as happy about this state of affairs as those who are consulted about rules. *(1966, p. 107)*

Other researchers *(Bandura & Walters, 1959; Westley & Elkin, 1957)* have uncovered similar degrees of family solidarity. Westley and Elkin, for example, studied the inhabitants of an upper-middle-class suburb near Montreal and found that teenagers there and their parents were in substantial agreement about almost every major issue in life: career aspirations, marriage goals, financial matters, and so forth. The normal controls in the previously cited study by Bandura and Walters presented much the same picture. To be sure, this comparatively "well-adjusted" group of teenagers reported disagreeing with their parents—and even raising their voices from time to time. But they also expressed admiration for their mothers and fathers, got along well with them on the whole, and described their family relationships as gratifying and happy.

Student activists   Even when we turn to that group of adolescents who could most accurately be described as "rebellious," student activists, no marked estrangement between parent and child appears. The protesters of the late 1960s and early 1970s may indeed have been challenging the established order, but they claimed to get along very well, on the whole, with their parents. In a survey of studies on activist youth, Block, Haan, and Smith *(1968)* determined that the typical student radical was likely to come from an upper-middle-class home, precisely the sort of environment in which liberal attitudes are inclined to flourish. Consequently, many radicals reported that, far from rebelling against their parents, they were simply putting into practice the values they had been brought up with *(Flacks, 1967; Keniston, 1968; Solomon & Fishman, 1964)*. And there is some impressionistic evidence to support this claim of familial esprit de corps as well. In an article devoted to examining various nuances of the "generation gap," Adelson observes that in "letters written to the press by parents of the students expelled by Columbia and Chicago, the rhetoric . . . reveals how strong the bond of political sympathy is between parents and their children" *(1970, p. 11)*. While expressing some concern over their fate, these parents generally commended their youngsters for calling attention to social problems.

Parent Versus Peer: The Adolescent Subculture

But in the popular view, adolescent rebellion is not limited solely to a revolt against one's parents. As he begins to defy parental authority (so the story goes), the teenager is supposed to rely increasingly on his peers. Indeed, some prominent observers of the "youth scene" *(Coleman, 1961; Friedenberg, 1959)* have contended that there is actually an adolescent "subculture," a subculture that exists quite apart from adult society, with its own distinctive mores and standards of taste. Perhaps the strongest advocate for this point of view is James Coleman:

In our modern world of mass communication and rapid diffusion of ideas and knowledge, it is hard to realize that separate subcultures can exist right under the noses of adults—subcultures with languages all their own, with special symbols, and, most importantly, with value systems that may differ from adults'. Any parent who has tried to talk to his adolescent son or daughter recently knows this, as does anyone who has recently visited a high school for the first time since his own adolescence. To put it simply, these young people speak a different language. What is more relevant to the present point, the language that they speak is becoming more and more different. *(1961, p. 3)*

Once again, however, when we consult the facts, the image of adolescents and adults squared off against each other in an intergenerational struggle or segregated into two hostile camps loses much of its credibility. Undeniably, as they grow older, teenagers report spending more time with their friends and less time with their families *(Douvan & Adelson, 1966; Offer, 1969)*, but the peer group does not seem to loom as a monolithic force in the life of the adolescent. Existing research suggests instead that the youngster relies on the judgment of his friends for ordinary, day-to-day decisions, but tends to consult his parents on more critical matters. Bowerman and Kinch, for instance, studied a sample of fourth through tenth graders and attempted to tap three different areas: identification, association, and norm orientation. The researchers defined each of these areas as follows:

For identification, subjects were asked which group (family or friends) understood them better and whether, when they grew up, they would rather be the kind of persons their parents are or the kind they think their friends would be. For association orientation, they were asked which group they most enjoyed doing things with, and which they would rather spend their time with in the evening and on weekends. The norm orientation question asked whose ideas were most like theirs with respect to decisions of right and wrong, things that are fun to do, the importance of school, and what they would do if one group wanted them to do something that the other did not approve of. *(1959, p. 207)*

Although with increasing age the subjects tended to report that they were *associating* more with their friends and even relying upon them more for making decisions, a majority of the tenth graders (52 percent) still reported that they were most strongly *identified* with their parents. Though tenth graders might be spending much more time with their friends than were fourth graders, and though they might be turning to their friends for advice with increasing frequency, they still wanted to *be* like their parents.

Similarly, Brittain *(1963)* asked a sample of adolescent girls whether their parents' or their friends' opinions would carry more weight with them in a variety of situations: deciding which course to take in school, whether to report a classmate who had damaged school property, how to dress for a football game and party, which part-time job to take, and so forth. He discovered that there was no *overall* preference either for parents or peers. For some decisions, the girls reported that they would be influenced more by their friends, for others by their parents. In matters of taste, dress, and the like, they relied on their friends. However, parents were seen as the appropriate arbiters for more serious decisions. Brittain concluded that far from being alienated from adults, teenagers actually have a kind of dual orientation, with parents and friends each being assigned their respective areas of expertise.

Meissner's findings *(1965)* are essentially comparable. He studied a group of Roman Catholic teenage boys in Grades 9 through 12 and discovered that though there was a slight tendency for the older boys to be more critical of their parents, the vast majority of his subjects (80 percent or more) declared themselves to be very happy at home.

What sort of amalgam can we make of these disparate facts— that is, while adolescents spend increasing amounts of time with their friends as they grow older and turn to them for day-to-day decisions, they still retain positive feelings for their parents? Clearly the popular notion that adolescents retreat into their own exclusive and hostile subculture requires some qualification. Rather than becoming increasingly *estranged* from their parents, we suspect, teenagers become increasingly *differentiated* from them. The studies we have cited suggest that the younger child tends to view his parents with considerable awe and to award them the final say-so on all decisions. However, to the teenager, his mother and father appear less godlike. Though they remain an important force in the youngster's life, he begins to recognize other points of reference as well, not the least of which is contained in his own circle of friends. But the overall picture is one of quiet disengagement rather than of cold war.

The Generation Gap

Closely related to the concepts of youthful rebellion and adolescent subculture is the notion of a generation gap: the assumption that adolescents and adults (including the parents of adolescents) have widely divergent opinions. As might have been expected from the previous discussion, this time-honored corollary to the storm and stress myth also turns out to be more apparent than real. Indeed, from the material we have presented so far, such a conclusion would seem well-nigh inescapable. The warm feelings and respect which most teenagers evince for their parents make it difficult to believe that there is any wholesale challenge to the established values of society during adolescence.

But does this mean that there is virtually no difference between the views of most youngsters and those of most adults? Much as we may distress those with a strong need for certainty, perhaps the most enlightening answer we can give is that it all depends—on which youngsters, which adults, and which issues are under consideration. As we have already seen, student activists may be in revolt against the standards that are cherished by a great many adults, but they are not necessarily rebelling against their own *parents*. And to complicate matters still further, there are a few specific issues that do seem to divide the younger generation from the older—and even to set adolescents apart from ther own parents.

While it is difficult to gather any ironclad figures on drug usage, Adelson *(1970)* surmises that drugs are one area in which those under 30 years old and those over that untrustworthy age probably differ. He notes that while a majority of teenagers have not actually smoked marijuana (a fairly recent survey cited by Brecher, *1972*, puts the number at between 15 and 20 percent), they are a good deal more tolerant about its usage than are their elders. A similar pattern emerges when we examine attitudes toward sexual expression. In this area too, the media are fond of promoting the impression that there is a "sexual revolution" underway and that today's adolescents are far more free-wheeling than their parents were. But once again, the gap, insofar as it exists, would seem to have more to do with philosophy than with actual practice. Reviewing a few of the surveys that have appeared in "teen magazines," Mussen, Conger, and Kagan *(1969)*, for instance, conclude that the incidence of premarital intercourse among girls under twenty has not increased very much since Kinsey published his data back in 1953. Kinsey's research indicated that among women born after 1900, 21 percent had engaged in premarital intercourse before the age of twenty. A survey conducted by *Seventeen* magazine in the late 1960s (perhaps not the most reliable source for such facts, but a source nonetheless) puts the percentage for the current crop of under twenty year olds at around 25 percent *(Lake, 1967)*. And although still more recent surveys *(Sorenson, 1973; Zelnik & Kantner, 1972)* have claimed somewhat higher rates (in both of these studies approximately 45 percent of the female subjects reported engaging in premarital intercourse by age twenty), the increase scarcely constitutes a "sexual revolution."

On the other hand, if we consider the issue of whether or not premarital relations are *ever* permissible, a clear difference of opinion appears—both between adolescents and adults in general and between adolescents and their parents. In one of the best-known studies in this area, Reiss *(1960)* queried samples of high school students and a national sample of adults about a variety of sexual activities, ranging from kissing to intercourse. All subjects were asked to state whether or not the activity was acceptable *for a male* before marriage under the following four conditions: if the couple in question was (1) engaged to be married, (2) in love, (3) felt strong affection for each other, or (4) had no particular affection for each other. For the most part, the high school students were more likely to approve *all* forms of sexual expression before marriage, regardless of what kind of commitment the couple under consideration might have for each other. However, the question of premarital intercourse evoked one of the most striking differences. A fairly substantial proportion of the high school students (52 percent of the males and 44 percent of the females) approved of full sexual intimacy for engaged couples whereas a comparatively small fraction of the adults (19 percent of the men and 17 percent of the women) did.

The findings of Lerner and his associates *(Lerner, Karson, Meisels, & Knapp, 1975; Lerner, Pendorf, & Emery, 1971; Lerner, Schroeder, Rewitzer, & Weinstock, 1972)* are essentially comparable. In a series of attitude surveys designed to examine the dimensions of the "generation gap," these researchers discovered that there was, in general, surprisingly little disagreement between the younger and the older generation on a wide variety of issues—except for sex. In this area alone, high school students and college freshmen alike expressed opinions that were considerably more liberal than those of adults.

However, despite this manifestation of the "generation gap," most adolescents appear to retain a degree of conservatism with regard to sexual matters. Comparatively few of the students in Reiss's study (21 percent of the male high school students and only 11 percent of the females) indicated much approval for casual liaisons—even for *boys*. And Mussen, Conger, and Kagan concluded *their* survey with the following observations:

> It should be noted that in no study available to us did a majority of the students approve of premarital sexual relations for couples who are not in love or engaged, and in most studies, less than 50 percent approved even where there was a formal engagement. . . . Contrary to popular adult stereotype, it appears reasonably clear that promiscuity is widely disapproved by both adolescent boys and girls of all ages. *(1969, pp. 641–642)*

Parent-child differences Studies of college students, admittedly a more select group, have unearthed some sharper differences of opinion, in this case between parents and children specifically rather than between adolescents and adults in general. In a survey of 217 coeds and their mothers *(Bell & Buerkle, 1961)*, 88 percent of the parents but only 34 percent of the students declared that it was "generally important" for a girl to be a virgin when she married. Similarly, 83 percent of the mothers expressed the view that it was "very wrong" for a girl who was engaged to have sexual relations with her fiance but only 35 percent of the coeds thought so.[1]

In an unpublished study, the author of the present book *(Gallatin & Canter, 1970)* revealed comparable levels of disagreement. In this survey, the overriding issue was whether or not the dormitory regulations of a midwestern university should be revised. At the time that the study was undertaken, male and female students were, for all intents and purposes, prohibited from visiting each other's rooms. (Open houses were permitted every now and then, but the doors were to remain ajar and resident advisers patrolled the halls.) Six hundred students and their parents were queried about proposed revisions of the so-called visitation rules, the students having questionnaires administered to them in person by the head residents in their respective dormitories, the parents being contacted by mail. Only about 40 percent of the parents actually responded. However,

---

[1] And even here, the discrepancy between parent and child was less sharp than it might appear. There were actually three choices in the Bell and Buerkle study: very wrong, somewhat wrong, and not wrong. A substantial number of the coeds chose the middle-of-the-road answer.

when their responses were compared with those of their own children, some pronounced discrepancies were observed. Not surprisingly, perhaps, the students were inclined to advocate total freedom to come and go as they pleased, expressing very little concern about the possible inconvenience of having boys and girls circulating in each other's living quarters at all hours of the night and day. The parents who took the trouble to return the questionnaire viewed the proposed amendments in the visitation code with a more jaundiced eye and claimed to be quite well satisfied with the existing, if somewhat draconian, set of rules.

Nonetheless, when parents and offspring were compared on a somewhat less explosive topic, the purpose of education, the differences of opinion became notably less marked. The students and their parents showed themselves in rather close agreement about educational goals. We should note that this latter finding substantiates the work of Bengston *(1970)* and Lubell *(1968)*. These researchers questioned college students about their relations with their parents, and both discovered an astonishing degree of harmony and good will. In Bengston's study, 79 percent of the students reported feeling somewhat close or very close to their families, 81 percent regarded communication with them as good, and 78 percent believed that their parents understood them most of the time. Lubell came up with essentially the same results: Only about 10 percent of the college students he interviewed recounted any serious clashes with their parents. Hence, over and over again, even among less typical groups of adolescents like college students, the same pattern tends to prevail. There may be disagreement between parent and child over day-to-day affairs and even some disagreement over issues of conventional morality, but by and large a sense of continuity and solidarity predominates between the generations.

Perhaps the crowning irony is that even in the absence of a large-scale generation gap, parents and teenagers themselves appear to assume that there is one. Several studies *(Canter & Meisels, 1971; Hess, 1959–1960; Hess & Goldblatt, 1957; Maxwell, Connor, & Walters, 1961)* have revealed that parents expect their teenage children to evaluate them less favorably than their children actually do—and vice versa. (Indeed, adolescents seem to expect adults in *general* to rate them rather unfavorably.)

Adolescence and Social Criticism

What is also paradoxical is that while the media are inclined to portray the typical adolescent as unruly and rebellious, an entire school of specialists *(Douvan & Adelson, 1966; Friedenberg, 1959;*

Keniston, 1960) has arisen to deplore the alleged apathy and blandness of contemporary youth. Douvan and Adelson imply that it is potentially harmful for the adolescent to be so accommodating and that he may be robbed of important opportunities for character development:

> Traditionally, adolescence has been the age in which the child readied himself to leave home; and when we read accounts of adolescence in the earlier part of the century we very often note between father and son a decisive encounter, a decisive testing of wills, in which the son makes a determined bid for autonomy, either by leaving home, or threatening to do so, and meaning it. The adolescent then had little of the freedom he has today; he was kept under the parental thumb but he used his captivity well, to strengthen himself for a real departure and a real autonomy. Nowadays the adolescent and his parents are both made captive by their mutual knowledge of the adolescent's dependency. They are locked in a room with no exit, and they make the best of it by an unconscious quid pro quo, in which the adolescent forfeits his adolescence, and instead becomes a teenager. He keeps the peace by muting his natural rebelliousness through transforming it into structured and defined techniques for getting on people's nerves. The passions, the restlessness, the vivacity of adolescence are partly strangled, and partly drained off in the mixed childishness and false adulthood of the adolescent teen culture. *(1966, p. 354)*

Whether or not we agree with this analysis (and there is probably a lot to quibble with in it), it does raise two serious questions about the nature of adolescence in contemporary American society. Why, if the teenage years are *not* a period of storm and stress, do we persist in viewing them as such? And *if* adolescence is not a tumultuous phase of life, *should* it be?

Romanticism and the Adolescent

Those who have addressed themselves to the first question, the persistence of the myth of storm and stress, seem fairly well agreed upon the answer. The image of adolescent turmoil predominates (in contradiction to the facts, we might add) because it is romantic, a theme that captures the imagination of novelists, social scientists, journalists, and even, perhaps, most more or less ordinary adults.

Adelson *(1964, 1970)* is one of the most articulate spokesmen for this point of view. In particular, he stresses the connection between our impressions of youth and the prevailing political climate. During the Eisenhower years, a period of comparative economic stagnation and general apathy, he notes that social critics and some journalists as well complained about the "spinelessness" of the younger generation. (Ironically, this was also an era in which concern over juvenile delinquency earned teenagers in general a bad press.) Our high schools and universities, so the argument went, were turning out a crop of docile and unquestioning "solid citizens." Far from questioning the established order, they would fit themselves into it like so many cogs in a giant machine, and American society would thereby lose much of its potential for creative change. Under the Kennedy administration, Adelson observes, the political climate was briefly one of optimism and idealism—and the image of youth was revised accordingly. During the early 1960s, the young Peace Corps volunteer and Freedom Rider received a lion's share of the publicity. However, with the advent of the Vietnam war and the growing number of demonstrations on college campuses, the media began to convey the impression that the great mass of teenagers were radicals and hippies. Whatever the reason, Adelson argues, we tend to project both our political hopes and fears upon the young. Hence as world conditions fluctuate so does our overall vision of adolescence. (In this connection it is interesting to note that with the decline of the Vietnam war as a political issue, adolescents are once more being characterized as "conservative"—and even as "studious.")

However, some of Adelson's sharpest criticism is reserved not for the media, but for social scientists themselves. Those who have ostensibly been studying adolescents have done as much, he suggests, to promote the myth of storm and stress as the "sensationalistic" press:

Having attended, to my sorrow, many convocations of experts on the young, I can attest that most of us are experts on atypical fractions of the young: on heavy drug users, or delinquents, or hippies, or the alienated, or dropouts, or the dissident—and above all, on the more sprightly and articulate youngsters of the upper middle class. By and large, our discourse at these meetings, when it is not clinical, is a kind of gossip: the upper middle class talking to itself about itself. The examples run: my son, my colleague's daughter, my psychoanalytic patient, my neighbor's drug using son, my Ivy League students. Most of us have never had a serious and extended conversation with a youngster from the working or lower-middle classes. . . . What we know deeply are the visibly disturbed, and the more volatile, more conspicuous segments of the upper middle class. These are the youngsters with problems, or with *panache*—makers and shakers, shakers of the present, makers of the future. Their discontents and their creativity, we hear it said, produce the new forms and the new dynamics of our social system. Thus, they allow us to imagine the contours of a hopeful new order of things, or, contrariwise, permit us visions of Armageddon. *(1970, p. 36)*

In other words, the upper-middle-class psychologist surveying, for the most part, only upper-middle-class adolescents (those adolescents who have the greatest *opportunity* and *leisure* to engage in several years of "finding themselves" or "acting out") tends to extrapolate too freely from his observations. Many of the adolescents he sees are undoubtedly going through a tempestuous phase, but they are, as Adelson puts it, an "atypical fraction." For most teenagers, the transition from childhood to adulthood is apparently neither particularly stressful nor especially romantic. We should add in this connection that two other psychologists who have also attacked the myth of storm and stress *(Bandura, 1964; Offer, 1969)* concur with Adelson in castigating their own colleagues.

Should Adolescence Be a Period of Storm and Stress?

But if the teenage years are not (at least for most youngsters) notably traumatic, we might still ask whether or not they ought to be. Is it healthy, as Douvan and Adelson imply, to rebel against one's parents? Do docile adolescents necessarily turn out to be bland and unfulfilled adults? Certainly this has been the fear of a number of social critics, the most vocal of whom is probably Edgar Friedenberg. In a book entitled, appropriately enough, *The Vanishing Adolescent (1959)*, Friedenberg admitted that the notion of "adolescent storm and stress" was a myth, but only with great regret. He acknowledged that in the United States adolescence was not a period of conflict and that the youngsters he had observed, albeit rather casually, did not appear to be in rebellion against the established order. But, he insisted, that absence of turmoil constituted a tragedy for American society. If adolescence was *not* filled with *sturm und drang* it ought to be, for how else could a young person discover who he was:

A youngster who has abandoned the task of defining himself in dialectical combat with society and becomes its captive and its emissary may be no rarity; but he is a casualty. There is not much more to be said about him: one can only write him off and trust that the world will at least feed him well if it cannot keep him warm. The promise of maturity must be fulfilled by those who are strong enough to grow into it at their own rate as full bargaining members.
Must there be conflict between the adolescent and society? The point is that adolescence *is* conflict—protracted conflict—between the individual and society. There are cultures in which the conflict seems hardly to occur; but where it does not, the characteristic development of personality which we associate with adolescence does not occur either. *(1959, p. 32)*

And in his study of alienated Harvard undergraduates, Keniston *(1960)* has come forward with a similar indictment of American culture, accusing it of encouraging teenagers to become disturbingly "cool" and detached in meeting the problems of life.

On the other hand, Offer *(1969)*, to whom we have referred several times previously, refuses to adopt such a gloomy and pessimistic view of the normal adolescent. On the basis of his own study, Offer concludes that the teenage years are a period neither of "blind acquiescence" nor of undue turbulence. There are definitely adjustments that must be made during adolescence—developing a degree of autonomy from parents, finding appropriate outlets for sexual drives, establishing relationships with members of the opposite sex—but, Offer insists, normal adolescents are able to meet these challenges without excessive strain. Nor does the absence of conflict necessarily doom the youngster to a constricted and unfulfilled adulthood. Quite the contrary, Offer declares:

> The transitional period of adolescence does present the adolescent with a special burden, a challenge, and an opportunity. He has to individualize, build up confidence in himself and his abilities, make important decisions concerning his future, and free himself of his earlier attachments to his parents. Our observations have led us to conclude that the majority of teenagers in our sample cope with these tasks successfully. They lack the turmoil of the disturbed adolescent precisely because their ego is strong enough to withstand the pressures. In their task they are greatly helped by their parents. If other subjects are found to have exaggerated turmoil and be just as well adjusted or normal as our students, they will have chosen a separate path to maturity.
>
> Yet our subjects were not devoid of problems. They did not go through life sheltered and unscathed. It seems to us that someone might eventually raise the objection concerning our subjects that, because of their low level of turmoil, they are cases of arrested development. Certain investigators have interpreted their findings somewhat differently than we have. . . . Implicitly these investigators have adopted the position that lack of turmoil is a bad prognostic sign and must necessarily prevent the adolescent from developing into a mature adult. All our data, including the psychological testing, point in the opposite direction. The adolescents not only adjusted well; they were also in touch with their feelings and developed meaningful relationships with others. *(1969, p. 184)*

Bandura *(1964)* also sharply attacks the notion that adolescence need necessarily be a period of great turbulence and turmoil. Indeed, he cites his own work *(Bandura & Walters, 1959)* with both aggressive and "well-adjusted" teenagers as a basis for rejecting any semblance of an "ages and stages" approach to human development.

The adolescent who acts up, Bandura insists, is not simply "going through a phase" and thus completely normal. Such a youngster is instead a prime example of "faulty learning patterns." Insufficient training early in childhood, rather than some mysterious developmental factor, is responsible for his problems. Bandura argues—thereby implying that stability is more the norm than turmoil during adolescence.

Overview

While we do not wish to go nearly as far as Bandura and to reject the developmental approach to adolescent psychology altogether, it is clear at this point that our attempt to reconcile theory with data has run into some difficulties. Our three representative theorists, Hall, Anna Freud, and Sullivan, all assumed, whatever other points they might have disputed, that adolescence was a period of sexual conflict in particular and emotional storm and stress in general. Existing research does not bear out this assumption (which, as we have seen, is also very popular among the lay public and the mass media). Furthermore, in the course of surveying the data on adolescent turmoil (or its absence), we have unearthed some other problems. It has become apparent by now that the experiences of the typical adolescent boy are rather different from the experiences of the typical adolescent girl. It is also apparent that a controversy exists as to whether adolescence *should* be a period of storm and stress.

And beyond these difficulties, there are others. Though we have examined various facets of adolescence—intellectual growth, moral and social development, sexual maturation, storm and stress—there are other dimensions that we have not as yet had an opportunity to explore. We have not mentioned vocational aspirations, for instance, or given much attention to political development or self-concept. And we have been able to refer to the real problems of adolescence (drugs, delinquency, dropping out) only in passing. Is there a theory that will permit us to resolve the dilemmas we have uncovered and at the same time allow us to broaden the scope of our discussion? In the succeeding chapters we shall examine one which, in our opinion, comes closest to constituting a comprehensive theory of adolescent development: Erik Erikson's.

REFERENCES

ADELSON, J. The Mystique of Adolescence. *Psychiatry*, 1964, **27**, 1–5.

ADELSON, J. "What Generation Gap?" *New York Times Magazine*, Jan. 18, 1970, 10 *ff*.

ALDRIDGE, J. M. *In the Country of the Young*. New York: Harper & Row, 1970.

BANDURA, A. The Stormy Decade: Fact or Fiction? *Psychology in the Schools*, 1964, **1**, 224–231.

BANDURA, A., & WALTERS, R. H. *Adolescent Aggression*. New York: Ronald, 1959.

BARDWICK, J. *The Psychology of Women*. New York: Harper & Row, 1971.

BELL, R. R., & BUERKLE, J. V. Mother-Daughter Attitudes to Premarital Sexual Behavior. *Marriage and Family Living*, 1961, **23**, 390–392.

BENGSTON, V. The Generation Gap: A Review and Typology of Social-Psychological Perspectives. *Youth and Society*, 1970, **2**, 7–32.

BLOCK, J., HAAN, N., & SMITH, M. B. Activism and Apathy in Contemporary Adolescents. In J. F. Adams (Ed.), *Understanding Adolescence*. Boston: Allyn & Bacon, 1968. Pp. 198–231.

BLOS, P. *On Adolescence: A Psychoanalytic Interpretation*. New York: Free Press, 1962.

BOWERMAN, C. E., & KINCH, J. W. Changes in Family and Peer Orientation of Children between the Fourth and Tenth Grades. *Social Forces*, 1959, **37**, 206–211.

BRECHER, E. M. (Ed.). *Licit and Illicit Drugs: The Consumers Union Report*. Mount Vernon, N.Y.: Consumers Union, 1972.

BRITTAIN, C. V. Adolescent Choices and Parent-Peer Cross-Pressures. *American Sociological Review*, 1963, **28**, 385–391.

CANTER, F., & MEISELS, M. A Note on the Generation Gap. *Adolescence*, 1971, **6**, 523–530.

COLEMAN, J. S. *The Adolescent Society*. New York: Free Press, 1961.

DOUVAN, E., & ADELSON, J. *The Adolescent Experience*. New York: Wiley, 1966.

FEUER, L. *The Conflict of Generations: The Character and Significance of Student Movements*. New York: Basic Books, 1969.

FLACKS, R. The Liberated Generation: An Exploration of the Roots of Student Protest. *Journal of Social Issues*, 1967, **23**, 52–75.

FRIEDENBERG, E. *The Dignity of Youth and Other Atavisms*. Boston: Beacon, 1965.

FRIEDENBERG, E. *The Vanishing Adolescent*. New York: Dell, 1959.

GALLATIN, J., & CANTER, F. Parent-Child Attitudes and the Revision of Visitation Rules. Unpublished manuscript, 1970.

HESS, R. D. Parents and Teenagers: Differing Perspectives. *Child Studies*, 1959–1960, **37**, 21–23.

HESS, R. D., & GOLDBLATT, I. The Status of Adolescents in American Society: A Problem in Social Identity. *Child Development*, 1957, **28**, 459–468.

JACOBS, J. *Adolescent Suicide*. New York: Wiley, 1971.

JOSSELYN, I. M. *The Adolescent and His World*. New York: Family Service Association of America, 1952.

KENISTON, K. *The Uncommitted: Alienated Youth in American Society*. New York: Delta, 1960.

KENISTON, K. *Young Radicals: Notes on Committed Youth*. New York: Harcourt Brace Jovanovich, 1968.

KINSEY, A. C., POMEROY, W., & MARTIN, C. *Sexual Behavior in the Human Male.* Philadelphia: Saunders, 1948.

KINSEY, A. C., POMEROY, W., MARTIN, C., & GEBHARD, P. H. *Sexual Behavior in the Human Female.* Philadelphia: Saunders, 1953.

LAKE, A. Teenagers and Sex: A Student Report. *Seventeen,* July 1967, p. 88.

LERNER, R. M., KARSON, M., MEISELS, M., & KNAPP, J. Actual and Perceived Attitudes of Late Adolescents and Their Parents. *Journal of Genetic Psychology,* 1975.

LERNER, R. M., PENDORF, J., & EMERY, A. Attitudes of Adolescents and Adults Toward Contemporary Issues. *Psychological Reports,* 1971, **28,** 139–145.

LERNER, R. M., SCHROEDER, C., REWITZER, M., & WEINSTOCK, A. Attitudes of High School Students and Their Parents Toward Contemporary Issues. *Psychological Reports,* 1972, **31,** 255–258.

LUBELL, S. That "Generation Gap." In D. Bell and I. Kristol (Eds.), *Confrontation.* New York: Basic Books, 1968.

MAXWELL, P. H., CONNOR, R., & WALTERS, J. Family Member Perceptions of Parent-Role Performance. *Merrill-Palmer Quarterly,* 1961, **7,** 31–37.

MEAD, M. *Coming of Age in Samoa.* New York: Dell, 1928.

MEISSNER, W. W. Parental Interaction of the Adolescent Boy. *Journal of Genetic Psychology,* 1965, **107,** 225–233.

MUSSEN, P., CONGER, J., & KAGAN, J. *Child Development and Personality.* (3rd ed.) New York: Harper & Row, 1969.

OFFER, D. Attitudes Toward Sexuality in a Group of 1500 Middle Class Teen-Agers. *Journal of Youth and Adolescence,* 1972, **1,** 81–90.

OFFER, D. *The Psychological World of the Teenager.* New York: Basic Books, 1969.

POMEROY, W. *Dr. Kinsey and the Institute for Sex Research.* New York: Harper & Row, 1972.

POWELL, M. Age and Sex Differences of Conflict within Certain Areas of Psychological Adjustment. *Psychological Monographs,* 1955, **69** (Whole No. 387).

REISS, I. L. *Premarital Sexual Standards in America.* New York: Free Press, 1960.

SANFORD, R. N. *et al.* Physique, Personality, and Scholarship. *Monographs of the Society for Research in Child Development,* 1943, No. 1.

SHIPMAN, G. The Psychodynamics of Sex Education. *Family Coordinator,* 1968, **17,** 3–12.

SHORT, J. F. Juvenile Delinquency: The Socio-Cultural Context. In L. W. Hoffman and M. L. Hoffman (Eds.), *Review of Child Development Research.* Vol. II. New York: Russell Sage, 1966.

SOLOMON, F., & FISHMAN, J. R. Youth and Peace: A Psychosocial Study of Student Peace Demonstrators in Washington, D. C. *The Journal of Social Issues,* 1964, **20,** 54–73.

SORENSON, R. C. *Adolescent Sexuality in Contemporary America.* New York: Harcourt Brace Jovanovich, 1973.

SPIEGEL, L. Review of Contributions to a Psychoanalytic Theory of Adolescence. *Psychoanalytic Study of the Child,* 1951, **6,** 375–393.

SULLIVAN, H. S. *The Interpersonal Theory of Psychiatry.* New York: Norton, 1953.

TOOLEY, K. M. Ego Adaptation in Late Adolescence. Unpublished doctoral dissertation, University of Michigan, 1966.

WEINER, I. *Psychological Disturbance in Adolescence.* New York: Wiley, 1970.

WESTLEY, W. A., & ELKIN, F. The Protective Environment and Adolescent Socialization. *Social Forces,* 1957, **35,** 243–249.

ZELNIK, M., & KANTNER, J. E. Survey of Female Adolescent Sexual Behavior Conducted for the Commission on Population, Washington, D.C., 1972.

Erikson's Theory of Personality

Biographical Notes

Of all the theorists we have consulted so far, Erikson has had perhaps the most varied and least classically "academic" career. He was born in Hamburg in 1902 to Danish parents. His parents separated shortly after his birth, but he was subsequently adopted by his stepfather, a Jewish pediatrician. Though he was genuinely fond of his stepfather, he has remarked in an autobiographical study *(1970)* that his mixed background created some "identity problems" for him. Being tall and blond he was labeled a "gentile" by his Jewish friends at the local synagogue, and as the son of a Jewish physician, he was teased for being a "Jew" by his gentile classmates at school.

Nor did Erikson apparently feel much at home in the traditional and formal German educational system. Though he attended the Gymnasium (more or less the equivalent of a private, college-preparatory high school in the United States), he decided after graduation to enroll in art school rather than in a university. However, he found that he could not "take hold" as an artist either, and he spent much of his late adolescence and early adulthood wandering from country to country, alternately painting and supporting himself by tutoring. When Erikson was in his mid-twenties, Peter Blos, a friend from Hamburg whom he had encountered now and again in his travels, invited him to join the staff of a small progressive school in Vienna.[1] The school was financed by Dorothy Burlingham, a wealthy American who had developed a strong interest in psychoanalysis, had gone to Vienna to be analyzed by Sigmund Freud, and had remained there to become a lay analyst.[2]

Through Mrs. Burlingham, Erikson was introduced to other members of the famous "Vienna Circle," among them Sigmund Freud's daughter Anna, who was also actively involved in the school. Anna Freud, in fact, was so impressed with Erikson's talents that she eventually urged him to undertake training in psychoanalysis and herself served as his analyst. After additional study at the Vienna Institute, Erikson became a practitioner in his own right and began to specialize in treating children. However, in the early 1930s political events connected with the rise of Hitler made him uneasy, and he left Vienna, settling for a brief time in Copenhagen and ultimately emigrating to the United States. He has resided in this country ever since, teaching at such prestigious institutions as the Menninger Foundation, Harvard University, and the University of California at Berkeley, writing, and pursuing his practice as a psychoanalyst.

Characteristically, some of the most important influences on Erikson's thinking have come from outside the university altogether. In 1938, Scuder Mekeel, a close friend of his and an anthropologist, invited him to participate in a series of field investigations. Traveling to various reservations in Nebraska, Erikson gained an opportunity to observe the life of the Sioux Indians at firsthand and to study a culture radically different from any he had known before. These contacts with the Sioux, perhaps more than anything else, began to convince him that psychoanalytic theory was limited in certain respects. It could account quite plausibly for *extremes* of behavior within a particular culture, but it did not contain the conceptual machinery necessary to deal as adequately with the normal and commonplace. As far as the Sioux were concerned, for instance, Erikson thought he could detect a connection between a bloody religious ritual in adulthood and some rather harsh feeding practices in early infancy. This connection made sense within the traditional psychoanalytic framework. However, in describing his observations, Erikson found himself compelled to add:

[1] Interestingly enough, Blos also became a distinguished psychoanalyst and is currently regarded as a specialist in the treatment of disturbed adolescents.

[2] Most analysts in the United States are MDs who have undertaken residencies in psychiatry and have followed them up with training at analytic institutes. However, in the early days of psychoanalysis, it was possible for people who were not physicians to obtain training at an institute and to be certified as "lay analysts."

But if we try to define the state of relative equilibrium between these dramatic extremes, if we ask what characterizes an Indian when he does not do much more than just calmly be an Indian bent on the daily chores of the year's cycle, our description lacks a fitting frame of reference. *(1968, p. 51)*[3]

The impression that psychoanalysis could explain otherwise "bizarre" actions much better than normal behavior was strengthened a few years later. While serving as a consultant to the armed forces during World War II, Erikson became very much impressed with human *adaptability*. There is perhaps no more unnatural habitat than a submarine, with its comings and goings beneath the ocean and its cramped quarters. Yet, after coming into contact with a number of submarine crews, Erikson could not conceal his amazement at the extent to which they made the best of their grotesque living conditions:

With astonishing tact and native wisdom, silent arrangements are made by which the captain becomes sensory system, brains, and conscience for the whole submerged organism of minutely tuned machinery and humanity, and by which the crew members mobilize themselves in compensatory mechanisms (for example in the collective use of the generously provided food), permitting the crew to stand monotony and yet to be ready for instant action. *(1968, p. 52)*

Once again, psychoanalytic theory, oriented as it was to conflict and pathology, could not provide a satisfactory explanation for this kind of healthy adjustment.

Nor, Erikson finally concluded, could psychoanalysis completely explain an individual's *failure* to cope with the stresses of war. There were soldiers who returned to the United States from combat disturbed and strangely out of touch with themselves.

Through long nights they would hang between the Scylla of annoying noises and the Charybdis of anxiety dreams which would startle them out of finally achieved moments of deep sleep. In the daytime they would find themselves unable to remember certain things; in their own neighborhoods they would lose their way or suddenly detect, in conversation, that they had unwittingly misrepresented things. *(1950, p. 41)*

Using the psychoanalytic framework, we might surmise, of course, that the dreadful events of war had reactivated some long-

[3] In our account of Erikson's theory we have taken most of our excerpts from his most recent book on adolescence, *Identity: Youth and Crisis.* This book is essentially a compendium of Erikson's writings over the past 30 years.

forgotten and deeply repressed "complex" of childhood in these men and that they now felt in danger of being overwhelmed by their unconscious conflicts. However, what struck Erikson as equally, if not more, important was that: "They could not rely on the characteristic processes of the functioning ego by which time and space are organized and truth is tested" *(1950, p. 41)*. The shocks these veterans had undergone, in addition, perhaps, to stirring up old childhood conflicts, had somehow robbed them of the ability to categorize and integrate experience. They had lost, as Erikson was later to put it, "a sense of personal sameness and historical continuity" *(1968, p. 17)*. Each was suffering, in short, a "crisis of identity."

Drawing upon his anthropological and wartime observations, Erikson began to formulate a theory that was less "mechanistic" and less preoccupied with pathology than psychoanalysis. While he agreed that early experiences were extremely important, he began to envision personality development as a dynamic and continuing process, a process that continued, for better or for worse, from the cradle to the grave. And while he agreed that the gratification of certain instincts was a key force in life, he concluded that something called "ego synthesis"—the ordering and integration of experience —was equally significant.

The Contributions of Hartmann

To be sure, Erikson was not the only member of the Vienna Circle who came to entertain such ideas. Even before he left Austria, Erikson recalls in his autobiographical study *(1970)*, Anna Freud and another member of the Circle, Heinz Hartmann, had been engaged in a theoretical debate over the nature of the id and the ego. Anna Freud, as might have been expected, represented the more orthodox psychoanalytic position. According to this view (as we have already pointed out in Chapter 3), the ego, though defined as the rational part of the personality, is completely dependent upon the id. The skills subsumed under the concept of ego—thinking, perceiving, coordinating, moving about in space, performing tasks—are alleged not to exist even in rudimentary form at birth. Instead, the newborn infant is supposed to consist of nothing but an id—an untidy conglomeration of drives and impulses. Only as the infant is frustrated in his desire to have these drives gratified immediately, do the various ego skills develop, and the ego is therefore, according to the classical Freudian model, fundamentally "dependent" upon the id. All its energies are ultimately derived from defending against the demands of the id. (An example of this line of reasoning, as we have seen, is Anna Freud's contention that the adolescent's increased powers of intellect are solely the result of "intellectualization.")

Hartmann noted, however, that there are a great many human activities and skills that do not seem to be tied in, except under very unusual conditions, with "defense." Although they can be disrupted, these skills—walking, talking, reading, driving an automobile —seem for the most part and for most people to become "autonomous" and "conflict-free." Perhaps, Hartmann suggested, the ego acquired the capacity to "liberate" or, in his words, to "neutralize" energy from the id and turn it to adaptive rather than defensive purposes. Or perhaps there is even some "free energy" at birth, Hartmann went on to propose (1939). Even the tiniest infant can perceive gross changes in his surroundings (e.g., sudden changes in illumination, loud sounds, wetness). It was possible that what psychoanalysis called the ego was derived, at least in part, from these rudimentary capacities, or "ego apparatuses" as Hartmann called them. In short, the infant might be more than a mere "bundle of drives" at birth, and what was to become the ego might depend in part upon *inborn* capacities.

Furthermore—and this was the notion that probably had the greatest impact on Erikson—since the infant possessed such inborn capacities, since he was able at birth to respond, however primitively, to changes in his environment, it might be useful to think of him as being born "preadapted" to that environment and hence requiring that the world treat him with a degree of order and consistency. Radical shifts in his surroundings, inconsistent handling, abuse might make it difficult for his "adaptive" skills to develop normally.

In any case, Erikson was aware of this debate between Anna Freud and Hartmann and of Hartmann's proposed revisions in psychoanalytic theory. But it was only his own experiences in the field— his anthropological excursions and wartime observations—that convinced him of the validity of this new "ego psychology." Once assimilated into his own thinking, however, these concepts became the basis for a singularly comprehensive theory of personality development. What is important to keep in mind for our purposes in particular is that this theory

1. Contains elements of all the others (e.g., Hall's, Freud's, and Sullivan's) which we have reviewed
2. Portrays adolescence as a pivotal period in personality development

3. Provides a possible solution to the dilemma of storm and stress
4. Furnishes a conceptual umbrella for many facets of adolescent development, normal and abnormal

In fact, about the only area of adolescence that it does not do justice to is feminine development. The theory is also, precisely because it portrays personality development as an on-going and never-ending process, a singularly complex and intricate one. Hence it is more than ever necessary to examine Erikson's ideas about adolescence within the context of his more general formulations.

Key Principles of Eriksonian Theory

If psychoanalytic theory can properly be described as "mechanistic," then the corresponding label for Eriksonian theory would be "organic." As we have indicated, a variety of experiences and influences apparently convinced Erikson that there was too much emphasis on the "pathological" and the "defensive" aspects of human nature and not enough on the "adaptive" and "creative." Analysts had originally assumed that they could learn a great deal about the normal personality from studying the *abnormal* personality and figuring out just where the disturbed individual's development had gone awry. Sigmund Freud himself was supposed to have remarked, in justifying this approach, that "we see a crystal's structure only when it cracks." But Erikson informs us that there is a difference between the crystal, which is inanimate, and a living, breathing organism. The organism "cannot be broken up without a withering of the parts" *(1968, p. 276).* Consequently, Eriksonian theory concentrates less on breaking the personality down into its constituent elements (i.e., "id," "ego," and "superego") and more on describing how the personality is gradually organized and built up. This emphasis on personality as an "organic whole" no doubt helps to explain why Erikson extends his account of human development from infancy to old age (rather than trailing off, like most other theorists, in early adulthood).

The Three Dimensions of Personality Development

In Erikson's view, what we call "personality" results from the continuous interaction of three great systems: the biological, the social, and the individual. These three systems are inseparable and mutually interdependent. None can exist without the others.

The biological dimension As far as the biological level is concerned, Erikson agrees with psychoanalysis that the newborn human being is invested with a powerful set of drives and impulses. However, having been influenced by Hartmann (and his notion that the infant is born preadapted to an "average expectable environment"), Erikson adds to this basic set of instincts a need for order and consistency, a need for "continuity of experience," as he describes it. And, like practically every other "stage theorist," he believes that human development occurs in a more or less predictable sequence and that it is governed in part by some kind of innate mechanism or "maturational" factor.

In fact, Erikson believes that this sort of mechanism underlies *all* organic development—human or otherwise—and refers to it as the *epigenetic principle*: "Somewhat generalized, this principle states that anything that grows has a ground plan, and that out of this ground plan the parts arise, each part having its time of special ascendancy, until all the parts have arisen to form a functioning whole" *(1968, p. 92)*.

The social dimension However, this ground plan cannot unfold in vacuo. Indeed, particularly for human beings, who are born in a state of great helplessness and dependency, the biological dimension makes no sense without assuming a social dimension as well. The infant's drives cannot be satisfied, his sense of order and consistency cannot be maintained, and his own peculiar potentialities cannot begin to become manifest in the absence of other people. If he is to survive, he must be cared for, and if he is to thrive, those who take on this responsibility must do so in a way that meets his needs:

> It must be added that a baby's weakness gives him power; out of his very dependence and weakness he makes signs to which his environment, if it is guided well by a responsiveness combining "instinctive" and traditional patterns, is peculiarly sensitive. A baby's presence exerts a consistent and persistent domination over the outer and inner lives of every member of the household. It is as true to say that babies control and bring up their families as it is to say the converse. A family can bring up a baby only by being brought up by him. His growth consists of a series of challenges to them to serve his newly developing potentialities for social interaction. *(1968, pp. 95–96)*

It is also apparent that the baby, if he is to become what is known as a "civilized human being," has to make all sorts of adjustments to the rest of his family as well. Just as they have to learn something about his habits and demands, he has to learn something about theirs. The social dimension of personality development, in short, involves a series of *mutual* accommodations.

Cultural relativity   Erikson's anthropological training, of course, makes him well aware that the precise *nature* of this accommodation may vary considerably from culture to culture. The infant's needs and vulnerabilities determine the "outer limits" of this relationship with his family—he cannot be permitted to starve and he cannot be severely abused—but between these limits there is leeway for a great variety of child-rearing practices and styles. Erikson sums up this principle of "cultural relativity" as follows:

> Now, while it is quite clear what must happen to keep a baby alive— the minimum supply necessary—and what must not happen, lest he be physically damaged or chronically upset—the maximum of early frustration tolerable—there is a certain leeway in regard to what *may* happen and different cultures make extensive use of their prerogatives to decide what they consider workable and insist upon calling necessary. *(1968, p. 98)*

And he gives a number of examples:

> Some people think that a baby, lest he scratch his own eyes out, must necessarily be swaddled completely for most of the day and throughout the greater part of the first year, and think he should be rocked or fed whenever he whimpers. Others think that he should feel the freedom of his kicking limbs as early as possible, but also that, as a matter of course, he should be forced to cry "please" for his meals until he literally gets blue in the face. *(1968, pp. 98–99)*

Not that the culture—whatever culture it happens to be—necessarily indulges the infant or imposes its will upon him in a completely arbitrary fashion. No matter how irrational, nonsensical, and even cruel a particular society may appear to the outside observer, there is, Erikson insists, "a logic—however instinctive and prescientific— in the assumption that what is 'good for the child,' what *may* happen to him, depends on what he is supposed to become and where" *(1968, p. 99)*. An American infant who is "destined" by his parents to become a "hard-working and law-abiding" adult may find comparatively early in life that he is expected to "keep to a schedule" as far as all of his bodily needs are concerned. Conversely, the parents of a Samoan infant may envision a less hectic existence for their child —and hence subject him to less regimentation.

Still, each culture must respect, at least to some extent, the basic "ground plan" of the human infant, and though each culture may have a different formula for dealing with this ground plan, all cultures have a common aim: to transform their "helpless children" into "mature adults." Hence, the social life of a human being tends to take on a similar pattern no matter what specific culture he resides in. In early infancy he interacts primarily with a few adult caretakers, indeed, sometimes principally with only one parent, his mother. As his social skills develop, partially through the care he receives and partially as a result of "unfolding" or "maturation," his range of acquaintance broadens. He becomes capable of interacting with more and more people, people of various ages and stations, and he enters into an increasing variety of relationships. By the time he reaches adulthood, he has taken his place in a society with a more or less complex set of customs and institutions. And, of course, even during adulthood, as he undergoes the biological phenomenon of aging, an individual's relationships with others and his status in society continue to evolve.

It is this interaction between the biological and the social in all cultures that produces what we call the "human personality." Hence, in rephrasing the basic "epigenetic principle" and applying it specifically to personality development, Erikson declares: "Personality, therefore, can be said to develop according to steps predetermined in the human organism's readiness to be driven toward, to be aware of, and to interact with a widening radius of significant individuals and institutions" *(1968, p. 93)*.

The individual dimension However, despite the existence of a basic biological and societal ground plan, no two people ever develop identical personalities. Though all human beings are born with a need to categorize and organize experience, no two are born with precisely the same equipment for doing so. Each will perceive and respond to the world slightly differently, and each will be perceived and responded to slightly differently. Consequently, no two people, even identical twins residing in the same home, ever have precisely the same experiences, and no two people ever integrate those experiences in precisely the same way. Thus there is, in addition to the biological and social dimensions, an "individual," or "ego," element in personality development.

The Concept of Identity

If these three systems—the biological, the social, and the individual—are properly coordinated, the result will be a so-called healthy person, a person who: "*actively masters* his environment, shows a *certain unity of personality*, and is able to *perceive* the world and himself correctly" *(1968, p. 92)*.[4] Indeed, Erikson, as we have seen, views the three systems as being inseparable, a point that becomes all the more evident when we examine the concept which is primarily responsible for his fame: the concept of identity. The psychologically healthy human being, Erikson declares, is one who has developed a "firm sense of identity." Such an individual has managed to place himself in what Erikson calls "ego-space-time." This involves the recognition that he is a particular person, within a particular society, with a particular past, present, and future. Those who cannot integrate their experiences in such a manner are, at the very least, less whole and unified than they might otherwise be, and if the breakdown in ego synthesis is serious enough, they may become severely disorganized. The overall unity of the personality thus depends upon a firm sense of identity.

Indeed, in a bit of anthropological and archaeological speculation, Erikson suggests that human evolution made the development of a sense of identity essential. As civilization advanced, each tribe had to conceive of itself as being superior, perhaps to sort out and make sense of all the differences in color, custom, and appearance that had emerged. It had to view itself as what Erikson terms a *pseudospecies*:

> First each horde or tribe, class and nation, but then also every religious association has become *the* human species, considering all others a freakish and gratuitous invention of some irrelevant deity. To reinforce the illusion of being chosen, every tribe recognizes a creation of its own, a mythology and later a history: thus was loyalty to a particular ecology and morality secured. *(1968, p. 41)*

And what was true of the group became true of each separate human being as well. Each developed the need to feel "special" or "unique" within his own particular group. Erikson admits that he has purposely left the precise meaning of the term "identity" somewhat ambiguous, but operating out of this evolutionary or "psychosocial" perspective, he defines it as

a. a conscious sense of individual uniqueness
b. an unconscious striving for continuity of experience
c. a solidarity with group ideals *(1968, p. 208)*

In other words, identity, like personality development in general, has a biological, a social, and an individual (or ego) dimension.

This formulation also helps us to understand how a person manages to construct an identity in the first place. Erikson implies

---

[4] Erikson credits his colleague Marie Jahoda with originally advancing this definition of the healthy personality.

that each human being has a need to feel special, a need that pre-sumably arises out of the "unconscious striving for continuity of experience." But he cannot develop this feeling of being special and having his own unique destiny in the absence of a culture. The culture provides, as we have already remarked, the care and con-sistency necessary for the development of an ego, and it *also* furnishes the set of labels and guidelines that permit the ego, as it develops, to formulate an identity. Therefore, if an individual's identity is to have a sturdy foundation, he must enjoy a feeling of "solidarity with group ideals." From a very early point in life, he must believe that he is following his culture's guidelines successfully and that they are leading him in meaningful directions: ". . . the growing child must derive a vitalizing sense of reality from the awareness that his individual way of mastering experience, his ego synthesis, is a successful variant of a group identity and is in accord with its space-time and life plan" *(1968, p. 49)*.

To illustrate the complex interaction that occurs between the child's ego, his developing body, and the surrounding social milieu, Erikson examines the consequences of learning to walk:

A child who has just found himself able to walk . . . becomes aware of the new status and stature of "one who can walk" with whatever connota-tion this happens to have in the co-ordinates of his culture's life plan—be it "one who will swiftly run after fleeing prey," "one who will go far," "one who will be upright," or "one who might go too far." To be "one who can walk" becomes one of the many steps in child development which through the coincidence of physical mastery and cultural meaning, of func-tional pleasure and social recognition, contribute to a realistic *self-esteem.* *(1968, p. 49)*

And it is this self-esteem—the result of the child's perception that his maturing skills and traits confer a certain status—which provides the basis for a firm sense of identity. If all goes well, this self-esteem "gradually grows into a conviction that the ego is capable of inte-grating effective steps toward a tangible collective future, that it is developing into a well-organized ego within a social reality" *(1968, p. 49)*.

Adolescence and identity   Since Erikson's is an organic theory —one that views personality development as a process that con-tinues from infancy to old age—he describes identity formation as

. . . always changing and developing: at its best it is a process of increasing differentiation, and it becomes ever more inclusive as the individual grows aware of a widening circle of others significant to him, from the maternal person to "mankind." The process "begins" somewhere in the first true meeting of mother and baby as two persons who can touch and recognize each other, and it does not "end" until man's power of mutual affirmation wanes. *(1968, p. 23)*

Of primary importance to us, of course, is the fact that Erikson designates *adolescence* as a particularly crucial period for identity formation. Not until this stage, Erikson insists, can the individual truly begin to place himself in ego-space-time, recognizing that he has had a distinctive past and envisioning a distinctive future for himself. To be sure, what happens during adolescence "is in many ways determined by what went before," but it also "determines much that follows" *(1968, p. 23)*. And since adolescence occupies this pivotal position in Erikson's theory—as the period that simultaneously *recapitulates* all the earlier stages of development and *anticipates* all those to come—it is impossible to discuss his account of adolescent development without examining his account of the entire human life cycle first. Hence, we turn at this point to a review of the "eight ages of man."

The Eight Ages of Man

Like Anna Freud and like Sullivan, Erikson believes that all human existence revolves around the need to maintain a certain *equilibrium.*[5] For Anna Freud, this equilibrium has to do with the gratification of various psychosexual impulses, for Sullivan, with the need to be free of anxiety. Erikson, as we have seen, focuses on the ego and seems to consider "continuity of experience" the most critical variable in personality development. If an individual is to achieve the "unity of personality" that Erikson talks about, if he is to be "whole," then he must succeed in relating the memories and experiences of one stage of life to those of every other stage. Upon close examination, it turns out that what is involved in this "striving for continuity" is an attempt to establish a whole *series* of equilibria. Each stage of life, unfolding as it does in accordance with a definite and at least partially inborn ground plan, presents its own distinctive challenge to the individual. And since the ground plan cannot unfold at all in the absence of a supporting social milieu, each stage presents a challenge to society as well.

The concept of normative crisis Erikson describes these challenges as *normative crises* or *nuclear conflicts* and asserts that there are eight of them to be resolved between birth and death.

---

[5] Of course, we have encountered this principle in the work of Jean Piaget as well.

However, just as no person can ever be completely "gratified" or utterly "anxiety free," no one can ever resolve a nuclear conflict "once and for all." It is instead a matter of tipping the balance more in one direction than in another. Consequently, each conflict or crisis leaves its mark upon the individual (indeed, it would *have* to if he is going to achieve any continuity of experience), and since the human life cycle and human civilization have, of necessity, evolved together, each conflict also leaves its mark upon society. For each of the eight ages of man, there are corresponding societal institutions and values.

Basic trust versus mistrust   A discussion of the first three ages of man reveals the extent to which Erikson's theory incorporates and elaborates upon ideas we have encountered elsewhere—specifically in Anna Freud and Sullivan. For these earliest phases, which occupy the same time span as the oral, anal, and phallic phases in psychoanalytic theory, Erikson has replaced the concept of *instinct* with that of *modality*. Erikson uses the term "modality" to describe the way in which the child's ego relates to the world, and hence it is a broader concept than "instinct."

For instance, during the age of man that corresponds to the oral stage in psychoanalytic theory, Erikson admits that the child is preoccupied with gratifying certain oral instincts, but he insists that this concern is only part of a larger one. The real issues the child faces go beyond "eating" and "sucking" and involve a much more general kind of "drinking in":

It is clear that in addition to the overwhelming need for food, a baby is, or soon becomes, receptive in many other respects. As he is willing and able to suck on appropriate objects and to swallow whatever appropriate fluids they emit, he is soon also willing and able to "take in" with his eyes whatever enters his visual field. His senses, too, seem to "take in" what feels good. *(1968, p. 98)*

One might say, in other words, that during this very early period, the infant's mode of integrating experience—in addition to his instincts—is "oral" or "incorporative" in character.

Since he is limited, for the most part, simply to taking in sensations, he must also depend very heavily on other people. His ego, which is barely beginning to form at this point, cannot provide him with much of a sense of continuity. Therefore he must rely on others to make the world sufficiently predictable and orderly:

Yet babies are sensitive and vulnerable too. In order to insure that their first experiences in this world will not only keep them alive but will also help them to co-ordinate their sensitive breathing and their metabolic and circulatory rhythms, we must see to it that we deliver to their senses stimuli as well as food in their proper intensity and at the right time; otherwise their willingness to accept may change radically into diffuse defense or into lethargy. *(1968, p. 98)*

Because of his helplessness and dependency, the infant has to have some assurance that his needs will be taken care of with reasonable promptness as they arise, for ironically, this is the only way that he can begin to overcome that initial helplessness and dependency. From having other people attend to him regularly and consistently, he builds up a storehouse of memories, images, and expectations. And once he learns that he can count on other people to appear, he also learns that he can "trust" them to disappear:

The infant's first social achievement, then, is his willingness to let the mother out of his sight without undue anxiety or rage, because she has become an inner certainty as well as an outer predictability. Such consistency, continuity, and sameness of experience provide a rudimentary sense of ego identity. . . . *(1950, p. 247)*

Erikson's first age of man is thus characterized by a nuclear conflict between trust and mistrust. No infant is probably ever so completely indulged that he completely overcomes his initial "mistrustfulness," and indeed, since the world in which he is to participate presents some very real dangers and pitfalls, a certain residue of mistrust is no doubt essential. However, to launch the child's ego properly in the arduous process of constructing an identity, it is desirable to have the balance tilt in the direction of trust.

This conflict between trust and mistrust is obviously an *interpersonal* one. In the earliest period of life the child is learning to count (or not to count) on other *people.* His interactions with them provide, in part, the basis for his own identity. Hence we detect in Erikson's concept of nuclear conflict a distinct resemblance to Sullivan. This resemblance has rarely been pointed out *(Goethals & Klos, 1970)*, and Erikson himself refers to Sullivan only in passing in his writings, but it is notable nonetheless.

Erikson, however, elaborates on this interpersonal theme somewhat differently than Sullivan did. To a greater extent than Sullivan, he introduces sociological and anthropological considerations into his account of personality development. Each age of man, as we have mentioned, is systematically correlated with a specific human "strength" or "virtue" and a more general cultural institution.

With regard to the first age of man, Erikson asserts that just as infants never quite resolve the conflict between trust and mistrust, neither do adults. The need to trust in a higher power is almost universal among adults, and hence the cultural institution derived from this first stage is religion. In a related vein, Erikson alleges that the infant's sense of trust also is a precursor of the simple and basic virtue of *faith* in adulthood:

As we overcome our universal amnesia for the frightening aspects of childhood, we may well also acknowledge gratefully the fact that, in principle, the glory of childhood also survives in adult life. Trust, then, becomes the capacity for *faith*—a vital need for which man must find some institutional confirmation. Religion, it seems is the oldest and has been the most lasting institution to serve the ritual restoration of a sense of trust in the form of faith while offering a tangible formula for a sense of evil against which it promises to arm and defend man. *(1968, p. 106)*

Autonomy versus shame and doubt Erikson's account of the second age of man reveals a similar blending of the psychoanalytic, the interpersonal, and the anthropological. He acknowledges the importance of excretory functions and "toilet training" during this stage, which occupies the same time span as the "anal phase" (roughly the ages of 18 months to 3 years). However, once again, he insists that it is the modality, the way in which the child's ego processes experience, rather than the specific id instinct, that is critical. At this point, to be sure, the child (and his parents) is likely to be much preoccupied with his anal and urethral activities, but what is reflected here is, for Erikson, only part of a much broader challenge. Having progressed beyond the passive receptiveness of the first stage, the child is now confronted with the issues of "holding on" and "letting go" in general. This is the way his sphincters operate, and in many respects, so does his ego.

The over-all significance of this second stage of early childhood lies in the rapid gains in muscular maturation, in verbalization, and in discrimination and the consequent ability—to co-ordinate a number of highly conflicting action patterns characterized by the tendencies of *"holding on"* and *"letting go."* In this and in many other ways, the still highly dependent child begins to experience his *autonomous will.* *(1968, p. 107)*

The child has advanced significantly by this stage, but he is still, as Erikson puts it, "highly dependent." Consequently, his desire to assert himself may often outstrip his ability to exert control. Almost inevitably, he finds himself at odds with his parents: "At this time sinister forces are leashed and unleashed, especially in the guerrilla warfare of unequal wills, for the child is often unequal to his own

violent will and parent and child are often unequal to each other"
(1968, p. 107). If the child attempts to be more autonomous than his
parents consider appropriate—if he persists in "holding onto" a
forbidden object, for instance, or "letting go" with a tantrum—he
may be reminded with embarrassing forcefulness that he is still
comparatively weak and helpless. Thus Erikson speaks of the nuclear
conflict of the second age of man as a struggle between a sense of
"autonomy" on the one hand and a sense of "shame and doubt" on
the other. And once again he claims (as in the case of trust versus
mistrust) that although the healthy child requires more of the former
than of the latter, it is still necessary to strike a balance:

> This stage, therefore, becomes decisive for the ratio between loving
> good will and hateful self-insistence, between cooperation and willfulness,
> and between self-expression and compulsive self-restraint. . . . Only
> parental firmness can protect [the child] against the consequences of his
> yet untrained discrimination and circumspection. But his own environment
> must also back him up in his wish to "stand on his own feet," while also
> protecting him against the now newly emerging pair of estrangements,
> namely that sense of having exposed himself prematurely and foolishly
> which we call shame or that secondary mistrust, that "double take" which
> we call doubt—doubt in himself and doubt in the firmness and perspicacity
> of his trainers. *(1968, pp. 109–110)*

Only through his interactions with his parents, then, can the child
hope to achieve a successful equilibrium between autonomy and self-
doubt. They must continue to furnish considerable support for his
still somewhat limited ego, trying not to restrict him too much, yet
often making judgments for him. Whereas before, all that was
required of them was a certain consistency and predictability, they
must now begin to instill a healthy (but not too oppressive) respect
for rules and regulations.

Accordingly, this second stage of man, like the preceding one, has
a lasting impact both on society and human nature. Because it is the
period when the child's autonomous will, his desire to do things his
way, first becomes apparent, Erikson traces the origin of "will" or
"will power" in adulthood to this stage. Since it is also the age of
man in which control and "regulations" first enter the picture significantly, Erikson draws a parallel between the parent-child conflict
and the institution of law and order: "Man's basic need for a delineation of his autonomy seems to have an institutional safeguard in the
principle of *law and order*, which in everyday life as well as in the
courts of law, apportions to each of his privileges and his limitations,
his obligations and his rights" *(1968, p. 113)*.

Initiative versus guilt   During the third age of man, the child faces a conflict similar to that of the second age. His dependence on his parents continues slowly to lessen, his skills become more refined, and his awareness of differences between his own anatomy and that of others increases. Consequently, it is natural for him to develop a personal interest in his own genitalia and an interpersonal interest in the parent of the opposite sex. But the overriding issue of the period (which corresponds to the "phallic stage" in Freudian theory) goes far beyond these rather narrow preoccupations. The Oedipal complex, Erikson asserts, is only one consequence of the many physical changes that have taken place. By the time he is three or four, the child is capable of thrusting himself into the world much more forcefully than before. His ego now functions (as his genitals will) in an "intrusive" fashion:

> The intrusive mode dominating much of the behavior of this stage characterizes a variety of configurationally "similar" activities and fantasies. These include (1) the intrusion into space by vigorous locomotion; (2) the intrusion into the unknown by consuming curiosity; (3) the intrusion into other people's ears and minds by the aggressive voice; (4) the intrusion upon or into other bodies by physical attack; (5) and, often most frightening, the thought of the phallus intruding the female body. *(1968, p. 116)*

All of these activities, not just the patently sexual ones, contribute to an emerging sense of initiative.

However, it is obvious at this point that the attempt to translate psychosexual instincts into ego modalities has run into a major problem. Only the little boy possesses a potentially "intrusive" set of genitals. The little girl's genitals are and will remain "receptive" by contrast. Clearly, if Erikson is to continue drawing parallels between the way certain parts of the body (i.e., the mouth, the anus, and the genitals) function and the way in which the ego develops, his theory must accommodate this basic difference.

His theory does, in fact, contain such accommodation, but it is one which remains surprisingly close to the orthodox psychoanalytic model:[6]

> Girls often undergo a sobering change at this stage, because they observe sooner or later that although their locomotor, mental, and social intrusiveness is as vigorous as that of the boy's, thus permitting them to

---

[6] This issue is perhaps the most controversial aspect of Erikson's theory, and we shall take a more detailed look at it in Chapter 12.

become perfectly good tomboys, they lack one item, the penis, and with it, important prerogatives, in most cultures and classes. While the boy has this visible, erectable, and comprehensible organ to which he can attach dreams of adult bigness, the girl's clitoris only poorly sustains dreams of sexual equality, and she does not even have breasts as analogously tangible tokens of her future. *(1968, p. 117)*

Erikson does not mean to imply, apparently, that the little girl's anatomical peculiarities will hopelessly cripple her efforts to establish a sense of initiative. But he is forced, because of his ties to orthodox psychoanalysis on this point, to designate two *kinds* of initiative, an intrusive "masculine" type and a receptive "feminine" type. As they enter the third age of man, Erikson declares, the little boy and the little girl begin to relate to the world in distinctly different ways. While the male child can actively seek what he wants in life, the girl must adopt a more passive means of satisfying her needs:

The ambulatory stage, that of play and infantile genitality, adds to the inventory of basic social modalities in both sexes that of "making," first in the childlike sense of "being on the make." There are no simpler, stronger words to match the basic social modalities of Basic English. The words suggest enjoyment of competition, insistence on goal, pleasure of conquest. *In the boy the emphasis remains on making by head-on attack; in the girl it may turn to "catching" either by aggressive snatching or by making herself attractive and endearing. The child thus develops the prerequisites for masculine or feminine initiative and, above all, some sexual self-images which will become essential ingredients in the positive and negative aspects of his future identity.* *(1968, p. 118, italics added)*

Whatever differences in personal style they may acquire during this period, however, children of both sexes must learn to temper their activities somewhat. As in the preceding period, their efforts to assert themselves inevitably meet with certain obstacles. Using the Oedipal situation once more as an example, Erikson describes the likely outcome of the child's efforts to compete for and with the parents:

. . . initiative brings with it *anticipatory rivalry* with those who were there first and who may therefore occupy with their superior equipment the field toward which one's initiative is first directed. Jealousy and rivalry, those often embittered and yet essentially futile attempts at demarcating a sphere of unquestioned privilege, now come to a climax in a final contest for a favored position with one of the parents: the inevitable and necessary failure leads to guilt and anxiety. *(1968, pp. 118–119)*

Thus, Erikson characterizes the nuclear conflict of the third age of man as a struggle between initiative and guilt. To be sure, guilt, like initiative, can be overdone. Simply because the child has become so much more active and expansive, he can imagine himself committing horrible offenses and suffering equally horrible punishments. But a certain restrained sense of guilt is nonetheless necessary to act as a counterweight to unbridled initiative.

This sense of guilt is, furthermore, more "internalized" and "mature" than the sense of shame which emerged during the second stage. It permits the child to take greater responsibility for his own actions: "The child . . . now not only feels afraid of being found out, but he also hears the 'inner voice' of self-observation, self-guidance, and self-punishment, which divides him radically within himself: a new and powerful estrangement. This is the ontogenetic corner-stone of morality" *(1968, p. 119)*.

Whether the balance is tipped too much toward guilt depends, in large part, on the child's interaction with his parents. They can overburden his young conscience and stifle his developing sense of initiative in the process, or they can help him to channel his energies constructively. Although they must discourage some of the child's attempts to compete with them directly, Erikson declares, it is equally important for the parent to indicate what he *can* do:

> . . . the play age relies on the existence of some basic family, which teaches the child by patient example where play ends and irreversible purpose begins and where "don'ts" are superseded by sanctioned avenues of vigorous action. For the children now look for new identifications which seem to promise a field of initiative with less of the conflict and guilt which attach to the hopeless rivalry of the home. *(1968, p. 121)*

Adults can tell stories of the "big life" beyond the nuclear family and the "great past" of significant dreams and achievements, thus stimulating the child's imagination with visions of what he might become someday. If all goes well, the third age of man "eventually results not only in a moral sense constricting the horizon of the permissible; it also sets the direction toward the possible and the tangible which attaches infantile dreams to the varied goals of tech-nology and culture" *(1968, p. 121)*.

By imparting to him some impression of the life he can hope to lead "when he grows up" and of the goals he can aspire to, the parent eases some of the pain and frustration of this period for the child, and this in turn benefits the culture. Childish "dreams of glory," Erikson suggests, become the foundations for ambition in adulthood, and without ambition a society would become dull and lifeless. Hence, although the clash between initiative and guilt does not leave its mark upon society in the form of a particular institution like religion or a specific principle like law and order, Erikson does believe that a general *ethos of action* can be traced to this third normative crisis. In other words, the problem of how to channel human energies may originate in childhood, but it remains an issue for adults as well, and each culture must furnish certain guidelines for adult activity. Furthermore, children must begin to feel, and adults must retain the feeling, that their actions serve some *purpose*. Thus, in addition to the ethos of action, Erikson derives the mature virtue of "purposefulness" from the third age of man.

Industry versus inferiority   If Erikson's account of the first three stages of the human life cycle contain some strong psychoanalytic overtones, his description of the fourth phase represents a notable departure. Although he remarks that this phase (which corresponds to "latency" in psychoanalytic theory) "differs from the earlier ones in that it is not a swing from an inner upheaval to a new mastery" *(1968, p. 126)*, he still considers it to be a far more significant period than do the orthodox Freudians—and in this respect he once more resembles Sullivan. Erikson's fourth age of man encompasses the "elementary school years" (roughly the ages of six to twelve), and like Sullivan, he emphasizes the impact that education can have during these years. But Erikson's approach is again more "anthropological." Sullivan limits his analysis, for the most part, to American society. Erikson makes it clear that he considers the nuclear conflict of this phase universal:

> When they reach school age, children in all cultures receive some systematic instruction, although it is by no means always the kind which literate people must organize around teachers who have learned how to teach literacy. In preliterate people much is learned from adults who become teachers by acclamation rather than by appointment and much is learned from older children, but the knowledge gained is related to the basic skills of simple technologies which can be understood the moment the child gets ready to handle the utensils, the tools, the weapons (or facsimiles thereof) used by the big people. He enters the technology of his tribe very gradually but also very directly. *(1968, pp. 112–113)*

To be sure, the educational system in more advanced societies is usually a more formal one, but Erikson insists that the difference is only a matter of degree:

> More literate people, with more specialized careers, must prepare the child by teaching him things which first of all make him literate. He is then given the widest possible basic education for the greatest number of

possible careers. The greater the specialization, the more indistinct the goal of initiative becomes, the more complicated the social reality, and the vaguer the father's and mother's role in it. Between childhood and adulthood, then, our children go to school, and school skill seems to many to be a world all by itself, with its own goals and limitations, its achievements and disappointments. *(1968, p. 123)*

In all cultures, the channeling and direction of the child's energies that began during the previous stage must continue. Only at this point does the ultimate goal become clearer. As he enters the "school years" (whether formally or informally), the child begins to acquire the skills needed to *work* within his particular society. Even in the more advanced cultures, these skills remain the prosaic ones of reading, writing, and arithmetic. Even in the most highly industrialized society, they are the basic building blocks, or what Erikson calls the "tools" of technology. But to learn these skills requires a degree of discipline (the same kind of discipline that will presumably be applied later, "on the job"). Hence, during the fourth age of man, all societies, especially the more technologically specialized ones, are faced with the task of transforming the sense of initiative into a "sense of industry."

The entire process, of course, is not without its pitfalls. A child who has been overprotected by his family "may still want his mommy more than knowledge; he may still prefer to be the baby at home than the big child at school" *(1968, p. 124)*. Or he may find that the educational system has no particular use for his talents: ". . . school life may fail to sustain the promises of earlier stages in that nothing he has learned to do well so far seems to count with his fellows or his teacher. And then again, he may be potentially able to excel in ways which are dormant and which, if not evoked now, may develop late or never" *(1968, p. 124)*. But what is perhaps most serious is that the youngster inevitably begins to learn something at school about society's "pecking order"—and hence about prejudice and discrimination:

It is at this point that wider society becomes significant to the child by admitting him to roles preparatory to the actuality of technology and economy. Where he finds out immediately, however, that the color of his skin or the background of his parents rather than his wish and will to learn are the factors that decide his worth as a pupil or apprentice, the human propensity for feeling unworthy may be fatefully aggravated as a determinant of character development. *(1968, p. 124)*

During the fourth age of man, then, the child's sense of industry must always compete against a "sense of inferiority." However, it is important to stress once more that neither, according to Erikson, should be allowed to become overpowering. The disadvantages of permitting youngsters to develop a sense of inferiority are already well known to educators, but it is also possible to produce a child who is too industrious.

The demands of the period thus place a special burden on teachers, who represent to the child a whole new class of adults outside the family. If they are too much bent on maintaining discipline and "making early school life an extension of grim adulthood," the child may

become entirely dependent on prescribed duties. He may thus learn much that is absolutely necessary and he may develop an unshakable sense of duty. But he may never unlearn an unnecessary and costly self-restraint with which he may later make his own life and other people's lives miserable, and in fact spoil, in turn, his own children's natural desire to learn and to work. *(1968, p. 126)*

On the other hand, some amount of guidance, however gentle and unobtrusive, is probably necessary. The trend toward permissiveness, for example, in American education, "when carried to an extreme, leads not only to the well-known popular objection that children do not learn anything any more but also to such feelings in children as those expressed in the by now famous question of a metropolitan child: 'Teacher, *must* we do today what we want to do?' " *(1968, pp. 126–127)*. The balance to be struck between industry and inferiority is, in short, a delicate one, and like all nuclear conflicts this one too purportedly leaves its mark upon human nature and society. The more fortunate child emerges from the fourth stage of life with his self-esteem intact and a sense of industry that can later, Erikson claims, be translated into a sense of *competence.* He also begins to learn a good deal about the kinds of work his society considers valuable and where he himself may hope to fit within the occupational hierarchy. In Erikson's words, he begins to grasp the prevailing *technological ethos* of his culture.

Identity versus identity confusion   During the four ages of man which we have outlined so far, the youngster's ego, assuming no disasters have occurred, has gradually added to its repertoire of skills and faculties. It has gradually become more and more capable of synthesizing and integrating experience. Since the need for continuity is supposed to be such a strong one, the ego will presumably *continue* to develop during the remaining four ages of man. However, as we have noted, Erikson considers adolescence, the fifth age of man, a kind of "critical" period in this respect. Since the child's ego has already been set upon a certain course, the events of this period are partially predetermined. But Erikson claims that what happens during adolescence will itself determine "much that follows."[7]

Up to this point, as the child has continued to mature and assimilate the customs and values of his culture, he has inevitably learned a good deal about himself. His interactions with other people have begun to give him an impression of the characteristics he shares with others and also of those that are unique to him alone. He has begun, in short, to formulate an identity. This process is, however, exceedingly complex, involving the ego in a continuous series of back and forth maneuvers:

> . . . identity formation employs a process of simultaneous reflection and observation, a process taking place on all levels of mental functioning, by which the individual judges himself in the light of what he perceives to be the way in which others judge him in comparison to themselves and to a typology significant to them; while he judges their way of judging him in the light of how he perceives himself in comparison to them and to types that have become relevant to him. *(1968, pp. 22–23)*

(Sullivan, of course, outlines a similar set of mental operations in his account of "supervisory patterns," but he refers to such phenomena primarily to explain "socially appropriate" behavior.) Nor can this process result in an identity, a "conscious sense of individual uniqueness," prior to adolescence.

Why is adolescence such a crucial period for identity formation? Erikson mentions several reasons, but the basic one seems to hinge upon the capacities of the adolescent ego. In order for a person to formulate an identity, in order for him to determine the extent to which he is:

a. like all other people
b. like some other people
c. like no other person

he must be able to entertain a number of different alternatives in quick succession.[8] He must be able to place his existence within what Erikson has termed an "historical perspective," evaluating the sort of individual he has been in the past, the sort of individual he is at present, and the sort he has some chance of becoming in the future. This entire process, which involves weighing a great many possibilities and alternatives simultaneously, is obviously

---

[7] We may observe parenthetically that this notion is similar to Sullivan's concept of "developmental thresholds."

[8] This formula is, of course, a paraphrase of Kluckhohn and Murray. See Chapter 2, p. 191.

rather taxing intellectually. It depends upon a complex set of cognitive skills, and these skills, as we know from our discussion of Piaget's work, do not develop until adolescence.

Indeed, Erikson himself refers to Piaget in his examination of the crystallization of an identity during adolescence:

> The cognitive gifts developing during the first half of the second decade add a powerful tool to the tasks of youth. Piaget calls the gains in cognition made toward the middle teens the achievement of "formal operations." This means that youth can now operate on hypothetical propositions and can think of possible variables and potential relations—and think of them in thought alone, independent of certain concrete checks previously necessary. . . . Such cognitive orientation forms not a contrast but a complement to the need of the young person to develop a sense of identity, for, from among all possible and imaginable relations, he must make a series of ever-narrowing selections of personal, occupational, sexual, and ideological commitments. *(1968, p. 245)*

Erikson points out that the adolescent, in addition to possessing the necessary skills to decide upon an identity, is also faced with certain *pressures* to do so. His ego is able to synthesize his perceptions and memories better than the child's ego, and it also has more perceptions and memories to synthesize. Having entered a stage that is "transitional" between childhood and adulthood, he is made aware of all the adjustments—personal, occupational, sexual, and ideological—that will be required of him before he reaches maturity. As Erikson observes:

> This is unavoidable at a time of life when the body changes its proportions radically, when genital puberty floods body and imagination with all manner of impulses, when intimacy with the other sex approaches and is, on occasion forced on the young person, and when the immediate future confronts one with too many conflicting possibilities and choices. *(1968, pp. 132–133)*

If he is not to be overwhelmed by choice, the adolescent simply must begin to define himself along certain dimensions. He can build upon the identifications of the past in this endeavor—the feelings of trust, autonomy, initiative, and industry that have hopefully resulted from his attempts to cope with other normative crises—but he must look ahead to the nuclear conflicts of adulthood as well as develop his *own* strategies for meeting them. Consequently, the identity that is finally settled upon toward the end of adolescence "is superordinated to any single identification with individuals of the past:

it includes all significant identifications but it also alters them in order to make a unique and reasonably coherent whole of them" *(1968, p. 161)*.

Since so much is happening at once, since the adolescent must make a great many decisions about himself not merely on the basis of what he has become but also upon his best guess of what he is *likely* to become as well, there is considerable potential during this period for indecision and disorientation. Erikson therefore describes the nuclear conflict of the fifth age of man as "identity versus identity confusion."

We have already examined the precursors of this conflict in our discussion of the previous four stages. But the adolescent's conflict also contains intimations of the three to follow—the crises of intimacy, generativity, and integrity. Hence it is necessary to take a brief look at them—these three nuclear conflicts of adulthood which are anticipated during adolescence—before examining the identity crisis itself more closely.

Intimacy versus isolation   Since Erikson considers social interaction one of the inescapable and fundamental influences on personality development, we can scarcely accuse him of neglecting this particular factor. Indeed, we have several times drawn comparisons between his theory and Sullivan's, which also places a great deal of emphasis on the interpersonal. However, Erikson's account of the sixth nuclear conflict, "intimacy versus isolation," reveals an interesting difference, and it is one that serves to clarify the concept of identity.

Sullivan speaks of a "need for intimacy" which arises during the preadolescent era (a phase that overlaps Erikson's fourth stage to some extent). He argues that the preadolescent's need for a close relationship propels him in the direction of a "chum," and that through interacting with his chum, the youngster clarifies his own self-image. Erikson insists that a sturdy self-image is necessary first, and that rather than being a *result* of intimacy, identity is instead a *prerequisite*. Without knowing something about his own peculiar needs, quirks, passions, and aversions, a person cannot appreciate anyone else's. Nor is he likely to find anyone who will appreciate his. And since an individual's identity is not supposed to take on its decisive stamp before the end of adolescence, in Erikson's theory there is no mention of "intimacy" before young adulthood.

As Erikson describes it, "true intimacy" is "really a counterpointing as well as a fusing of identities" *(1968, p. 135)*. What passes for closeness in adolescence—the "teenage romance"—is often mere fusion instead. The teenage couple who cannot bear to be apart betray the fact that they are still somewhat unsure of themselves: "To a considerable extent adolescent love is an attempt to arrive at a definition of one's identity by projecting one's diffused self-image on another and by seeing it thus reflected and gradually clarified. This is why so much young love is conversation" *(1968, p. 132).* There may, on the other hand, be equally marked attempts to exclude others during adolescence, to seek a sense of identity through simple "counterpointing":

> Clarification can also be sought by destructive means. Young people can become remarkably clannish, intolerant, and cruel in their exclusion of others who are "different," in skin color or cultural background, in tastes and gifts, and often in entirely petty aspects of dress and gesture arbitrarily selected as the signs of an in-grouper or out-grouper. *(1968, p. 132)*

As the oscillation between these two extremes gradually subsides and the youngster's identity takes shape, a true capacity for intimacy emerges. But this capacity must itself be weighed against a sense of *isolation.* In Erikson's view, a successful young adult must be able to express warmth and affection for others, and he must be able to distinguish his friends from his enemies, but he must also feel sufficiently secure about himself to endure—and even to enjoy—being by himself. The two major preoccupations of adulthood, love and work, require a balance between these two opposing trends:

> Freud was once asked what he thought a normal person should be able to do well. The questioner probably expected a complicated "deep" answer. But Freud simply said, *"Lieben und arbeiten"* ("to love and to work"). It pays to ponder this simple formula: it grows deeper as you think about it. For when Freud said "love," he meant the generosity of intimacy as well as genital love; when he said love and work, he meant a general work productiveness which would not preoccupy the individual to the extent that he might lose his right or capacity to be a sexual and a loving being. *(1968, p. 136)*

The individual who fears closeness may withdraw from others and use his work as a protective shield. But the person who cannot bear to be alone, who can never shut others out, cannot work.

Ideally, this age of man, with its emphasis on love and productivity, is characterized by a broadening of social horizons. In young adulthood, the individual has typically moved out beyond the confines of the parental home and into a larger and more variegated community. In the healthy young adult this new sense of participation encourages a kind of fellow feeling and solidarity which did not exist before. If the virtue that is derived from this stage is "love," then,

Erikson declares, the societal institution associated with young adulthood is a *system of ethics*. For (as we have seen from Kohlberg's work) this sort of system reaches beyond principles like "duty" and "obedience" and underscores instead the inherent dignity of all mankind:

> ... as the areas of adult responsibility are gradually delineated, as the competitive encounter, the erotic bond, and merciless enmity are differentiated from each other, they eventually become subject to that *ethical sense* which is the mark of the adult and which takes over from the ideological conviction of adolescence and the moralism of childhood. *(1968, p. 136)*

Generativity versus stagnation   But although the young adult is more actively engaged in the community than the adolescent, his participation is still somewhat limited. Newly capable of intimacy, recently initiated into the world of work, he has yet to make his contribution to society in a larger sense. Ideally, this contribution is made during the seventh age of man. Erikson, in fact, hints that it *must* occur if the mature adult is to retain his sense of wholeness and purpose:

> Evolution has made man a teaching as well as a learning animal, for dependency and maturity are reciprocal: mature man needs to be needed, and maturity is guided by the nature of that which must be cared for. *Generativity*, then is primarily the concern for establishing and guiding the next generation. *(1968, p. 138)*

Perhaps the most obvious way of demonstrating concern for the next generation is to *produce* it, and for many people (particularly women) the most visible sign of generativity is raising a family. Indeed, in his account of childhood and adolescence, Erikson continually makes indirect references to the seventh stage of life. Adults are, after all, necessary to ensure proper development through all of the more dependent ages of man. Without their care, no sense of trust, autonomy, initiative, industry—no sense of identity itself—is possible. Their conviction that what they are doing is meaningful, and their feeling that it is somehow consistent with their goals in life, support the child's attempts to integrate his experiences:

> We have already suggested that the infant's sense of trust is a reflection of parental faith; similarly, the sense of autonomy is a reflection of the parents' dignity as autonomous beings. For no matter what we do in detail, the child will primarily feel what it is we live by as loving, cooperative, and firm beings, and what makes us hateful, anxious, and divided in ourselves. *(1968, p. 113)*

In his account of this mature stage of life, Erikson underscores once more his dictum that "a family can bring up a baby only by being brought up by him," but he seems to imply that human beings *need* to form families and bring up children as well.

However, although Erikson is particularly partial to child care as a vehicle for generativity, he admits that it is not the sole means of enhancing society. His acknowledgment of other contributions sounds a bit backhanded, but he observes nonetheless: "There are, of course, people, who from misfortune or because of special and genuine gifts in other directions, do not apply this drive to offspring of their own, but to other forms of altruistic concern and creativity which may absorb their parental drive" *(1968, p. 138)*.

He is also well aware that the simple act of producing a child is not sufficient to ensure a feeling of generativity:

On the other hand, the mere fact of having or even wanting children does not "achieve" generativity. Some young parents suffer, it seems, from a retardation in the ability to develop true care. The reasons are often to be found in early childhood impressions, in faulty identifications with parents; in excessive self-love based on a too strenuously self-made personality; and in the lack of some faith, some "belief in the species" which would make a child appear to be a welcome trust. *(1968, p. 138)*

Indeed, those who have children merely because it is the "thing to do" may find themselves, in later life, oppressed by a sense of *stagnation*—as may those who discover themselves locked into boring and unrewarding jobs. Stagnation, then, is the negative counterpart to generativity. (Although in keeping with Erikson's assertion that the resolution of each nuclear conflict represents a balance or equilibrium, we might assume that it is the *fear* of stagnation which helps to keep people productive.)

It should be evident by now that "care" is the adult virtue which Erikson attributes to the seventh age of man. But because "care" implies an all-encompassing concern, Erikson does not limit himself to describing a single institution which can be traced to this period. He claims instead that generativity is inherent in *all* cultural standards and values:

As to the institutions which reinforce generativity and safeguard it, one can only say that *all* institutions by their very nature codify the ethics of generative succession. Generativity is itself a driving power in human organization. And the stages of childhood and adulthood are a system of generation and regeneration to which institutions such as shared households and divided labor strive to give continuity. *(1968, p. 139)*

Integrity versus despair As has no doubt become apparent, there is a philosophical and "humanistic" quality to Erikson's work, and this is precisely the note upon which he concludes his account of the human life cycle. If one of the paramount needs in human existence is to find meaning and continuity in experience, nowhere is it more evident than in this eighth and final stage of man.

In our culture and in many others (though by no means in all), this final reckoning often brings images of *despair* to mind. The old person is thought to have lost his health and faculties. He is portrayed as becoming too weak, too disorganized, or too "set in his ways" for productive work, too much a relic of a generation past. No doubt people who must suffer through their last years in such a state are left to wonder if their lives did indeed have much validity:

> Clinical and anthropological evidence suggest that the lack or loss of this accrued ego integration is signified by *disgust* and *despair*: fate is not accepted as the frame of life, death not as its finite boundary. Despair expresses the feeling that time is short, too short for the attempt to start another life and try out alternate roads to integrity. Such despair is hidden behind a show of disgust, a misanthropy, or a chronic contemptuous displeasure with particular institutions and particular people—a disgust and displeasure which, where not allied with a vision of a superior life, only signify the individual's contempt of himself. *(1968, p. 140)*

However, as Erikson reminds us, even as he describes the ravages that time can inflict, there is another side to the nuclear conflict of old age and an alternative to despair. If the elderly person can believe that he has met the crises of the previous stages with good grace and reasonable success, if he can believe that his has been a unique and worthwhile destiny, then a sense of *integrity* may predominate. His ego and his identity have come through the life cycle intact, and his own life can be placed at long last in truly historical perspective:

> In the aging person who has taken care of things and people and has adapted himself to the triumphs and disappointments of being, by necessity, the originator of others and the generator of things and ideas—only in him the fruit of the seven stages gradually ripens. I know no better word for it than *integrity*. Lacking a clear definition, I shall point to a few attributes of this stage of mind. It is the ego's accrued assurance of its proclivity for order and meaning—an emotional integration faithful to the image-bearers of the past and ready to take, and eventually to renounce, leadership in the present. It is the acceptance of one's one and only life cycle and of the people who have become significant to it as something that had to be and that, by necessity permitted of no substitutions. It thus means a new and

different love of one's parents, free of the wish that they should have been different, and an acceptance of the fact that one's life is one's own responsibility. It is a sense of comradeship with men and women of distant times and of different pursuits who have created orders and objects and sayings conveying human dignity and love. Although aware of the relativity of all the various life styles which have given meaning to human striving, the possessor of integrity is ready to defend the dignity of his own life style against all physical and economic threats. For he knows that an individual life is the accidental coincidence of but one life cycle with but one segment of history and that for him all human integrity stands and falls with the one style of integrity of which he partakes. *(1968, pp. 139–140)*

And inspired by the example of those who have achieved integrity in old age, Erikson designates *wisdom* as the enduring human virtue of this final epoch in the life cycle, and he describes *tradition*, the standard that to some extent must serve as a yardstick for all lives, as its monument to society.

Here is a fitting place to repeat Erikson's persistent theme— that human nature, social institutions, and the survival of the human race are all mutually interdependent. The normative crises in life arise from the interaction between the biological ground plan of the species and the social organization we call "culture." The culture exists to ensure and guide the successful unfolding of the ground plan but it relies for its future existence upon this same ground plan. It is upon the integration of the two, then, that the "sequence of generations" depends:

From the stages of life, then, such dispositions as faith, will power, purposefulness, competence, fidelity, love, care, wisdom—all criteria of vital individual strength—also flow into the life of institutions. Without them, institutions wilt; but without the spirit of institutions pervading the patterns of care and love, instruction and training, no strength could emerge from the sequence of generations. *(1968, p. 141)*

We have identified all the virtues listed except the fifth one, fidelity. It is hence appropriate to recall at this point that Erikson assigns to the fifth age of man, adolescence, a central role in the entire complicated cycle of human life. Indeed, his characterizations of adolescence and old age are curiously similar in this respect. Old age provides the final measure of identity. Near the end of his life, the individual can determine how successful he was in coordinating his unique talents with his opportunities. But what happens (or does not happen) during adolescence, according to Erikson, may decide to a considerable degree what the assessment will be in old age. The elderly individual strives to put his entire past in perspective, with the realization that there is little left of the future. The adolescent attempts to put both his past and future in perspective and to come to some conclusions about his prospects. The sense of identity that is derived from these attempts will become a key force in shaping that future. And having reviewed the basic concepts and broad outlines of Erikson's theory, we are ready to focus more exclusively on the period that he considers so important.

REFERENCES

ERIKSON, E. Autobiographic Notes on the Identity Crisis. *Daedalus*, 1970, **99**, 730–759.

ERIKSON, E. *Childhood and Society.* New York: Norton, 1950.

ERIKSON, E. *Identity: Youth and Crisis.* New York: Norton, 1968.

GOETHALS, G., & KLOS, D. *Experiencing Youth.* Boston: Little, Brown, 1970.

HARTMANN, H. *Ego Psychology and the Problem of Adaptation.* New York: International Universities, 1939.

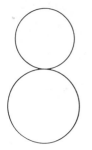

Erikson's Theory of Adolescent Development

Adolescence is accorded its position of special importance in Eriksonian theory basically because it is considered to be a particularly decisive period for identity formation. A firm sense of identity is, as we have seen, essential for "further and truly individual maturation" *(Erikson,1968, p. 89)*—for a really meaningful adult life—and only at the end of adolescence can such a sense of identity emerge. To be sure, the other stages of life present their crises too—crises of trust, autonomy, industry, and integrity, for example—but "not until adolescence does the individual develop the prerequisites in physiological growth, mental maturation, and social responsibility to experience and pass through the crisis of identity" *(1968, p. 91)*.

This crisis, furthermore, incorporates elements of all the others. It is foreshadowed to some extent in each of the four nuclear conflicts that precede it; it, in turn, recapitulates all of them, and it *also* anticipates the three nuclear conflicts of adulthood that are to follow. Identity formation, in short, entails a very complex set of relationships among the various stages of the human life cycle, and adolescence sits Janus-like in the middle of it all.

The Epigenetic Chart

To clarify the entire process, Erikson has devised an "epigenetic chart," which we reproduce in Figure 2. There are a vertical axis (squares I,5–V,5), a horizontal axis (squares V,1–V,8), and a diagonal (squares I,1; II, 2; III,3; IV, 4; V, 5; VI, 6; VII, 7; and VIII, 8). The diagonal is readily recognizable as consisting of the eight ages of man. The vertical axis represents the specific contributions of the four childhood stages to the adolescent identity crisis, and the horizontal axis represents the various aspects of the identity crisis itself. Having already reviewed the diagonal (which describes the eight ages of man), we can now turn to the vertical and horizontal axes.

The Vertical Axis

In addition to leaving its mark upon human nature and society, each of the first four ages of man has an impact on the adolescent identity crisis, as might be expected. In fact, the chart implies that if the child's experiences in any one of these four stages are devastating enough, his identity may be irrevocably "foreclosed." He may arrive at adolescence with too great a sense of *isolation, doubt, inhibition,* or *futility* to carry out the complex integration necessary for development of a truly viable identity. If the youngster is fortunate, however, each stage of childhood contributes more on the positive than on the negative side: "namely, the primitive *trust* in mutual recognition; the rudiments of a *will* to be oneself; the *anticipation* of what one might become; and the capacity to *learn* how to be, with skill, what one is in the process of becoming" *(1968, p. 180).* These precursors of identity constitute, in part, the basis for a "conscious sense of individual uniqueness" in adolescence.

The Horizontal Axis

However, since we are focusing on adolescence, it is the horizontal axis that is our chief concern, for it describes the adolescent identity crisis and reveals its relationship to all the other normative crises of the human life cycle. The nuclear conflict of adolescence as outlined in Eriksonian theory involves the resolution of seven "part conflicts,"[1] each of which mirrors one of the four nuclear conflicts of childhood *or* one of the three crises of adulthood. A firm sense of identity requires the successful resolution of all seven. Only in this way can the individual come to terms with his past and adequately prepare himself for the future. Although the adolescent must struggle with many part conflicts simultaneously, it would no doubt be useful to examine each of them separately.

Temporal perspective versus time confusion   The reconciliation of the past with the future obviously hinges upon a sense of time, and this reconciliation is fittingly the first part conflict that Erikson outlines in his description of the adolescent identity crisis. In order to formulate a coherent plan for his adult life, the adolescent must examine what he has become and ponder what he would like to become. He must, in order to direct his energies, be able to estimate on the basis of his past experience how long it will take him to achieve what he has chosen to. One essential component of a viable identity, then, is a sense of *temporal perspective.* But because the youngster must sort through a multitude of memories, anticipations, and possibilities in coordinating his past with his future, there is ample potential for *time confusion:*

> . . . every adolescent, I would believe, knows at least fleeting moments of being thus at odds with time itself. In its normal and transitory form, this new kind of mistrust quickly or gradually yields to outlooks permitting and demanding an intense and even fanatic investment in a future, or a rapid succession in a number of possible futures.   *(1968, p. 181)*

The attempt to match previous history with future prospects represents a kind of balancing act for the adolescent, but this problem is not an entirely new one.

Indeed, Erikson compares these youthful efforts with those of the infant during the very first age of man: "The experience of time arises only from the infant's adaptation to initial cycles of need tension, delay of satisfaction, and satiation" *(1968, p. 181).* The infant gains a very primitive impression of the continuity that we call "time" from the comings and goings of those who care for him. Hopefully, he learns to "trust" these figures to reappear consistently and punctually rather than falling victim to "mistrust," with all its attendant disorganization and unpredictability. The adolescent's

---

[1] The term "part conflict" is ours, rather than Erikson's. However, we feel fairly safe in having coined it. When Erikson describes the syndrome of "acute identity confusion" (which we shall review in Chapter 11), he refers to the various manifestations as "part-symptoms."

	1	2	3	4	5	6	7	8
VIII								INTEGRITY versus DESPAIR
VII							GENERATIVITY versus STAGNATION	
VI						INTIMACY versus ISOLATION		
V	Temporal Perspective versus Time Confusion	Self-Certainty versus Self-Consciousness	Role Experimentation versus Role Fixation	Apprenticeship versus Work Paralysis	IDENTITY versus IDENTITY CONFUSION	Sexual Polarization versus Bisexual Confusion	Leader- and Followership versus Authority Confusion	Ideological Commitment versus Confusion of Values
IV				INDUSTRY versus INFERIORITY	Task Identification versus Sense of Futility			
III			INITIATIVE versus GUILT		Anticipation of Roles versus Role Inhibition			
II		AUTONOMY versus SHAME, DOUBT			Will to Be Oneself versus Self-Doubt			
I	TRUST versus MISTRUST				Mutual Recognition versus Autistic Isolation			

Figure 2. Erikson's Epigenetic Chart. (From Erik Erikson, *Identity: Youth and Crisis*, New York: Norton, 1968. Copyright © 1968 by W. W. Norton & Company, Inc.

efforts to put the time clock of his own life in perspective, although much more elaborate, thus enlarge upon the original nuclear conflict.

Self-certainty versus self-consciousness Erikson highlights a similar parallel in his account of the second part conflict of adolescence. Assimilating the past and planning for the future implies a certain self-confidence. The youngster has to believe that his previous history fits together and makes sense, and he also has to feel that he stands a reasonable chance of accomplishing his aims in adulthood. Erikson calls this inner conviction *self-certainty.*

Self-certainty, however, can be acquired only through self-examination, and therein lies a particular danger. In his attempts to weigh his assets and liabilities, the adolescent may find himself suffering from a painful *self-consciousness*:

Self-consciousness is a new edition of that original doubt which concerned the trustworthiness of the parents and of the child himself—only in adolescence such self-conscious doubt concerns the reliability of the whole span of childhood which is now left behind and the trustworthiness of the whole social universe now envisaged. The obligation now to commit oneself with a sense of free will to one's autonomous identity can arouse a painful over-all ashamedness somehow comparable to the original shame and rage over being visible all around to all-knowing adults—only such shame now adheres to one's having a public personality exposed to age mates and to be judged by leaders. *(1968, p. 183)*

For most young people, Erikson contends, the conflict is resolved more or less happily: "All of this in the normal course of events is outbalanced by *self-certainty* now characterized by a definite sense of independence from the family as the matrix of self-images and a sureness of anticipation" *(1968, p. 183)*. But as is clear, this second part conflict harks back to an earlier nuclear conflict. In his attempts to achieve a mature sense of self, the youngster elaborates upon the basic sense of autonomy that emerged during the second crisis of childhood. There is an echo in the self-awareness of the adolescent of the toddler's dim recognition that he is an autonomous being. Similarly, the adolescent's self-consciousness recalls the more primitive shame and doubt of this earlier period.

Role experimentation versus role fixation The adolescent, of course, has a much more complicated world to deal with than the small child, and many more possibilities and alternatives to sift through. Before settling into his niche in society, it is desirable for the youngster to assess all these choices and to try out many of the roles he is to play. Only in this way can he discover where his true tastes and talents lie. Erikson thus speaks of the importance of *role experimentation* during adolescence.

And here too there is a parallel with an earlier phase. During the third age of man, the child's increased mobility and his developing verbal skills encourage a sense of initiative. The teenager's "experiments" thus recall the more tentative explorations of the child. Similarly, the sense of guilt that belongs to the third age of man may foreshadow a more pervasive sense of inner restraint. The youngster who finds himself bewildered by too many possibilities or restricted by too few may experience a kind of *role fixation.*[2] Indeed, such an adolescent may discover that it is easier to

derive a sense of identity out of a total identification with that which he is least supposed to be than to struggle for a feeling of reality in acceptable roles that are unattainable with his inner means. The statement of a young man that "I would rather be quite insecure than a little secure" and that of a young woman "at least in the gutter I'm a genius" circumscribe the relief following the total choice of a negative identity. *(1968, p. 178)*

Fortunately, most youngsters—even in their wildest antics—are not compelled to make such a drastic choice. Society institutionalizes their experimentation under the guise of "sowing wild oats": "The normal expression of relatively guilt-free and in fact more or less 'delinquent' initiative in youth, however, is an experimentation with roles which follows the unwritten codes of adolescent subsocieties and thus is not lacking a discipline of its own" *(1968, p. 184)*.

Apprenticeship versus work paralysis   And, of course, one of the most important choices to be weighed and tested during adolescence has to do with work. Certainly, the occupation eventually chosen constitutes a rather critical element in the youngster's emerging identity. Once entered into, his job will play a large part in determining his view of himself and his place in society. And again, as in the case of the previous part conflict, it is desirable for the adolescent to have a kind of trial period, an opportunity to "try out," before deciding: "Social institutions support the strength and distinctiveness of the budding work identity by offering those who are still learning and experimenting a certain status of *apprenticeship*, a moratorium characterized by defined duties and sanctioned competition as well as by special license" *(1968, p. 185)*. And it is

[2] In earlier accounts of the identity crisis, Erikson refers to "role fixation" as "negative identity." We must confess to preferring the latter term to the former.

even easier to detect in this apprenticeship the residue of an earlier nuclear conflict. The fourth age of man, which just precedes adolescence, is, after all, associated with the development of a sense of industry. It seems reasonable to assume that in pondering and exploring his future vocation, the adolescent relies on skills he has acquired during this previous stage.

Nor is it difficult to see how a child's sense of inferiority could become the basis for a feeling of *work paralysis* in youth. Although most teenagers eventually find a place in the occupational hierarchy, those who consider themselves ill-equipped may be unable to muster the necessary energy for either school *or* a job:

> This disbelief that they could ever complete anything of value . . . is especially marked in those who, for some reason or other, do not feel that they are partaking in the technological identity of their time. The reason may be that their own gifts have not found contact with the productive aims of the machine age or that they themselves belong to a social class (here "upper-upper" is remarkably equal to "lower-lower") that does not partake of the stream of progress. *(1968, p. 185)*

And judging from the lack of enthusiasm with which many people view their work, Erikson is probably correct to imply that some degree of work paralysis is normative—not only in adolescence but in adulthood as well.

In any case, the youth who successfully wrests a sense of temporal perspective, self-certainty, role experimentation, and apprenticeship from these first four part conflicts of the identity crisis is enlarging upon the experiences of an earlier era. All these aspects of identity can be traced back to a childhood precursor (i.e., trust, autonomy, initiative, and industry). However, this identity crisis is particularly important because it *also* contains three part conflicts that represent *preliminary* versions of crises that are to follow.

Sexual polarization versus bisexual confusion   The nuclear conflict of young adulthood is, for instance, intimacy versus isolation. Whether or not things actually turn out this way, it is assumed that the vast majority of adults will find their most intimate relationship with a person of the opposite sex. (At any rate, American society with all its emphasis on "marriage and togetherness" seems to make this assumption.) Consequently, Erikson suggests, in anticipation of this future heterosexual intimacy, a kind of *sexual polarization* occurs among adolescents, and they engage in attempts to define and redefine what it means to be "male" and "female." Erikson admits that there are wide cultural differences in this respect—

"the sexual mores of cultures and classes make for immense differences in the psychosocial differentiation of masculine and feminine in age, kind, and ubiquity of genital activity" *(1968, p. 186)*. But he adds: "These differences cannot obscure the common fact . . . that the development of psychosocial intimacy is not possible without a firm sense of identity" *(p. 186)*. And a clear identification with one sex or the other—a feeling of confidence in one's own "femininity" or "masculinity"—presumably contributes significantly to a firm sense of identity.

There is another (and more controversial) reason for Erikson to emphasize the phenomenon of sexual polarization during adolescence. A firm delineation of sex differences in adulthood, he declares, is vital to society. To ensure that the community functions smoothly, men and women must be willing to assume their proper roles: ". . . mutual genital love faces toward the future and the community. It works toward a division of labor in that life task which only two of the opposite sex can fulfill together: the synthesis of production, procreation, and recreation in the primary social unit of some family system" *(1968, p. 72)*. Hence, though in most cultures men and women display similarities of "consciousness, language, and ethics," they must also manage to be "maturely different" *(1968, p. 137)*.

In the course of trying to sort out all of these similarities and differences, the adolescent may begin to suffer from a sense of *bisexual confusion* and become unsure of himself or herself. He or she may express this insecurity either by plunging prematurely into physical intimacy or withdrawing from sexual encounters altogether:

> . . . young people in confusion may foreclose their identity development by concentrating on early genital activity without intimacy; or, on the contrary, they may concentrate on social, artistic, or intellectual aims which underplay the genital element to an extent that there is a permanent weakness of genital polarization with the other sex. *(1968, pp. 186–187)*

However, Erikson acknowledges that it is not unusual for adolescents to go through *periods* of "promiscuous genital activity," "complete abstinence," or (more commonly, we suspect) "sexual play without genital engagement." And he implies that these periods represent temporary adjustments that will hopefully permit the balance to swing more toward intimacy than toward isolation in young adulthood.

Leadership and followership versus authority confusion   In the same way, the adolescent's expanding social horizons, his participation in an ever-widening community, help to determine how he will meet the crisis of generativity versus stagnation in his middle years. His experimentation with various roles, his work apprenticeship, his tentative encounters with the opposite sex all help him to locate his individual niche in society and to anticipate his future contributions to that society—as a citizen, worker, and parent. He learns to take on *leadership* responsibilities, when appropriate, and he also learns to assume an attitude of *followership* when that is called for. In this way, the authority of the home, so significant to the child, is gradually replaced to some extent by a more general allegiance to the community, and the values originally transmitted to the child by his parents are refined and elaborated.

However, in his expanded circle of social contacts, the adolescent may become aware of the fact that there are a number of different and competing claims on his allegiance. The state, his sweetheart, his employer, his parents, and his friends all have their own impact upon him, and as a result he may begin to experience a sense of *authority confusion*. To resolve such confusion, he must compare these divergent values with his own and formulate a personal creed.

Ideological commitment versus confusion of values   The sixth part conflict (leadership and followership versus authority confusion) then is closely related to the seventh. In order to anchor himself solidly in his community, in order to bring his past and present experiences firmly in line with his future aspirations, the adolescent must enjoy what Erikson terms a feeling of *ideological commitment*. He must believe that what he has done, what he is doing, and what he plans to do are all compatible, that they may all be measured against the same yardstick. He must also believe that his own goals make sense within the context of a larger society, that his society approves these goals, and that it will, as it governs, provide him with the necessary support. Just as it can help him to overcome a sense of authority confusion, this "personal ideology" can help the adolescent to avoid a *confusion of values*.

Indeed, Erikson suggests, the formulation of an ideology or personal philosophy permits the young person to resolve *all* the part conflicts of identity crisis:[3]

---

[3] The reader will note here that the "match" between aspects of ideology and part conflicts is not a perfect one. Apparently some nuclear conflicts are to be included as well. We assume that the first conflict corresponds to temporal perspective versus time confusion, the second to basic trust versus mistrust, the third to self-certainty versus self-consciousness, the fourth to role experimentation versus role fixation, the fifth to apprenticeship versus work paralysis, the sixth to identity versus identity confusion, the seventh to sexual polarization versus bisexual confusion, and the eighth to leadership and followership versus authority confusion.

From what has been said so far we can ascribe to ideology the function of offering youth (1) a simplified perspective of the future which encompasses all foreseeable time and thus counteracts individual "time confusion"; (2) some strongly felt correspondence between the inner world of ideals and evils and the social world and its goals and dangers; (3) an opportunity for exhibiting some uniformity of appearance and behavior counteracting individual identity-consciousness; (4) inducement to a collective experimentation of roles and techniques which help to overcome a sense of personal guilt; (5) introduction into the ethos of the prevailing technology and thus into sanctioned and regulated competition; (6) a geographic-historical world image as a framework for the young individual's budding identity; (7) a rationale for a sexual way of life compatible with a convincing system of principles; and (8) submission to leaders who as superhuman figures or "big brothers" are above the ambivalence of the parent-child relation. *(1968, pp. 187–188)*

And in facilitating the resolution of all the subsidiary conflicts of the identity crisis, the construction of an ideology during adolescence touches upon all the nuclear conflicts of the life cycle as well. As we have seen, the sense of integrity in old age requires a similar kind of integration. Erikson therefore suggests that the crisis between ideological commitment and confusion of values in youth foreshadows the nuclear conflict of integrity versus despair during the last age of man.

The Virtue of Fidelity

The crystallization of an identity, as Erikson describes it, is obviously an enormously complex process, one that reflects and is influenced by every institution in a particular culture. However, he is able to identify a single human virtue or strength that originates in adolescence. From each of the many conflicts he faces, the adolescent must salvage something genuine, something that will enhance his own sense of individuality and uniqueness. Erikson calls this effort the "search for fidelity":

The evidence in young lives of a search for something and somebody to be true to can be seen in a variety of pursuits more or less sanctioned by society. It is often hidden in a bewildering combination of shifting devotion and sudden perversity, sometimes more devotedly perverse, sometimes more perversely devoted. Yet in all youth's seeming shiftiness, a seeking after some durability in change can be detected, whether in the accuracy of scientific and technical method or in the sincerity of obedience; in the veracity of historical and fictional accounts or the fairness of the rules of the game; in the authenticity of artistic productions and the high fidelity of reproduction, or in the genuineness of convictions and the reliability of commitments. This search is easily misunderstood, and often it is only dimly perceived by the individual himself, because youth, always set to grasp both diversity in principle and principle in diversity, must often test extremes before settling on a considered course. *(1968, pp. 235–236)*

In keeping with his conviction that the life cycle of the individual, the sequence of generations, and the structure of society are all intimately intertwined, Erikson also attaches a kind of evolutionary significance to this search: ". . . fidelity is that virtue and quality of adolescent ego strength which belongs to man's evolutionary heritage, but which—like all basic virtues—can arise only in the interplay of a life stage with the individuals and social forces of true community" *(1968, p. 235)*.

The adolescent's quest for fidelity must take place within a community, but it may also ultimately enhance the community. The young people who manage to develop a sturdy sense of identity generally take what they can from the "older generation"—the traditions, values, and customs of the past—and put their own decisive stamp on what they have taken. Those who have achieved a "conscious sense of individual uniqueness" retain a "solidarity with group ideals," but they also recognize that the way in which they have integrated their own experiences and perceptions is somehow distinctive. Thus, there is a creative aspect of identity formation, and societies depend for their vitality upon this creative—and oddly unpredictable—aspect:

> In youth, ego strength emerges from the mutual confirmation of individual and community, in the sense that society recognizes the young individual as a bearer of fresh energy and that the individual so confirmed recognizes society as a living process which inspires loyalty as it receives it, maintains allegiance as it attracts it, honors confidence as it demands it. Let us go back, then, to the origins of the combination of drivenness and disciplined energy, of irrationality and courageous capability which belong to the best discussed and most puzzling phenomena of the life cycle. The puzzle, we must grant throughout, is the essence of the phenomenon. For the unity of the personality must be unique to be united, and the functioning of each new generation unpredictable to fulfill its function. *(1968, pp. 241–242)*

Eriksonian Theory and Issues in Adolescent Psychology

Having completed a review of Erikson's theory, we may return to those still unresolved issues in adolescent psychology which we identified earlier. It is already clear that Erikson's theory draws upon a number of others—Freudian psychoanalysis and ego psychology, for example—and it also bears a certain resemblance to Sullivan's interpersonal theory. Indeed, we can even detect an echo of G. Stanley Hall in Erikson. Although Hall's rambling observations never constituted anything remotely like a coherent theory, he did believe that adolescence contained the "bud of promise" for the human race —and so, as it turns out, does Erikson.

But the really critical question is whether or not Erikson's theory can help to extricate us from the problem areas we have identified. Does it provide a solution to the controversy over storm and stress? Can it serve as a "conceptual umbrella" for research? And can it resolve the problem of sex differences?

The Issue of Storm and Stress: Norm and Ideal

In our opinion, Erikson's theory goes a long way toward resolving the issue of storm and stress. This issue, of course, proved to be a stumbling block for all three of the other theories of adolescence we reviewed, and it remains one for many psychologists and laymen. There is, as noted, a glaring discrepancy between the popular image of adolescence—turbulent, rebellious, explosive—and the actual data on teenagers. The data appear to indicate that whatever adjustments adolescents may have to make, they do not usually undergo serious emotional upheaval; for the most part, they do not hate their parents; and they are not in a continual state of rabble-rousing rebellion. Precisely because it is so complex and allows for so many different contingencies, these stubborn facts create, it seems to us, relatively little difficulty for Erikson's theory. The problem of storm and stress is actually two problems in one: storm and stress as a norm and storm and stress as an ideal, and Erikson appears to take care of both.

Storm and stress as a norm and normative crisis Hall, Anna Freud, and Sullivan all assumed that adolescence, whether by virtue of biological changes, inner conflict, or interpersonal difficulties, would be a disordered and disorderly period. All of them, in other words, considered storm and stress during adolescence to be more or less the *norm*. Though Erikson, true to his clinical training, draws many of his illustrations from the ranks of disturbed youth,[4] he does not claim that these youngsters are necessarily "typical." Indeed,

---

[4] As we shall note later in Chapter 11, Erikson includes only one case history of a normal teenager in his writings.

his theory, with all its emphasis on uniqueness and individuality, seems to imply that there is no such thing as a "typical teenager." He might go so far as to agree that each adolescent faces a similar crisis in the transition between childhood and adulthood—and thus that the crisis itself is "normative" in the sense that each adolescent must resolve more or less the same issues. But however complex this crisis may be (and we have seen that it is supposed to be very complex indeed), it is only one of many. There are eight others in the course of the normal human life cycle, according to Erikson.

Furthermore, although the changes and problems that occur during adolescence are distinctive, they are envisioned as part of an ongoing process. Identity formation may have its normative crisis in adolescence, but it is something that begins in infancy and need not end until "man's power of mutual affirmation wanes"—presumably in old age.

Finally, because of its very nature, every adolescent who undergoes this crisis resolves it somewhat differently. Each brings a slightly different host of experiences, opportunities, assets, and liabilities into the fray, and the identity that results is by definition a "unique product." In Erikson's own words:

> Adolescence is the last stage of childhood. The adolescent process, however, is conclusively complete only when the individual has subordinated his childhood identifications to a *new kind of identification*, achieved in absorbing sociability and in competitive apprenticeship with and among his age mates. These new identifications are no longer characterized by the playfulness of childhood and the experimental zest of youth: with dire urgency they force the young individual into choices and decisions which will, with increasing immediacy, lead to commitments "for life." *The task to be performed here is formidable. It necessitates, in different individuals and in different societies, great variations in the duration, intensity, and ritualization of adolescence.* (1968, p. 155, italics added)

As Erikson sees it, there is a certain *potential* for storm and stress during adolescence. Identity formation is, after all, a "formidable task." Nonetheless, severe emotional upheaval is not *inevitable*; it may or may not occur. If a youngster's childhood has been relatively benign and he can look forward to a reasonably stimulating and rewarding adulthood, then he may be able to carry out the assorted tasks of adolescence without undue pain and suffering. On the other hand, if the foundation the teenager is trying to build upon is a shaky one, if the experiences of childhood have made it difficult for him to resolve earlier nuclear crises successfully, and if adulthood holds little promise of compensation or redress, then his adolescent years may indeed prove turbulent. (And there are obviously a great many other possible variations as well.)

There is no doubt, of course, that some youngsters *as a group* stand a better chance than others of coming through the experience unscathed. In a society like ours, Erikson acknowledges, the more privileged, educated, and talented adolescents are likely to fare better than the deprived, the uneducated, and the unskilled:

> Adolescence, therefore, is least "stormy" in that segment of youth which is gifted and well trained in the pursuit of expanding technological trends, and thus able to identify with new roles of competency and invention and to accept a more implicit ideological outlook. . . . On the other hand, should a young person feel that the environment tries to deprive him too radically of all forms of self expression which permit him to develop and integrate the next step, he may resist with all the wild strength encountered in animals who are suddenly forced to defend their lives. For, indeed, in the social jungle of human existence there is no feeling of being alive without a sense of identity. *(1968, pp. 129–130)*

In recognizing these cultural differences, in acknowledging that adolescence can be something other than traumatic, Erikson's theory provides an alternative to the "storm and stress" theories we have reviewed and found wanting. His theory alone is not "embarrassed" by (or at any rate, is least embarrassed by) the data on adolescence. The concept of "normative crisis" goes a long way toward accommodating the awkward fact that most teenagers manage to pass through their youth relatively unperturbed.

We might add that Offer, whose research on normal adolescents *(1969)* has been cited several times, holds similar views about the usefulness of Erikson's theory. Offer, it may be recalled, does not conclude that the adolescent boys in his study were "bland" or "constricted." He admits that they had their share of "emotional problems" and "conflicts." However, the existence of *some* problems and conflicts during adolescence does not, he insists, justify a diagnosis of "adolescent turmoil":

> It seems to us that Erikson's concept of normative crisis is more applicable to our subjects than the concept of turmoil. "Crisis" is defined by Webster's *New Twentieth Century Dictionary* (1956) as "decisive or crucial time; a turning point." In other words, "normative crisis" does not imply chaos but typifies the kind of problems one sees in any of the major transitional periods in life. *(1969, p. 182)*

The ideal of storm and stress and the concept of moratorium
However, coming to terms with the norm of storm and stress resolves only part of the dilemma. We still have the ideal to contend with, and this point constitutes a somewhat stickier dilemma.

As we have seen, Friedenberg readily admits that adolescence

(adolescence in the *United States* at any rate) is not unduly turbulent *(1959)*, but rather than rejoicing in the fact, he despairs. If most teenagers do not experience any fine, romantic agonies, they ought to, he declares. For without such conflict there can be no true self-definition. And without self-definition, adult existence becomes, very simply, a meaningless treadmill. Although their views are less extreme and they expound them in a less polemical fashion, Douvan and Adelson *(1966)*, Keniston *(1960)*, and Anna Freud *(1958)* have all adopted a similar position.

Where does Erikson stand on this issue? In his theory, it seems to us, the ideal of storm and stress is replaced by that of the *moratorium*. So far, in discussing role experimentation and apprenticeship during adolescence, we have referred to this concept only fleetingly and indirectly. We consider it, however, a very useful notion. Erikson defines "moratorium" as a kind of breathing space for the adolescent, a period in which to experiment with various alternatives and forestall adult commitments. As noted in our biographical sketch, Erikson himself enjoyed a rather lengthy "adolescent moratorium," and he appears to view it as a desirable experience for *all* teenagers:

A moratorium is a period of delay granted to somebody who is not ready to meet an obligation or forced on somebody who should give himself time. By psychological moratorium, then, we mean a delay of adult commitments, and yet it is not only a delay. It is a period that is characterized by a selective permissiveness on the part of society and of provocative playfulness on the part of the youth, and yet it also often leads to deep, if often transitory, commitment on the part of youth, and ends in a more or less ceremonial confirmation of commitment on the part of society. *(1968, p. 157)*

But always the individualist and cultural relativist, he adds: "Such moratoria show highly individual variations, which are especially pronounced in very gifted people (gifted for better or worse), and there are, of course, institutional variations linked with the ways of life of cultures and subcultures" *(1968, p. 157)*.

Erikson, we conclude, believes that adolescence should truly be a period of transition—that the teenager should have the opportunity to explore, test out, and experiment before assuming his adult responsibilities. If he is forced into adulthood too soon, whether through economic necessity, emotional insecurity, or sheer misfortune, he may have to forgo certain experiences forever and leave certain aspects of himself unexplored. When adulthood is inflicted upon a youngster rather than being "grown into," his sense of identity may be prematurely "foreclosed." (Teenagers who "have to get married" and settle down unexpectedly to the business of raising a family probably offer prime examples of such "foreclosure.")

Erikson also seems to recognize that the sort of moratorium he has described as being particularly beneficial for the adolescent is something of an ideal, that it cannot be enjoyed by all. As we have seen, he recognizes that there are wide "individual variations," and he also hints that for most young people the transition from childhood to adulthood is fairly uneventful: "Each society and each culture institutionalizes a certain moratorium for the majority of its young people. For the most part, these moratoria coincide with apprenticeships and adventures that are in line with the society's values" (1968, p. 157).

Of course, we have still not quite resolved the basic issue. Is Erikson right, or is Friedenberg? Should adolescence be characterized by severe storm and stress, by wholesale rebellion against society, or should it be instead a period of extensive self-exploration —which may or may not be accompanied by a degree of turmoil? This issue is more difficult to decide than the previous one. We can determine fairly readily which theory best accommodates a given set of facts on storm and stress. But to declare what adolescence ought to be like—whether the ideal should be one of turmoil or moratorium—involves a value judgment, and such judgments are less easily put to an empirical test. To an extent we are forced simply to give our opinion—although there are some facts we can adduce as well.

As far as "hard data" are concerned, Offer's study, as noted, appears to demonstrate that teenagers can turn out to be reasonably decent and interesting human beings without undergoing severe emotional upheaval. In a similar vein, Weiner (1970), who has had ample opportunity to observe disturbed adolescents, flatly contradicts the notion that such upheaval is beneficial. Though rather few in number, the studies in this area seem to show that seriously disturbed youngsters do not simply outgrow their problems and emerge as mature, fulfilled, well-balanced adults. Although some manage to overcome their difficulties, a large number of adolescents with severe emotional problems have equally severe problems as adults.[5]

In addition, there have been some tentative, but nonetheless interesting, efforts to apply some of the concepts from Eriksonian theory directly, for example, "identity," "identity confusion," "foreclosure," and "moratorium." Working with college students, Marcia

[5] We shall review such specific studies in Chapter 11.

(1966) and his associates *(Podd, 1972; Waterman & Waterman, 1971)* have developed an interview that distinguishes between four different "identity statuses." Those who are judged on the basis of the interview to have passed through a true moratorium, formulating a personal system of values (i.e., an ideology) and choosing an occupation in the process, are termed "identity achievers." Students who are apparently still undergoing an identity crisis and trying to decide upon such matters are called "moratoriums." "Foreclosures" are students who have adopted an ideology and decided upon a vocation seemingly *without* undergoing an identity crisis. Presumably they have merely accepted a set of values rather than thrashing things out for themselves. And those students who appear generally confused and unable to come to grips with either task of adolescence are labeled "identity diffusions."

As would be predicted by the theory, students who have "achieved" an identity, that is, by permitting themselves a moratorium in which to resolve certain issues, generally appear the "healthiest" of the lot. In one experiment *(Marcia, 1966)* these "identity achievers" outperformed all the other three groups under pressure on a concept-attainment task. In another study *(Podd, 1972)*, they tended to score higher than any of the other groups on various measures of moral judgment. There are, as we shall see, some problems with this kind of research,[6] but the results do provide at least tentative support for Eriksonian theory.

However, even without Offer, Weiner, and Marcia, we would be tempted to favor the ideal of "moratorium" over that of "turmoil." It makes better sense, in our opinion, to advise that adolescents have a "breathing space" than to demand that they suffer severe storm and stress. In all probability, the kind of personal growth which promotes a firm sense of identity cannot occur without some degree of conflict. We suspect that in order to develop the qualities which are highly prized in Western culture—tolerance, sympathy, ambition, trustworthiness—the youngster must remain open to and even expose himself to a variety of experiences and ideologies. Some degree of experimentation (with alternative life styles, value systems, vocations) and indecision are probably necessary if a youth is to discover just what sort of individual he is. But we wonder if it is reasonable to expect adolescents to undergo tremendous upheavals and still emerge "whole" and "sound" in adulthood. Furthermore, we wonder if it is *desirable.* The concept of moratorium, it seems to us, furnishes a more workable standard for evaluating the

---

[6] Marcia's research has been limited to college students and appears to hold up better for men than for women.

adolescent experience. It is unlikely that all adolescents can enjoy the sort of moratorium that Erikson describes as ideal, but we believe that the vast majority of them could benefit from it.

A More Detailed Look at Adolescence

Having disposed of the issue of storm and stress, we still have two related issues to consider: Can Erikson's theory serve as an umbrella for existing research on adolescence, and can it account for sex differences in adolescent development? These questions may seem rather simple, but like the issue of storm and stress, they require extensive discussion, and we propose to devote the next few chapters to them.

REFERENCES

DOUVAN, E., & ADELSON, J. *The Adolescent Experience.* New York: Wiley, 1966.

ERIKSON, E. *Identity: Youth and Crisis.* New York: Norton, 1968.

FREUD, A. Adolescence. *Psychoanalytic Study of the Child,* 1958, **13**, 255–277.

FRIEDENBERG, E. *The Vanishing Adolescent.* New York: Dell, 1959.

KENISTON, K. *The Uncommitted: Alienated Youth in American Society.* New York: Delta, 1960.

MARCIA, J. E. Development and Validation of Ego-Identity Status. *Journal of Personality and Social Psychology,* 1966, **3**, 551–558.

OFFER, D. *The Psychological World of the Teenager.* New York: Basic Books, 1969.

PODD, M. H. Ego-Identity Status and Morality: The Relationship Between Two Developmental Constructs. *Developmental Psychology,* 1972, **6**, 497–507.

WATERMAN, A. S., & WATERMAN, C. K. A Longitudinal Study of Changes in Ego Identity. *Developmental Psychology,* 1971, **5**, 167–173.

WEINER, I. *Psychological Disturbance in Adolescence.* New York: Wiley, 1970.

Erikson's Theory as a Conceptual Umbrella: PART I

Erikson's description of adolescence is, to say the least, comprehensive. The nuclear conflict of adolescence, identity versus identity confusion, is portrayed as multifaceted and complex, elaborating on the concerns of earlier stages and foreshadowing crises that will eventually arise. We have already suggested that this description, incorporating as it does the concepts of normative crisis and moratorium, rather neatly resolves the issue of storm and stress. The question before us here is whether or not it can help to resolve some of the other problems we have identified.

Clearly, Erikson's account of adolescence outlines many aspects of adolescent development that commonly find their way into textbooks. There are references, either implicit or explicit, to almost all the phenomena we reviewed in Chapter 5: cognitive growth, physical and sexual maturation, social development. Equally important, Erikson also touches upon aspects of adolescence that we have *not* had an opportunity to examine. As far as more or less normal development is concerned, we have not yet discussed the research on such topics as time perspective, self-concept, achievement, vocational interests, religion, and political development. And despite the preoccupation with adolescent turmoil, we have paid only the most cursory attention to some of the more familiar "teenage problems": suicide, drugs, delinquency, underachievement, dropping-out, and alienation. We have been unable to address these topics primarily because none of the other theories we consulted referred to them in any detail.[1] By contrast, Erikson mentions them all. Consequently, it seems logical at this point to see if his theory can furnish us with a "conceptual umbrella" for research on adolescence.

Research Previously Reviewed

There is little doubt, in our opinion, that Erikson's theory can accommodate most of the research that has already been reviewed. In Chapters 5 and 6 we explored a number of significant changes that occur during adolescence. We saw that youngsters typically undergo a growth spurt somewhere around the beginning of this period, that they acquire the capacity to reproduce, and that some of them, at least, become capable of formal (or "hypothetico-deductive") thought. We observed that they acquire more sophistication about morality, by and large, and that they gradually but rather quietly differentiate themselves from their parents. And we also learned that although they are not necessarily traumatized by sex, it does cause them some difficulty. In their early teens at least, youngsters tend to worry about sex and to complain that they receive too little information about it. As a related concern, many of them admit to feeling awkward and inadequate in their initial encounters with the opposite sex, and, typically, they do not achieve any great degree of "heterosexual intimacy" until comparatively late in adolescence.

Most of these developments, we contend, can be accommodated under one or more "part conflicts" of the adolescent identity crisis. The growth spurt, the appearance of primary and secondary sexual characteristics, the increased preoccupation with sexuality, and the ups and downs of dating could all, for instance, be placed under the heading of "sexual polarization versus bisexual confusion." The shift in friendship patterns during adolescence—from same-sex (isophilic) to opposite-sex (heterophilic) friendships—might also come under this heading. Similarly, other aspects of social development— evolution of moral values, increased ability to differentiate between parents and peers—could be subsumed under "leadership and followership versus authority confusion." And although there is no single part conflict that might be designated for cognitive develop-

---

[1] We should amend this assessment slightly. G. Stanley Hall, of course, mentioned many of these problems, but his theory is 70 years old and was never very coherent to begin with.

ment, Erikson is obviously well aware of this particular phenomenon and its significance. Indeed, he refers to Piaget explicitly and declares that it is the adolescent's capacity for formal thought that makes a true identity crisis possible in the first place. In order to formulate an identity, a youngster must be able to place his entire life in perspective, and he cannot do so, in Erikson's opinion, before he has acquired certain intellectual skills. Prior to adolescence, his ego is simply not sufficiently mature to perform such a task.

We might conclude, then, that changes in cognition associated with adolescence would underlie *all* the part conflicts of the identity crisis. At the very least, a youngster would have to draw upon certain cognitive skills in developing a "temporal perspective" or an "ideological commitment"—and this point brings us to our next major concern. In addition to furnishing a "conceptual umbrella" for the research we have already reviewed, the part conflicts of the identity crisis provide us with a framework for examining many aspects of adolescent development we have so far been forced to ignore. We can, for example, discuss the development of a sense of time under "temporal perspective versus time confusion," changes in self-concept under "self-certainty versus self-consciousness," and vocational development under "apprenticeship versus work paralysis."[2] (In Chapter 10 we shall take up "sexual polarization versus bisexual confusion," "leadership and followership versus authority confusion," and "ideological commitment versus confusion of values," while Chapter 11 will be devoted to "adolescent problems."[3])

Temporal Perspective Versus Time Confusion

Relatively few psychologists have examined the particular subject of temporal perspective, but the small amount of research that has been done appears to substantiate Erikson's claim that significant changes in the sense of time do take place during adolescence. Once again, it is Piaget who has laid the groundwork in his studies with children *(1946)*. Piaget observes that very young children display only the most rudimentary sense of time. Indeed, the typical five year old continually confuses notions of "time" with other variables—like distance. If a child of this age is, for instance, shown a blue car and a green car, both of which start out at the same point

[2] As we shall explain later, "role experimentation versus role fixation" is not used as a specific heading in this chapter because it encompasses almost *all* aspects of adolescent development.

[3] Once again, we do not claim to provide an exhaustive review of the existing research—but we do think that the studies to be cited are representative.

in time and stop at the same point in time while traveling at unequal speeds, he will declare that the car that has gone farther (i.e., has been driven at a faster rate of speed) has been traveling "longer" than the other car. Only at the age of eight or nine, when this kind of intuitive thinking is replaced by "concrete operations," is the child capable of making the necessary allowances for differences in speed and concluding that the two cars have been on the road the same amount of time.

Picking up where Piaget leaves off, Fraisse (1963) contends that a true sense of time does not actually emerge until relatively late in adolescence—around age 15 or 16. A true sense of the concept, Fraisse insists, involves the recognition that time is simply a convention, a man-made system for ordering events. To substantiate his conclusion, he cites the following experiment by another researcher (Michaud, 1949). A group of children and teenagers aged 10 to 15 are asked the question: "What happens to time when we put the clock forward an hour in spring and jump suddenly from 11:00 P.M. to midnight?" Do they suddenly become older? Even up to the age of 13, a substantial number of subjects reply that they have abruptly become an hour older or that, at the very least, they have "lost" an hour of time. However, a majority of the fifteen year olds (approximately 60 percent) assert by contrast that arbitrarily shifting the hands of the clock has no effect upon time itself at all. It is simply that people have agreed for the sake of convenience to say that it is an hour later. This response, Fraisse observes, demonstrates an understanding of the principle that "time is an underlying thread of uniform nature which is independent of human actions" (1963, p. 279).

Once the adolescent recognizes the distinction between the measurement of time and time itself, he can begin to acquire a perspective about his own "stay on earth" that is quite different from that of the child. Time itself may be infinite, but the amount allotted to any given human being is finite and limited. Hence, as the adolescent becomes aware of the difference between the man-made convention and the phenomenon of nature, he might be expected to become more preoccupied with the allocation of time during his own life span. We might expect him, that is, to show more concern than the child about his own future and also more interest in actually planning for the future.

Time and "Life Plans"

There is some research to indicate that this concern does, in fact, tend to appear during adolescence. Leblanc, for instance, conducted a study *(1969)* in which he compared a wide variety of subjects—children, adolescents, college students, businessmen, and senior citizens. He discovered that the college students—in effect, a late adolescent population—made the most accurate judgments in an experiment requiring them to estimate "one minute of clock time." In another experiment, which involved making up stories to selected T.A.T. cards, the college students also made more references to the future than any other group.

We should add that Leblanc's subjects were all Americans. In a study of Dutch youngsters (aged 14–21), Monks *(1968)* uncovered some similar trends. All subjects were asked to compose essays describing their future aspirations and life plans. Late adolescents, by and large, exhibited a much more complex and differentiated set of perspectives than did early adolescents. There was a marked tendency for the younger subjects (over 80 percent of them) to write only about their own personal plans—almost as if they were envisioning a world in which they would exist alone and isolated. Although a substantial number of the twenty-one year olds (54 percent) adopted this same rather narrow perspective, their essays, taken as a group, contained references to a considerably wider range of concerns—relations with other people, religion, society, science, and so forth.

Sex differences   There were also, as usual, some intriguing sex differences. As might have been expected, girls were more likely to describe "marriage, home, and family" as playing a key role in their life plans, and boys were more likely to concentrate on educational and occupational aspirations. However, Monks hints that the girls' essays also made somewhat less scintillating reading than those of the boys. The average boy touched upon a larger number of topics than the average girl and managed to remain comparatively "objective" and "factual" in the process. Girls apparently took up more space in writing their "future autobiographies"—but they ultimately had less to say.

Although their subjects were somewhat younger (approximately 14–18) than Monks' subjects, Douvan and Adelson report comparable findings for American teenagers. When questioned about their future plans, the male subjects in this famous study *(Douvan & Adelson, 1966)* outlined an increasingly specific set of expectations and aspirations. They reported worrying about grades, expressed concern about their eventual "status" in the workaday world, and had usually already begun to formulate a set of definite occupational and educational plans. When asked, for instance, what they hoped to become, boys were often able to pinpoint a specific job. Furthermore, their plans for future schooling were generally in accord with their occupational aims. Those who were interested in middle-class professions (lawyer, doctor, engineer) also declared a firm intention to attend college, whereas those with "working class" aspirations (skilled tradesman, factory worker, truck driver) usually did not. All in all, the boys struck the researchers as having a rather well-organized and "realistic" view of the future—and the older they were the more apparent this orientation became.

By contrast, the female adolescents seemed to retain a much hazier perception of the future. Their plans were generally less well articulated than the boys' plans and there was no particular correspondence, curiously enough, between their occupational plans and their educational aspirations. Although the vast majority of girls expressed interest in "working for a while" at some type of white collar job, they were much less likely than the boys to have a specific *career* in mind. Most of their vocational choices, Douvan and Adelson report, involved jobs "which require little skill and continuing contact in order to maintain skills once they are acquired" *(Douvan & Adelson, 1966, p. 39)*. (Presumably, the researchers were referring to jobs like "secretary," "bookkeeper," and "sales clerk." Their presentation of the data makes it somewhat difficult to tell.)

Furthermore—and this point was probably the more critical—a girl's expressed intention to attend college was much less likely to coincide with her career plans (or lack of them) than was a boy's. It was not unusual for a girl to declare that she hoped to become a telephone operator (not a job which requires much formal education) and still say that she also intended to enroll at a university. We could argue, of course, that this lack of congruence between occupational aspirations and educational plans does not necessarily reflect a "hazy" or "unrealistic" view of the future.

As Douvan and Adelson themselves admit, male and female adolescents might be expected to develop rather different "life plans." Traditionally, a boy does not *choose* to work. He knows very well that as an adult he will be *compelled* to support himself (and quite possibly a number of other people as well). The only choice usually open to him in this context is *which* job to pursue—not whether or not to pursue a job. In addition, the kind of status he achieves in life is likely to be bound up with his own efforts to "succeed" in his chosen occupation—not with someone else's efforts.

For a girl, the situation contains a larger number of imponderables. She may elect to work or, as an alternative, to "get married" and "become a homemaker." Consequently, *her* position in life may result from her own efforts directly (as a "career girl") *or* indirectly from her husband's (depending upon whom she marries). To complicate matters still further (and this variable is neglected for the most part by Douvan and Adelson), a girl's prospects for a successful working career may *realistically* be somewhat more limited than those of a boy. Recent surveys *(World Almanac, 1973)* reveal that women who *are* employed are likely to be underpaid in comparison with similarly qualified men. And judging from the small number of women in certain "prestige" fields (e.g., medicine and law), we may assume that it is also difficult—very likely for a variety of reasons that we shall explore later—for women to gain access to some of the higher-status occupations. Nonetheless, although we may dispute Douvan and Adelson's conclusion that girls are less "realistic" about the future than boys, their research does reveal the impact of a variable like sex on the development of "temporal perspective."[4]

Social-class differences Other researchers *(Klineberg, 1967; Mischel, 1962)* have observed similar effects for social class. Mischel asked a sample of lower-lower-class boys (many of them delinquent) and middle-class boys to perform a series of tasks. They were offered a choice of reward: a small chocolate bar that would be awarded on the spot or a larger chocolate bar a week from the date of the experiment. The lower-class adolescents typically decided upon the smaller but more immediate prize, while the middle-class subjects more often chose the larger but more distant one. Klineberg reports much the same result in his study of French adolescents and concludes, like Mischel, that middle-class children learn to "delay gratification" in the present in order to maximize their possibilities for success in the future. This capacity for restraint presumably permits them to develop a more highly articulated set of life plans.

The Sense of Time and the Eriksonian Model

How can we relate these findings to Erikson's theory? Are concepts like "temporal perspective" and "time confusion" useful? In our opinion, they do at least give a sense of the process that youngsters must undergo in order to locate themselves in "ego-space-time." Fraisse's work suggests that the typical sixteen or seventeen year old possesses the necessary mental equipment to pinpoint his future, but as we have seen, not all adolescents do so with great precision. Judging from Douvan and Adelson's research, boys—

---

[4] We should reiterate that it may be more "realistic" for girls to remain "vague" about the future, a point that will be explored in Chapter 12.

whether middle class or working class—have a more extended sense of time than do girls and more specific plans for themselves. This difference occurs, we suspect, because the actual alternatives (e.g., work, college, etc.) are clearer for boys: They know what is expected of them. When the expectations are less definite (as in the case of adolescent girls) or the alternatives somewhat restricted (as in the case of delinquent youngsters), the sense of time remains, if not more "confused," at least more "diffuse."[5]

Seif-certainty Versus Self-consciousness

In Erikson's account of the adolescent identity crisis, "temporal perspective" is closely associated with "self-certainty." Presumably, as the youngster acquires the capacity to envision his own future life (however ambiguous his prospects may be), he also acquires the capacity to envision *himself in* the future. As Erikson himself puts it:

The young person, in order to experience wholeness, must feel a *progressive continuity between that which he has come to be during the long years of childhood and that which he promises to be in the anticipated future*; between that which he perceives himself to be and that which he perceives others to see in him and expect of him. *(1968, p. 87, italics added)*

Self-certainty

Once again, research in this particular area proves to be rather sparse. However, what there is of it does appear to indicate that any changes in self-concept that occur during adolescence are "continuous" rather than "discontinuous." Most teenagers do, in fact, seem to perceive a strong connection between what they have become in the past and what they promise to be in the future. Engel *(1959)*, for instance, gave several measures of self-concept to a sample of eighth, ninth, and tenth graders, retesting them two years later. Although there were some shifts the second time through, she obtained a correlation of .53 between the two sets of self-ratings. The teenagers in Engel's study, in other words—at least when taken as a group—did *not* see themselves as having changed radically over a two-year period. Quite the contrary, their self-descriptions displayed a fair degree of consistency and "continuity."

[5] Actually, in earlier accounts of the adolescent identity crisis, Erikson himself refers to "time confusion" as "time diffusion."

Even more intriguingly, any shifts that did occur tended to be in a *positive* rather than a negative direction. The adolescents who had given themselves favorable assessments in the first round of Engel's study tended to view themselves in an even rosier light the second time around. And those whose self-evaluations had been predominantly negative were considerably easier on themselves two years later, thus lending support to Erikson's contention that for most adolescents, the balance tips more toward "self-certainty" than toward "self-consciousness" with increasing age.

More to the point as far as both "self-certainty" and "continuity" are concerned is the research of Guardo and Bohan *(1973)*. Rather than resorting to pen and pencil tests, they simply questioned a group of adolescents directly (à la Piaget) about their own self-perceptions. The subjects (40 male and female high school students in grades 9 and 11 and a sample of 30 college freshmen) were each asked whether he or she had been the same person since birth and whether he or she would continue to be the same person in the future. Each was also asked whether he or she could ever assume the identity of another person. Though most of the subjects saw themselves as continuously changing in some respects, these changes were viewed as "evolutionary" rather than "revolutionary." The vast majority of youngsters felt that there was a definite connection between what they had been in the past and what they were in the present (although there was a slightly weaker relationship between these two self-perceptions and what they "promised to become" in the future). Indeed, 30 percent of them explicitly characterized the self as having an "unchanging core." Furthermore, there was a pronounced tendency for all subjects to see themselves more and more as separate and distinct *individuals* with increasing age.[6]

Adolescent "Self-consciousness"

However, although "self-certainty" may carry the day, we should not forget that adolescence is also depicted as a period of considerable "self-consciousness." In the course of discovering what sort of individual he is and what sort of niche he can be expected to occupy in society, Erikson suggests, the teenager may be assailed by an almost painful self-awareness. He may feel at times as if the whole world is scrutinizing him and finding fault with his in-

---

[6] We should point out that Guardo and Bohan's study was cross-sectional rather than longitudinal; that is, it compared youngsters in *different* age groups rather than comparing the *same* youngsters at different points in time. However, we suspect that a longitudinal study would produce very similar results.

adequacies. Here, of course, Erikson's characterization merges to some extent with the popular stereotype of the "awkward adolescent."

Existing research does, in fact, provide some support for this traditional stereotype, particularly the studies that have concerned themselves with the adolescent's *physical* self-image. Frazier and Lisonbee *(1950)* and Stolz and Stolz *(1951)* asked high school students to check off adjectives (e.g., "fat," "thin," "tall," "short," etc.) that accurately described their own physical appearance. The subjects were also asked if they would like to change themselves in any way and whether or not they were especially worried about any specific feature. In both studies, about two-thirds of the subjects admitted that they *would* like to "improve" their appearance. In the Frazier and Lisonbee study specifically, girls typically yearned to have "curvier" figures, boys more "masculine" physiques, and both sexes confessed to worrying about alleged "defects": blemishes, prominent noses, receding chins, irregular teeth, birthmarks, and the like. The following excerpts furnish two rather typical examples of this kind of self-consciousness:

> *Tenth grade girl:* My hips and legs are too large and fat. If I could have smaller hips and legs I'd have a much better figure. I'd also like to be a *little* more developed above the waist than I am, but I'm not flat. I wish I didn't have so many pimples or had to wear glasses. *(Frazier & Lisonbee, 1950, p. 93)*
>
> *Tenth grade boy:* I would make myself look handsomer and not fat. I would have wavy black hair. I would change my whole physical appearance so that I would be handsome, with a good build. *(Frazier & Lisonbee, 1950, p. 96)*

Significantly, more girls than boys expressed dissatisfaction with their looks. Other researchers *(Dwyer & Mayer, 1968–1969)* have interpreted this finding as evidence that girls experience more pressure than boys to present an attractive facade. They remark, "A common route to upward social mobility for a woman is to marry a man of higher social rank. Any positive attribute such as a pleasing appearance, a good voice, or intelligence increase the chances of this happening" *(Dwyer & Mayer, 1968–1969, p. 67)*. However, related studies of "early maturers versus later maturers" seem to indicate that *boys* may suffer more emotional distress from being physically out of phase with their peers than girls do.

In a piece of research that has been widely cited, Mussen and Jones *(1958)* compared the T.A.T. protocols of 33 boys, 16 of whom were considered physically "advanced" for their age (i.e., taller, heavier, and more muscular than the norm) and 17 of whom were classified as "physically retarded" (i.e., shorter, slighter, and less muscular than the norm). The early maturers were, on the whole, a self-confident lot. Their T.A.T. stories contained little evidence of emotional conflict, ill will toward their parents, or feelings of inadequacy. For the late maturers, the situation was largely reversed. Most of them appeared to be riddled with self-doubt—frustrated by their parents, childishly dependent, and fearful of rejection.

Mussen and Jones reasoned that the psychological differences between the two groups had resulted in large part from differences in physique. The early maturers could take pride in the fact that they looked uncommonly "masculine" and "grown-up" for their years. The late maturers, knowing that they appeared unusually "babyish" and "weak" for their age, were doomed to feel correspondingly miserable about themselves. So for boys, at least, there is some evidence that the kind of self-awareness that emerges during adolescence can lead either to pleased self-certainty or painful self-consciousness— depending upon how the youngster feels he measures up. Indeed, there is also some indication that the self-image that develops during the teens can be rather persistent. Jones *(1957)* conducted a follow-up study on her early and late maturers when they had all reached their early thirties and detected some of the same differences in personality.

Those who have reviewed the studies on early-maturing and later-maturing *girls (Rogers, 1972; Wattenberg, 1973)* have found the results somewhat contradictory. Jones and Jones *(1962)* summarized data from the California Adolescent Growth Study, which was conducted during the late 1930s and early 1940s. They concluded that early maturing girls, in marked contrast to their male counterparts, were likely to suffer a distinct disadvantage socially and emotionally. However, Stone and Barker *(1937)*, who undertook a study at roughly the same time, drew substantially the opposite conclusion. They compared a sample of girls who were already menstruating with a group who were still "premenarcheal." (The two groups were, of course, matched in age. Otherwise, the results would have been impossible to interpret.) When their responses to a number of "developmental inventories" were compared, the postpubescent girls generally displayed a more "mature" set of attitudes and interests than did the prepubescent girls. Woronoff *(1962)*, who collected *his* data in the early 1960s, reports findings that, at first glance, appear to support those of Stone and Barker. He had *teachers* rate a group of adolescent school girls and discovered that "fast-growing" youngsters were judged more self-confident and "better-adjusted" than those who were physically less advanced. And finally, to complicate matters still further, we shall present a study by Faust *(1960)*. She asked grade school and junior high school girls to rate *one another* on the Guess Who test (which consists of items like "Here is someone whom everyone thinks a lot of who influences the group. What she says or does is important to the group"). In sixth grade, "early maturing" girls (i.e., those who had already begun to menstruate) were evaluated less favorably than were those who were still "prepubescent." However, the situation was largely reversed in the three upper grades. In the seventh, eighth, and ninth grades, the more "mature" girls received higher "prestige" scores than did those who were less "mature."

We can certainly agree with Rogers and with Wattenberg that these data are "inconclusive" or "confusing"—but largely, we believe, because they are not completely *comparable.* This seemingly "mixed bag" of findings shows, it seems to us, what can happen when researchers use different criteria to define something as nebulous as "maturity." Jones and Jones were probably referring to girls who were "overdeveloped" (i.e., too "sexy-looking") in comparison to their peers—girls who could be *expected* to feel awkward and conspicuous. Stone and Barker, as we have seen, compared postmenarcheal and premenarcheal girls, without any attention whatsoever to their appearance. And as far as their results are concerned, it is not unreasonable to assume that girls who already saw themselves as "young ladies" would exhibit more "grown-up" interests and attitudes than those who did not. Woronoff, for all we know, may simply have been measuring the effects of "height." Furthermore, in his study the girls' *teachers*, rather than the girls themselves, furnished the data on emotional adjustment. Finally, Faust used the criterion of menstruation in different age groups, perhaps illustrating the point that what is considered "odd" very early in adolescence may become quite acceptable later on. In any case, it is not difficult to see why something of a muddle results when these studies are simply compared piecemeal—without any regard to their differences.

Role Experimentation Versus Role Fixation

A somewhat similar problem arises when we try to decide which research to discuss in connection with the next part conflict of the adolescent identity crisis. Like "maturity," "role experimentation" implies a broad range of phenomena. In a sense, it describes almost all the activities commonly associated with adolescence—attending school, dating, going places with friends, discussing religion and politics, formulating life plans, trying to decide upon a job. These activities can all be seen as a kind of preparation for future adult responsibilities. Consequently, most of the research we have reviewed and will review could be placed under the general heading of "role experimentation." (We believe this concept will be further clarified when we take up its counterpart, "role fixation," in our discussion of "adolescent problems.")

Apprenticeship Versus Work Paralysis

Putting the general topic of role experimentation aside for the moment, let us consider specifically one of the most important roles an adolescent can prepare himself for: his role as a worker. Indeed, we have already seen how significantly work and the preparation for it loom in the future plans of the adolescent boy. In a sense, of course, the child begins to equip himself (although not necessarily *her*self) for a job from the very first moment he enters school—which is precisely the point Erikson has in mind when he describes the fourth nuclear conflict, industry versus inferiority. During the rather long period prior to the "adolescent identity crisis," the educational system is supposed to play a particularly prominent part in the child's life, making him aware of a larger social reality outside the home, teaching him about his culture, and providing him with certain essential skills. The school, in short, furnishes the child with what Erikson calls the "tools of technology."

But the child, years away from any "gainful employment," can imagine only dimly what it will be like to participate actively in this technology. For the adolescent, such participation becomes a very real possibility. He is at an age when the responsibilities of adulthood are no longer quite so distant, and his increased cognitive abilities permit him to anticipate better than the child what it will be like to hold a job. (Indeed, he may even decide to secure a part-time job at this point.) The adolescent's connection with work thus goes considerably beyond the schoolroom. To be sure, the kind of education he receives will help to determine his place in the occupational "rat race." But attending school represents only an intermediate step in the teenager's eventual career. Also to be taken into account are the aspirations (or "achievement motivation") he develops and the specific occupations he finds himself gravitating toward. Therefore, under "apprenticeship versus work paralysis" we shall take up the following three topics: schooling, achievement motivation, and vocational choice.

Schooling

School systems have probably never enjoyed an extremely good reputation, but the American school system in particular seems to have been singled out for criticism. Hall's complaints of 70 years ago (see Chapter 2) have been echoed and elaborated all the way up to the present era. Friedenberg, in fact, holds the schools chiefly responsible for turning the American adolescent into a "vanishing species":

Its motives are weighted toward administrative experience rather than toward awareness of what is going on in the youngster and respect for what he is and what he may become, even though these more humane motives are now stronger than in the past. Where a full human response to him would previously have been blocked by arrogance, rigidity, and punitiveness, it is now blocked by status anxiety, manipulativeness, and the absence of a firm habit of respect for individuality of any kind. The school has lost confidence in its authority to maintain order, and has specially trained experts to crawl inside the miscreant, exorcise him from himself, and engineer his consent to its guidance. *(1959, p. 91)*

Even more recently, Silberman has declared that there is a virtual "crisis in the classroom"—and interestingly enough, quotes Erikson to buttress his argument:

"The most deadly of all possible sins," Erik Erikson suggests, "is the mutilation of a child's spirit." It is not possible to spend any prolonged period visiting public school classrooms without being appalled by the mutilation visible everywhere—mutilation of spontaneity, of joy in learning, of pleasure in creating, of sense of self—because adults take the schools so much for granted, they fail to appreciate what grim, joyless places most American schools are, how oppressive and petty are the rules by which they are governed, how intellectually sterile and esthetically barren the atmosphere, what an appalling lack of civility obtains on the part of teachers, what contempt they unconsciously display for children as children. *(1970, p. 10)*

In view of this indictment, we might expect most teenagers to express something less than wild enthusiasm about their schools. No doubt many of them are frustrated and "turned off" by the system. As we shall learn later, even in this era of mass education a surprisingly high percentage of youngsters drop out before receiving their diplomas.

However, those who remain in school—a majority of the nation's adolescents, we might add—counteract this impression of "grim joylessness" to some extent. Drawing upon the Purdue Opinion Poll (which has been querying a representative sample of teenagers since 1942), Leidy and Starry *(1967)* report that although the percentage of youngsters who claimed to "like school very much" had declined from 32 percent to 16 percent in recent years, the percentage who declared that they "didn't like it very much" or that they just plain disliked it had remained almost constant at 27 percent. The slack had been taken up largely by those who said they like school "most of the time," who constituted 43 percent of the sample in 1953 and 57 percent in 1967. This mild increase in dissatisfaction scarcely amounts to a vote of no confidence.

Similarly, in a *Life* survey of high school and college students ("The Unradical Young," *1971*), 84 percent of the respondents stated that they were generally satisfied with their educational experiences to that point. Furthermore, fully 66 percent of the high school students indicated that they hoped to *continue* their educations in college. And indeed, it may be the college-bound who are best served by the system. Youmans queried a sample of college-preparatory students in rural Kentucky and obtained the following evaluation:

> Nine-tenths of them said their teachers showed a great deal of interest in them. Although one-fifth said the teachers were too easy with them, four-fifths said they were about right in strictness. Approximately four-fifths of the youths planning on going to college said their teachers treated them fairly, never embarrassed them greatly, and never hurt their feelings badly. *(1958, p. 155)*

It is entirely possible, of course, that this group of farming-community youngsters do not represent the opinions of the entire college-preparatory population, but the degree of approval is, nonetheless, impressive.

We should also point out that some critics deplore the "anti-intellectual" atmosphere of the American educational system but blame the students themselves rather than the schools. James Coleman *(1961)* is perhaps the most celebrated of these critics, and he presents what appear to be some very convincing data. He asked students in eight different high schools how they would like to be remembered at their alma mater. Although there was considerable variation from school to school, only 31 percent of the boys and 28 percent of the girls wished to make their mark as "brilliant students." These figures compared with 45 percent of the boys who preferred to be immortalized as "athletic stars" and 72 percent of the girls who preferred the epithet "most popular." Coleman concludes somewhat gloomily:

> The relative unimportance of academic achievement, together with the effects shown above, suggest that the adolescent subcultures in these schools exert a rather strong deterrent to academic achievement. In other words, in these adolescent societies, those who are seen as "intellectuals," and who come to think of themselves in this way, are not really those of highest intelligence, but are only the ones who are willing to work hard at a relatively unrewarded activity.
>
> The implications for American society as a whole are clear. Because the high schools allow adolescent societies to divert energies into athletics, and the like, they recruit into adult intellectual activities many people with a rather mediocre level of ability, and fail to attract many with high levels of ability. *(1961, p. 265)*

However, Friesen *(1968)* takes issue with this assessment and claims that Coleman simply failed to ask the proper questions. Working with a large (over 10,000) sample of Canadian[7] high school students, he posed a *variety* of questions about academic success. With one set of items, he obtained results almost identical to those of Coleman. When he inquired, for instance, what sort of characteristics it took to become a member of the "leading crowd," 51 percent of his subjects replied "friendliness," and only 7 percent mentioned scholastic ability. Academic achievement fared a bit better on a similar question ("What characteristic do you think is most important for success in life?"); 15 percent of the subjects identified it as the critical attribute. But a vastly greater proportion (57 percent) cited "personality" instead.

However, when Friesen asked his subjects point-blank how they wished to be remembered and *also* what characteristic they saw as most important for their future success, his results were markedly different. Though there was some variation by region, the largest proportion of youngsters in each school (44–61 percent) wished to go down in history as "outstanding students" rather than as "athletic stars" (22–26 percent) or "most popular" (15–31 percent). Similarly, more than 80 percent declared that "academic achievement" (as opposed to athletics or popularity) would play the largest part in determining their future. On the basis of his own data, Friesen concludes that Coleman may have misinterpreted his results. There

---

[7] The fact that Friesen's subjects were Canadian (rather than American, like Coleman's) introduces an independent source of variation into his study. However, we shall assume for the sake of argument that Canadian high school students do not differ radically from their American counterparts.

is a difference, Friesen points out, between wanting to be a member of the "leading crowd" in high school and appreciating the value of an education.

In any case, even Coleman is willing to assign some degree of influence to the school system—for instance, in shaping plans for further education. Whether or not a youngster plans to attend college, he declares, depends far more on the type of high school he goes to (e.g., urban and upper class versus rural and lower class) than his father's education. Although Boyle (1966) is not as emphatic as Coleman (he notes that research in this area has been somewhat inconclusive, some studies indicating that the high school has the most significant impact on college plans, others apparently finding that the parents' level of education is more important), he too concludes that the high school can have *some* influence on a youngster's intentions to attend college. In a study of Canadian schoolgirls,[8] Boyle discovered that there was a correlation of .25 between the type of high school a student was attending and her stated intention to enroll in college even when other factors (e.g., the socioeconomic status of the subject's parents) were held constant. In other words, a girl who went to a relatively "high status" school (one with a large proportion of upper-middle-class students) was more likely to set her sights on college than a girl who was attending a relatively "low status" school—regardless of her own family background.) Oddly enough, this relationship prevailed only in metropolitan school districts. In rural districts, there was virtually no correlation between the "status" of the school and the proportion of students planning to attend college. Boyle speculates that rural schools, more easily controlled by a strong central administration, were less likely to fall prey to "residential segregation" and hence were more uniform in character).

Of course, as is only too evident, the high school is not alone in determining the nature of an adolescent's "apprenticeship" and the type of job training he seeks. Intelligence, social class, and sex all enter the picture as well. For reasons that are not altogether clear, social class has received the most attention—perhaps because researchers assume, simply as a matter of common sense, that the more intelligent students will enroll in college and because concern over the educational status of women has revived only recently (Rossi, 1964). In any case, a whole host of investigators, including Boyle (1966), have pointed to the substantial relationship be-

---

[8] Boyle does not explain why he limited his study to girls, and because, as we shall see, fewer girls than boys attend college, it is a little difficult to interpret his results. They are nonetheless interesting.

tween a youngster's socioeconomic standing and his educational objectives—or lack of them *(Hollingshead, 1949; Nelson, 1963; Sewell, Haller & Straus, 1957; Thomas, 1956; Youmans, 1956)*. In general, teenagers from the more affluent and educated families make up a disproportionate percentage of the student body at any given university, and those from less privileged backgrounds either opt for trade schools or end their training altogether after the twelfth grade. (Indeed, a substantial number of lower-class youngsters drop out of high school even *before* the twelfth grade.)

Why? Why is it, to quote an old platitude, that "the rich get richer and the poor get poorer"? Abrahamson *(1952)* hints, in what sounds like a more temperate echo of Friedenberg, that the school system itself may be to blame. He notes that the upper-class youngsters carry off a staggeringly large share of the honors in any given high school—grades, citizenship awards, class officers, general popularity—and suggests that this record is not strictly a matter of coincidence. It is not unreasonable to assume that the lower class teenager (not to mention the black teenager), is in fact subjected to a degree of discrimination. Hollingshead *(1949)*, in his pioneering *Elmtown's Youth*, detected a clear preference on the part of teachers for the scrubbed, well-dressed children of the upper class as opposed to those from the "wrong side of the tracks," and Friedenberg *(1959)* presents some anecdotal material to the same effect.

However, in an excellent article on the development of occupational motives and roles, Borow *(1966)* cautions against any hasty oversimplifications. If teachers know that an adolescent comes from a "good family" they may be inclined to favor him over less privileged students, but the family itself "as the child's primary reference group tends to define his occupational universe by a) furnishing work role models with which the child can identify and b) by transmitting a set about work in general and types of work in particular" *(Borow, p. 382)*. Since these models and values are generally derived from *two* parents and a number of siblings, the decision to attend or not to attend college may be based on influences that are more complex than they might seem at first glance. To illustrate his point Borow cites the work of Kraus *(1964)*.

Kraus surveyed a group of 700 middle-class and lower-class high school seniors shortly before they were to be graduated. Although the middle-class students were generally more likely to seek higher education, there were some intriguing differences in this respect among lower-class youths. For instance, of the lower-class youngsters whose mothers were working at nonmanual jobs, 53 percent intended to enroll in college; the figure for youngsters whose mothers were employed in manual jobs, by contrast, was only 29 percent. If a lower-class youth's mother had worked before marriage, the odds were 50–50 that he was planning on college, whereas if she had not worked, they dropped to one chance in three. Father's education; disparity between father's and mother's education, if any; school plans of friends; and school plans of siblings were all found to have a differential impact on a youth's own plans. Indeed, with regard to friends and siblings Borow notes:

> Eighty-one per cent of those reporting all friends going to college also planned to attend; only 10 per cent of those reporting all friends not going to college planned to attend themselves. Of those lower-class seniors having college-going older siblings, 53 per cent were college bound; half this percentage was found for those subjects without siblings who had gone to college. *(1966, p. 387)*

So much for glib generalizations about the relationship between social class and educational aspirations!

Aspiration and Achievement

So far we have examined some aspects of the adolescent's educational milieu, but this milieu is only one facet of his "apprenticeship." His family background and the high school he attends may have considerable impact on his plans for future training, but his own attitudes toward achievement—his aspirations in a larger sense—are important as well. His general orientation toward work, his drive, his competitiveness or lack of it will all help to determine what he does with that training and how effectively he can put it to use.

Socioeconomic differences in achievement motivation Once again, and probably not surprisingly, social class enters the picture. Indeed, just as concern with future plans is thought to be something of a middle class syndrome (see our discussion of "temporal perspective"), so is what McClelland and Atkinson *(1953)* call the "achievement motive." Indeed, it is not difficult to see the connection. In order to attain success in the world—or what is defined as "success" in Western culture—an individual must generally work his way into one of the more prestigious occupations. (He or she, most likely she, can also *marry* someone in one of the more prestigious occupations, but this is a separate point that we shall take up later in the chapter.) A good education undoubtedly counts for something

—although not perhaps as much as we may think.[9] But McClelland and Atkinson argue that liberal doses of the "Protestant ethic" are required as well: hard work, willingness to give up immediate pleasures for more distant goals, willingness to compete, and so forth. They speculate—and this speculation has been confirmed to some extent by other researchers *(Winterbottom, 1958)*—that the "motive to achieve" (commonly abbreviated "n-ach") is more readily instilled by middle-class than by lower-class parents. Middle-class families, they suggest, are more likely to be concerned about having their children "move up in the world" and are perhaps better versed as well in the general tactics of competition.

Douvan *(1956)* has, in fact, uncovered some evidence that the "need to achieve" is a more generalized motive (i.e., less sensitive to and dependent upon external rewards) in middle-class adolescents than in lower-class adolescents. Employing an instrument for measuring n-ach developed by Atkinson, she compared a sample of middle- and lower-class teenage boys. The subjects were given a battery of tests and told that these same tests were being administered to high school students "in different parts of the country." In the "nonreward" condition of the experiment, the investigator then declared, "After each test I'll give you the average score of high school students on that test, so you'll know how you're doing as we go along." To a second group of subjects in the "material reward" condition, the experimenter followed up these directions with the announcement that a $10 prize would be awarded to any subjects whose score exceeded a certain level. After the subjects in both groups were permitted time to complete the "tests" (which were, of course, simply experimental tasks with no bearing whatsoever on scholastic aptitude), they were provided with an artificially high set of "average scores for high school students in the country." This maneuver, it was hypothesized, would create a "nonsatiated state of the achievement motive" since very few subjects had been able to score anywhere near the alleged "average."

Following this empirically induced "failure," the subjects were given McClelland and Atkinson's test for need achievement (very similar to the Thematic Apperception Test, but scored according to a rather complex formula). In the nonreward condition, the n-ach scores of the lower-class teenagers remained relatively low. However, the lower class youngsters who had been treated to the prospect of a $10 prize, scored relatively high in n-ach. The scores

[9] Riesman and Jencks *(1968)* maintain that the correlation between income and education is only a modest .4.

of the middle-class teenagers, by contrast, were much less volatile and remained high *whether or not* a material reward had been offered. The middle-class youngsters, in other words, demonstrated a more global need to achieve than the lower-class youngsters.

Personality differences and achievement   Quite apart from considerations of social class, there is some indication that adolescents who are "highly achieving"—that is, those who manage to earn grades in line with or even above their tested aptitudes—are better "put together" than those who work below their capabilities. Finger and Silverman *(1966)* studied a population of junior high school students and found (somewhat dishearteningly, we think) that 45 percent were receiving grades lower than those they had earned in elementary school. However, those youngsters who had *improved* upon their performance in elementary school had higher "persistence," more ambitious "academic plan," and better "self-control, deliberateness" scores on a personal-values inventory. These qualities were also more in evidence among adolescents who had *maintained* high grades in both elementary school and junior high school. In addition, the experimenters hypothesized (à la Coleman, very likely) that students who had suffered a decline in achievement would be substantially more involved in the "youth culture"—presumably an anti-intellectual influence—but, interestingly enough, this hypothesis was not confirmed: further evidence, perhaps, that poor scholarship cannot always be blamed on "bad company."

Ringness *(1967)* and Gawronski and Mathis *(1965)* also observed a good deal of what looks like the "Protestant ethic" in the personality profiles of "high achieving" adolescents—particularly in comparison with the "normal" or "under" achiever. In both studies, teenagers who were doing well in school (in some cases, considerably above their tested aptitudes) appeared generally better adjusted (i.e., more independent, less rebellious, and more optimistic about the future) than those who were either working just at or below their capabilities. Not surprisingly, the highly successful students were also the most "achievement-oriented" and had the best study habits. The underachievers, by contrast, judging from their responses to personality inventories and questionnaires, created the impression of being rather anxious, emotionally "needy," and disorganized.

All in all, a healthy sense of apprenticeship, or at any rate, an orientation toward schoolwork that permits a teenager to make the most of his abilities, seems to be tied in with a sense of self-certainty. And the converse also appears to be true. What we might call "work paralysis" (i.e., "underachievement") appears to be associated with self-doubt and emotional discomfort. This correlation is, of course, precisely what the Eriksonian model of adolescent development would predict.

A related study highlights the possible relationships of various adolescent part conflicts even more vividly. Douvan and Adelson *(1958)* were interested not so much in achievement motivation as in the phenomena of "upward" and "downward" mobility. They identified a sample of upwardly and downwardly mobile adolescent boys simply by determining their socioeconomic status (i.e., lower-middle class or lower class) and then asking them what sort of adult job they aspired to. The adolescents who were labeled "upwardly mobile" were those who indicated that they planned to enter occupations that would permit them to rise above their present social standing. Conversely, adolescents who chose occupations that would result in a loss of status were designated "downwardly mobile." Though Douvan and Adelson do not refer explicitly to Erikson in their research, the results of their study correspond remarkably well with the various dimensions of the adolescent identity crisis. The boys who had high levels of aspiration also had a much firmer orientation toward the future (temporal perspective versus time confusion) and a more positive self-image (self-certainty versus self-consciousness) than those whose level of aspiration was overly modest. The upwardly mobile boys were also engaged in more activities than their downwardly mobile counterparts (role experimentation versus role fixation) and gave some evidence of being better adjusted sexually; that is, they were more likely to be dating (sexual polarization versus bisexual confusion). The more ambitious group of adolescents were obviously more "achievement oriented" as well (apprenticeship versus work paralysis).[10]

Vocational Choice

The Douvan and Adelson study also touches upon the third major topic to be taken up under the heading of "apprenticeship": vocational choice. Sooner or later, no matter what his level of achievement in school or his aspirations, an individual must decide to enter some sort of occupation. (For the moment, but only for the moment, we shall exclude all the possible exceptions: girls who make a career

[10] We do not mean to imply that there is anything especially meritorious about being either upwardly or downwardly mobile. We are simply reporting the psychological correlates that Douvan and Adelson observed.

of homemaking, chronic misfits, the mentally defective, the disabled, and the unskilled.) Several experts on vocational psychology *(Borow, 1966; Ginzberg, 1951; Super, 1957)* and a leading developmental psychologist *(Havighurst, 1964)* have suggested that adolescence is really *the* critical period for this decision. Indeed, Super's, Ginzberg's, and Havighurst's formulations all have distinctly "Eriksonian" overtones.

In contrast to Roe *(1956)*, who has hypothesized that a person's occupational preferences are determined by the kind of child-rearing practices he was subjected to in infancy, Super *(1957)* argues that self-concept is the key variable. According to his theory, an individual tends to choose a career that will suit him, that is, be consistent with his own self-image. However, Super insists, though the self-concept begins to emerge early in childhood, it does not begin to take on a definitive stamp until adolescence. Only at the age of fourteen or so ("the all-important ninth grade" as Super refers to it) does the youngster know enough about himself to have any basis for choosing a vocation.

Ginzberg's theory, which is based on a lengthy series of interviews with 64 upper-class adolescents over a period of a decade or more, is very similar. In fact, Ginzberg's work complements that of Super by describing the process of vocational choice in detail. Drawing inferences from his own data, Ginzberg outlines three major phases that precede the selection of a particular occupation in adulthood. Prior to the age of eleven, the child's occupational plans (assuming he has any at all) retain an air of unreality. They are, for all intents and purposes, largely a matter of *fantasy*. If asked what he wants to become, the child is likely to reply with a few stereotyped choices ("fireman," "policeman," "doctor"). He displays very little understanding of the skills, interests, or personal qualities required for a particular job and seems to assume that he can enter any line of work he wishes to at will.

However, between the ages of eleven and seventeen, the youngster finds himself in a very important and eventful *tentative* period. In an excellent summary, Borow describes what is supposed to occur during this phase:

> Ginzberg believes that the child's rationalized basis for choice shifts predictably as he moves through adolescence. It progresses from a consideration of compatible interests as the sole relevant qualification for job entry to a consideration of ability and training prerequisites (ages thirteen and fourteen); then to a consideration of the place of personal values in choice (ages fifteen and sixteen); and, finally, at about age sixteen or seventeen to a recognition of the need for a synthesis of interest, ability, and value factors in relation to one's goals. At about age seventeen, the

youth finds himself in a transition stage in which the compelling realities of the outside world begin to influence his thoughts about occupational choice. *(1966, p. 399)*

And finally, during the third stage, which follows this more tentative period, the adolescent (by this time a late adolescent) incorporates what he has learned about his own job preferences and sets about trying to make a *realistic* choice. This process also turns out to be rather complicated. First, Ginzberg maintains, the youth engages in *exploration*, acquiring information and experiences that will give him a taste of various occupations. (One of the most common examples of this sort of experimentation is the college student who takes courses in a number of different areas while attempting to decide upon a major.) Such exploratory activities result in what Ginzberg terms *crystallization*. At this point, the adolescent ceases to experiment and begins to prepare himself for commitment to a particular vocation (e.g., by selecting a major in college). The final step following this narrowing of choices is *specification*, the actual decision to enter a single occupation.

Havighurst advances a similar, though considerably less elaborate scheme. Merging his own notion of "developmental tasks" with what is readily recognizable as Erikson's concept of "normative crisis," Havighurst outlines a kind of "occupational ages of man" (see Table 1).

As is apparent, Havighurst, like Super and Ginzberg, regards adolescence as a "formative period" in the development of voca-

Table 1. Typal Hierarchies of Vocational Values for Each Sex and Age

	Stage of Vocational Development	Representative Vocational Developmental Task
Age		
5–10	Identification with a worker	Concept of working becomes an essential part of the ego ideal
10–15	Acquiring the basic habits of industry	Learning to organize one's time and energy to get chores and school work done
15–25	Acquiring identity as a worker	Choosing and preparing for an occupation
25–40	Becoming a productive person	Mastering the skills of one's occupation

Source: From H. Borow, "Development of Occupational Motives and Roles." In L. W. Hoffman and M. L. Hoffman (eds.), *Review of Child Development Research*, Vol. II. New York: Russell Sage, 1966. Reprinted by permission.

tional choice. We should mention once more at this point that not everyone who has studied the phenomenon shares their views. As noted, Roe (1956) believes the really critical influences on occupational choice are to be found in early childhood. However, Borow (1966) indicates that although researchers have failed to uncover much support for Roe's position, there *are* studies which provide corroboration for the more or less "Eriksonian" models of Super, Havighurst, and Ginzberg.

In a rather simple cross-sectional study, Nelson (1963) asked third, fifth, seventh, ninth, and eleventh graders to state how much they knew about each of 16 different occupations. They were also asked to indicate which of these jobs they might like to hold as an adult. In the realm of occupational choice, the younger children proved very easy to please. They expressed a liking for practically every vocation on the list. The older children were much more selective, expressing fairly definite preferences and aversions by the time they had reached midadolescence.

In a considerably more elaborate study, Gunn (1964) asked a sample of 240 boys in grades 1 through 12 to rank 11 occupations and then to *justify* their rankings. She obtained results reminiscent of both Erikson and Piaget. The very youngest subjects (first and second graders) gave very personal reasons for their choices and in general responded quite positively to every occupation, no matter how lowly its actual position on the career ladder. In other words, the youngest children were essentially unable to *rank* occupations. Beginning in the third grade and increasingly through the fourth, fifth, and sixth grades, a kind of order began to emerge, but the "goody-goody" quality still persisted to a degree. In this age range, the subjects expressed a kind of naïve idealism and indicated a preference for "service" occupations (i.e., jobs like "policeman" and "fireman") that they described as helping the community in some global way. However, beginning in the seventh grade, a real status hierarchy started to appear. From this point on, the subjects demonstrated awareness that some occupations were more *prestigious* than others, registering contempt by the tenth grade for what might be considered an "inferior" job. In fact, the rankings of tenth graders were approximately the same as those by adults, Gunn reports.

In a study restricted exclusively to adolescents, Gribbons and Lohnes (1965) obtained similar results. They asked a sample of boys and girls in grades 8 through 12 to state what they would look for in a vocation. The researchers concluded (in explicit support of Super) that a firm set of occupational values had already been established by ninth grade. These "values" and the rankings assigned them are described in Table 2.

Table 2. Typal Hierarchies of Vocational Values for Each Sex and Age

| | 8th Grade | | | | 10th Grade | | | | 12th Grade | | | |
| | Girls (N = 57) | | Boys (N = 54) | | Girls (N = 57) | | Boys (N = 54) | | Girls (N = 57) | | Boys (N = 54) | |
Values	Rank	f	Rank	f	Rank	f	Rank	f	Rank	f	Rank	f
Satisfaction	1	48	1	47	2	50	1	51	1	51	2	50
Interest	2	47	2	44	1	51	2	47	2	49	1	51
Marriage and family	7.5	9	11	4	7	14	12	4	3	30	4	22
Personal contact	3.5	24	6	11	3	35	5	16	4	25	6.5	14
Social service	3.5	24	5	12	4	26	8	13	5	23	8	10
Preparation, ability	9	5	7.5	10	9	7	6	16	6	15	6.5	14
Advancement	12	0	10	7	12	4	11	7	7	14	9	7
Salary	11	3	3	19	9	7	3	25	8	13	3	41
Personal goals	5	14	7.5	10	6	13	4	20	9.5	8	10	6
Demand	10	4	12	3	11	6	10	9	9.5	8	11	4
Location, travel	6	12	9	8	5	15	9	12	11.5	3	12	2
Prestige	7.5	9	4	13	9	7	7	15	11.5	3	5	16

Girls versus boys: Rho = .50   Rho = .52   Rho = .62

For Girls: 8th vs. 10th, Rho = .95; 8th vs. 12th, Rho = .46;
            10th vs. 12th, Rho = .52

For Boys: 8th vs. 10th, Rho = .84; 8th vs. 12th, Rho = .68;
            10th vs. 12th, Rho = .50

Source: From W. D. Gribbons and P. R. Lohnes, "Shifts in Adolescents' Vocational Values," *Personnel and Guidance Journal,* **44,** pp. 248–252. Copyright 1965 American Personnel and Guidance Association. Reprinted with permission.

These data also provide support for Ginzberg's assertion that adolescents become increasingly "realistic" about vocational matters as they mature. The eighth graders rather idealistically rank *social service* and *personal goals* relatively high on their list, whereas in twelfth grade these factors have given way to the more pragmatic considerations of *marriage and family, preparation and ability,* and *advancement.* Hall *(1963),* O'Hara and Tiedeman *(1959),* and, of course, the much-cited Douvan and Adelson *(1966)* furnish additional evidence for the growth of "occupational realism" during adolescence. In all three of these studies, teenagers (particularly teenage *boys*) showed increasing awareness of the necessity of choosing a specific line of work, demonstrating at the same time increasing appreciation of their own talents and liabilities. Thus, all in all, the term "apprenticeship" does seem a felicitous one to apply to the process of vocational choice during adolescence.

Aspiration and outcome   However, we have yet to examine the actual *outcome* of the adolescent apprenticeship. Is there, we might ask, any connection between the type of training and a career a teenager *says* he plans to pursue and his eventual job? Since longitudinal data are notoriously difficult to obtain, there are relatively few studies we can draw upon for an answer—and the existing ones are somewhat contradictory. Apparently, adolescents cannot predict with any great degree of accuracy the precise slot they will occupy a decade later. Kuvlesky and Bealer *(1967)*, for instance, traced the work histories of a sample of rural adolescents over a 10-year period and concluded that there was very little relationship between aspiration and actual attainment. The vast majority of young men (as in most studies of this type, the sample was exclusively male) were not pursuing the careers they had planned on in high school— although not surprisingly the more modestly motivated had been more "successful" in realizing their aims than the more ambitious. Of the teenagers who had originally aspired to enter the professional class, only 26 percent were actually employed at this level ten years later, whereas 48 percent of those who had wanted to become unskilled laborers were able to do so.

On the other hand, we cannot apparently dispense with aspiration altogether. When Kuvlesky and Bealer turned their inquiry around and asked those who were *already* employed in a particular occupation what their original intentions had been, their results were revealingly different. Of those who had managed to gain access to one of the professions, 52 percent had expressed such a preference as teenagers. Among those who were working as unskilled laborers, the corresponding figure was 13 percent. So although not all adolescents who are "called" to a specific vocation are chosen, at least *some* of the called are chosen.

Furthermore, when we examine some broader kinds of predictions, an even stronger relationship between aspiration and attainment becomes apparent. In a seven year follow-up study of Wisconsin high school students (also exclusively male), Haller and Miller *(1963)* reported a correlation of .52 between levels of aspiration and years of college completed. The correlation between "prestige of occupation" and aspiration level was almost as large—.46. Similarly, Little *(1967)*, who reviewed the later careers of a huge sample (more than 35,000) of graduating high school seniors, discovered that 82 percent of those planning to enroll in college did so and that 67 percent of those not planning to enroll did not. We might conclude, then, that within certain wide limits, there is a definite connection between the "apprentice" adolescent's stated intentions and his eventual accomplishments.

The impact of social class and sex   As might be anticipated from our earlier discussion (e.g., of schooling and achievement motivation), social class appears to exert a considerable impact on vocational choice. Although Borow *(1966)* reminds us that this issue is very complex, it is safe to say that, in general, adolescents from working-class backgrounds are more likely to set their sights on the less prestigious "manual" occupations and that those from the middle class are likely to opt for the esteemed "white collar" or "professional" occupations. To a certain extent, these differences may reflect a difference in values. In Gunn's study *(1964)*, for example, which is cited above, lower-class tenth, eleventh, and twelfth graders rated "teacher" lower on the status ladder than "gas-station attendant" and "electrician." Actual differences in opportunity no doubt play a part as well.

Indeed, the model of vocational choice advanced by Ginzberg, Havighurst, and Super (and hence the kind of ideal "apprenticeship" described by Erikson), has a distinctly middle-class flavor. According to this model, particularly the variant proposed by Ginzberg, the adolescent gradually becomes aware of his own interests and values, tentatively identifies several occupations that might suit him, and finally, after a period of experimentation and preparation, settles upon one. But we suspect that affluent youngsters have more of a chance—and much more leisure—to proceed in this fashion. A lower-class youngster who lacks either the means or the educational background to attend college may find his options considerably more restricted. Economic exigency or lack of training may force him into a routine manual job before he has had the opportunity to discover what truly "suits" him. Certainly this lack of opportunity has been and remains a very pressing problem as far as black youngsters are concerned *(Goldberg, 1963; Osborne, 1960; Siller, 1957)*.

The model that has been presented is also a decidedly *masculine* one, which brings us face to face once more with the ubiquitous topic of sex differences. These differences are, if anything, more striking than the variations that can be attributed to social class. Indeed, we have already encountered them earlier in the chapter in another context. Douvan and Adelson *(1966)*, it may be recalled, came to the conclusion that girls had "fuzzier" and more tentative perceptions of what the future would bring them than did boys. As might have been expected, they also found girls less ambitious. Though a surprisingly large percentage (10 percent versus 3 percent of the boys) rather unrealistically expressed the wish to secure "glamorous jobs" —model, stewardess, movie star—considerably fewer girls than boys (24 percent versus 40 percent) aspired to any of the professions—doctor, lawyer, engineer. Nor were girls as preoccupied with salary and opportunities for advancement. Paramount among their concerns were "nice working conditions" and "co-workers I can get along with." The Gribbons and Lohnes study *(1965)* contains some similar findings. Consulting Table 2 once again, we discover that for boys "salary" and "prestige" are the most important occupational considerations and that for girls "personal contact" and "social service" take precedence.

Such disparities are neither surprising nor very mysterious. As Douvan and Adelson are quick to acknowledge—and they are joined by a host of other prominent researchers *(Bardwick, 1971; Horner, 1972; Komarovsky, 1950)*—the typical adolescent girl's conception of her future remains somewhat vague and tentative because her future is in fact somewhat vague and tentative. At the risk of belaboring the point, we must emphasize once more that her status in society is likely to depend more upon the man she marries and what *he* does than upon her own efforts. Furthermore (assuming she marries and has children, of course) she will very likely spend a substantial number of her "working years" essentially unemployed—or employed only part-time. (Cleaning house and caring for children, to be sure, can be rather strenuous, but they are not considered "work" and rewarded with a formal salary unless the housewife hires someone *else* to do what are usually regarded as "her chores.")

There are probably a number of other related and, indeed, interlocking factors which influence the female adolescent's occupational plans—or lack of them. Perhaps because it is assumed that a girl will spend a good deal of her young adulthood as a "wife and mother," society appears to put a damper on her ambitions. Although more girls than boys actually finish high school, substantially fewer of them enroll in college *(Rossi, 1964)*. Furthermore, in the study of high school students that we have already alluded to, Coleman *(1961)* reports that it was "much less acceptable" for girls to be considered "brilliant scholars" than for boys. (We ought to add, however, that Friesen finds only mild trends to this effect in his research on Canadian youngsters, *1968*).

Komarovsky, in a more impressionistic survey of high school and college-age women *(1950)*, obtained similar results. Her study revealed that it was not at all unusual for girls who were in fact earning high grades to lie about them (i.e., turning actual "A"s into fraudulent "C"s) or otherwise conceal them from their boyfriends. And in a study which is rapidly assuming the status of a classic, Horner *(1968)* discovered that a staggeringly large percentage of female undergraduates at a prestigious midwestern university displayed an unconscious "fear of success." Horner asked her subjects—a mixed group of male and female undergraduates—to write stories in response to the following cue: "After term finals, Ann finds herself at the top of her medical class." The males were given essentially the same lead, but in their case the protagonist was named John. More than 65 percent of the girls produced stories that indicated a degree of discomfort with Ann's success—describing her as worried about losing her boyfriend, overcompensating for her unattractiveness, becoming the target of hostility from her fellow students, and so forth. Fewer than 10 percent of the boys predicted such dire consequences for John. Thus, not only is it "unnecessary" for the adolescent girl to commit herself to an independent career ("After all, she'll just get married and have to give it all up"); it may also be "unfeminine."

To complicate matters still further, the female adolescent can *realistically* expect less success in a full-time career than her male counterpart—at least if income is considered a criterion. Again, perhaps because society has adopted the belief that "women do not need to work" or that they will be providing "only a second income," there is considerable evidence that women are discriminated against occupationally. According to the *World Almanac*, a college-educated woman employed full-time could expect to earn roughly half the salary of a comparably educated man in 1973.

Overview

So far our attempt to translate Erikson's theory into a "conceptual umbrella" seems to have met with a fair degree of success. The changes implicit in the "adolescent identity crisis"—a firming up of temporal perspective, increased self-awareness, the development of vocational skills and goals—are all confirmed by the research on teenagers. Furthermore, *interrelationships* among various aspects of adolescent development that would also be predicted by the theory have begun to appear. We have seen, for instance, that, for boys at least, vocational objectives are likely to figure prominently in a teenager's future plans. In addition, we have seen that teenagers who "stand out" in one area—achievement in school, level of aspiration, even physical maturity—are likely to be quite solid in others as well, and vice versa. However, it is apparent that certain variations in development—particularly sexual variations—continue to be a problem. Indeed, these variations are brought directly into the spotlight in the next chapter, which is devoted to the part conflicts of "sexual polarization versus bisexual confusion," "leadership and followership versus authority confusion," and "ideological commitment versus confusion of values."

REFERENCES

ABRAHAMSON, S. Our Status System and Scholastic Rewards. *Journal of Educational Sociology*, 1952, **25**, 441–450.

BARDWICK, J. *The Psychology of Women*. New York: Harper & Row, 1971.

BOROW, H. Development of Occupational Motives and Roles. In L. W. Hoffman and M. L. Hoffman (Eds.), *Review of Child Development Research*. Vol. II. New York: Russell Sage, 1966.

BOYLE, R. P. The Effect of High School on Students' Aspirations. *American Journal of Sociology*, 1966, **71**, 628–639.

COLEMAN, J. S. *The Adolescent Society*. New York: Free Press, 1961.

DOUVAN, E. Social Status and Success in Striving. *Journal of Abnormal and Social Psychology*, 1956, **52**, 219–223.

DOUVAN, E., & ADELSON, J. *The Adolescent Experience*. New York: Wiley, 1966.

DOUVAN, E., & ADELSON, J. The Psychodynamics of Social Mobility in Adolescent Boys. *Journal of Abnormal and Social Psychology*, 1958, **56**, 31–34.

DWYER, J., & MAYER, J. Psychological Effects of Variations in Physical Appearance During Adolescence. *Adolescence*, 1968–1969, **3**, 353–360.

ENGEL, M. The Stability of Self-Concept in Adolescence. *Journal of Abnormal and Social Psychology*, 1959, **58**, 211–215.

ERIKSON, E. *Identity: Youth and Crisis*. New York: Norton, 1968.

FAUST, M. S. Developmental Maturity as a Determinant in Prestige of Adolescent Girls. *Child Development*, 1960, **31**, 173–184.

FINGER, J. A., & SILVERMAN, M. Changes in Academic Performance in the Junior High School. *Personnel and Guidance Journal*, 1966, **45**, 157–164.

FRAISSE, P. *The Psychology of Time*. New York: Harper & Row, 1963.

FRAZIER, A., & LISONBEE, L. Adolescent Concerns with the Physique. *School Review*, 1950, **58**, 397–405.

FRIEDENBERG, E. *The Vanishing Adolescent*. New York: Dell, 1959.

FRIESEN, D. Academic-Athletic Popularity Syndrome in the Canadian High School Society. *Adolescence*, 1968, **3**, 39–52.

GAWRONSKI, D. A., & MATHIS, C. Differences between Over-Achieving, Normal-Achieving, and Under-Achieving High School Students. *Psychology in the Schools*, 1965, **2**, 152–155.

GINZBERG, E., et al. *Occupational Choice*. New York: Columbia University Press, 1951.

GOLDBERG, M. L. Factors Affecting Educational Attainment in Depressed Urban Areas. In A. H. Passow (Ed.), *Education in Depressed Areas*. New York: Columbia University Press, 1963.

GRIBBONS, W. D., & LOHNES, P. R. Shifts in Adolescents' Vocational Values. *Personnel and Guidance Journal*, 1965, **44**, 248–252.

GUARDO, C., & BOHAN, J. Personal communication, 1973.

GUNN, B. Children's Conceptions of Occupational Prestige. *Personnel and Guidance Journal*, 1964, **42**, 558–563.

HALL, D. W. The Vocational Development Inventory: A Measure of Vocational Maturity in Adolescence. *Personnel and Guidance Journal*, 1963, **41**, 771–774.

HALLER, A. O., & MILLER, I. W. *The Occupational Aspiration Scale: Theory, Structure, and Correlates*. (Technical Bulletin 288) East Lansing: Michigan State University Agricultural Experience Station, 1963.

HAVIGHURST, R. J. Youth in Exploration and Man Emergent. In H. Borow (Ed.), *Man in a World at Work.* Boston: Houghton Mifflin, 1964.

HOLLINGSHEAD, A. B. *Elmtown's Youth.* New York: Wiley, 1949.

HORNER, M. Sex Differences in Achievement Motivation and Performance in Competitive and Non-Competitive Situations. Unpublished doctoral dissertation, University of Michigan, 1968.

HORNER, M. Toward an Understanding of Achievement-Related Conflicts in Women. *Journal of Social Issues,* 1972, **28,** 157–176.

JONES, H., & JONES, M. C. Individual Differences in Early Adolescence. In *Individualizing Instruction: Sixty-First Yearbook of the National Society for the Study of Education, Part I, 1962.* Chicago: University of Chicago Press, 1962.

JONES, M. C. The Later Careers of Boys Who Were Early- or Late-Maturing. *Child Development,* 1957, **28,** 113–128.

KLINEBERG, S. L. Changes in Outlook on the Future between Childhood and Adolescence. *Journal of Personality and Social Psychology,* 1967, **7,** 185–193.

KOMAROVSKY, M. Functional Analysis of Sex Roles. *American Sociological Review,* 1950, **4,** 508–516.

KRAUS, I. Sources of Educational Inspiration among Working-Class Youth. *American Sociological Review,* 1964, **29,** 867–879.

KUVLESKY, W. P., & BEALER, R. C. The Relevance of Adolescent's Occupational Aspirations for Subsequent Job Attainment. *Rural Sociology,* 1967, **32,** 290–301.

LEBLANC, A. F. Time Orientation and Time Estimation: A Function of Age. *Journal of Genetic Psychology,* 1969, **115,** 187–194.

LEIDY, T. R., & STARRY, A. R. The American Adolescent—A Bewildering Amalgam. *National Education Association Journal,* 1967, **56,** 8–12.

LITTLE, K. The Occupations of Non-College Youth, *American Educational Research Journal,* 1967, **4,** 147–153.

McCLELLAND, D. C., ATKINSON, J. W., CLARK, R. A., & LOWELL, E. *The Achievement Motive.* New York: Appleton, 1953.

MICHAUD, E. *Essai sur l'organization de la connaissance entre 10 et 14 ans.* Paris: Vrin, 1949.

MISCHEL, W., & METZNER, R. Preference for Delayed Reward as a Function of Age, Intelligence, and Length of Delay Interval. *Journal of Abnormal and Social Psychology,* 1962, **64,** 425–431.

MONKS, F. Future Time Perspective in Adolescents. *Human Development,* 1968, **11,** 107–123.

MUSSEN, P., & JONES, M. C. The Behavior-Inferred Motivations of Late- and Early-Maturing Boys. *Child Development,* 1958, **29,** 61–67.

NELSON, R. C. Knowledge and Interests Concerning Sixteen Occupations among Elementary and Secondary School Students. *Educational Psychology Measurement,* 1963, **23,** 741–754.

O'HARA, R. P., & TIEDEMAN, D. V. The Vocational Self-Concept in Adolescence. *Journal of Counseling Psychology,* 1959, **6,** 292–301.

OSBORNE, R. T. Racial Differences in Mental Growth and School Achievement: A Longitudinal Study. *Psychological Reports,* 1960, **7,** 233–239.

PIAGET, J. *Le Développement de la notion de temps chez l'enfant.* Paris: Presses Universitaires, 1946.

RIESMAN, D., & JENCKS, C. *The Academic Revolution.* New York: Doubleday, 1968.

RINGNESS, T. A. Identification Patterns, Motivation, and School Achievement of Bright Junior High School Boys. *Journal of Educational Psychology,* 1967, **58,** 93–102.

ROE, A. *The Psychology of Occupations.* New York: Wiley, 1956.

ROGERS, D. *Adolescence: A Psychological Perspective.* Monterey, California: Brooks/Cole, 1972.

ROSSI, A. Equality between the Sexes: An Immodest Proposal. In R. J. Lifton (Ed.), *The Woman in America.* Boston: Beacon, 1964.

SEWELL, W. H., HALLER, A. O., & STRAUS, M. A. Social Status and Educational and Occupational Aspiration. *American Sociological Review,* 1957, **22,** 67–73.

SILBERMAN, C. *Crisis in the Classroom.* New York: Random House, 1970.

SILLER, J. Socioeconomic Status and Conceptual Thinking. *Journal of Abnormal and Social Psychology,* 1957, **55,** 365–371.

STOLZ, H. R., & STOLZ, L. M. *Somatic Development in Adolescent Boys.* New York: Macmillan, 1951.

STONE, C. P., & BARKER, R. G. Aspects of Personality and Intelligence in Post Menarcheal and Premenarcheal Girls of the Same Chronological Ages. *Journal of Comparative Psychology,* 1937, **23,** 439–455.

SUPER, D. E. *The Psychology of Careers.* New York: Harper & Row, 1957.

THOMAS, L. *The Occupational Structure and Education.* Englewood Cliffs, N.J.: Prentice-Hall, 1956.

THE UN-RADICAL YOUNG. *Life Magazine.* Jan. 8, 1971, 22–30.

WATTENBERG, W. W. *The Adolescent Years.* (2nd ed.) New York: Harcourt Brace Jovanovich, 1973.

WINTERBOTTOM, M. R. The Relation of Need for Achievement to Learning Experiences in Independency and Mastery. In J. W. Atkinson (Ed.), *Motives in Fantasy, Action, and Society.* Princeton: Van Nostrand Reinhold, 1958.

THE 1973 WORLD ALMANAC. New York: Newspaper Enterprise Association, 1973.

WORONOFF, I. An Investigation of Some Pre-Adolescent Developmental Factors to Adolescent Social Adjustment. *Journal of Educational Research,* 1962, **56,** 164–166.

YOUMANS, E. G. Backgrounds of Rural Youth Planning to Enter College. *Journal of Educational Sociology,* 1958, **32,** 152–156.

YOUMANS, E. G. Occupational Expectations of Twelfth Grade Michigan Boys. *Journal of Experimental Education,* 1956, **24,** 259–271.

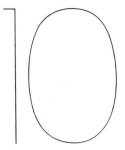

Erikson's Theory as a Conceptual Umbrella: PART II

As our review of research on adolescent development has already revealed, boys tend to be more "ambitious, assertive, realistic about the future, and purposeful," whereas girls are more "passive, modest, vague about the future, and retiring." In formulating an identity, Erikson declares, it is vital for the teenager to take account of such differences and (we assume) to act in accordance with them. Without a firmly established sense of "masculinity" or "femininity," he or she may be seriously hampered in dealing with the nuclear conflict of young adulthood, intimacy versus isolation.

Indeed, Erikson hints that it is necessary for the teenager to become aware of *and* to accept sex differences for an even deeper and more fundamental reason. Society depends for its survival, he claims, upon a "division of labor," and the specific division of labor which occurs between the sexes—men going out into the world and assuming the duty of breadwinner, women staying at home to keep house and care for children—is particularly important in the general scheme of things. Therefore, in order to prepare themselves for the distinctive contributions they will presumably make to society, it is imperative for teenagers of both sexes to come to terms with their proper "gender roles."

Sexual Polarization Versus Bisexual Confusion

Whether or not we agree with this assessment, one fact is certain. In addition to the obvious anatomical differences, there are some distinct differences in personality between the sexes. What *produces* these differences may be a matter of considerable controversy (more about that in Chapter 12), but there can be little question that they exist. In fact, the research devoted to this area grows more voluminous with each passing year *(Garai & Scheinfeld, 1968; Kagan, 1964; Maccoby, 1966)*.

In his summary of the data on "sex-role typing," Kagan presents a good deal of evidence that children have begun to acquire the concepts of "male" and "female" long before they reach adolescence. There are indications, for instance, that they become attuned to differences between their parents—two of the most significant men and women in their lives—rather early in life. Typically, children between the ages of three and eight report that their fathers are more "punitive" and "forbidding" and that their mothers are "friendlier" and "easier to get along with" *(Hawkes, Burchinal, & Gardner, 1957; Kagan, 1956; Kagan & Lemkin, 1960)*, presumably laying the foundation for the acquisition of sexual stereotypes later on. Indeed, these stereotypes seem to be quite firmly entrenched by middle childhood. Hartley *(1960)*, for instance, reports that elementary school children characterize women in *general* as being more "nurturant" and men as being more "aggressive."

Nor should it come as any great surprise to learn that little boys and girls themselves exhibit some of the same distinctively "male" and "female" traits. By the not very advanced age of four or so, children begin to display marked preferences for toys. When offered a choice between playing with a doll or a truck, for example, little boys opt for the truck in overwhelming proportions, and little girls are almost equally insistent upon having the doll *(Hartup & Zook, 1960; Honzik, 1951)*. Similarly, Kagan *(1964)* remarks that "it is difficult to find a sound study of preschool or school-age children in which aggressive behavior was not more frequent among boys than among girls" *(1964, p. 140)*—and then cites an impressive number *(Bandura, 1962; Bandura, Ross, & Ross, 1961; Dawe, 1934; Hattwick, 1937; Maccoby & Wilson, 1957; Muste & Sharpe, 1947)* to substantiate his claim. There are, in fact, researchers who maintain that boys are simply *born* more aggressive and that this difference can be attributed at least in part to hormones *(Bardwick, 1971; Diamond, 1965)*.

Sexual Stereotypes

But whatever their origins, sex differences appear early and persist, so that by adulthood men and women have settled, sometimes comfortably, sometimes regretfully, into their prescribed roles. In a study that drew upon a very heterogeneous group of subjects— teenagers and middle-aged, single and married, grade-school and college-educated people—the results were remarkably similar. The investigators *(Broverman, Vogel, Broverman, Clarkson, & Rosenkrantz, 1972)* discovered that no matter what their age, marital status, or educational level—not to mention sex—all subjects adhered, for the most part, to the conventional sex-role stereotypes. When asked to characterize the typical man or woman, they described men as "lacking in interpersonal sensitivity, warmth, and expressiveness" in comparison to women, and women were described as "relatively less competent, less independent, less objective, and less logical" than men *(1972, p. 75)*. Furthermore, the men and women in the study characterized *themselves* in much the same terms (i.e., as opposites in many respects). Several other researchers *(Bennett & Cohen, 1959; Elman, Press, & Rosenkrantz, 1970; Garai & Scheinfeld, 1968; McKee & Sherriffs, 1959)* report comparable findings. All in all, we may conclude that "sexual polarization" is an integral part of modern life.

However, this sort of categorization contains some disturbing elements as well (disturbing at least to those who believe in full sexual equality). As with many such prejudices, there is some evidence that "male" tends to be equated with "good" and "female" with "bad." Broverman and her colleagues *(1972)* have observed that though men might be perceived as comparatively cold and insensitive, in general, the traits assigned to men were judged to be more admirable and desirable than those assigned to women. When the researchers asked their subjects to *rate* the adjectives they had used to characterize the typical man or woman, those used to describe men were evaluated more favorably than those employed to describe women. In other words, labels like "strong," "competent," "fearless," and "dominant" counted for more than labels like "weak," "incompetent," "anxious," and "passive." Broverman and her colleagues argue that since the women in the study assigned many of these same "typically feminine" qualities to *themselves*, they were, in effect, designating themselves as inferior to men. Indeed, Bennett and Cohen *(1959)* provide some corroborating data. They report that in their comparison of a sample of men and women, the female subjects considered themselves "less adequate" and "more fearful" than the male subjects.

Even more troubling is a study which implies that even *psychologists* may share these preconceptions. Broverman, Broverman, Clarkson, Rosenkrantz, and Vogel *(1970)* asked a group of male and female therapists to describe the "healthy adult male," "the healthy adult female," and "the healthy adult person." Dismayingly but perhaps not surprisingly, the resulting profiles of "healthy male" and "healthy person" resembled each other far more than either resembled the profile for "healthy female."

Sexual Polarization During Adolescence

Most central to our own inquiry, of course, is the possible impact of "sexual polarization" during adolescence. We have seen that sex differences begin to appear in early childhood and that they have already become firmly cemented in adulthood, but what happens in between? Although Erikson acknowledges that early experience plays a crucial role in the development of such differences (see the account of "initiative versus guilt" in Chapter 7), he implies that an individual's sexual identity actually *crystallizes* only during adolescence.

In this area, as in a number of others, "the facts" are not easy to come by. However, what research there is certainly indicates that by the time they reach adolescence, most youngsters have managed to get the appropriate sex role stereotypes "down pat." Whether asked to describe the typical man and woman *(Broverman et al., 1972)*, to rate their own "personality strengths" *(Otto & Healy, 1966)*, or to list the values they consider most important *(Rosenberg, 1965)*, they reveal the same polarities. Adolescents invariably assign the more "dominant, aggressive, rational, and controlled" characteristics to boys and the more "dependent, passive, emotional, and sympathetic" characteristics to girls.

Nor is there much difference between lower-class adolescents and the relatively affluent young. Lower-class teenagers may draw sharper distinctions between "male" and "female" *(Pope, 1953)*, but the same stereotypes crop up among the more privileged as well. When a sample of college students were asked what they thought were the "proper roles" for men and women *(Wright, 1967)*, the vast majority declared that the male ought to concentrate on being a "hard-driving and responsible" provider and the female a "sympathetic and understanding" wife and mother. While a slightly larger percentage of the coeds in this study expressed the view that women ought to be able to pursue careers regardless of their failure or success in the marriage market, their responses closely resembled those of the males.

Perhaps the most startling piece of research along these lines is an informal study carried out at an illustrious women's college (*reported in Douvan & Adelson, 1966*). When 50 students at this school, which prides itself on its distinguished and productive alumnae, were asked to envision what their lives would be like 10 years later, over 90 percent of the resulting essays mentioned the following themes:

1. Marriage to a successful professional man or junior executive
2. Three or more children
3. A home in the suburbs
4. Daily activities including chauffeuring, shopping, and food preparation
5. Family income of $20,000 a year or more
6. A station wagon
7. Membership in community organizations

(Douvan & Adelson, 1966, p. 235)

Virtually none of the girls had any plans for a serious career.

Douvan and Adelson comment a trifle acerbically on these findings:

> The group of upper-middle-class talented girls in this study have much greater access to alternative patterns of feminine adjustment than any other group in our culture. They have talent and training which open professional opportunities to them; many of them are daughters of women who took an active interest in increasing women's rights; they certainly have greater opportunity than most girls for choosing life goals that are glamorous or in the grand manner of deviant ladies in earlier historical periods. But even they have been swept by the force of the popular image into strongly conventional choices. *(1966, pp. 235–236)*

It is possible, of course, to exaggerate the degree of sex-typing in American society. Otto and Healy assert that the self-descriptions of the male and female adolescents in their study were "more similar than dissimilar," and Rosenberg, who asked teenagers to list the values that were most important to them, makes much the same claim. There is even evidence that times are changing and that some female adolescents, principally those who are gifted and affluent enough to be attending first-rate universities, are breaking the conventional patterns to an extent. In a study of coeds at a number of well-known eastern schools, Josselson *(1972)* found that while few of her subjects were committed to a professional career, most had serious occupational plans for after graduation. The majority also exhibited relatively little of the desperation regarding marriage that is commonly attributed to college seniors. (Oddly enough, the women's movement appeared to be implicated only indirectly in this shift. Josselson reports that out of a sample of 48, only 3 coeds claimed to be a member of any feminist organization.) Nonetheless, those who are worried about the advent of a "unisex" world in which all sexual differences are virtually obliterated would appear to have little cause for alarm.

Adolescence and the Crystallization of Sex Differences

The data reviewed so far clearly indicate that adolescents, like younger children, are well acquainted with sex role stereotypes. However, we have still not determined whether the teenage years are, as Erikson asserts, a decisive period for the development of a sexual identity. In addition to the research already cited, there are further indications that influences early in life, influences which are still not too well understood, also play an extremely significant part.

Studies on hermaphroditism provide perhaps the most fascinating data in this regard. Hermaphrodites are individuals who, through some genetic quirk, are born with the reproductive organs of both sexes. (We should add that in most instances, the infant in question has male and female genitalia but only a rudimentary or incomplete set of both.) Consequently, it is possible (although very rare) for a baby to appear to be female when he is in fact biologically closer to being male—and vice versa. What is particularly fascinating about such individuals is that if they are brought up as boys, they consider themselves boys, and if they are brought up as girls, they consider themselves girls—*regardless* of which gender they incline to biologically. Furthermore, once set in childhood, their sexual identity does *not* seem to be reversible in adolescence *(Hampson & Hampson, 1961; Money, 1961)*.

Marmor *(1965)*, for example, reports the case of a "girl" whose hermaphroditism was not recognized until she reached the age of fifteen. By this time her own feminine identification was so firmly established that even when the facts were explained to her, she was unable to accept them. (Her reproductive system, as it turned out, was actually closer to being "male" than "female.") Though biologically "masculine," she was psychologically "feminine." In fact, she married and then complained to her physicians when she failed to become pregnant—which was, of course, impossible.

Less dramatic, but equally interesting, are the results of the Fels study *(Kagan & Moss, 1962)*. As we have already learned, certain qualities, principally those having to do with being "active" and "aggressive," are habitually associated with "maleness" and the opposite traits of "passivity" and "dependency" are commonly identified as "female." The Fels study was designed to determine, among other things, whether children who displayed such sex-typed traits early in life would also exhibit them in adulthood. The subjects were a group of boys and girls who were observed intensively (at home, in nursery school, at summer camp, and in grade school) between the ages of three and fourteen. They were also interviewed as adults, their ages at that time ranging from 20 to 30. What the researchers discovered was that for women there was a moderately high correlation between "passivity and dependence" in childhood and "passivity and dependence" in adulthood. For *men* there was a moderately high correlation between "aggressiveness" in childhood and the appearance of the same trait in adulthood. (Indeed, using the ages of six through ten as a base line, the researchers found correlations of .44 for dependency in women and .63 for aggression in men.) However, there was *no* correlation between overtly "aggressive" behavior in childhood and overt "aggression" in adulthood for women, and the same was true for dependency in men. This suggests, perhaps, that not only were dependent little girls permitted to remain that way, but that boisterous little girls were encouraged to forsake their "tomboy" habits—and the same might be inferred for "aggressive" and "timid" little boys respectively. In any case, such data undoubtedly strengthen the argument that a great deal of "sex-role typing" occurs in childhood.

Nonetheless, adolescence should not be written off altogether. Although the correlations in the Fels study are impressively high, they are not *perfect*, an indication perhaps that influences entering the picture *between* childhood and adulthood may also have had an impact on the growth of "sex role appropriate" behavior.[1] Though it is difficult to specify precisely what these influences might be, we have already seen that adolescent girls do not develop as strong a "career orientation" as adolescent boys. In addition, we have observed that while teenagers of both sexes become more "self-conscious" about their physical appearance during adolescence, girls

---

[1] If two variables turn out to be correlated, it does not mean, of course, that one has necessarily *caused* the other to vary in a particular direction. A correlation simply indicates the degree of relationship between two variables. That is why we remain rather cautious in discussing the possible connection between "sex" and "sex-role appropriate" behavior.

worry more about being "attractive" than boys do. Supplementing these data are other studies which suggest that youngsters become increasingly aware of the distinctions between "masculine" and "feminine" as they approach adulthood.

Sex differences in orientation There are certain corollaries which follow from the fact that boys are, as a rule, more aggressive and independent and that girls are, for the most part, more passive and dependent. The independent person is distinguished by the ability to judge situations for himself and to make his own decisions —regardless of what his parents or the rest of the crowd might think. It is thought that this kind of autonomy requires a strong set of personal values, or to put it another way, a strongly *internalized* set of values. Dependency, on the other hand, is thought to be associated with a more *externalized* orientation. With his intense need for love and approval, the dependent person is usually portrayed as being content to have *other* people make his decisions for him. At the same time, the desire to be accepted is alleged to render him more sensitive to the needs and wishes of others. Hence, if the culture dictates that men ought to be more "independent and aggressive" and women more "dependent and passive," then the psychologically "healthy" adolescent boy and his female counterpart ought to be somewhat differently oriented. In anticipation of the responsibilities he will be expected to shoulder, the well-integrated adolescent male ought to display an "autonomous" set of moral values, and the corresponding mark of adjustment in the adolescent female would be a kind of "social sensitivity" and "responsiveness" to others. (We might add that this line of reasoning—often associated with *social-learning theory*—dovetails with Erikson's claim that women enhance society chiefly by becoming "nurturant," and men by becoming "competitive.")

There are, in fact, data which lend support to this hypothesis. In a study that was later incorporated into the more comprehensive survey by Douvan and Adelson *(1966)*, Douvan *(1960)* discovered that among teenage boys "ego integration" and "internalization" went hand in hand, while among teenage girls "ego integration" was related to "interpersonal skill." In other words, the boys who demonstrated a capacity to resolve moral issues on their own were also judged to be more self-confident and energetic, while in girls these same qualities were more likely to be correlated with an ability to get along with other people.

Furthermore, Carlson *(1963, 1965)* furnishes evidence that this kind of difference in ego styles emerges during and not prior to adolescence. She reasoned that because they receive more encouragement to engage in activities on their own, boys ought to appear more self-absorbed or "personally oriented." Conversely, because the emphasis for girls is upon being "sensitive to others," *they* ought to appear more "socially oriented." But when Carlson attempted to confirm this prediction with a group of preadolescents *(1963)*, she obtained essentially negative results. Preteens of both sexes tended to be more "personally oriented," that is, when asked to describe themselves they were more likely to mention solitary concerns ("I like to figure things out for myself") than social pursuits ("My friends spend a lot of time at my house"). However, when Carlson tested this same group six years later as high school seniors, a somewhat different pattern appeared. As might have been expected, there was considerable attrition from the original sample. Many of the subjects had moved away, and a substantial number did not care to participate a second time. Nonetheless, the twelfth grade girls who remained in the study proved to be significantly more "socially oriented," and the remaining boys were significantly more "personally oriented." (These findings, of course, corroborate Douvan and Adelson's observation—cited in Chapter 5—that girls develop more intimate friendships than boys during the course of adolescence.)

An additional indication that this dichotomy between "internalized" and "externalized" takes on added meaning during adolescence comes from the unlikely area of perception. It is contained in the research on "field-dependence" by Witkin and his associates *(Witkin, Dyk, Faterson, Goodenough, and Karp, 1962)*. These investigators have devised a number of techniques for determining how an individual organizes his perceptual world—whether he relies on so-called "internal" cues or on "external" ones. Perhaps the most dramatic and revealing test involves placing a subject in an experimental room with a chair, both of which can be tilted. When the subject is first seated in the chair, the room is upright. Subsequently, it is tilted and the chair is tilted in a different direction. The subject is then asked to right himself. Some people—presumably because they are relying more upon external cues—bring themselves into alignment with the walls of the *room*, but since these walls are at an angle, the chair is in actuality still tilted. However, other subjects are apparently able to ignore their immediate environment and (presumably responding to some still mysterious set of internal cues) return the chair to a truly vertical position. Although there are wide variations in this respect (indeed, Witkin and his colleagues argue that differences between the sexes are relatively small when compared with variations within each sex), preadolescent children of both sexes tend to be field-*independent*. They seem to be responding, that is, to internal rather than to external cues. However, as they approach the teens, girls, almost as if they were beginning to march to a different drummer, become significantly more field-dependent than boys.

Sex differences in self-concept and self-esteem   Corresponding differences in self-concept and self-esteem might be expected to appear during adolescence. As noted, Broverman and her colleagues *(1972)* have found that the qualities typically assigned to the masculine half of the human species tend to be valued more highly than those relegated to the feminine half—even by trained psychologists. If adolescence is the decisive period for putting the finishing touches on a youngster's sexual identity, then this distinction ought to make some kind of impact. But precisely what kind? We can advance a fairly clear set of predictions for boys, but for girls the situation is (as usual) more complicated.

We might anticipate, for instance, that boys who do not fit into the masculine mold—who are not tall, strong, active, ambitious, and dominant—will pay for these "deficiencies" with lower self-esteem. Indeed, we have already encountered data that point in this direction. The Mussen and Jones study *(1958)* cited in the previous chapter demonstrated that the boy who is a late maturer is likely to be "under par" emotionally as well—perhaps because of his awareness that he does not measure up physically. And there are a whole host of other studies (also referred to in the previous chapter) which indicate that the "highly motivated," "energetic," and "upwardly mobile" youth is a healthier psychological specimen than his "under-achieving," "apathetic," and "downwardly mobile" counterpart *(Douvan & Adelson, 1966; Gawronski & Mathis, 1965; Ringness, 1967)*. Hence it is no great surprise to learn that Connell and Johnson *(1970)*, who investigated the relationship between "sex-role identification" and self-esteem more directly, came up with comparable results. In their study of early adolescents (average age 13.5), boys who were strongly masculine in orientation—that is, who scored high in "masculinity" on a personality inventory—also appeared to be significantly more self-confident than boys whose masculine identification was rather weak.

It is more difficult to make any straightforward predictions for girls. One could argue that they are subjected to the same kinds of pressures boys are, that just as boys are encouraged to become "masculine," they are encouraged to develop "typically feminine" traits. Following this line of reasoning, we might anticipate that girls who were highly identified with the appropriate sex role would exhibit greater self-esteem than those who were not. However, such reasoning ignores the "ringer" discussed earlier. As has already been pointed out, many (not all, by any means, but many) of the qualities commonly attributed to women bear the connotation of "inferior." It is, we frequently hear, "just like a woman" to be weak, illogical, emotional, passive, unambitious, and incompetent. So, in a sense, the girl who successfully assumes her prescribed role may incorporate a view of herself as something of a "failure"—and vice versa. To achieve the same sort of success as a man—presumably by growing up to be strong, logical, controlled, assertive, and ambitious—a girl may have to resign herself to becoming a "failure" as a woman. Helson, in fact, observes *(1972)* that in the early 1950s there was a tendency to describe the more dedicated career women in precisely such terms—as "unfulfilled" or even as "unfeminine and aggressive."

This peculiar paradox of femininity may help to clarify the data on self-esteem in girls, which is, at first glance, inconsistent and contradictory. What the relevant studies indicate, one suspects, is that the two opposing forces we have described tend to cancel each other out. The girl who is "highly feminine" may be pleased with her ladylike image, but in accepting it she may admit to a number of qualities that are not so highly prized. Conversely, the girl who is "nonfeminine" may feel uncomfortable about her relative lack of womanliness, but perhaps she also escapes having to perceive herself as somehow "inferior" to men. Consequently, we might expect that because both types find themselves in a kind of "double-bind," there would be no marked differences in self-esteem between "highly feminine" and "nonfeminine" adolescent girls. (For a similar assessment of the relationship between femininity and self-esteem —arrived at quite independently, we should add—see *Marshall & Karabenick, 1973, and Stein & Bailey, 1973.*)

Both the Carlson *(1965)* and the Connell and Johnson *(1970)* studies cited above lend some support to this post hoc hypothesis. Carlson asked the adolescents in her study to describe their "ideal" selves and their "real" selves and derived a measure of self-esteem from the discrepancy between the two. Despite the fact that there had been a significant shift in orientation among the girls (from "personal" to "social"), she did not observe any sex differences in self-esteem. However, she *did* find that the girls who had already adopted a "social orientation" in preadolescence (apparently there were a number who had "precociously" adopted the approach that was to become more characteristic of girls during adolescence) had suffered a significant *drop* in self-esteem six years later. If the female role, with all its emphasis on being attuned to other people were all that rewarding, we might expect just the opposite result.

Connell and Johnson report results that are intriguingly similar, if not identical. Though these researchers, as we have seen, discovered that "nonmasculine" boys felt a good deal less adequate than "highly masculine" boys, they did *not* turn up a corresponding difference for girls. The "nonfeminine" girls apparently believed themselves to be just as worthwhile as the "highly feminine" girls.

There are factors other than the ambiguity of the female role which might help to account for these curious findings. We have already observed that *adult* women are generally lower in self-esteem than adult men *(Bennett & Cohen, 1959)*. Connell and Johnson turned up much the same kind of disparity among their early adolescents. The highly masculine boys were more self-confident than the nonmasculine boys, and they *also* appeared more self-assured than *both* the highly feminine and the nonfeminine girls. No matter how feminine or unfeminine she may be, a girl can scarcely be completely unaware of the fact that she is a girl—and therefore perhaps "inferior" to men in some respects. If girls are already generally lower in self-esteem than boys (at least than more "masculine" boys) by the time they reach adolescence, it may not make much difference whether they identify strongly with their own sex role or shun it.

There is some evidence, however, that the full impact of sexual polarization is not experienced until relatively late in adolescence or even in young adulthood. Bohan *(in press)* compared boys and girls in each of four age groups: fourth grade, sixth grade, eighth grade, and tenth grade. She discovered that the tenth-grade girls had the lowest self-esteem of all—significantly lower than any other group. Similarly, Monge *(1973)*, in his investigation of "developmental factors" in self-concept, found a rather marked drop in what he called "adjustment" for girls between sixth and twelfth grade. And finally, perhaps the most interesting (or depressing, depending on one's point of view) study is one by Nawas *(1971)*. Employing the T.A.T., another researcher had tested 125 male and female high school seniors in 1952 and retested them eight years later in 1960. Nawas scored both sets of T.A.T. protocols for "ego sufficiency" and "ego complexity." While men increased significantly on both measures, there was a "highly significant" *decrease* on both for women. Is it possible, we wonder, that as girls grow increasingly aware of what is expected of them—indeed, as they assume more and more the life style prescribed for them by society—they become subject to a more and more pervasive sense of inferiority? We can only speculate, of course, but such data are nonetheless provocative.[2]

In the interest of giving an opposing point of view its due, we should note that Douvan and Adelson (1966) describe the relationship between femininity and self-esteem in much more favorable terms. We are already familiar, in fact, with Douvan's smaller-scale study (1960), which revealed that girls high in "interpersonal skill" (a "feminine" trait) were likely to display a sounder "ego integration" than girls who were not. In the later, more comprehensive investigation, Douvan and Adelson report that the girl who obtained a high score on their index of femininity also appeared to be the most mature in certain respects. "She has," they remark,

a rather highly developed sense of self, and her adolescent adjustment . . . is an active and energetic one. She is passive, if at all, only in interpersonal situations, and here the passivity holds only at the level of overt activity. While she is less given to active disruptive gestures and to aggressive assertion of individuality in relationships, she is very active on a psychological level in trying to maintain existing relationships by handling problems and conflicts that arise, by absorbing some of the burden of these conflicts rather than expulsively shunting her own hostility or anxiety into the relationships. (1966, pp. 240-241)

But Douvan and Adelson also admit some difficulty in doing justice to all the nuances and complexities of the female identity. In addition to their "unambivalent" feminine girl, they identified no less than *five* other "types" within their sample of female adolescents. And upon closer examination, even their model "unambivalent" girl turns out to be a complicated—and ultimately somewhat disturbing—creature. It is not astonishing to learn that she has rather traditional goals: marriage to a presentable young man, a comfortable home, children. However, there is some evidence that this orientation, with all of its emphasis on living through others, exacts its own emotional price. Reading the footnotes of the Douvan and Adelson study, we discover that the highly feminine girls exhibit a peculiar preoccupation with painful experiences:

Feminine girls worry more than other girls, and name more disappointments they have suffered. According to their reports, the feminine girls have more often experienced a major tragedy: illness, death, or divorce

[2] On the other hand, women may have their "revenge" in old age. In a study of elderly men and women, Gutmann (1970) reports that female subjects appeared to enjoy more robust psychological health—quite possibly because the men were being confronted with the trauma of retirement.

in the family. We know from other information that femininity groups do not differ in the incidence of parental death or divorce. It seems that they hold on to the experience longer and more consciously than other girls do. We also find a consistent relationship between femininity and reported discomfort during menstruation. *(1966, p. 239n)*

In our efforts to examine the development of sex-role identity during adolescence, we have obviously raised more questions than we have answered. However, despite the issues to be resolved (see Chapter 12 for a further attempt), the data clearly support Erikson's assertion that "sexual polarization" is an important aspect of adolescent development—particularly in the sense of cementing the familiar masculine and feminine stereotypes.

Intimations of Intimacy

But we should not forget that such distinctions between male and female are supposed to have a larger significance—and that, whatever their actual impact, they are regarded as beneficial and desirable in some respects. In any case, there can be no doubt that Erikson espouses this particular point of view, and in so doing he is simply elaborating on the venerable "complementarity theory." This theory, which has been most closely associated with the anthropologist Ralph Linton *(1936)*, asserts that male and female roles are essentially, and perhaps of necessity, "complementary." To buttress his position, Linton observes that in almost all cultures—and ours is scarcely an exception—the two sexes, though opposite in many respects, are neatly matched. The man's aggressiveness is balanced by the woman's receptiveness; her emotionality serves as a counterweight to his hard-boiled rationality. While he must be controlled, even to the point of austerity, she can be nurturant and sympathetic. Each, particularly in a more advanced civilization, can seek in the other qualities that he or she lacks, their mutual relationship thus furnishing each of them with a vital outlet. Or as the old saw puts it, "Opposites attract."

Whether or not close relationships between men and women actually reflect this sort of complementarity is debatable.[3] But it is nonetheless assumed that the vast majority of young people will,

[3] In a review of the research on "complementarity versus similarity" in marriage partners, Burchinal *(1964)* concludes that the motto "Opposites attract" is somewhat oversimplified. Actually, the studies on the subject indicate that people seek combinations of differences *and* common interests in the individuals they marry.

sooner or later, seek out *some* kind of intimate relationship—most likely with people of the opposite sex. Thus, Erikson implies, the differentiation or "polarization" of the sexes that occurs during adolescence is a necessary prelude to a more harmonious interchange in young adulthood.

The sexual aspect It is also assumed that *physical* intimacy will play a significant part in this exchange. Erikson himself seems to view sexual intercourse as one of the most basic expressions of human affection and closeness:

> Genitality consists in the capacity to develop orgastic potency which is more than the discharge of sex products in the sense of Kinsey's "outlets." It combines the ripening of intimate sexual mutuality with full genital sensitivity and with a capacity for discharge of tension from the whole body. This is a rather concrete way of saying something about a process which we really do not quite understand. But the experience of the climactic mutuality of orgasm clearly provides a supreme example of mutual regulation of complicated patterns and in some way appeases the hostilities and potential rages caused by the daily evidence of the oppositeness of male and female, of fact and fancy, of love and hate, of work and play. *(1968, p. 137)*

In our chapter on storm and stress (Chapter 6), we have already examined some of the steps the typical adolescent takes in his halting journey toward adult sexuality. But we did not explore the matter in depth, and our description was somewhat negative in tone. The increase in worries about sex during adolescence *(Offer, 1972; Shipman, 1968)*, the discomforts of dating *(Burchinal, 1964)*, and the inadequacies of sex education *(Bandura & Walters, 1959; Douvan & Adelson, 1966; Kinsey, 1948; Offer, 1969; Shipman, 1968)* commanded most of our attention. Since the youngster is not (in our culture at least) supposed to engage in much sexual activity until he or she is long past puberty and comfortably ensconced in a marriage, such strains and anxieties are probably inevitable. But we must assume that there is a positive side to the sexual awakening as well. Early in adolescence the youngster may feel compelled to inhibit his (or her) impulses, but if he (or she) is ever to take any pleasure in sex—specifically, the kind of pleasure Erikson describes —he or she must undo these inhibitions somewhere along the line.

There are a few studies to indicate that this is, in fact, what does happen. As is usual for controversial subjects, the "hard data" are rather sparse. However, the study by Offer *(1972)* already cited suggests that—among middle-class adolescents at any rate—the anxieties and taboos regarding sex grow less troublesome during the normal course of adolescence. Younger subjects (ages 13–14) in the predominantly middle-class sample were more likely to confess that they found sex "hard to handle," that it frightened them, and that they were put off by dirty jokes. Older subjects appeared to have put such childish worries aside and were also more likely to agree unequivocally with the statement "Sex gives me pleasure." Furthermore, there is evidence that by the time they reach late adolescence, a substantial number of teenagers have adopted the ethic which links sexual expression with love. In this connection, it is worthwhile to consider Reiss's findings *(1960)* once again. As may be remembered (see Chapter 6), he discovered that in a sample of high school seniors, 44 percent of the girls and 52 percent of the boys believe that premarital intercourse was permissible if the couple involved was engaged. It turns out that *almost* as many of them approved of such intimacies when the couple in question was merely "in love" (39 percent of the girls and 48 percent of the boys). Smigel and Seiden *(1968)*, who investigated the sexual attitudes of college students, report similar findings.

The double standard   We should point out, however, that there is a "catch" in all of this. The standards for premarital intercourse that we have cited are for *males.* Adolescents and young adults of *both* sexes usually back down somewhat when asked to give their views on what is permissible for females *(Reiss, 1967; Smigel & Seiden, 1968)*. Reiss maintains that it is males who insist the most strenuously on this all too familiar double standard, but Smigel and Seiden present data that put more of the burden on females. No matter who is responsible, the double standard does seem to persist to some extent, even in the face of the so-called sexual revolution. The notion that male adolescents may "sow their wild oats" premaritally while females must "save themselves for marriage" is thus one of the most durable aspects of sexual polarization.

A recent and somewhat irreverent piece of research by Pearsall *(1973)* outlines the complicated maneuvering and fencing that can result from the application of this "separate but unequal" standard. In a study of junior college students which sought to trace the development of premarital relationships from first meeting all the way to marriage, he discovered approximately 10 levels of involvement:

1. *The Meeting and Looking Stage*, which was uniformly described as difficult. Young people of both sexes complained about their lack of opportunities for contact, although in the course of "cruising," they eventually managed to encounter someone attractive enough to arrange a date with.

2. *The First Date.* Pearsall describes this as a "prearranged meeting" of some sort and notes that the vast majority of first dates took place in settings that made intimacy of any sort extremely awkward. Conversation was usually restricted or impossible (e.g., drowned out by a rock band), and a surprising 80 percent of the respondents reported that they did not kiss.

3. *Going out With.* Once the ice-breaking first date was out of the way and a couple had developed the expectation that they would continue to see each other, the young man would make some preliminary attempts at physical contact (Pearsall refers to this in the vernacular as "trying to get some") and would generally encounter at least token resistance. This stage was also marked for the first time by "statements of noncommitment," in which one or both of the partners declared that they were either "not involved" or that they wished to limit their involvement.

4. *Going With.* Assuming the relationship proceeded past phase 3, this was the first stage in which actual genital contact usually occurred—typically well short of intercourse. At this point, the couple had an understanding that they would see each other regularly, and the first signs of "exclusiveness" or "jealousy" began to appear. As a result, partners reported that they began to lie and "cover up," if necessary, glossing over any unexplained absences and concealing any "extracurricular" dates.

5–6. *Going Steadily and Going Steady.* Phases 5 and 6 were marked by increasing intimacies (heavy petting, oral-genital contact) short of actual intercourse and redoubled efforts to keep the other partner from finding out about any adventures "on the side." Males in particular were likely to complain of frustration and physical discomfort (often in the form of genital soreness) during both of these stages. Pearsall suggests that the dilemma for the couple during this period is "how to go all the way without going all the way."

7. *Semiengaged.* At this point, the couple, who were often still refraining from sexual intercourse, began to speak of marriage and related issues (children, houses, etc.). If coitus did not occur during this stage (and Pearsall reports that for many couples it did not), the period was marked by more sexual experimentation and more frustration, and, frequently, by arguments.

8. *Engaged.* Assuming the relationship had not been broken off in the preceding stage, the couple made a commitment to marry at this point and often marked it formally with the presentation of an engagement ring. (Pearsall calls this the "Stone Stage.") The critical issue for the girl at this juncture was generally

whether or not to have intercourse with her fiancé now that marriage was definitely in the picture. (This is referred to as the "Should I let him have it?" dilemma.)

9. *Going to Get Married.* As the wedding date was set, the couple came under increasing pressure to carry out their plans, even if one or both of the partners was beginning to suffer from "cold feet." (This was identified as the "We've got the hall" stage.) Oddly enough, perhaps because of the anxieties surrounding the impending event, sex tended, for the first time, to be relegated to the background.

10. *Married.* For a good many couples, this was the first stage in which sexual intercourse actually took place. While it was generally assumed that such intimacies would become a regular occurrence, there were sometimes still signs of the "barter psychology" that had been so much in evidence throughout. As one of the male subjects remarked about the physical side of his own marriage, "At least you can get it when you want it without trouble—*maybe.*"

If nothing else, this account confirms Ehrmann's *(1959)* observation that women tend to view sexual intimacy as properly occurring only after a strong commitment has been made and men tend to prefer the intimacy *first* and to make the commitment (if ever) later.

Attitudes toward marriage   The mention of commitment brings us to our next topic. As is evident from Pearsall's study, the question of physical intimacy and the question of marriage frequently coincide. Indeed, marriage is widely considered the only legitimate setting for such intimacy. It is also generally assumed—however naïvely or idealistically—that marriage furnishes the best vehicle for emotional intimacy and, for both these reasons, that most young people will eventually want to enter into it. Hence, in addition to serving as a proving ground for sexuality, adolescence is supposed to prepare the individual for marriage.

Indeed, by midadolescence an overwhelming proportion of teenagers declare that they do plan to marry. In a study of ninth graders *(Garrison, 1966)* virtually 100 percent of the girls and 90 percent of the boys reported such intentions. However, the fact that 10 percent of the boys did *not* points up the existence of another double standard, one which is undoubtedly much related to the double standard so prominent in the Pearsall study. On the whole, adolescent girls appear to be distinctly more interested in marriage than do adolescent boys. In Garrison's survey, for instance, two-thirds of the girls expected the event to occur somewhere between the ages of 20 and 24, while only half the boys anticipated being wed by this time. Similarly, Broderick *(1965)* queried a group of male and female subjects between the ages of ten and seventeen. At virtually every age level, the girls claimed that they were "looking forward to marriage" in significantly greater numbers than the boys. (Interestingly enough, this difference did not hold up among the black adolescents included in Broderick's research population. Black males, for the most part, expressed just as much enthusiasm for matrimony as did their female counterparts.)

Continuing in the same vein, Douvan and Adelson *(1966)* note that a girl develops increasingly articulated and specific ideas of what she wants in a mate during her teens. Only early in adolescence is she apparently much engrossed with fantasies of Prince Charming. Thereafter, superficial qualities like "good looks" drop out of the picture, and by the time she is sixteen the typical adolescent girl reports that she would like her prospective husband to be a good companion—and above all a good *provider*:

The ideas these girls have of their future husbands correspond to the jobs they want these young men to hold. They are looking for men who have social skill and consideration for others, intelligence and responsibility, all characteristics that are tied to success in middle-class professional jobs.

We cannot fail to be impressed with the consistency that marks the girls' views. They want to attain middle-class jobs for themselves, they want their husbands to have high status jobs, and they have a personal image of the future husband which conforms to the requirements of these same occupations. *(Douvan and Adelson, 1966, p. 44)*

There is also some indication that by the time she reaches late adolescence the girl is surveying the field with a more active and practiced eye than a boy of the same age. Coombs and Kenkel *(1966)* set about arranging blind dates for 500 male and 500 female college students. When questioned about their preferences, the girls produced a more demanding set of criteria—with one notable exception. For a coed, the ideal date was a man who was popular, a good dancer, a good student, and a member of the same race or religion. There was no objection either to his being active in a fraternity and a "sharp dresser." By contrast, the boys were more particular than the girls in only one area. Probably much to the distress of those who complain about women being "mere sex objects," the male students expressed more concern than the females about obtaining a date who was good looking.

There are no doubt several reasons why the female adolescent displays a somewhat disproportionate interest in marriage—most of which have already been taken up. The prohibition on premarital intercourse and the "sexual bartering" that go along with it, the expectation that she will live her life "nurturantly" through others, the encouragement of her own "passivity and dependency," the cultural stereotypes that contribute to a sense of inferiority—all of these probably influence her to seek the security and status of marriage.

However, it is possible that we are also encountering a degree of "experimenter bias." Very likely, adolescent girls are more pre-occupied with dreams of matrimony than boys, but whatever fantasies boys *do* have remain shrouded in mystery, mainly because researchers rarely address any questions on the subject. At least this is true of the two most widely cited and intensive studies of adolescents, Offer's *(1969)* and Douvan and Adelson's *(1966)*. Offer's interviews with teenage boys contain only the vaguest refer-ences to marriage and create the impression that this was not a topic the researchers were particularly interested in probing. In the Douvan and Adelson study, the male sample served to some extent as a "pilot group" for the female sample. By the time the girls were approached, the researchers had added some items on marriage, items that were not, for whatever reason, administered to the boys. The few comparative studies referred to earlier *(Broderick, 1965; Garrison, 1966)* have been of the "forced choice" paper and pencil variety, the kind which simply ask male and female adolescents if they plan to marry and if they are "looking forward" to the event. So the picture we have of premarital development during adolescence is by no means complete.

We are not, it might be noted, alone in drawing such conclusions. In his intensive survey of research on dating patterns, premarital relationships, and courtship, Burchinal *(1964)* remarks, "Different views exist about the possible outcomes of preadolescent and adolescent cross-sex interaction" *(1964, p. 632)*. But different views are apparently about all that exist, for a little later he observes, "At this point, we simply need more comprehensive, and, preferably, longitudinal studies to determine the various outcomes of different dating histories and patterns" *(1964, p. 632)*. Following an equally exhaustive survey, Elder *(1968)* expresses much the same opinion. Thus, from the data we have reviewed, one might infer that adoles-cence is an important period for the establishment of harmonious and intimate relationships between the sexes (as Erikson implies), but the really critical research (à la Pearsall, perhaps, but less impressionistic) is probably yet to come.

Leadership and Followership Versus Authority Confusion and Ideological Commitment Versus Confusion of Values

Nor has the next area—the development of values and ideol-ogies—been exactly "overresearched." In its heyday, student activism created quite a flurry among psychologists and sociologists, but even at its height, student activism was a rather specialized topic, involving only a minute fraction of the total adolescent population. Nonetheless, Erikson considers "ideological commit-ment" a singularly important—perhaps the *most* important—aspect of identity formation. For it is allegedly the development of a personal philosophy that permits the adolescent to integrate *all* the other dimensions of his identity: his outlook on the past, present, and future; his self-concept; the various roles he is expected to play as an adult; his occupational aspirations; his orientation toward sexuality; and finally, his probable niche in society. In fact, Erikson regards this last-named facet of the identity crisis—leadership and followership versus authority confusion—as being so closely related to the problem of ideological commitment versus confusion of values that he runs them together in his account, and we will follow his lead.

As far as "leadership and followership versus authority con-fusion" is concerned, we have already seen (in Chapter 6) that the adolescent (particularly the male adolescent) gradually differen-tiates himself from the members of his family, remaining close to them emotionally but learning to make his own decisions *(Bowerman & Kinch, 1959; Brittain, 1963; Meissner, 1965).* The ideology he formulates during adolescence presumably helps to determine what many of those decisions will be.

Adelson *(1971)* observes that the term "ideology" can be defined either loosely or strictly. In the narrowest sense it connotes a "highly structured, hierarchically ordered, internally consistent body of principles from which specific attitudes follow" *(1971, p. 120).* According to the broader definition, an ideology is simply a "body of attitudes roughly consistent with each other, and more or less organized in reference to a more encompassing, though perhaps tacit set of principles" *(1971, p. 121).* Erikson's use of the term is less specific still. He remarks that an ideology can be either "explicit or implicit" and that it may be associated with a wide variety of different values—historical, moral, occupational, ethical, religious, and political. However, when he elaborates on the subject, the religious and political themes—particularly the political—receive the most attention:

Ideologies, then, seem to provide meaningful combinations of the oldest and newest in a group's ideals. They thus channel the forceful earnestness, the sincere asceticism, and the eager indignation of youth toward that social frontier where the struggle between conservatism and radicalism is most alive. . . . But ideologies must ask, as the price for the promised possession of a future, for uncompromising commitment to some absolute hierarchy of values and some rigid principle of conduct, be that principle total obedience to tradition, if the future is the earthly kingdom of the ancestors; total resignation, if the future is to be of another world altogether; total martial discipline, if the future is reserved for some brand of armed superman; total inner reform, if the future is perceived as an advanced facsimile of heaven on earth; or finally (to mention only one of the ideological elements of our time) complete pragmatic abandon to human teamwork and to the processes of production if unceasing production seems to hold the present and future together. *(1968, pp. 190–191)*

Hence, it seems reasonable to concentrate on religion and politics as we review the research on "ideological commitment" during adolescence—especially since they are supposed to incorporate the temporal, moral, and occupational values discussed elsewhere.

Interest in Religion and Politics

When the question is how much adolescents are preoccupied with either of these two realms, one might conclude that religion and politics are both rather peripheral concerns. In a summary of research on the religious interests of American youth, Bealer and Willits *(1967)* report that although most adolescents (approximately 70 percent) attend church fairly regularly and an even larger percentage believe in God, relatively few seem to assign to religion a central role in their own lives. Only 38 percent of the teenagers in a national survey, for instance, agreed with the statement that faith was superior to logic for solving a person's problems. Similarly, although a high percentage (80 percent) credited God with watching over them, considerably fewer (60 percent) believed He was actively engaged in protecting them. (As might be expected, there were marked differences among members of the major denominations; Roman Catholic youngsters appeared to be the most devout, Jewish youngsters least so, and Protestants somewhere in between.)

With regard to politics, the same lack of interest seems to prevail. High school students may follow a few issues in the newspaper or on television, but relatively few of them become actively involved. Nor does the social studies curriculum appear to make much impact. Jennings and his associates *(Jennings & Niemi, 1968; Langton &*

Jennings, 1968) conducted an extensive survey of secondary school students and found that those who had taken several civics courses apparently did not know much more about politics—at least in the sense of being able to answer factual questions—than those who had taken only one. Similarly, the students who had been through the more "issue-oriented" American Problems course were only slightly more concerned about politics and social matters than those who had limited themselves to the more traditional American History course. In trying to account for their findings, the researchers reasoned that their subjects might have received all the political socialization they were going to receive *before* they had even reached high school. Conceivably, their attitudes had been so strongly molded in childhood that they were no longer accessible to change.

This view has, in fact, been rather popular among American researchers, particularly those who have studied the development of political thinking in children *(Easton & Hess, 1962; Hess & Torney, 1967)*. By the time he is twelve or thirteen, the argument goes, the youngster has acquired his "basic orientation" to the political system, and he is not likely to alter such a rock-ribbed set of values very much.

The Development of Religious Ideas

However, this school of thinking (again associated with *social-learning theory* to some extent) ignores the very important changes in cognition that occur during adolescence. There is a difference between being a devout churchgoer and cherishing certain religious ideals. There is also a difference between being able to rattle off the names of all 100 senators and exhibiting a grasp of certain political concepts. From reviewing the work on moral development *(Piaget, 1932; Kohlberg, 1964; Kohlberg & Kramer, 1969)*, we know that there is a marked shift in orientation between childhood and adolescence. The child's approach to questions of right and wrong is generally punitive and harsh, the adolescent's approach increasingly reasonable and humanitarian.

The same pattern can be observed as far as religion and politics are concerned. In a somewhat dated but interesting study, Kuhlen and Arnold *(1944)* explored the religious beliefs of sixth-, ninth-, and twelfth-graders. The younger children were inclined to be somewhat literal about most religious issues, agreeing wholeheartedly with statements like, "Hell is a place where you are punished for your sins on earth," "Every word in the Bible is true," and "God is someone who watches you to see that you behave yourself and punishes you if you are not good." With increasing age, there was a corresponding increase in skepticism, a majority of the twelfth graders indicating that they either disagreed with such assertions or that they at least "wondered" about their validity. The oldest adolescents were, for instance, far more likely to agree with the statement "It is not necessary to attend church to be a Christian" and to disagree with the dictum "People who go to church are better than people who do not go to church."

Significantly, this retreat from fundamentalist views was not accompanied by any marked loss of religious faith. Whereas 94 percent of the sixth graders believed in God, the percentage at twelfth grade stood at a still substantial 79 percent, and of the remaining twelfth graders, only 2 percent declared flatly that they were atheists, the rest simply admitting that they "wondered" about the existence of a Divine Being. Even more notable is the fact that the number of subjects who agreed with the statement "Prayers are a source of help in times of trouble" actually increased between sixth grade and twelfth grade from 74 percent to 83 percent.

Equally interesting, and perhaps more to the point, Elkind *(1971)* has concluded that the development of religious thought closely parallels the classical Piagetian stages (see Chapter 5 for a detailed discussion of Piaget). Drawing his conclusions both from his own studies and from those of other researchers, Elkind describes three phases of religious development. During the first stage (encompassing roughly the ages of five to seven), the child displays only a "global, undifferentiated" concept of religion. For example, he confuses his own denomination with his nationality. This rather vague comprehension gives way, usually sometime between the ages of seven and nine to a "concretely differentiated" view of religion. At this stage the child is capable of describing what members of various religious sects *do* (e.g., go to mass or celebrate Hanukkah), but he is unable to articulate what they actually *believe*. However, with the approach of adolescence, generally somewhere between the ages of ten and twelve, the child begins to exhibit an "abstract, differentiated conception" of religion. In a rudimentary sense, at least, he is able to identify the doctrine associated with his own faith. In response to the question of "What is a Jew?" for instance, he is capable of replying, "A person who believes in one God and doesn't believe in the New Testament" *(Elkind, 1971, p. 678)*.

The Development of Political Ideas

Though generally directed at a somewhat older population of subjects, research on the development of political thinking reveals comparable findings. As an indication of how "underresearched" this particular area has been, we note that the first studies which concentrated specifically on adolescents were undertaken within the last decade *(Adelson & O'Neil, 1966; Adelson, Green, & O'Neil, 1969)*. In these studies, which included 120 American boys and girls in grades 5, 7, 9, and 12, the subjects were asked (again à la Piaget) to imagine the following situation: A group of 1000 people had grown dissatisfied with their country and had moved to an island in the Pacific. Once there, they were portrayed as being confronted by a host of political, legal, and social issues—what form of government to have, what kinds of laws, what sort of school system and health care, what to do about crime. Each subject was asked how these issues might be resolved. As might have been expected, there was a shift from a punitive and categorical stance during childhood to a more humanitarian and idealistic orientation during adolescence. (Indeed, the resemblance to Kohlberg's research is unmistakable.)

The younger respondents, assuming they were even able to understand the problem at hand, answered questions in a generally moralistic and authoritarian manner. By late adolescence, a "social contract" mentality was much more in evidence. Instead of being perceived as a kind of superpoliceman, the government had come to be viewed primarily as a facilitator and arbiter, an agency which saw to it that various interests were balanced and that people got along harmoniously. The following replies to the question, "What is the purpose of law?" illustrate the changes in conceptualization that occur between fifth grade and twelfth grade:

Eleven years old: Well, so everybody won't fight and they have certain laws so they won't go around breaking windows and stuff and getting away with it.

Thirteen: To keep people from doing things they're not supposed to like killing people and like . . . if you're in the city like speeding in the car and things like that.

Fifteen: To help keep us safe and free.

Eighteen: Well, the main purpose would be just to set up a standard of behavior for people, for society living together so that they can live peacefully and in harmony with each other.

(Adelson, Green, & O'Neil, 1969, p. 328)

More extensive studies have yielded similar results. Though they observed some national variations, Gallatin and Adelson *(1970, 1971)* found much the same progression in political ideation among a sample of British and German youngsters. The pattern also held up in a sample of black and white American teenagers four times the size of the one employed by Adelson and O'Neil *(Gallatin, 1972)*. In this project, in fact, the age differences were by far the most impressive; ethnic, social class, *and* sex differences proving to be relatively minor.

This research *(Gallatin, 1972)* also provided evidence that the changes that had taken place by late adolescence were "ideological" in nature—at least if "ideology" is defined in its weaker sense as a body of related attitudes and values. No matter what area they were being questioned about—government, law, political parties, poverty, crime, police-community relations—younger subjects responded in a more categorical and authoritarian fashion, older subjects in a more informed and humanitarian manner. Indeed, the older subjects seemed to have incorporated many of the principles inherent in the Bill of Rights. *(See Tapp & Levine, 1972, for a study that reports comparable findings.)*

Values and education   Perhaps this is also the place to raise once more the question of *why* such changes occur during adolescence. The problem is undoubtedly a complicated and elusive one. As noted (see the discussion of "intelligence" in Chapter 5), the factors that influence cognition are difficult to identify and isolate. Very likely, the adolescent's increasing political sophistication and idealism result from a combination of forces: neurological changes in the brain (obviously most difficult to measure), increasing independence from the family, anticipation of becoming a voting citizen. However, there are indications, controversial and debatable as they may be, that education may have something to do with it. Trent and Craise *(1967)*, for example, paired a group of high school seniors who were college-bound with a group who were planning to take jobs immediately following graduation; they tested them on a number of standardized scales: thinking introversion, complexity, nonauthoritarianism, and social maturity. At that point there were no significant differences between the two samples. However, four years later the differences had become quite marked. The working group was, if anything, less flexible and liberal than it had been in high school, the college-educated group significantly more so.[4]

Ideology and Emotional Health

One final issue remains. Erikson asserts that the formulation of an ideology is supposed to permit the adolescent to resolve all the

---

[4] Again, we must point out that the results of this study do not indicate that education *produced* the differences in values between the two groups. The data merely imply that education was *associated* with these differences in some way.

part conflicts of the identity crisis. If so, there ought to be some sort of connection between commitment to an ideology and "psychological health." Those adolescents who have managed to work out and settle upon a set of values ought to appear "better integrated" than those who have not.

Marcia's research *(1966; Marcia & Friedman, 1970)* on identity status (already alluded to in Chapter 6) has unearthed some provocative findings in this connection. In his work with male college students, it may be remembered, Marcia identified four different types: Identity Achievements, Moratoriums, Foreclosures, and Diffusions. The Identity Achievements were defined specifically as individuals who have "experienced a crisis period and are committed to an occupation and an ideology" *(Marcia & Friedman, 1970, p. 250)*. The Moratoriums seemed still to be grappling with such issues and were thus judged to be in the *process* of making a commitment. The Foreclosures seemed simply to have adopted their *parents'* values wholesale without ever having undergone a crisis. And the Diffusions were described as lacking "both a sense of struggle and attempts to make commitments" *(Marcia & Friedman, p. 250)*. (We should add that students were assigned to a particular status on the basis of their replies to a standardized interview.)

On the whole, just as Eriksonian theory would predict, the Achievements gave evidence of being the "best adjusted"—that is, best able to perform under stress and most resistant to any attempted manipulations of self-esteem. Furthermore, as would also be predicted, the adjustment ratings of the three other statuses declined from those of the Achievements in the following descending order: Moratoriums, Foreclosures, and Diffusions. As we shall see (Chapter 12), somewhat different results were obtained with a group of female students, but these data on males nonetheless lend support to Erikson's assertions about the relationship between ideological commitment and psychological well-being.

Better known, perhaps, but more impressionistic, are Keniston's investigations of "alienated" undergraduates *(1960)* and idealistic "young radicals" *(1968)*. Keniston discovered his group of alienated subjects within a sample of Harvard freshmen who were (ironically enough) participating in a study of "normal personality development during late adolescence." These disaffected youngsters were bright, talented, often impeccably upper middle-class—and characterized by a disturbing inability to formulate a workable philosophy of life. The absence of ideological commitment seemed to be accompanied by conflicts in a number of other key areas. The future plans of the alienated youths remained notably fuzzy and diffuse. They exhibited symptoms of "work paralysis," most having to force themselves to study, some being compelled to drop out of school altogether. Their self-esteem, moreover, appeared fragile and their sexual identities correspondingly shaky.[5]

Some years later, when Keniston conducted a series of intensive interviews with a small group of young war protesters, a strikingly different configuration emerged. While by no means entirely free of problems, these youngsters, who were all involved in a "Vietnam Summer" project, appeared far more intact than their uncommitted counterparts. To be sure, they had questions about the fate of society and their future roles in it, but they were also clearly aware of the possible choices and alternatives. In addition, they gave the impression of being self-confident and energetic, displaying little of the sexual confusion that had been so prominent among the alienated students.

Other researchers *(Flacks, 1967; Heist, 1965; Trent & Craise, 1967; Watts & Whittaker, 1966)* have claimed to confirm the relationship between ideological commitment and emotional well-being, especially for leftist-leaning youngsters.[6] As proof, student activists have been portrayed as getting better grades and being more open-minded than their less "committed" confreres, and they themselves have consistently reported being on good terms with their parents.

Nonetheless, there are a number of caveats to be observed with respect to this particular issue. In the first place, almost all research on activism and commitment has been conducted with college students, often those attending the more élite and exclusive universities. This is a very select population, to say the least, and it might well be hazardous to generalize from such a group to the great mass of late adolescents. Second, activists do not always show up as thoroughly exemplary citizens. Haan, Smith, and Block *(1968)* surveyed a group of radicals at Berkeley, California, most of whom had been active in the Free Speech Movement and some of whom had actually been arrested in the course of a sit-in. These radical students were compared with a number of other groups: a random sample from another California university, Peace Corps volunteers, and so forth. All subjects were asked to respond to a special form of Kohlberg's Moral Dilemmas (see Chapter 5 for a review of

---

[5] We shall have more to say about these alienated students in Chapter 11.

[6] The picture is somewhat cloudier for conservatively oriented students. A study by Schiff *(1966)* found a sample of them to be somewhat constricted and defensive, but since conservative students have been studied so much less frequently than leftist-leaning students, it is difficult to draw any definitive conclusions about them.

Kohlberg's work), a biographical questionnaire, and a child-rearing practices report. They were also requested to describe themselves, both as they were and as they would like to be, on an adjective check list.

The activists turned out to be an intriguingly mixed lot. A disproportionate number, relative to the other groups, turned up at *either* end of Kohlberg's Scale of Moral Values. In line with the findings of the other researchers cited, a relatively high percentage of the radicals were judged to be "postconventional" or "principled" thinkers. They exhibited, in other words, a kind of "social contract" mentality. However, a smaller but still considerable percentage of the radicals were judged to be functioning at a "premoral" or comparatively primitive level. *Their* evaluations of right and wrong were based purely on expedience and utility.

As might have been expected, these two groups also differed markedly in other respects. The "idealistic" radicals closely resembled those who have been described in other studies. They reported harmonious relationships with their parents and characterized themselves as being conscientious, open-minded, and sympathetic. Their premoral counterparts presented a very different picture altogether. These youths admitted a great deal of conflict with their parents and characterized themselves as rebellious, stubborn, and aloof—but also as "creative." Thus, it appears that adolescents—even a comparatively homogeneous group like students attending the same college—can become involved in political activities for rather different reasons. The "principled" radicals may well have participated in sit-ins out of deep and abiding conviction that they were doing the right thing. We suspect, however, that their premoral "fellow travelers" had somewhat less admirable motives—such as seeking a convenient vehicle for their own rebelliousness and hostility.

Haan, Smith, and Block also caution against confusing political idealism with simple participation in a cause. They point out that the students who permitted themselves to be arrested in the sit-in at Berkeley included individuals at all three levels of Kohlberg's Scale: premoral and idealistic students and an in-between group of "conventionals." And as we have already noted (see Chapter 6, p. 122), Keniston himself *(1970)* issues a similar warning. It is important, he observes, to distinguish between mere commitment to a cause and moral rectitude. Many of the Hitler Youth in Germany who pledged their allegiance to fascism thought they had discovered a coherent and admirable philosophy of life, but their actions can scarcely be judged to have been ethical or humane.

Sex differences and ideology A sex difference that became apparent in the Haan, Smith, and Block study throws another interesting sidelight on the entire question of ideology and emotional adjustment. Kohlberg and Kramer *(1969)* report that in general fewer girls than boys forsake the "conventional" level of moral reasoning for the supposedly more advanced "principled" level, and Haan, Smith, and Block's research contains some clues that may help to account for this disparity. We have noted that the "principled" thinkers in their study presented, in many respects, a picture of robust emotional good health—but this was true mainly of the *men.* The women who scored at this level on Kohlberg's Scale presented themselves to the researchers as "guilty," "doubting," "restless," "impulsive," and relatively lacking in "foresight" or "ambition." (As might have been expected, they also described themselves as "altruistic" and rejected the adjective "stubborn.")

To add to this rather bleak portrait, the "principled" girls described themselves as "less feminine" than women at either of the other two levels (i.e., "conventional" and "premoral") and reported more conflict with their parents—precisely the reverse of the pattern for men. So, once again, what is "healthy" for a man is revealed to be somewhat "unhealthy" for a woman *(see Broverman et al., 1972).* It is possible that a female adolescent pays a higher price emotionally for formulating her own personal philosophy and code—which in turn might explain why fewer girls than boys appear to do so. Such an explanation is certainly compatible with a good deal of the research on feminine development that has already been discussed, research that indicates that girls are generally lower in self-esteem than boys and encouraged to be more dependent and less ambitious. Indeed, Haan, Block, and Smith themselves emphasize the connection:

> The social milieu and expectations for women encourage dependency, which is one form of irresponsibility. Consequently, the development of autonomous, principled morality may be a more difficult task for girls because it involves conflict with the culturally defined feminine role. The principled women's dysphoria and their admission of disappointing their parents may be a manifestation of their moral growing pains. *(1968, p. 198)*

We should not, on the other hand, push the differences that appear in Kohlberg's research and in Haan, Smith, and Block's too far. The closely related research in political thinking by Adelson and his associates *(Adelson, Green, & O'Neil, 1969; Adelson & O'Neil, 1966; Gallatin & Adelson, 1970, 1971; Gallatin, 1972)* has not uncovered *any* notable variations between boys and girls. Nonetheless, the "principled" coeds in the Haan, Smith, and Block study, with their "dysphoric" self-images, do at least remind us that adolescent development is a complicated affair.

Overview

Judging by the review we have conducted in this chapter and the previous one, Erikson's theory accommodates such complexities quite neatly. The problems of the teenage girl are still, and will remain, with us, but Erikson's model of the adolescent identity crisis, with all of its interlocking part conflicts, does seem to describe many of the important dimensions of adolescent development. We have seen that the part conflicts outlined in the model (e.g., self-certainty versus self-consciousness, apprenticeship versus work paralysis, sexual polarization versus bisexual confusion, and so forth) correspond to many significant changes—in temporal perspective, self-concept, vocational orientation, sex-role identification, and values—that occur during the teenage years. We have also seen that many of these changes seem, as the model implies, to be inter-related. Self-concept appears to be related to sex role, achievement motivation to self-esteem, and ideological commitment to emotional adjustment, to mention just a few of the possible connections that have turned up.

However, thus far in our attempt to use Erikson's theory as a conceptual umbrella, we have concentrated on the more "normative" aspects of adolescent development, catching only a glimpse, for the most part, of any of the more disturbing elements. This approach has been justified, in our opinion, because we believe that most adolescents do pass through their teens more or less unscathed. But some are undoubtedly not so fortunate, and it is to these that we now direct our attention.

REFERENCES

ADELSON, J. The Political Imagination of the Young Adolescent. *Daedalus*, 1971, **100**, 1013–1050.

ADELSON, J., GREEN, B., & O'NEIL, R. P. Growth of the Idea of Law at Adolescence. *Developmental Psychology*, 1969, **1**, 327–332.

ADELSON, J., & O'NEIL, R. P. Growth of Political Ideas in Adolescence: The Sense of Community. *Journal of Personality and Social Psychology*, 1966, **4**, 295–306.

BANDURA, A. Social Learning through Imitation. In M. R. Jones (Ed.), *Nebraska Symposium on Motivation, 1962*. Lincoln: University of Nebraska Press, 1962.

BANDURA, A., ROSS, D., & ROSS, S. A. Transmission of Aggression through Imitation of Aggressive Models. *Journal of Abnormal and Social Psychology*, 1961, **63**, 575–582.

BANDURA, A., & WALTERS, R. H. *Adolescent Aggression*. New York: Ronald, 1959.

BARDWICK, J. *The Psychology of Women*. New York: Harper & Row, 1971.

BEALER, R. C., & WILLITS, R. K. The Religious Interests of American High School Youth. *Religious Education*, 1967, **62**, 435–444.

BENNETT, E. M., & COHEN, L. R. Men and Women: Personality Patterns and Contrasts. *Genetic Psychology Monographs*, 1959, **60**, 101–153.

BOHAN, J. Age and Sex Differences in Self-Concept, *Journal of Youth and Adolescence*, in press.

BOWERMAN, C. E., & KINCH, J. W. Changes in Family and Peer Orientation of Children between the Fourth and Tenth Grades. *Social Forces*, 1959, **37**, 206–211.

BRITTAIN, C. V. Adolescent Choices and Parent-Peer Cross-Pressure. *American Sociological Review*, 1963, **28**, 385–391.

BRODERICK, C. B. Social Heterosexual Development among Urban Negroes and Whites. *Journal of Marriage and the Family*, 1965, **27**, 200–203.

BROVERMAN, I. K., BROVERMAN, D. M., CLARKSON, F. E., ROSENKRANTZ, P., & VOGEL, S. R. Sex Role Stereotypes and Clinical Judgments of Mental Health. *Journal of Consulting Psychology*, 1970, **34**, 1–7.

BROVERMAN, I., VOGEL, S. R., BROVERMAN, D., CLARKSON, F. E., & ROSEN-KRANTZ, P. S. Sex-Role S ₃reotypes: A Current Appraisal. *Journal of Social Issues*, 1972, **28**, 59–78.

BURCHINAL, L. G. The Premarital Dyad and Love Involvement. In H. T. Christensen (Ed.), *Handbook of Marriage and the Family*. Chicago: Rand McNally, 1964.

CARLSON, R. Identification and Personality Structure in Preadolescents. *Journal of Abnormal and Social Psychology*, 1963, **67**, 566–573.

CARLSON, R. Stability and Change in the Adolescent Self-Image. *Child Development*, 1965, **36**, 659–666.

CONNELL, D. M., & JOHNSON, J. E. Relationship between Sex-Role Identification and Self-Esteem in Early Adolescents. *Developmental Psychology*, 1970, **3**, 268–273.

COOMBS, R. H., & KENKEL, W. F. Sex Differences in Dating Aspirations and Satisfaction with Computer-Selected Partners. *Journal of Marriage and the Family*, 1966, **28**, 62–66.

DAWE, H. C. An Analysis of 200 Quarrels of Preschool Children. *Child Development*, 1934, **5**, 139–157.

DIAMOND, M. A Critical Evaluation of the Ontogeny of Human Sexual Behavior. *Quarterly Review of Biology*, 1965, **40**, 147–175.

DOUVAN, E. Sex Differences in Adolescent Character Processes. *Merrill-Palmer Quarterly*, 1960, **6**, 203–211.

DOUVAN, E., & ADELSON, J. *The Adolescent Experience*. New York: Wiley, 1966.

EASTON, D., & HESS, R. D. The Child's Political World. *Midwest Journal of Political Science*, 1962, **6**, 229–246.

EHRMANN, W. W. *Premarital Dating Behavior*. New York: Holt, Rinehart & Winston, 1959.

ELDER, G. H. *Adolescent Socialization and Personality Development*. Chicago: Rand McNally, 1968.

ELKIND, D. The Development of Religious Understanding in Children and Adolescents. In M. P. Strommen (Ed.), *Research on Religious Development*. New York: Hawthorn, 1971.

ELMAN, J. B., PRESS, A., & ROSENKRANTZ, P. Sex-roles and Self-Concepts: Real and Ideal. Paper presented at the meeting of the American Psychological Association, Miami, August 1970.

ERIKSON, E. *Identity: Youth and Crisis.* New York: Norton, 1968.

FLACKS, R. The Liberated Generation: An Exploration of the Roots of Student Protest. *Journal of Social Issues,* 1967, **23,** 52–73.

GALLATIN, J. *The Development of Political Thinking in Urban Adolescents.* (Final Rep., Office of Education Grant 0-0554) Washington, D.C.: National Institutes of Education, 1972.

GALLATIN, J., & ADELSON, J. Individual Rights and the Public Good: A Cross-National Study of Adolescence. *Comparative Political Studies,* 1970, **3,** 226–242.

GALLATIN, J., & ADELSON, J. Legal Guarantees of Individual Freedom: A Cross-National Study of the Development of Political Thought. *Journal of Social Issues,* 1971, **27,** 93–108.

GARAI, J. E., & SCHEINFELD, A. Sex Differences in Mental and Behavioral Traits. *Genetic Psychology Monographs,* 1968, **77,** 169–299.

GARRISON, K. C. A Study of the Aspirations and Concerns of Ninth-Grade Pupils from the Public Schools of Georgia. *Journal of Social Psychology,* 1966, **69,** 245–252.

GAWRONSKI, D. A., & MATHIS, C. Differences Between Over-Achieving, Normal-Achieving, and Under-Achieving High School Students. *Psychology in the Schools,* 1965, **2,** 152–155.

GUTMANN, D. Female Ego Styles and Generational Conflict. In E. L. Walker (Ed.), *Feminine Personality and Conflict.* Belmont, Calif.: Brooks/Cole, 1970.

HAAN, N., SMITH, M. B., & BLOCK, J. Moral Reasoning of Young Adults: Political and Social Behavior, Family Background and Personality Correlates. *Journal of Personality and Social Psychology,* 1968, **10,** 183–201.

HAMPSON, J. L., & HAMPSON, J. G. The Ontogenesis of Sexual Behavior in Man. In W. C. Young (Ed.), *Sex and Internal Secretions.* Vol. II. Baltimore: Williams & Wilkins, 1961.

HARTLEY, R. E. Children's Concepts of Male and Female Roles. *Merrill-Palmer Quarterly,* 1960, **6,** 83–91.

HARTUP, W. W., & ZOOK, E. A. Sex Role Preferences in Three and Four-Year-Old Children. *Journal of Consulting Psychology,* 1960, **24,** 420–426.

HATTWICK, B. A. Sex Differences in Behavior of Nursery School Children. *Child Development,* 1937, **8,** 343–355.

HAWKES, B. G., BURCHINAL, L. G., & GARDNER, B. Pre-Adolescents' Views of Some of Their Relations with Their Parents. *Child Development,* 1957, **28,** 393–399.

HEIST, P. Intellect and Commitment: The Faces of Discontent. Mimeograph, Center for the Study of Higher Education, University of California, Berkeley, 1965.

HELSON, R. The Changing Image of the Career Woman. *Journal of Social Issues,* 1972, **28,** 33–46.

HESS, R. D., & TORNEY, J. *The Development of Political Attitudes in Children.* New York: Aldine, 1967.

HONZIK, M. P. Sex Differences in the Occurrence of Materials in the Play Constructions of Preadolescents. *Child Development,* 1951, **22,** 15–35.

JENNINGS, M. K., & NIEMI, R. G. The Transmission of Political Values from Parent to Child. *American Political Science Review,* 1968, **62,** 169–184.

JOSSELSON, R. Identity Formation in College Women. Unpublished doctoral dissertation, University of Michigan, 1972.

KAGAN, J. The Child's Perception of the Parent. *Journal of Abnormal and Social Psychology*, 1956, **53**, 257–258.

KAGAN, J. Sex Typing and Sex Role Identity. In M. L. Hoffman and L. W. Hoffman (Eds.), *Review of Child Development Research.* Vol. I. New York: Russell Sage, 1964.

KAGAN, J., & LEMKIN, J. The Child's Differential Perception of Parental Attributes. *Journal of Abnormal and Social Psychology*, 1960, **61**, 446–447.

KAGAN, J., & MOSS, H. *Birth to Maturity.* New York: Wiley, 1962.

KENISTON, K. Student Activism, Moral Development, and Morality. *American Journal of Orthopsychiatry*, 1970, **40**, 577–592.

KENISTON, K. *The Uncommitted: Alienated Youth in American Society.* New York: Delta, 1960.

KENISTON, K. *Young Radicals: Notes on Committed Youth.* New York: Harcourt Brace Jovanovich, 1968.

KINSEY, A. C., POMEROY, W., & MARTIN, C. *Sexual Behavior in the Human Male.* Philadelphia: Saunders, 1948.

KOHLBERG, L. Development of Moral Character and Moral Ideology. In M. L. Hoffman and L. W. Hoffman (Eds.), *Review of Child Development Research.* Vol. I. New York: Russell Sage, 1964.

KOHLBERG, L., & KRAMER, R. Continuities and Discontinuities in Childhood and Adult Moral Development. *Human Development*, 1969, **12**, 93–120.

KUHLEN, R. G., & ARNOLD, M. Age Differences in Religious Beliefs and Problems During Adolescence. *Journal of Genetic Psychology*, 1944, **65**, 291–300.

LANGTON, K. P., & JENNINGS, M. K. Political Socialization and the High School Civics Curriculum in the United States. *American Political Science Review*, 1968, **52**, 852–867.

LINTON, R. *The Study of Man.* New York: Appleton, 1936.

MACCOBY, E. (Ed.). *The Development of Sex Differences.* Stanford: Stanford University Press, 1966.

MACCOBY, E., & WILSON, W. Identification and Observational Learning from Films. *Journal of Abnormal and Social Psychology*, 1957, **55**, 76–87.

McKEE, J. P., & SHERRIFFS, A. C. Men's and Women's Beliefs, Ideals, and Self-Concepts. *American Journal of Sociology*, 1959, **64**, 356–363.

MARCIA, J. E. Development and Validation of Ego-Identity Status. *Journal of Personality and Social Psychology*, 1966, **3**, 551–558.

MARCIA, J. E., & FRIEDMAN, M. L. Ego Identity in College Women. *Journal of Personality*, 1970, **38**, 249–263.

MARMOR, J. (Ed.). *Sexual Inversion: The Multiple Roots of Homosexuality.* New York: Basic Books, 1965.

MARSHALL, J. M., & KARABENICK, S. A. Self-Esteem, Fear of Success, and Occupational Choice in Female Adolescents. Unpublished manuscript, 1973.

MEISSNER, W. W. Parental Interaction of the Adolescent Boy. *Journal of Genetic Psychology*, 1965, **107**, 225–233.

MONEY, J. Sex Hormones and Other Variables in Human Eroticism. In W. C. Young (Ed.), *Sex and Internal Secretions.* Vol. II. Baltimore: Williams & Wilkins, 1961.

MONGE, R. Developmental Trends in Factors of Adolescent Self-Concept. *Developmental Psychology*, 1973, **8**, 382–393.

MUSSEN, P. H., & JONES, M. C. The Behavior Inferred Motivations of Late and Early Maturing Boys. *Child Development*, 1958, **29**, 61–67.

MUSTE, M. J., & SHARPE, D. F. Some Influential Factors in the Determination of Aggressive Behavior in Preschool Children. *Child Development*, 1947, **18**, 11–28.

NAWAS, M. M. Change in Efficiency of Ego Functioning and Complexity from Adolescence to Young Adulthood. *Developmental Psychology*, 1971, **4**, 412–415.

OFFER, D. Attitudes Toward Sexuality in a Group of 1500 Middle Class Teen-Agers. *Journal of Youth and Adolescence*, 1972, **1**, 81–90.

OFFER, D. *The Psychological World of the Teenager*. New York: Basic Books, 1969.

OTTO, H. A., & HEALY, S. L. Adolescents' Self-Perception of Personality Strengths. *Journal of Human Relations*, 1966, **14**, 483–490.

PEARSALL, P. Personal communication, 1973.

PIAGET, J. *The Moral Judgment of the Child*. London: Routledge & Kegan Paul, 1932.

POPE, B. Socioeconomic Contrasts in Children's Peer Culture Prestige Values. *Genetic Psychology Monographs*, 1953, **48**, 157–220.

REISS, I. L. *Premarital Sexual Standards in America*. New York: Free Press, 1960.

REISS, I. L. *The Social Context of Premarital Permissiveness*. New York: Holt, Rinehart & Winston, 1967.

RINGNESS, T. A. Identification Patterns, Motivation, and School Achievement of Bright Junior High School Boys. *Journal of Educational Psychology*, 1967, **58**, 93–102.

ROSENBERG, M. *Society and the Adolescent Self-Image*. Princeton: Princeton University Press, 1965.

SCHIFF, L. F. Dynamic Young Fogies, Rebels on the Right. *Trans-action*, November 1966, pp. 30–36.

SHIPMAN, G. The Psychodynamics of Sex Education. *Family Coordinator*, 1968, **17**, 3–12.

SMIGEL, E. O., & SEIDEN, R. The Decline and Fall of the Double Standard. *Annals of the American Academy of Political and Social Sciences*, 1968, **376**, 6–17.

STEIN, A. H., & BAILEY, M. The Socialization of Achievement Orientation in Females. *Psychological Bulletin*, 1973, **80**, 345–366.

TAPP, J. L., & LEVINE, F. J. Compliance from Kindergarten to College: A Speculative Note. *Journal of Youth and Adolescence*, 1972, **1**, 233–250.

TRENT, J. W., & CRAISE, J. L. Commitment and Conformity in the American College. *Journal of Social Issues*, 1967, **2**, 34–51.

WATTS, W. A., & WHITTAKER, D. N. E. Free Speech Advocates at Berkeley. *Journal of Applied Behavioral Science*, 1966, **2**, 41–62.

WITKIN, H. A., DYK, R. B., FATERSON, H. F., GOODENOUGH, D. R., & KARP, S. A. *Psychological Differentiation*. New York: Wiley, 1962.

WRIGHT, D. Junior College Students View Women's Roles. *Journal of the National Association of Women Deans and Counselors*, 1967, **30**, 71–77.

11 Erikson's Theory as a Conceptual Umbrella: PART III

The Darker Side of Adolescence

Although we have argued that Erikson's theory, with its concepts of "normative crisis" and "moratorium" conveys an impression of adolescence far less tempestuous and turbulent than the popular one, many psychologists, ironically, insist on lumping Erikson with the "storm and stress" theorists. The "normative" falls by the wayside, and the "crisis" aspects of the theory predominate. Monge, for example, asserts that Erikson describes adolescence as an essentially "discontinuous" period of development, one marked by "considerable" and "even dramatic" changes in self-concept *(1973, p. 382)*. And Weiner, an acknowledged expert on adolescent disturbances, offers us the following assessment of Eriksonian theory:

> Erikson ascribes a number of apparently maladaptive reaction patterns to the role diffusion that accompanies identity crisis, including labile and unpredictable behavior, lack of commitment, semideliberate experimentation with dangerous or deviant behavior, and experimentation with fantasy and introspection, the latter involving conscious awareness of many thoughts and impulses ordinarily repressed by adults. *Yet he maintains that such phenomena, although indicative of major psychopathology when they occur in adults, are normative and healthy in adolescents.* (1970, p. 44, italics added)

We have no intention of criticizing Monge and Weiner and mention them specifically here only for purposes of illustration, but we do

280

believe that they, like many other researchers and practitioners, have unwittingly misinterpreted Erikson—and that the theorist himself is, in part, responsible.

In describing the normative crisis of adolescence, Erikson does, it seems to us, allow for wide variations in development. He claims that this is the first period in which the youngster is sufficiently mature to begin perceiving himself as an individual (i.e., to experience a "conscious sense of individual uniqueness"). Or to put it another way, adolescence is, as Erikson describes it, that era of life in which the sense of identity begins to crystallize. And since he envisions identity formation as an enormously complex process, Erikson implies that it can vary tremendously from one individual to the next—that some teenagers may experience great storm and stress and others little or none.

However, there can be no question that he recognizes the *potential* for serious disturbance during adolescence. Each of the part conflicts he describes, after all, has both a positive and a negative aspect. To attain a sense of "temporal perspective," for example, the adolescent must allegedly combat a sense of "time confusion," and "ideological commitment" occurs as the alternative to a total "confusion of values." Erikson can even be accused, perhaps, of *dwelling* on the negative aspects of adolescent development, of giving more attention, in a way, to identity *confusion* than to identity *formation*. Offer, whom we have cited so often, once more puts his finger on the problem:

> It is of interest to note that where Erikson gives examples of eight problems or crises of the adolescent, he illustrates each by an example of psychopathology taken from the negative end of the continuum. Why are there no examples of healthy or adaptive responses to adolescence? Where are the examples of true "normative crisis"? It seems that for Erikson, too, it is easier to give clinical examples. *(1969, p. 183)*[1]

The point is well taken. Particularly in his earlier work on identity formation *(1959)*, Erikson does display a tendency to draw his illustrations from the pathological and omit the more typical. Consequently, it is not entirely surprising that he is often included (erroneously, in our opinion) among the "storm and stress" theorists. But we should add that in his most recent book on adolescence, Erikson himself seems to have become aware of the omission, and

---

[1] We are not quite sure what Offer has in mind in referring to eight problems. The only time, so far as we know, that Erikson specifically refers to eight problems is when he describes the eight aspects of ideology. See Chapter 8 of the present text.

he includes, for the first time, an account of a normal "identity crisis" and "moratorium" *(see the case of Jill, 1968, pp. 130–131).* He also promises us that other "normal" case histories will follow, although they have yet to appear in print.

Furthermore, while it may at times appear to emphasize the more troubling aspects of adolescence, we believe that Eriksonian theory is sufficiently flexible and comprehensive to accommodate *both* the normal and the pathological. Despite his criticisms, Offer applies the concept of normative crisis to his own study of teenage boys, and we have used it as an organizing principle for our research review in the two preceding chapters. Indeed, having examined the "brighter side" of adolescence, we may now turn our attention to the "darker side." Disturbed and problem-ridden youngsters may constitute a distinct minority, but they are an important (and sometimes all too visible) minority nonetheless.

A Closer Look at the "Crisis" in "Identity Crisis"

Weiner is at least partially correct in his claim that Erikson minimizes the seriousness of "pathological behavior" during adolescence. Erikson does not, it seems to us, consider wild antics and bizarre fantasies to be "perfectly normal" and "healthy" features of the period, but he does believe that such "symptoms" can be less *ominous* when they occur in adolescence rather than in adulthood. *Some* teenagers, definitely conflicted but "not too neurotic" as Erikson describes them, may engage in questionable and even hazardous activity simply to test limits and find out more about themselves. In these circumstances, what *looks* like severe disturbance, Erikson insists, may instead be a somewhat extreme variant of "role experimentation":

> The adolescent's leaning out over any number of precipices is normally an experimentation with experiences which are thus becoming more amenable to ego control, provided that they are not prematurely responded to with fatal seriousness by overeager or neurotic adults. The same must be said of the adolescent's "fluidity of defenses," which so often causes genuine concern on the part of the worried clinician. Much of this fluidity is anything but pathological, for adolescence is a crisis in which only fluid defense can overcome a sense of victimization by inner and outer demands and in which only trial and error can lead to the most felicitous avenues of action and self-expression. *(1968, p. 164)*

It is reasonably clear, we think, that in referring to "worried clinicians" that Erikson has adolescent *patients*, rather than normal, "garden variety" teenagers, in mind. On the other hand, he cautions clinicians (and others who must deal with adolescents) not to be too hasty in labeling a given youngster "sick." Though they are to be taken seriously, some young people who give the appearance of being "severely disturbed" may be suffering more from "developmental problems" than from any deep-rooted and long-festering conflicts of early childhood. They may have found the complexities of identity formation—with all the decisions and choices that are required—too much to cope with. Rather than being afflicted with "psychosis" or "severe neurosis," such adolescents are in a state of "acute identity confusion," and they may therefore, Erikson implies, stand a better chance of regaining their bearings:

> The clinically oriented reader will rightly feel that in my endeavor to understand identity confusion as a developmental disturbance, I neglect diagnostic signs which would mark a malignant and more irreversible condition. Identity confusion, of course, is not a diagnostic entity, but I would think that a description of the developmental crisis in which a disturbance has its acute onset should become part of any diagnostic picture, and especially of any prognosis and any statement concerning the kind of therapy indicated. *(1968, p. 166)*

The Signs of "Acute Identity Confusion"

Erikson goes on to describe four "symptoms" that are likely to be associated with this state of acute confusion—all of which are recognizable, with slight changes in terminology and emphasis, as negative aspects of the adolescent identity crisis. The disparities occur, we should add, because Erikson has a habit of including parts of older manuscripts in his most recent writings. Consequently, there is not always a perfect correspondence in terminology from one chapter of his most recent work on adolescence *(1968)* to the next. What is referred to as "bisexual confusion" or "role fixation" in one section of *Identity: Youth and Crisis* becomes "the problem of intimacy" or "negative identity" in another. To clarify matters, we shall use the older term for each symptom of "acute identity confusion" and put the newer label in parentheses beside it.

Diffusion of Time Perspective (Time Confusion)

Though more fortunate youngsters, as we have seen, develop a firm sense of time, those undergoing more acute forms of the identity crisis may suffer from a "diffusion of time perspective." A youth so afflicted appears to be particularly fearful of accepting the clock as a meaningful part of his life. The notion that his existence is finite—and hence that his alternatives are limited—seems to engender intense conflict. Confronted with the task of establishing some sort of framework for his own future, the youngster complains, on the one hand, of feeling helpless and "baby-like" and, on the other, of feeling "old beyond rejuvenation." It is as if the chance to accomplish anything significant and worthwhile had already passed— paradoxically at just the point where most adolescents believe they have "their whole lives before them":

> The contradiction is often expressed as a general slowing up which makes the patient behave, within the routine of his activities and of his therapy, as if he were moving in molasses. It is hard for him to go to bed and face the necessary restitution of wakefulness; it is hard to come to the therapeutic appointment, and hard to leave it. *(1968, p. 169)*

This kind of slowing up, apparently almost to the point of stupor in some youthful patients, is one of the classical symptoms of depression. And indeed, Erikson notes that adolescents who have lost their grip on time often consciously express the wish to "quit," to "give up,"—or even to "die."

Diffusion of Industry (Work Paralysis)

Young people may actually "quit" or "give up" in another respect. In American society, as in many others, Erikson notes, the concept of work is very much entwined with that of "competition." Youngsters who are confused about their identities may be put off by the thought of competing; some of them are afraid to fail, others skeptical about the real value of trying to succeed. Thus, in situations in which they are compelled to "prove themselves"—in school or on the job—they are likely to be stricken with an "inability to concentrate" or to apply themselves:

> Although the patients in question usually are intelligent and able and have shown themselves successful in office work, scholastic studies, and sports, they now lose the capacity for work, exercise, sociability and thus lose the most important vehicle of social play and the most significant refuge from formless fantasy and vague anxiety. *(1968, pp. 171–172)*

Revealing his psychoanalytic roots, Erikson also focuses on the possible "Oedipal" aspects of such diffusion of industry. For the little boy, in particular, his first model of vocational success is his father—who presumably goes off to work in some capacity every day. In resolving the conflict of initiative versus guilt (Erikson's own expanded version of the Oedipal struggle), he must master his desire to compete directly with and replace his father. If the child is unable to do this, if his feelings of frustration are never resolved and simply remain buried, or if all striving somehow takes on the connotation of battling his father for supremacy, the youngster may find himself unable to work at much of anything as he reaches adolescence. Any attempt to achieve a measure of vocational success for himself may be interpreted unconsciously as an attack on his father—and hence dangerous. Erikson gives us an example of this sort of conflict from his own clinical practice: "A young patient who had found himself blocked in college nearly read himself blind during the initial phase of his treatment, apparently in a destructive over-identification with father and therapist, both of whom were professors" *(1968, p. 172).*

The Problem of Intimacy (Bisexual Confusion)

We already know that Erikson views a strong sense of identity as a prerequisite for intimacy. Therefore it follows that the adolescent who is having difficulty "finding himself" may also have difficulty "finding" others. His own insecurity may make it dangerous for him to be "too close" to anyone else, for such closeness, Erikson suggests, threatens to blur what little sense of identity he has managed to salvage. Such a youngster may withdraw into his own protective shell, threatening to become a painfully "isolated" adult. Or he may plunge into "pseudointimate" physical relationships and become afflicted with a kind of "bisexual confusion":

True "engagement" with others is the result of the test of firm self-delineation. As the young individual seeks at least tentative forms of playful intimacy in friendship and competition, in sex play and love, in argument and gossip, he is apt to experience a peculiar strain, as if such tentative engagement might turn into an interpersonal fusion amounting to a loss of identity and requiring therefore, a tense inner reservation, a caution in commitment. Where a youth does not resolve such strain, he may isolate himself and enter, at best, only stereotyped and formalized interpersonal relations; or he may, in repeated hectic attempts and dismal failures, seek intimacy with the most improbable partners. . . . During love-making or in sexual fantasies a loosening of sexual identity threatens; it even becomes unclear whether sexual excitement is experienced by the individual or by his partner, and this applies in either heterosexual or homosexual encounters. *(1968, pp. 167–168)*

Negative Identity (Role Fixation)

And finally, some adolescents attempt to resolve all the confusion of an "acute identity crisis" by settling upon a "negative identity." A youngster whose parents have always placed more emphasis on what he should *not* become (rather than on what he should) is a prime candidate for such a choice—or attempted choice:

A mother who was filled with unconscious ambivalence toward a brother who had disintegrated into alcoholism again and again responded selectively only to those traits in her son which seemed to point to a repetition of her brother's fate, with the result that this "negative identity" sometimes seemed to have more reality for the son than all his natural attempts at being good. He worked hard at becoming a drunkard, and, lacking the necessary ingredients, ended up in a state of stubborn paralysis of choice. *(Erikson, 1968, p. 175)*

Similarly, an upper-class adolescent who has been pushed and manipulated by "morbidly ambitious" parents may, in his attempts to reclaim himself, decide to become a "nothing" rather than a "somebody." And a lower-class youth who has lost all hope of *ever* becoming "somebody" may discover himself "fixated" on much the same role in life. The point in all such cases, Erikson notes, is that where *positive* alternatives have been blocked, the youngster may be compelled to settle for negative ones:

The history of such a choice reveals a set of conditions in which it is easier for the patient to derive a sense of identity out of a total identification with that which he is least supposed to be than to struggle for a feeling of reality in acceptable roles which are unattainable with his inner means. *(1968, p. 176)*

An adolescent might presumably display other symptoms of "acute identity confusion," symptoms that would correspond to other facets of the identity crisis. Erikson does, in fact, refer fleetingly to "self-consciousness" and "confusion of values," but the four symptoms discussed here are the four he concentrates most of his attention upon.

The Usefulness of the Concept

The key question at this point, of course, is whether the concept of "acute identity confusion" can help to illuminate the "darker side" of adolescence. Earlier "normative crisis" was employed as a conceptual umbrella. Can we apply the concept of "identity confusion" in a similar fashion? Actually, the question may be divided in two:

1. First, how useful is the concept of identity confusion, taken as a whole? Is it true that the strain of trying to synthesize an identity may cause some youngsters to become disturbed? Do such strains make the disturbed adolescent seem "crazier" than he really is? In short, how much of what appears to be pathology during adolescence can be attributed to youthful "experimentation" and how much to deep-seated emotional conflicts?
2. Can the various part-symptoms of identity confusion—the failures in time perspective, work, intimacy, and role-experimentation— be related to some of the more serious problems of adolescence (e.g., adolescent schizophrenia, suicide, drug abuse, delinquency, underachievement, and alienation)?

The Diagnostic Significance of Identity Confusion

Erikson obviously believes that "adolescing" can be an exceedingly complicated task. Can the demands of this whole enterprise precipitate a serious emotional disturbance (or what looks like one), and is such a disturbance likely to be more reversible when it occurs during adolescence than it is at some other point in life?

Judging from Weiner's figures *(1970)* on the diagnosis of emotional illness among the young, many clinicians apparently think so. Weiner notes that a suspiciously disproportionate number of adolescents evaluated at psychiatric clinics are diagnosed as "transient situational disorders." In comparison with "neuroses" or "psychoses," these are considered to be relatively minor disturbances, brought on largely by "situational" factors. Once these factors have been alleviated, the disorder is supposed to clear up pretty much on its own—and with a minimum of therapeutic intervention. Thus, when applied to adolescents, "transient situational disorder" is probably more or less the equivalent of "growing pains." In any case, a sizable 36 percent of adolescent clinical patients as opposed to a minuscule 4–6 percent of all adult patients are assigned to this diagnostic category.

However, according to Weiner, youngsters diagnosed as "transient situational disorders" are just as likely to receive psychotherapy and are likely to remain in it just as long as those who are judged to be suffering from more serious ailments, such as "neurosis," "psychosis," "personality disorder." Consequently, he concludes, the fact that a disproportionate number of adolescents have this particular label applied to them probably says more about *clinicians* than about adolescents. Almost as if they were heeding Erikson's warnings, many professionals seem disinclined to call a

youngster with problems "sick." Eying the statistics on diagnosis
and treatment, Weiner remarks: "the high incidence of treatment in
these patients suggests that the frequent impression of 'transient
situational personality disorder' reflected more a reluctance to apply
other diagnostic labels than a conviction that these youngsters had
self-limiting disturbances for which they did not require treatment"
(p. 84).

Citing several studies by Masterson and his associates (Masterson, 1967a, 1967b, 1968; Masterson, Corrigan, Kofkin, & Wallenstein,
1966; Masterson & Washburne, 1966), Weiner also discounts the
notion that disorders which become manifest during adolescence
are necessarily less ominous than those which occur earlier or later
in life. He notes, for instance, that when a group of teenage clinic
patients were carefully matched with a group of teenagers who were
not undergoing therapy, it was remarkably easy to distinguish the
patients from the controls. The disturbed adolescents were not
simply more extreme versions of their "normal" counterparts. Many
more of the patients gave signs of being severely neurotic, schizophrenic, or dangerously impulsive, and they also had a much higher
incidence of psychosomatic complaints. These youngsters were
furthermore markedly more likely to be enmeshed in an unhappy
and fundamentally unrewarding family situation. Their parents were
often characterized as either neglectful or domineering, and there
had typically been long-standing disputes over basic issues like life
style and personal philosophy.

The normal teenagers, by contrast, enjoyed a considerably more
harmonious home life. For the most part these youngsters got along
well with their families. If there were any conflicts, they usually
revolved around such matters as dress, curfews, allowances, and
dating—typical, run-of-the-mill, parent-child disputes, in other words.
In fact, Weiner notes, these normal adolescents closely resembled
the "typical teenagers" interviewed by Douvan and Adelson (1966).
(We might point out that they also resemble the normal controls in
Bandura and Walters' 1959 study of "adolescent aggression.") Not
that the nonpatient group went through their lives with nary a care,
surveying the world through rose-colored glasses. During the period
they were observed, 65 percent of them presented evidence of being
"anxious" and 41 percent of being depressed at one time or another.
However, anxiety and depression seem rather common, if un-
welcome, appurtenances of human existence. Weiner claims that
normal *adults* complain of such symptoms in almost exactly the same
proportions. So except for their normal human failings, the non-
patients appeared to be a much healthier lot than the patients.

Nor did the disturbed group exhibit much of a tendency to "outgrow" their problems. Masterson *(Masterson & Washburne, 1966)* reevaluated these young patients twice in a five year period. Although more than half the group had been undergoing some form of psychotherapy, 62 percent were judged to be "moderately or seriously impaired" by the time of the second follow-up. And to puncture the "growing pains" hypothesis still further, Weiner marshals an impressive array of studies on adolescents who had been diagnosed as schizophrenics *(Annesley, 1961; Carter, 1942; Masterson, 1956; Warren, 1965)*. Reviewing the findings from all these investigations, he concludes that "other things being equal, about one-fourth of adolescent schizophrenics will recover, another one-fourth will demonstrate some improvement, and the remaining one-half will fail to improve" *(1970, p. 140)*—scarcely the most encouraging set of statistics. All in all, the "don't worry about them they'll grow out of it" school of adolescent psychopathology does not receive much support. Teenage disturbances are apparently not to be dismissed lightly, and the troubled teenager shows a disturbing tendency to become an equally troubled adult.

What implications do these data have for the concept of "identity confusion"? Probably they create less trouble for the concept than might seem to be the case at first glance. Eriksonian theory would not necessarily be embarrassed, it seems to us, by the finding that a group of adolescents who were not receiving psychotherapy differed markedly from a group who were. While Erikson claims that there is *potential* for identity confusion in all adolescents, nowhere does he suggest that they all inevitably fall prey to serious disturbances—or even that a large proportion of them do. He also does not claim that his account of "acute identity confusion" is based on normal adolescents. It is instead derived, as we have seen, from his observations of psychiatric patients, many of whom were probably "borderline" or "prepsychotic."

The figures on prognosis are more problematic. Erikson *does* seem to be somewhat overoptimistic about the future prospects of severely disturbed youngsters. He speaks, for instance, of "specific conditions which may have forced a transitory regression on the individual as an attempt to postpone and to avoid, as it were, a psychosocial foreclosure" *(1968, p. 167)*. Judging from Weiner's review of the data, regressions during adolescence are rarely "transitory." Even with treatment, the majority of emotionally troubled adolescents carry their symptoms with them into adulthood.[2]

---

[2] This point, too, is less damaging than it may seem, for Erikson himself never specifically predicts the recovery rates for disturbed adolescents. He merely implies that for *some* adolescents the immediate strains of the identity

Part-Symptoms: The Common-Sense Level

Eriksonian theory fares rather better once again when we examine possible connections between developmental changes and some of the more familiar "adolescent problems"—for example, drugs, suicide, and delinquency.

There is, of course, a purely "common sense" level that cannot be ignored. Earlier it was suggested that adolescents can generally be distinguished from children by virtue of their comparative biological, physical, and intellectual maturity. They look and act more like adults than children do, and large numbers of them are (technically) at an age where they can reproduce. Consequently, they can also get themselves into many of the same difficulties as adults, difficulties which are comparatively rare among children. Because of their smaller size and stature, children cannot usually inflict as much damage to property as adolescents (or adults) can. Usually they cannot wield knives or firearms without being overpowered. And it is a very unusual child who can become pregnant—or cause anyone else to become pregnant. Adolescents, in short, can experiment with *all* adult roles—both positive and negative—more readily than children.

Developmental changes and adolescent problems can be related in more subtle ways as well. And here it becomes useful once more to refer to the various symptoms of "acute identity confusion": emotional isolation, diffusion of time and work, and fixation on the negative alternatives in life.

Emotional Isolation and Adolescent Schizophrenia

Though Weiner is inclined to be somewhat critical of concepts like "identity confusion," he unwittingly provides support for the concept in his discussion of adolescent schizophrenia. One of the most ominous signs of possible disturbance during adolescence is an inability to establish friendships. The youngster who cannot relate to others or develop an interest in the usual teenage pursuits is, Weiner claims, a prime candidate for adolescent schizophrenia.

---

crisis may be a more significant factor than any deeply rooted emotional conflicts. And this claim cannot be proved or disproved simply by quoting the statistics on recovery. "Some" can mean 1 percent or 99 percent of all disturbed adolescents. However, by hedging his bets in such a fashion, we have to concede that Erikson has probably weakened his case. In the final analysis, his observations on prognosis seem a bit shakier than most of his other formulations.

Youngsters who later become schizophrenic often display "striking immaturity and a general failure of social development" *(1970, p. 119)*. Alternatively, they may manage to conceal their inability to reach out to other youngsters behind a mask of "pseudomaturity," developing startlingly adult interests in an effort to avoid the more typical adolescent ones. Though the teenager's peers may sense his shortcomings and ostracize him, such a facade can sometimes succeed in deceiving his elders altogether:

A 15-year-old boy, an only child, attributed his being viciously teased by his classmates to "how unruly young people are today." He referred to his parents' social engagements as, "We had some of our friends over yesterday." Although his measured IQ was 90 and he had virtually never engaged in any activity other than in the company of his parents, except for attending school, a number of people who had discussed his peer-group difficulties with him—principal, guidance counselor, minister—had consistently introduced their initial impressions of him with such statements as, "This bright, alert, clean-cut young man discussed the situation with me in a very open, sensible, and mature manner." *(Weiner, 1970, p. 120)*

In some instances, the prepsychotic teenager's "front" is even more unobtrusive, and parents and teachers remain unaware of the insidious emotional retreat that is taking place, or the pressures that are building up within the youngster:

At times the immaturity and basic social inadequacy underlying the pseudomature pattern comes suddenly to the fore in episodes of poor judgment or psychological collapse that come as a total surprise to the parents and teachers. The apparently mature and sophisticated young lady of 16 goes into a frenzied panic when a boy tries to kiss her, because she has never progressed beyond the childhood fantasy that kissing causes pregnancy; or the seemingly self-reliant 14-year-old boy goes off to camp for the first time and must be rescued by his parents after a week in which he has made no friends, clung to his counselor's side, and cried himself to sleep at night. *(Weiner, 1970, p. 121)*

Indeed, Weiner substantially confirms Erikson's more general observation that the inability to face the role demands of young adulthood—intimacy, work, self-sufficiency—can ultimately precipitate a breakdown, even with adolescents who are outwardly very gifted. The anticipation and strains at long last expose the sad fact that the youngster's identity has failed to crystallize:

Some youngsters who mask an underlying schizophrenic disturbance with a facade of adequacy may avoid overt breakdown until late in their adolescence and then decompensate in the face of increasing demands for independent and self-assured behavior and decreasing availability of parental support and protection . . . such youngsters may achieve apparent social and academic successes during most of their teenage years, only to have the emptiness of these achievements exposed near the close of their adolescence when they are unable to muster the necessary self-confidence and object-relationship capacity to attain an adequate adult adjustment. *(Weiner, 1970, p. 121)*

At this point in our knowledge, it is impossible to specify precisely what part the various demands of adolescence and approaching adulthood may play in bringing about a psychosis. Does the prospect of intimacy, both sexual and social, prove too much for a youngster who is only marginally adjusted to begin with, or is his marginal adaptation simply exposed for the first time as he drifts farther and farther out of the teenage mainstream? We cannot really say. Some preschizophrenic adolescents probably fit the former pattern and others the latter.

It is important to recognize, of course, that some youngsters may not fit *either* pattern. Weiner concedes that the inability to form close relationships or to develop the "normative adolescent concerns" do not always precede a psychosis. But he does consider these to be rather troubling signs, *especially* in teenagers who present other evidence of disturbance, and he thus identifies a possible "developmental factor" in adolescent schizophrenia.

Suicide, Love, and Time

We can also relate aspects of Erikson's theory to the increasingly gloomy statistics on teenage suicides. The most cursory glance at the figures would suggest *some* connection between adolescence and suicide. To be sure, it is comparatively rare for a teenager to take his own life. Judging from the prevalence of depression during adolescence, many probably contemplate doing so, but few actually make the attempt. Nonetheless, as noted in Chapter 6, suicide remains one of the most serious problems of adolescence. It is the third leading cause of death among teenagers in general, and among college students it is estimated to be the second leading cause of death *(Coleman, 1972)*.

Even more striking is the fact that *children* almost never try to kill themselves. The *Vital Statistics of the United States* for the year 1965 reports only one suicide by a child under 10 years of age. However, once past the age of ten, the rate begins to climb alarmingly. Among ten to fourteen year olds, there were 103 suicides in 1965, and the corresponding figure for the fifteen to nineteen year old group was 685, a sevenfold increase. We should qualify these figures by pointing out that the suicide rate for adolescents is generally lower than for adults. However, the steep rise that occurs during adolescence cannot be ignored. Nor do the figures on "successful" suicides tell the whole story. Balser and Masterson (1959) estimate that while teenagers account for only 3.7 percent of all "completed" suicides, they make 12 percent of all attempts.

The dynamics of adolescent suicide   What is it that might account for this unhappy set of statistics? Why does the propensity for self-destruction increase so dramatically during the teenage years? Weiner observes that, traditionally, adolescent suicide, like so many other youthful afflictions, has been accommodated under the general heading of "storm and stress." A number of clinicians, he notes, have implied that suicidal behavior in teenagers is yet another manifestation of "adolescent impulsiveness," of the flightiness and unpredictability that are supposed to characterize all youngsters in their teens simply as a matter of course (Gould, 1965; Jacobinzer, 1960, 1965; Schneer & Kay, 1961). This same "impulsivity" is also invoked to explain the disparity between "completions" and "attempts." Gould (1965) suggests, for example, that for most adolescents the suicide attempt is a spur-of-the-moment and ill-conceived affair—and hence less likely to be lethal.

In assessing the facts, however, Weiner (1970) comments rather drily that although such explanations may be appealing on the surface, "they do not stand up well to close examination" (1970, p. 182). As in so many other instances, the actual data do not confirm the myth. Careful studies (Jacobs, 1971; Jacobs & Teicher, 1967) indicate that the vast majority of youngsters who try to take their own lives are grimly and deadly serious. The suicide attempt is usually not an impulsive, hastily conceived act. It tends instead to be carefully thought out and weighed against other alternatives. It is also generally a last-ditch measure.

The teenager resorts to suicide, Jacobs (1971) asserts, only after he has tried to advertise his plight in more conventional ways and only after he has become convinced that "nothing else will work." Suicide is seen as the single remaining alternative, as this pathetic note so poignantly bears witness:

Dear folks:
    I know this won't seem the right thing to you but from where I stand it seems like the best solution, considering what is inevitably in store for the future.

You know I am in debt. Probably not deeply compared to a lot of people, but at least they have certain abilities, a skill or trade, or talents with which to make a financial recovery. Yes, I am still working but only "by the grace of the gods." You know how I feel about working where there are a lot of girls. I never could stand their cattiness and I couldn't hope to be lucky enough again to find work where I had my own office and still have someone to rely on like Harriet. And above all, most jobs don't pay as well as this one for comparable little work. I get so tired at typing for instance, that I couldn't hold a straight typist position. . . .

. . . How I wish I could make "small talk" or "party chatter" like some girls do. But I can't compete with most of them for many reasons and after trying to enter social activities with kids in my age range, especially the past year, I find I can't compete with most of them. Even if I had all the clothes to look the part I still wouldn't be able to act the part. Sorry I'm such a disappointment to you folks.

I'm saying these things so you'll understand why it's so futile for me to even hope for a better job. And as long as I go on living there will be "working conditions" when there are so many other better places for the money. I don't mean to sound unappreciative of all you folks have done all through the years to keep us kids well and healthy. It's just that I can't see the sense of putting money into a losing game. *(Jacobs, 1971, pp. 90–91)*

This note also vividly portrays some of the circumstances that are likely to precede a teenager's decision to end it all, ironically at a point where most young people are described as "having everything to live for." As in adolescent schizophrenia, the interpersonal climate can be seen to play a large part, but with this difference: The schizophrenic or preschizophrenic youngster has been pictured as being fearful of closeness and lacking an interest in the normal adolescent pursuits. The note reproduced above provides convincing and tragic evidence that it is the *need for* rather than the *fear of* intimacy that underlies youthful suicides.

After reviewing the data from his own study of teenage suicide "attempters," Jacobs concluded that a youngster is likely to take his own life when he feels totally abandoned, effectively cut off from any hope of a "meaningful social relationship." Jacobs matched these suicidal adolescents with a group of "nonsuicidal" controls and discovered that the suicidal group had suffered one or more severe emotional blows prior to their attempts: broken romances, pregnancies, serious illnesses, deaths of loved ones, a divorce in the family, and so forth.

Even more significant (and here the Eriksonian model proves to be especially useful), the disruptions suffered by the suicidal adolescents were nothing new. In sharp contrast to their nonsuicidal counterparts, these youngsters had endured a long and bitter history of family troubles. Typically, their parents had divorced and re-married on several occasions—often there was a divorce pending at the time of the suicide attempt—they did not get along well with their parents or step-parents, and their families had made a large number of moves.

Interestingly enough, the simple fact of coming from a broken home did not appear to be decisive. A majority of the control subjects also had divorced parents (53 percent versus 71 percent for the "attempters"). But for the controls, this divorce had occurred early in childhood. Typically, their parents had quickly remarried, and their home lives thereafter had been comparatively stable and unharried. The suicidal adolescents, by contrast, had been subjected to an almost continuous emotional barrage, not the least of which involved having witnessed someone else's suicide attempt. For fully 44 per-cent of the suicidal adolescents, a close relative or friend was reported to have tried to take his own life—in many cases the youngster's own mother or father. There was no such precedent for *any* of the control subjects.

Furthermore, almost all the attempters had signaled their pro-found distress for months prior to the act. They began to fail in school, they picked fights with their parents, they stayed out after curfew, they ran away—apparently anything to draw attention to themselves. And finally, convinced that no other remedy existed, they tried suicide.

Jacobs's model of adolescent suicide is thus a kind of "straw that broke the camel's back" account. The youngster, he claims, has a long-standing history of conflict behind him; his problems have escalated recently, exacerbating a preexisting sense of isolation; and his distress signals have gone unheard. Furthermore, the conven-tional prohibitions against suicide are less likely to have a restrain-ing influence because other members of his family may have attempted it themselves. With all these predisposing forces converg-ing upon the adolescent, suicide becomes a chillingly logical alternative.

But Jacobs's model does not quite explain why the attempt occurs during adolescence rather than in childhood. Why is it only in his *teens* that the youngster's despair seems to overwhelm him? Eriksonian theory, we believe, provides a useful supplement to Jacobs's work in answering this particular question. As we have seen, Erikson claims that if he is to experience the "wholeness" of a sound identity, then "the young person . . . must feel a progressive continuity between that which he has come to be during the long years of childhood and that which he promises to become in the anticipated future" *(1968, p. 87)*. To be able to look forward to adult life, the adolescent must put both his past experience and his future prospects into perspective. But what if the past has been uniformly miserable and the future promises to be no better? Indeed, what if the adolescent has collected further "proof" (in the form of a broken romance, a divorce in the family, or continued and unremitting strife with his parents) that he can never expect any improvement? It might be reasonable for him to conclude, then, that it is preferable not to exist at all—or at the very least to inform the world that he has reached the end of his own emotional resources. He might be expected to hold this conviction all the more firmly if his family history contains the precedent of a suicide attempt. In sum, it may be the teenager's increased ability to *apply the lessons of the past and to anticipate the future* that explains the sharp rise in suicides and suicide attempts during adolescence. Ironically, it may be just his capacity to put his life in perspective that proves to be fatal. This theme is certainly prominent in the suicide note excerpted above, where the unfortunate girl recounts a long history of failure and states her belief that she can never expect anything better.

The inevitable sex differences   In the area of suicide, as in so many others, some notable sex differences become apparent. Girls *attempt* suicide about three and a half times as frequently as boys, but boys *succeed* in killing themselves almost three and a half times as frequently as girls. One probable reason for the discrepancy has to do with the respective methods employed. When girls try to kill themselves, they generally resort to poison, while boys are much more likely to use firearms or to hang themselves. Obviously, the more violent the means, the greater the possibility of "success."

Introducing a time-honored variant of the storm and stress hypothesis, Schneer and Kay (1961) have suggested that the "impulsive and histrionic" tendencies of adolescent girls may also be a factor. This would imply, of course, that when a female teenager resorts to suicide she does not really "mean it" and is simply dramatizing her emotional problems in a "characteristically feminine" way.

However, Jacobs (1971) reminds us that very few, if any, suicide attempts occur merely "for show." There is almost always an element of serious intent. Therefore, we suspect that the observed sex difference in adolescent suicides is yet another example of a more general phenomenon. For whatever reason, boys are inclined to be more aggressive and active than girls—certainly by the time they reach adolescence. Consequently, when a boy decides to do away with himself he may stand a better chance of accomplishing his aim simply because he is inclined to choose a more "aggressive" and "masculine" method. It is worthwhile to note in this connection that the ratio of attempts to actual suicides among teenage boys and girls closely parallels the ratio among adult men and women.

Drugs, Experimentation, and Time Diffusion

A problem of youth that has attracted far more attention recently than suicide is that of drugs. When it first became apparent that teenagers were beginning to sample hallucinogens like marijuana and LSD and amphetamines like methedrine and dexedrine (more commonly known as "speed"), there was a great public hue and cry. The drug problem was said to be reaching "epidemic proportions," and there were dire predictions that countless youngsters would suffer irreparable psychological damage—or, equally as bad, find themselves addicted to that most dread of all drugs, heroin. The tempest has died down somewhat, but the problem remains, and the principal question for us is whether Erikson's theory can shed any light upon it. Before we address ourselves to this issue, however, the whole subject of drugs must be put in perspective.

The extent of the problem Reliable data on drug use among adolescents are almost as hard to obtain as data on teenage sexuality —and for similar reasons. Drugs, like sex, represent a proscribed activity for adolescents. Indeed, in some states the legal penalties for simple possession of marijuana remain forbiddingly severe. In such circumstances, it becomes difficult to question teenagers about their consumption of drugs without alarming school officials and parents—and even, perhaps, running afoul of the law. Consequently, most research on the so-called drug problem has been restricted to an older and more accessible group of adolescents: college students. Unfortunately, as we are well aware by now, college students, being for the most part brighter and wealthier than average, are not exactly typical. Furthermore, a recent survey of what little research there is echoes a complaint which should have an all too familiar ring. Most of the data on teenage drug use, as Braucht, Brakarsh, Follingstad, and Berry (1973) observe, have been compiled piecemeal without any particular framework in mind.

Given these limitations, it is obvious that we cannot draw any firm conclusions about the extent of drug use and abuse during adolescence. One fact, however, does seem to stand out. On college campuses at least, smoking marijuana has become increasingly common. One of the earlier surveys (Suchman, 1968) reported that

21 percent of the students on the University of California campus at Santa Barbara had sampled "pot" at least once, and subsequent research has revealed a steady increase. Indeed, Davis *(1970)* found that 56 percent of a sample of college students at the relatively staid University of Connecticut had indulged at least once. Nor is pot smoking restricted to undergraduates. Surveys of medical students, law students, and servicemen have uncovered high levels of use, although such use has not necessarily proved to be excessive *(Brecher, 1972)*.

All in all, it seems reasonable to conclude that a substantial proportion of the young people in this country, particularly of the affluent young, have at least a nodding acquaintance with pot. But this conclusion does not really tell us much about the dimensions of the "drug problem." What about high school students? What about heavy drug consumption? And what about hard drugs like heroin?

High school students   As noted, the data on younger adolescents are not easy to come by. One of the few surveys we had been able to locate until very recently is summarized in a comprehensive study by Consumers' Union *(Brecher, 1972)*. The survey *(Bogg, Smith, & Russell, 1969)*—which may already be considerably out of date—questioned high school seniors in a variety of different settings (rural, urban, suburban, private school) in Michigan and found a wide variation in drug use. Thirty-three percent of the students at an exclusive private institution admitted to smoking marijuana on at least one occasion, whereas *none* of the students at two rural high schools had done so, a finding which substantiates the connection between the use of hallucinogens and social class. However, more revealing, and almost unnoticed in the furor over marijuana and LSD, were the figures on *alcohol* consumption. At all the high schools but one in the Michigan survey, a majority of the seniors admitted to drinking, at times quite heavily (half of those who drank reported that they had imbibed enough to become ill on at least one occasion). Even more intriguing, the percentage of "drinkers" at one of the rural high schools was almost exactly the same as at the private school—79 percent versus 81 percent—which suggests that alcohol is something of a leveler with respect to social class. At any rate, having compared the figures on marijuana and alcohol, the Consumer Reports Survey concludes: "These data suggest that, even in schools where marijuana use is widespread, alcohol remains the major drug *problem* among high school seniors" *(Brecher, 1972, p. 428)*.

An excellent study, which we discovered just before this book was scheduled to go to press, essentially confirms this general pattern. Johnston *(1973)* conducted an extensive survey of male high school students over a five-year period *(1966–1970)*. A mere 23 percent of the respondents reported *ever* having used marijuana or any other hallucinogen (and this included, of course, students who had only experimented with a particular drug once). By contrast, over 80 percent of the subjects indicated that they had sampled an alcoholic beverage on at least one occasion—and a third of them reported indulging at least once a week.

Of course, the raw statistics on marijuana and alcohol use still do not answer the most troubling question. The youngsters who undoubtedly cause the most concern (and receive the most attention in the news media) are the "heavy users," those who are chronic alcoholics, habitual pot smokers, LSD "trippers," and narcotics addicts. Who are they, how numerous are they, and what are their motives?

Statistics on heavy drug use   Judging from the rather limited statistics that are available, actual drug abuse is less widespread than might be supposed. Braucht and his colleagues *(1973)* report that the vast majority of teenagers are "light to moderate" drinkers and that only 2–6 percent might be labeled "problem drinkers," that is, individuals "for whom alcohol has come to occupy a more than simply incidental role in their lives" *(p. 92)*. Similarly, in his study of college students, Davis *(1970)* discovered that less than a fifth of his sample smoked marijuana "regularly" (i.e., more than once a week). Fewer still had "tripped" on LSD on even one occasion, and only two (out of a sample of more than 100) had ever experimented with heroin. (These subjects asserted, incidentally, that they had no intention of repeating the experiment.)

We should point out that because heroin use is highly illegal, the figures on heroin addiction among teenagers are the most difficult of all to obtain, but it is not surprising that Davis observed so little contact with the drug among college students. Narcotics addiction has long been regarded as a scourge of the ghetto *(Braucht et al., 1973; Brecher, 1972)*, and the few researchers who have actually studied narcotics addiction among adolescents *(Bender, 1963; Chein, 1959; Vaillant, 1966)* have found that most were indeed members of a minority community. Fortunately, like other forms of "problem drug use," narcotics addiction is probably relatively rare among teenagers. The *total* number of heroin addicts in this country is estimated at between 250,000 and 300,000 *(Brecher, 1972; "The Heroin Plague," 1971)*.

Motives underlying drug usage in general and heavy drug usage in particular   However, although only a small fraction of all adolescents appear to be engaged in any form of drug abuse, the need to understand this unfortunate few remains. The alcoholic teenager may become the alcoholic adult. The teenager who "trips" on LSD repeatedly may suffer severe psychological damage. The youthful addict must often steal and mug in order to support his habit—and he may "overdose" and kill himself. There is even some thought (though comparatively little reliable evidence, according to Brecher, *1972*) that heavy pot smoking may be harmful as well.

Drug usage in general   The figures that have been presented thus far offer little support for the hypothesis, rather commonly entertained, we suspect, that most drug taking during adolescence is a reflection of "youthful rebellion" or "alienation." Alcohol, widely accepted and tolerated by adults, is by far the most widely used (and probably the most frequently abused) drug. And although marijuana appears to have been sampled by a substantial proportion of the younger generation, the number of habitués has, in all likelihood, probably remained quite small.

We have an inkling, then, that most adolescent "users" have two eminently comprehensible motives underlying their behavior: imitation and fun-seeking. In the case of alcohol, it is important to remember that huge numbers of adults imbibe and that the "drug" is therefore widely available. In fact, when questioned about the circumstances surrounding their first drink, most teenagers report that they obtained it at home, sometimes with the express permission of their parents *(Maddox, 1970)*. Furthermore, it is logical to assume that, once having been introduced to liquor, adolescents continue to drink for substantially the same reason adults do: the effect. Throughout the centuries alcohol has been prized (and condemned) for its mind-altering attributes, its capacity to lift the spirit and to erase the cares of the world. There is no reason to suppose that the adolescents who consume it are, for the most part, any less eager than adults to enjoy its unique impact.

Marijuana, of course, has been less enthusiastically received by adults, and very few adolescents probably become acquainted with it through observing their parents. (There does seem to be an indirect connection. Adolescents who smoke marijuana are more likely to smoke cigarettes, and adolescents who smoke cigarettes are more likely to have *parents* who smoke cigarettes. See *Brecher, 1972*.) Marijuana is unlike liquor in another respect: It is illegal for *all* users, not just for minors. Nonetheless, teenagers probably sample it for at least some of the same reasons they sample alcohol. They want to find out what it is like (an interest that is only intensified by its questionable legal status), and it is alleged to bring on a "high." In short, most drug taking during adolescence is very likely a kind of testing out. It represents a desire to sample the "adult" pleasures of alcohol (which may or may not be legal for a teenager, depending on where he resides and precisely how old he is) or the forbidden pleasures of marijuana (which are flatly illegal, though rarely punished). In view of its probable benign character, most drug consumption during adolescence can be accommodated by the Eriksonian concept of "role experimentation." It is simply a part of the limits testing and experience collecting that Erikson claims are more or less a normal feature of the period.[3]

Motives underlying heavy drug usage and addiction   But what of the youngster for whom a "high" is a necessity rather than an occasional pastime or a one-shot experiment? What of the youngster who is frankly addicted to heroin or alcohol, who is tripping on LSD or who is frequently "stoned" on pot? Here we might expect the concept of "identity confusion" to be more applicable. Certainly the media have implied a connection between heavy drug use and some of the most prominent symptoms of identity confusion—emotional isolation, a "live for the present" mentality, a disinclination for work or any other "useful" activity.

Marijuana   Indeed, when marijuana first began to make its appearance on college campuses, some researchers, most notably Suchman *(1968)*, ascribed a kind of "hang loose" ethic to its devotees. However, upon close examination, the "hang loose" ethic turns out to bear only the mildest resemblance to "acute identity confusion." Suchman did discover some differences between marijuana users and nonusers on a California campus (at that time only 21 percent of those sampled admitted to any contact at all with the drug). In general, the pot smokers appeared to be more "antiestablishment" than nonsmokers. They were more likely to read underground newspapers (42 percent of the users versus 4 percent of the nonusers), to attend "happenings" (34 percent versus 17 percent), and participate in mass demonstrations (46 percent versus 15 percent). In addition, they expressed more criticism of the educational system—30 percent of the users agreed with the statement that what they were learning in school was a "waste of time" whereas only 13 percent of the nonusers agreed, and 28 percent of the users

---

[3] Not that all such experimentation is necessarily innocuous. The connection between drinking and traffic accidents is all too well known.

compared with 11 percent of the nonusers called for more student power. And there were also some slight indications that the pot smokers were not as strongly imbued with the "Protestant ethic" as their nonsmoking classmates. Those who had sampled marijuana were somewhat more likely to agree that it was "all right to get around the law so long as you don't actually break it" (35 percent versus 14 percent), to express approval of the "hippie way of life" (27 percent versus 11 percent), and to state that they expected to get as much satisfaction out of their leisure time activities as from civic or family pursuits once they left college (45 percent versus 12 percent).

As is apparent, nonetheless, the differences between smokers and nonsmokers could scarcely be described as extreme. We can assume, for instance, that if only 30 percent of the marijuana users decreed their college educations to be largely a waste, 70 percent did not—or were at least undecided. Thus it should not astonish us to learn that when Suchman asked his subjects a series of four questions designed to determine their degree of "alienation" (e.g., "If you don't watch yourself people will take advantage of you," "These days a person does not really know whom he can count on") there was no difference between smokers and nonsmokers. He was compelled to conclude: "The 'hang-loose' ethic, while it may represent antagonism to the conventional world, does not appear to create apathy and withdrawal. Subscribers to the ethic are not so much 'anomic' in regard to society in general as critical of the existing 'Establishment' in specific" (1968, p. 374). In Eriksonian terms, then, it could be said that although these early marijuana users seemed more committed to a particular *ideology* than nonusers, there were very few signs of anything like "acute identity confusion" among them.

Furthermore, when the majority of college students began to experiment with the drug, the differences between smokers and nonsmokers all but disappeared. Davis (1970), whose study of Eastern college students postdated Suchman's West Coast study by only two or three years, did not observe any appreciable differences in attitude when he compared pot smokers (including those who had tried marijuana only once) with nonsmokers. Such results are, we might add, not particularly baffling. A few years ago it was considered rather daring, in view of its illegal status, to smoke marijuana. Therefore, only the more adventurous and less conventional youngsters were likely to indulge. With the passage of time, the taboo became weaker and weaker, more and more students sampled the drug, and the differences between users and nonusers have probably all but washed out.

Hence, in view of marijuana's widespread popularity among

undergraduates, it would no doubt be more meaningful to compare "regular" or "heavy" users with the rest of the college population. Davis, in fact, did this and discovered that students who were more than casual smokers exhibited something like Suchman's "hang-loose" ethic. They were less apt than other students, for instance, to describe themselves as conventionally religious, and they also expressed less enthusiasm for "establishment" values. Davis also detected a few more hints of intensified "identity crisis" among the regular or heavy users. Significantly more of them reported being in psychotherapy and, judging from their scores on a personality inventory, they appeared slightly more "maladjusted." However, it seems unlikely that these regular smokers were suffering "acute identity confusion." Despite their ideological misgivings and their personal problems, their schoolwork remained curiously unaffected. Indeed, taken as a group, the regular and casual marijuana users had a significantly higher grade point than nonusers.

Such findings, of course, do not tell us much about the *long-term* effects of smoking marijuana. Indeed, according to the Consumer Reports Survey *(Brecher, 1972)* there are practically no reliable data on this question. It is possible that youngsters who indulge their taste for marijuana regularly—and heavily—over a period of years might begin to suffer something more than mild discomfort, but we have no way of knowing for sure at the present time. Certainly, there is little evidence to indicate that casual or moderate users are in grave danger—although here too we must await further research.

Alcohol, LSD, and heroin   When we turn to the more demonstrably dangerous drugs, a less benign picture emerges. Although the research in this area also leaves much to be desired *(see Braucht et al., 1973, for a detailed critique)*, what little there is indicates that teenagers who drink heavily, trip on LSD, or "shoot up" with heroin are neither notably stable nor well adjusted.

There is some evidence that teenage "problem drinkers"—like most adolescents who drink—acquire the habit from their parents. Although some adolescents who imbibe too heavily come from highly religious and abstemious backgrounds, the majority reside in households where liquor is used rather freely and there is no particular religious affiliation *(Gusfield, 1970; MacKay, 1961; Maddox, 1970)*. They are also likely to have friends who drink heavily *(Jessor, Collins, & Jessor, 1972)*. In addition, they exhibit characteristics that suggest a degree of identity confusion. Perhaps the most interesting research in this connection is a set of longitudinal studies by Jones *(1968, 1971)*. Comparing adolescents who were problem drinkers with those who were only moderate or light drinkers, she discovered that members of the problem group had appeared to be more impulsive, unstable, and unpredictable *before* they became involved with alcohol. And Jessor, Carman, and Grossman *(1968)* furnish some corroborative data. In their study of college students, they found that those who were pessimistic about their chances of achieving academic success and social recognition were significantly more likely to drink heavily than those who were more self-confident about such matters. So there are some indications at least that adolescents who habitually seek solace in alcohol are less sure of themselves—and it is also probable that they have had poorer models.

Among youthful LSD users an even more disturbing pattern becomes apparent. Several studies have uncovered evidence of serious pathology among teenage "acid-heads." Smart and Feier *(1969)* gave a group of LSD users the Minnesota Multiphasic Personality Inventory, a widely used clinical test, and on the basis of the resulting profiles concluded that many of their subjects were either "borderline" or suffering from "personality disorders." The findings of Blumenthal and Glickman *(1967)* are even more discouraging. They examined a group of hospitalized adolescents who had experimented extensively with LSD and discovered that 70 percent had previously undergone psychiatric treatment and that 80 percent had been diagnosed as either "psychotic" or "borderline." Similarly, a study of clinic patients by Hekiman and Gershon *(1968)* revealed that 50 percent of the LSD users in the sample had either been treated for schizophrenia or had been considered schizophrenic before they took the drug.

LSD, of course, is considered a dangerous drug, one that can cause severe personality disorganization if taken repeatedly. The data summarized here therefore raise the question of which comes first. Do adolescents who are suffering from what Erikson would term "acute identity confusion" take LSD hoping to "find themselves" in the course of some great mystical experience? Or does the drug itself produce their symptoms? The consensus among researchers seems to be the former: that many youngsters who turn to LSD are at least predisposed to serious psychiatric illness and that the drug merely aggravates their problems rather than causing them in the first place *(Braucht et al., 1973; Brecher, 1972.)*

Indeed, in the anecdotal accounts of many youthful LSD users, we can detect a deep desire to "make the world stand still" and a markedly diffuse sense of time. The following excerpt from the account of one such "ego-tripper" is revealing in this respect:

The weather forecaster had predicted sunshine and warmth for the day. As I carried the tape recorder into the pouring rain, everything began to make sense. I was really happy that it was raining. I felt that if it snowed, hailed, and hurricaned all at once, I would still be happy. Anything that nature did was happy; unhappiness was truly our own private creation. . . .

As I walked along the beach that makes up the Point, I felt that man's anxieties were based on a lack of evolutionary understanding. My mind went back to the realm of animals, where each beast was concerned only with his or her specific needs. Then as the process of evolution advanced and the brain became convoluted, these needs became more easily accessible resulting in the need for a new intellectual outlet. With the dawn of man, came leisure time. No longer was it necessary to spend every minute in a quest for satisfaction of life processes. Interpersonal relations began to supplant instinct as a prime mover, with the emerging ego as a corollary to this development. *(Goethals & Klos, 1970, p. 147)*

One other fact stands out as far as LSD users are concerned. Although their family backgrounds and home life have not been studied extensively, the vast majority of youngsters who take the drug are from the middle or upper class *(Braucht et al., 1973)*. And in this they differ markedly from the next group of "problem adolescents" we shall examine: teenage heroin addicts.

Youthful heroin users are predominantly poor, usually belong to an ethnic minority (e.g., black or Puerto Rican), and live in ghetto neighborhoods, where narcotics, though prohibitively expensive, are readily available *(Bender, 1963; Chein, 1959; Vaillant, 1966)*. However, though there is relatively wide agreement on this point (which conforms rather neatly to the popular stereotype), there is practically no consensus at all about the personality characteristics of teenage addicts *(Braucht et al., 1973)*. They have been described variously as "inadequate," "schizoid," "psychopathic," "highly anxious," "psychotic," and "neurotic." Yet at least one study *(Nyswander, 1956)* reports that the incidence of mental illness among addicts is *no* greater than among the population as a whole!

We suspect that this puzzling and inconsistent array of findings reflect both the nature of the drug in question and its highly questionable legal status. Incredible as it may seem, the painstaking Consumer Reports Survey *(Brecher, 1972)* does not cite any evidence that heroin *in and of itself* is harmful to the psyche. The only side effects that have consistently been detected are constipation and a somewhat diminished sex drive. (The deaths from so-called overdoses that have been reported in recent years are thought to result, not from heroin, but from substances which have been added to it.) Nor does the drug (unlike LSD) appear to produce a particularly dramatic "high." Although some addicts describe its effects as "thrilling" or "joyful," most simply state that it makes them feel "relaxed."

To be sure, the *lack* of heroin once an individual has become accustomed to it, can make him feel very miserable indeed—and here, we have an inkling, is where the real problem may lie. The "lift" or feeling of relaxation that follows an injection wears off quite rapidly, leaving in its wake the extremely unpleasant physical symptoms of withdrawal. Consequently, an addict must worry constantly about securing his next "fix." Since "fixes" are illegal and very expensive to obtain, he is forced into a singularly wretched way of life. He often steals to support his habit. He neglects his diet. He rarely exercises or goes out (except in search of more heroin). And he is generally regarded as one of the "lowliest of the low." Thus it is difficult to determine whether the psychological disorganization many researchers have observed in addicts results from a "character flaw" or "identity confusion" or is instead a kind of sociological by-product.

The need for perspective   That a youngster permits himself to become addicted to an illegal drug in the first place may well indicate a lack of judgment, foresight, and even intelligence. But so, according to the statistics on lung cancer, does taking up smoking. There is a tendency to speak of the "adolescent drug problem" as if drugs were a problem *only* for adolescents. Obviously, this is not the case. Adults become addicts and alcoholics as well. They also consume tranquillizers and sleeping pills, smoke large quantities of cigarettes, and drink enormous amounts of coffee, tea, and Coca-Cola—all of which contain drugs and all of which are harmful in large-enough doses. We live, in short, in a drug-laden culture.[4] The fact that many drugs begin to pose a serious problem only with the advent of adolescence is, no doubt, significant. As in the case of suicide and sex, it suggests that changes occur during adolescence that make youngsters susceptible to some of the same needs, cravings, and concerns as adults. Or, bringing our observations in line with Eriksonian theory, we find in the data on drug use fresh evidence that the problems of adolescence do indeed anticipate the problems of adulthood.

Delinquency and Negative Identity

There may be comparatively few studies as yet on "teenagers and drugs," but the same can scarcely be said of our next topic. As noted in Chapter 1, the concept of adolescence appeared relatively late in Western civilization. Nevertheless, once the distinction between "juveniles" (who were not responsible for their crimes) and

---

[4] Indeed, it has even been suggested (*Weil, 1973*) that all human beings need to experience altered states of consciousness.

adults (who were) was established, roughly in the 1880s *(See Platt, 1969, for a fascinating history of the juvenile court system)*, preoccupation with "youthful offenders" became more and more evident. Special rules and regulations for dealing with minors were formulated, and researchers, educators, and therapists increasingly turned their attention to so-called juvenile delinquency. G. Stanley Hall, as we have seen, was much concerned with the "faults and immoralities" of the young, and so are the experts of our own era. As testimony to its time-honored status, a large number of theories have been advanced to explain delinquency, and a considerable body of research exists. Despite the attention it has received, however, the subject retains an aura of controversy. Indeed, before attempting to relate the data on juvenile delinquency to the Eriksonian model, it would be useful to review some of the basic issues.[5]

The seriousness of the problem   As with suicide and drug use, the statistics are unequivocal on one point at least. With the approach of adolescence, there is a sharp rise in "youthful offenses." According to one fairly recent study *(Ball, Ross, & Simpson, 1964)*, the incidence of such crimes doubles between eleven and twelve and then triples between the ages of twelve and seventeen. Furthermore, teenagers appear to have actual run-ins with the law in rather disproportionate numbers. Examining the figures for all arrests, we discover that seventeen year olds account for the largest percentage, followed by eighteen year olds and then by sixteen year olds *(F.B.I., 1965)*. The majority of these arrests are for "crimes against property" (e.g., stealing and vandalism), and thus juveniles can be credited with a large share of the offenses in this category. Making the situation seem even more dire are the occasional claims that delinquency is rising steadily, not only in the United States, but throughout the world *(Sellin & Wolfgang, 1964)*. Nonetheless, it is difficult to determine just how serious the problem actually is.

Indeed, Weiner *(1970)* and Short *(1966)* both list a number of complications. First, the sizable number of adolescent property crimes notwithstanding, there is a certain class of transgressions that can be committed only by minors. Adults, for instance, cannot be arrested for "running away" or "being out after curfew." Second, it has been suggested that with the improvement of juvenile court facilities in this country, police are less reluctant to apprehend youngsters, the rationale being that special agencies exist to deal with them. Third, although teenagers may indeed account for a

[5] Our examination of delinquency must, of necessity, be somewhat brief. For more exhaustive accounts, see Short *(1966)* and Empey *(1967)*.

disproportionate number of all *arrests*, it has been argued *(Marwell, 1966)* that there is a great deal of hidden law breaking among adults —and that there is no evidence that adolescents actually commit illegal acts more frequently than adults do. They simply commit more of the easily detectable crimes and hence are caught more often. Finally, depending upon how the term is defined, the vast majority of teenagers (particularly boys) admit to having been "delinquent" at one time or another *(Offer, Sabshin, & Marcus, 1965)*.

Theories of juvenile delinquency   Nor do experts agree on the precise causes of juvenile delinquency. Sociologists have argued that it inevitably results from the increasing strains and impersonality of industrialized society *(Merton, 1957)*, that it arises out of a "delinquent subculture" *(Cloward and Ohlin, 1960; Cohen, 1955)*, and that it is caused by the frustration of middle-class aspirations *(Short, 1966)*. Psychologists have suggested that delinquency (which is thought to be more prevalent among males than among females) results from "inadequate male models" *(Bandura & Walters, 1959; Miller, 1958)*, unconscious "scapegoating" by parents *(Johnson, 1959)*, and (as in the case of suicide) desire to gain attention and affection *(Weiner, 1970)*. Biological and constitutional factors have even been invoked. Glueck and Glueck *(1956)* have pointed out that adolescents with "mesomorphic" (muscular) builds tend to be involved in law-breaking to a disproportionate degree, and Weiner *(1970)* suggests that some forms of brain damage may be associated with "delinquent acting-out." This summary includes, we should add, only a very partial listing of theories.

There is also, as might be inferred, considerable debate as to whether delinquency is primarily a lower-class phenomenon or whether it is visited with equal frequency on the middle and upper classes as well. Traditionally, teenage offenders have been pictured as poor and "underprivileged"—"depraved on account of being deprived," as the line from *West Side Story* puts it. Consequently, another convention has grown up. Delinquency among lower-class youngsters has usually been attributed to "sociological factors" (drug addiction, broken homes, alienation, delinquent subcultures, frustration of middle-class aspirations), whereas among middle-class youngsters "psychological factors" (unconscious conflicts, neurotic acting-out, parental scapegoating, "wild oats") have usually been cited. According to this line of reasoning, the lower-class youngster lives in the kind of baleful milieu that encourages crime, while the relatively comfortable middle-class youngster, by contrast, has to have some extraordinary excuse to break the law *(Haney & Gold, 1973)*.

As usual, the truth proves to be elusive. Despite the large number of theories, the causes of delinquency remain obscure, and the statistics on incidence are notoriously hazy *(Short, 1966)*. Offer, Sabshin, and Marcus *(1965)*, for instance, conclude that law breaking occurs with equal frequency among middle-class and lower-class adolescents—and it is a very high frequency at that. Seventy-five percent of the "typical teenagers" in their study (the same adolescents examined in greater detail by Offer, *1969*) admitted to at least one delinquent act or to associating with "known delinquents." However, we may receive these rather alarming conclusions with a degree of skepticism. Offer and his colleagues defined delinquency in very broad terms and included transgressions such as "kicking over trash cans after a football game."

The argument that a certain amount of middle-class delinquency goes undetected, thereby complicating the calculation of incidence rates, is probably more convincing. Simply because of their more "respectable" appearance, it has been suggested *(Haney & Gold, 1973; Short, 1966)*, middle-class youngsters are less likely to be picked up for various offenses. And even if they are apprehended, they are perhaps less likely to be charged. It is easier to believe that an adolescent who comes from a "good home" complete with "law-abiding" parents has acted "on a whim" or "gotten in with the wrong crowd." It is possible, in other words, that juvenile authorities themselves are more inclined simply to warn a middle-class youngster about an offense that would doom his lower-class counterpart to a term in the state reformatory. (A judge may also feel more confident about releasing the middle-class youngster "to the custody of his parents" and may see a foster home or reformatory as a preferable alternative for the more deprived lower-class adolescent.)

To be sure, there is some evidence that delinquency is, in fact, more common at one level of society than another. Glaser *(1965)* notes, for example, that in "mixed" neighborhoods containing both middle-class and lower-class adolescents, crime rates among juveniles are generally lower than in exclusively lower-class neighborhoods. And Coleman *(1972)* suggests that "socially disadvantaged" youngsters are more likely to be "repeaters." He goes on to claim that contrary to popular belief, there is *no* apparent difference between blacks and whites when social class is held constant. Despite the stereotypes that exist, lower-class black youngsters are no more likely to become delinquent than lower-class whites. Nonetheless, we are inclined to agree with Short *(1966)* that further study is required before any firm conclusions regarding the singularly complicated issue of incidence can be drawn.

Motives underlying delinquency Whatever the causes or incidence of juvenile law breaking, the Eriksonian model once again
proves useful when we turn to the delinquents themselves. In addition to his own work, Short *(1966)* cites considerable research to
support the concept of "negative identity" or "role fixation," at least
among lower-class delinquents, who are the most frequently studied.
These youngsters rarely act alone, preferring to carry out their
illegal activities as members of a "gang." Research *(Freedman &
Rivera, 1962; Gold, 1963; Short, 1964)* indicates that the typical gang
member, when matched with adolescents who are not members of
a delinquent gang, is something of a "loser." Indeed, there is little
evidence to support Cohen's well-known theory *(1955)* that the
delinquent's values and hence his forays into crime represent a
"reaction" against middle-class values. Gordon and his colleagues
(1963) report, for example, that gang members admire the same
kinds of people that other adolescents do—"people who work hard
for good grades at school" and "people who read good books," as
opposed to "criminals" and "dope-pushers." And Gold *(1963)* draws
much the same conclusions from his study of delinquent boys.

However, the delinquent youngster seems to lack the capability,
confidence, and opportunity to be like those he admires. Usually, he
has much more difficulty with school than his peers *(Short, 1964)*
and exhibits considerably less social poise *(Cartwright, 1962;
Gordon, 1965)*. Erikson himself *(1968)* has observed that adults in
the community—policemen, teachers, businessmen, and so forth—
often compound the potential delinquent's problems by "pegging"
him as a "good-for-nothing" and then responding to him accordingly.
As corroboration, he cites the following horrendous example:

JUDGE IMPOSES ROAD GANG TERM FOR BACK TALK

Wilmington, N. D. (UP)—A "smart alecky" youth who wore pegged
trousers and a flattop haircut began six months on the road gang today for
talking back to the wrong judge.

Michael A. Jones, 20, of Wilmington, was fined $25 and costs in Judge
Edwin J. Roberts Jr.'s Superior Court for reckless operation of an automobile. But he just didn't leave well enough alone.

"I understand how it was, with your pegged trousers and flattop haircut," Rogers said in assessing the fine.

"You go on like this and I predict in five years you'll be in prison."

When Jones walked over to pay his fine, he overheard Probation Officer
Gideon Smith tell the judge how much trouble the "smart alecky" young
offender had been.

"I just want you to know I'm not a thief," interrupted Jones to the judge.

The judge's voice boomed to the court clerk: "Change that judgment
to six months on the roads." *(1968, p. 255)*

A less impressionistic piece of work provides additional support for Erikson. Gold and Williams *(1969)* compared 35 teenagers who had been apprehended for a delinquent act with 35 controls who had committed similar offenses but had never been caught. For 20 of the 35 pairs, the youngster who had actually been processed through the courts subsequently engaged in *more* law breaking than his unapprehended counterpart. (In only 10 of the pairs was the situation reversed.) Quite possibly, then, a teenager who has "had the book thrown at him" accepts the label of "criminal"—and proceeds to live up to expectations. At any rate, in reflecting on these findings, Haney and Gold *(1973)* observe with more than a trace of gloom: "Whatever it is that the authorities do once they have caught a youth, it seems to be worse than doing nothing at all, worse even than never apprehending the offender. Getting caught encourages rather than deters further delinquency" *(1973, p. 52)*.

Other studies reveal a similar tendency for adults in a particular community to write gang members off. Short, Rivera, and Marshall *(1964)* and Short and Strodtbeck *(1965)* found in their interactions with such youngsters that neighborhood adults were unlikely to ask "how things were going in school" or "what they were planning to do with themselves when they got out of school." It was widely assumed that the gang members would "never amount to anything" and hence the adults reserved their more solicitous attentions for the more reputable youngsters.

Nor is the delinquent teenager unaware of his deficiencies. To illustrate how painfully self-conscious an allegedly "tough" gang member can feel, Short relates the following anecdote from his field study *(Short & Strodtbeck, 1965)*. The occasion was a YMCA banquet to which a neighborhood miscreant and his girl had been invited by a social worker:

> Duke and his girl friend were noticeably silent throughout the YMCA banquet. The accident of seating arrangements found them sitting at a table adjacent to the one where the worker sat. They never initiated conversation with the half dozen other guests at the table, and their responses to others' conversational efforts were brief and subdued. Throughout, Elaine seemed cowed by the experience, Duke less so, but obviously at some pains not to make a behavioral miscue. The two exchanged meaningful glances with one another during the course of the meal and the entertainment which followed. Their behavior was stiff and uncertain, quite a contrast to the generally relaxed and friendly atmosphere of the crowd. *(1965, pp. 220–221)*

Short concludes that with neither the skills nor the appropriate models for "making it" legitimately, the delinquent turns to the gang as a kind of compensation or "alternative status system" *(1966, p. 451)*. He may not be able to achieve a healthy sense of "apprenticeship" in the straight world, but in the gang, with all its excitement and aura of lawlessness, he can be "somebody"—even if he becomes a rather negative somebody.

Gold's assessment *(1963)* is essentially very similar, and Stinchcombe *(1964)* furnishes some additional corroborating data. In a little-known but extremely interesting study of high school students, Stinchcombe discovered that those who were most likely to be rebellious and antisocial were also those who perceived themselves as having the poorest prospects for success upon graduation. Effectively blocked in their quest for status, prestige, and fulfillment, these teenagers, the researcher reasoned, had ceased to recognize any connection between "conforming" and "behaving" in school and achieving any very satisfying long-range goals. Consequently, they had adopted a "live for the moment," hedonistic philosophy that continually got them into trouble with the authorities (further evidence, perhaps, of the interrelationship between "negative identity," "work paralysis," and "diffusion of time perspective").

Sex differences in delinquency   "Making it" financially and in an occupational sense is, of course, a predominantly male concern— and so, as we have seen, is delinquency. Although there are claims that female delinquency is on the rise *(Coleman, 1972)*, teenage girls still have far fewer brushes with the law than teenage boys, and the crimes that girls engage in even when they do commit an illegal act are generally far less serious. "Running away" is one of the more common reasons that female adolescents come to the attention of the juvenile authorities, and "sexual delinquency" is another. (Sexual delinquency tends to be rather ill defined but presumably includes promiscuity, illegitimate pregnancy, and prostitution.)

It is logical to assume that these differences in the incidence and type of delinquency reflect the basic sex differences we have remarked elsewhere. Whether by genetic design, cultural training, or some still unfathomed combination of the two, boys tend to be more aggressive than girls. Boys are also freer to come and go as they please, less concerned with social approval, generally more adventurous—and hence perhaps indirectly given more opportunity to run afoul of the law than girls are. The forms that delinquency takes in boys and in girls may also reflect this basic dichotomy. For the boy, the kind of "toughness" that is expressed in stealing and vandalism (not to mention fighting with other boys) may be aimed at reassuring himself about his own masculinity and assertiveness.

There can likewise be no greater testimony to a girl's femininity than a pregnancy or a large number of lovers.

Probably because it is comparatively rare, there have been few systematic attempts to study delinquency in female adolescents. In his excellent review of the literature on juvenile law breaking, Short *(1966)* mentions the "weaker sex" only in passing—and then only to note that their court appearances are only one fifth to one fourth as numerous as those made by teenage boys. One of the better-known works *(Konopka, 1966)*, while interesting and basically sympathetic to the plight of the delinquent girl, is somewhat short on analysis. And, as Hatcher *(1972)* points out, a certain bias seems to infuse the entire subject. Those who study illegitimate pregnancy or prostitution during adolescence, she notes, seem intent on linking it with some variant of psychopathology.

Weiner *(1970)* agrees that neurotic conflicts may be responsible for the "sexual delinquency" of *some* adolescent girls, but he gives considerable weight to other factors as well. The girl who becomes pregnant out of wedlock, he implies, may simply be "experimenting" with a role suggested to her by a sister or a mother who did precisely the same thing. Or she may be goaded into sexual misbehavior by an openly seductive father or brother. At any rate, Weiner observes, such family patterns have been found to be quite common among illegitimately pregnant teenagers *(Gottschalk, 1964)*.

There are also data to indicate that what has been termed "sexual acting out" is, in part, a "premature" (by present cultural standards, at least) attempt to establish intimacy. In a large survey of unwed mothers, Pope *(1967)* discovered that most had dated the father of their child exclusively and had believed that their attachments were genuine love relationships. Hatcher *(1972)* reports a similar dynamic among at least part of her very small sample of unmarried pregnant girls. Thus it is possible that the motives of many "female delinquents" do not differ markedly from those of adolescent girls in general. Delinquents too may have their dreams of love and marriage. But for further insight into this problem—like so many other "female problems"—we must await future research.

Dropping Out, Underachievement, and Work Paralysis

Though neither as dramatic nor as headline-worthy as delinquency, the twin phenomena of "dropping out" and "underachieving" are equally serious. Indeed, considering the vast number of youngsters affected, these problems may be *more* serious. Lichter and his colleagues *(1962)* claim that 40 percent of all teenagers in the United States fail to complete high school, and while recent estimates *(World Almanac, 1974)* put the figure at a more palatable 20 percent, this is still a singularly dismal statistic for a nation that prides itself on its extensive mass educational system. It has been estimated that at least half these drop-outs are of average intelligence, surely a waste of talent. Even more troubling is the fact that the very youngsters who are most likely to leave high school, the "under-privileged," are the ones who would presumably benefit most from staying. It has also been suggested that the drop-out rate has a good deal to do with the alarmingly high rate of unemployment among teenagers (30 percent in some ghetto neighborhoods), and we can be sure that dropping out does nothing to deter delinquency. (We have already seen that lower-class delinquents are likely to do comparatively poorly in school, leading us to suspect that a dispro-portionate number of them eventually leave without graduating.)

Mere physical presence in the classroom, of course, does not ensure that a youngster will actually learn anything. In our earlier comparison of "high-achieving" and "underachieving" adolescents, we detected some symptoms of "work paralysis" and "negative self-concept" in those who were unable to make the most of their talents (see Chapter 9). A more extensive review of the research on underachievement and dropping out only confirms this initial diagnosis. In a study which compared equally bright boys and girls in grades 10 and 12, Pierce and Bowman *(1960)* found that those who were working up to capacity valued the concepts of *school*, *work*, and *imagination* significantly more than did those who were not. Similarly, Hathaway and Monachesi *(1963)* report that when they asked a sample of male and female drop-outs why they had left school, many more cited sheer "lack of interest" than "low grades."

To be sure, *some* drop-outs probably do not have the ability to master the increasingly demanding curriculum of the high school. Combs and Cooley *(1968)*, for example, found that teenagers who had left school were more likely to score in the lowest quartile of an aptitude test than those continuing on to graduation. For many others, however, underachievers and drop-outs alike, emotional factors appear to take precedence.

In gaining perspective on the problem, it would be well to recall Erikson's claim that "work paralysis" during adolescence may arise from the failure to develop a firm "sense of industry" during middle childhood. There are, in fact, findings that support this supposition. Shaw and McCuen *(1960)* compared a group of "bright, achieving" and "underachieving" male adolescents and discovered that those who were unable to capitalize on their abilities had been poorer students since first grade. (They found a similar pattern upon comparing two groups of girls, but, significantly, it did not begin to show up until considerably later—in sixth grade.) Furthermore, once pegged as a poor student, a child has a tendency to go from bad to worse. In the Shaw and McCuen study, the records of the underachievers declined progressively the farther they went in school. And research by Marcus (1966) indicates that youngsters like these apparently find themselves trapped in a kind of vicious circle. His sample of bright twelve to fourteen year olds exhibited a variety of learning difficulties. As they tried to advance, their poor preparation made it increasingly arduous for them to learn. Such failures led to an increasingly negative assessment of themselves as students, which in turn made them less and less inclined to apply themselves.

What is it that contributes to the youngster's initial sense of inferiority? What is it that undermines his abilities in the first place? There are, no doubt, a number of possible determinants.

Sources of underachieving First, as already noted in our discussion of vocational development (see Chapter 9), an adolescent's aspirations tend to bear some relationship to his own socioeconomic status. If his parents are unskilled, unemployed, or uneducated, he may find it difficult to "rise above" them. And indeed, Bledsoe (1959) has observed that adolescents from such families do drop out of school in disproportionate numbers. Why this should be the case is not entirely clear—especially since uneducated parents often subscribe to the view that their youngsters ought to continue with their schooling in order to have "a better chance." Perhaps, as Jencks (1973) has recently suggested, such families are unable to create the proper climate for learning. Perhaps they simply provide poor models for scholarship during the long years when the child is purportedly trying to master the "tools of the technology." We have already reviewed research, of course, that suggests that middle-class parents manage more successfully to instill the homely virtues of the Protestant ethic in their children (see the discussions of "time perspective" and "achievement motivation" in Chapter 9). But whatever the reason, the relationship between socioeconomic class and dropping out persists.

However, we do not want to create the impression that middle-class adolescents are completely exempt from learning difficulties. Far from it. While middle-class families may be generally more effective in encouraging good scholarship and "orderly work habits," not all do so by any means. Morrow and Wilson (1961) furnish some particularly interesting data in this connection. In their study, a group of upper-class, middle-class, and lower-class underachievers were matched with a high-achieving group. The researchers discovered that regardless of social class, the overall morale and atmosphere of the family appeared to be better for high achievers. Significantly more often than their underachieving classmates, the boys (the subjects were all ninth graders and all male) who were doing well in school

(a) described their families as typically sharing recreation, ideas, and confidences; (b) described their parents as approving and trusting (the areas of sharpest difference between the two groups), affectionate, encouraging (but not pressuring) with respect to achievement, and relatively nonrestrictive and nonsevere; and (c) described themselves as accepting their parents' standards. *(Morrow & Wilson, 1961, p. 508)*

Cervantes *(1965)* reports similar findings. In a study that matched lower- and middle-class high school drop-outs with students who had remained in school, he observed that the drop-outs were considerably more likely to complain that their families did not understand them, did not encourage them, rarely took an interest in them, and on the whole spent very little time with them.

Indeed, more clinically oriented research has revealed that a family may display all the outward trappings of success and still be teeming with undercurrents that discourage competition. Sperry and his colleagues *(1958)* found that fathers of boys who were being treated for learning disabilities tended to regard themselves as failures, even though many of them were well established professionally. Grunebaum and his colleagues *(1962)* furnish us with comparable impressions, again from a clinical population. Striking an Oedipal theme, they concluded that fathers of underachieving boys, even those who appeared to have distinguished themselves, tended to view their sons as actual competitors for their wives' support and admiration. Consequently, they attempted unconsciously to discourage their sons from amounting to anything. We should point out that Erikson strikes precisely the same sort of Oedipal theme in his own discussion of work paralysis *(see pp. 284–285)*.

And Weiner *(1970)* confirms Erikson's observations about the impact of "morbidly ambitious" parents. Some of the most affluent underachievers, Weiner theorizes, may consider failure the only viable means of self-expression. Such youngsters often have parents who are extremely successful and socially prominent. They expect their children to get the "best grades" at the very "best schools," associating at all times with the very "best people." Thus coerced, these teenagers sometimes rebel, not directly or openly, but effectively nonetheless. In class after class and school after school, they manage to frustrate their families by quietly flunking out. The following case history is singularly instructive in this respect:

Paul, a bright 14-year-old boy from a successful and socially prominent family was about to be dismissed from boarding school because of his dismal academic record. His father, who had attended the same school and had gone on to an élite preparatory school and a distinguished university, had long planned that his son would follow in his footsteps. Discussions with Paul and his father revealed that his father was an emotionally cold, authoritarian figure who demanded outstanding accomplishment and absolute obedience from his son. Paul rankled under his father's constant criticism and lack of overt affection but—although he was active and assertive with his mother, sister, and peers—the prospect of ever raising his voice against, or disagreeing with, his father was out of the question for him ("I'd just get clobbered"). When in the course of exploring Paul's scholastic debacle the therapist suggested that this seemed to be the one area in which he could exert some control over his father, Paul smiled broadly, fully the Cheshire cat: "You said it; there's not a darn thing he can do about it; when he got the call from the headmaster he hit the ceiling, but he can't do a thing about it!" (Weiner, 1970, p. 268)

This youngster's desire to assert his own individuality—even at the risk of being branded a "failure"—is all too evident.

Intellectual factors in underachievement   However, although we have stressed the psychodynamic and socioeconomic aspects of underachievement, we cannot ignore the role of intellectual factors. As noted, a certain percentage of high school drop-outs are actually below average in intelligence and hence are not "underachievers" in the usual sense of the word. However, a large proportion of drop-outs *are*. These adolescents are of at least average intelligence but lack a number of critical skills, a lack that becomes increasingly frustrating and damaging as the years go by. Voss and his colleagues (1966) note that many potentially capable drop-outs are "poor readers." In elementary school, where their deficiency is not as great a handicap, they can manage to struggle through. However, in high school, where greater amounts of reading are required and course work is more demanding, they become discouraged. And as they become progressively disheartened, their skills (as we have seen) decline farther and farther. In fact, there are experts who claim that it is the deficiencies themselves that produce the emotional disturbance often associated with underachievement rather than the reverse. Gates (1941), a pioneer in the area of reading disabilities, takes this position, and Eisenberg (1962) concurs. "Emotional disorder," he declares, "is almost invariably a consequence of the repeated frustration entailed in trying, but being unable to read" *(p. 5)*. It is undoubtedly possible that many teenagers, unable to master this very basic "tool of technology," decide that it is preferable simply to leave their embarrassment behind them.

Sex differences   As in almost every area we have examined thus far, there are the inevitable sex differences. As far as underachievement is concerned, however, they are especially interesting. For reasons that have been widely debated but are still unexplained, girls suffer fewer scholastic difficulties overall than boys do. More verbally facile than boys from early infancy *(Maccoby, 1966)*, they are *much* less likely to have problems with reading. Indeed, perhaps as a consequence of their superior verbal skills, girls generally outperform boys all through school—although there is some evidence that the boys have caught up and even begun to draw ahead by twelfth grade. In any case, whatever underachievement exists among girls tends, as noted *(see Shaw & McCuen, 1960)*, to show up later than it does in boys, and more girls actually manage to complete high school *(World Almanac, 1974)*.

Furthermore, the girls who do drop out before receiving a diploma, list somewhat different reasons than boys for doing so. Forty percent of the girls in one study *(Perrella & Bogan, 1968)* and 53 percent in another *(Hathaway & Monachesi, 1963)* gave "marriage" or "pregnancy" as their excuse for leaving school. To be sure, some of the boys in these two studies also gave the former reason (obviously none could cite the latter)—but far fewer of them. (Boys, as might be expected from the statistics on underachievement, were more likely than girls to list "grades" or "lack of interest.")

These figures probably provide us with insight into yet another notable sex difference. Despite their generally creditable performance in high school, fewer girls than boys enroll in college, and a smaller proportion still go on to graduate programs. Indeed, women earn approximately 43 percent of the bachelor's degrees in this country, 36 percent of the master's degrees and a surprisingly low 14 percent of the doctoral degrees *("Degrees Awarded in Various Fields," 1973)*. Part of the discrepancy can no doubt be accounted for by the fact that, until recently, most colleges retained higher standards for female than for male applicants (a practice that is now supposedly forbidden by law). But in this instance, as in so many others, we can probably hold "marriage" primarily responsible. Girls tend to marry earlier than boys *(Bayer, 1968)*, and as we already know, girls display a general tendency to be more preoccupied with the whole matter than boys *(Douvan & Adelson, 1966; Garrison, 1966; Pearsall, 1973)*. Finally, although attitudes may be changing to some extent in this regard, marriage is still considered an acceptable "career" for a woman. Hence, adolescent girls may view a college education as less "relevant" to their particular goals in life than boys do—and so may those who might be expected to furnish financial support. Parents may be more reluctant to send their female offspring to college precisely because "they'll just get married anyway" or "they don't need it." Nor can we ignore the role of emotional conflicts, such as the widely touted "fear of success" *(Horner, 1968, 1972)*, which is supposed to plague a large proportion of young women. Whatever their reasons, female adolescents constitute something of an "underachieving" group as far as college degrees are concerned. Many who apparently have the ability to continue their educations choose not to—or are unable to.

College drop-outs This chapter is also perhaps the place to discuss the subject of college drop-outs, who constitute a surprisingly large proportion of those admitted to institutions of higher learning. It has been estimated that about half of all male high school graduates (roughly 40 percent of the male population aged 18 and 19) enter college, but that a very substantial proportion—40–50 percent—leave without a degree *(Summerskill, 1962)*. Recently, it has become fashionable to interpret these statistics as evidence of widespread apathy and alienation among the young. However, an examination of the reasons college drop-outs cite for their departure reveals more prosaic factors as well.

College is generally considered more strenuous academically than high school, and as possible testimony to the difference in standards, many more college than high school drop-outs list low grades as a factor in their decision (33 percent versus approximately 12 percent). In fact, among *male* undergraduates this factor tends to be the most commonly stated excuse. (Among female undergraduates, as might have been anticipated, marriage carries off the honors.) Furthermore, several studies *(Freehill, 1954; Iffert, 1957; Mercer, 1943)* indicate that students who drop out of college tend to have earned lower grades in high school. Indeed, it is interesting to note that high school achievement appears to play an even larger role than social class in determining drop-out rates at the university level. Lower-class youngsters do withdraw from college in larger proportions than middle-class youngsters, but in a study in which high school grades were controlled *(Suddarth, 1957)* this difference washed out. In other words, lower-class adolescents who had performed well in high school were no more likely to leave without their degrees than middle-class adolescents who had distinguished themselves in high school.

To be sure, dissatisfaction with school (lack of interest, lack of motivation, etc.) is the second most commonly stated reason for leaving college, and drop-outs do not seem, in general, to be as "tuned in" to the system as those who remain. Iffert *(1957)* reports, for instance, that students who lack definite vocational plans are less likely to graduate than those who do. However, sheer lack of finances looms large as the third most frequently mentioned reason for withdrawing (one that may become even more prevalent in an era of tightening budgets). All in all, such concepts as "time confusion," "work paralysis," and "negative identity" seem less applicable to this more affluent and highly selected group.

Alienation and Negative Identity

Not that college students are necessarily immune to identity problems. No doubt some of those who leave without a degree do so neither for lack of ability nor lack of money but for "personal reasons." Indeed, such comparatively privileged and gifted drop-outs have probably received more than their share of publicity. Keniston *(1960)*, whom we have mentioned several times, drew his conclusions about "alienated youth in America" from a sample of bright, well-to-do undergraduates at Harvard, and his work has had a significant impact upon our assessment of the past decade's "younger generation." The students in Keniston's study, as may be recalled, seemed curiously unable to arrive at a coherent philosophy of life, and their lack of commitment in this area was accompanied by symptoms of what we would now readily recognize as "identity confusion"—inability to work, diffusion of time perspective, and emotional isolation.

When Keniston attempted to determine the source of their difficulties, he uncovered a pattern similar to the one that has been described for chronic underachievers. Although the fathers of these students were, by and large, eminently successful men, their children often described them as empty and disappointing failures. The following written characterization is typical: "My father has always been more or less disinterested, except when an important decision or some breach of discipline came up. Recently, he has tried to become more of a friend or 'Dad,' but I am too independent and unemotional, and the result is always a miserable failure" *(Keniston, 1960, p. 116)*.

Mothers emerged, on the other hand, as "frustrated" and subtly domineering women. Intelligent and talented, they were frequently portrayed as having "given up everything" to assume the role of wife and mother, thus having no recourse but to fulfill their blocked ambitions vicariously through their sons. Some of these sons sympathized with their predicament:

I have always been sentimental about my mother, and "Gee, isn't it a pity" and all that. See, she never went to college. She got supergood marks in school, but she didn't get the scholarship she wanted, and she didn't go to college at all. She just stayed home, and home was this little town in Pennsylvania. So you have the feeling she's always been cramped. . . . Then she had my father to contend with. *(Keniston, 1960, p. 111)*

Other youngsters were less impressed by their mothers' "sacrifices" and accused them outright of trying to run their lives: "Her only defect is that she refuses to face such realities or incongruities as drinking, sex, not getting married, majoring in psychology . . . and the like. Her careful watching over my career and my life in general has had little effect, much as water running off a duck's back" *(Keniston, 1960, p. 112)*.

Keniston did not actually observe any of these parents, and he admits the limitations of having to rely on the students' descriptions. Nonetheless, he was struck by the malignant elements in this typical family portrait. Confronted by fathers whom they did not admire nor wish to be like and mothers who had "given up" so much for them, these adolescents appeared to have nowhere to go. Conventional success seemed meaningless to them, but there was nothing to replace it, as is apparent in one youth's harsh and negativistic account of himself:

I was again elected class president, though by this time I recognized it as a farcical honor. I used to think that if my classmates knew what a despicable creature I was they would never consider me for honors. . . . Apparently my junior-year classmates were too stupid to realize what I was, for in the spring I was awarded a medal which said that I best typified the boy in my class who has the highest scholastic record, the best character(!) etc. . . . There are other (honors) of which I am absolutely ashamed— when I can stop laughing. *(Keniston, 1960, p. 128)*

But Keniston carried his analysis far beyond these particular undergraduates and their families. In a long and thoughtful exposition, he sought to comprehend the social context in which they had gone astray. As pathological and distorted as these homes might be, perhaps they reflected something basically wrong with American society. Perhaps it was inevitable for people to become "alienated" in a culture that demands that successful men isolate themselves in their careers and that successful women be exiled to the suburbs. It was reasonable to assume that some of the adolescents who had been exposed to such an "unreal" set of values might well find themselves with nothing to look forward to in life.

Keniston's analysis was, as we have remarked, searching and perceptive. Other writers, however, did not prove to be as temperate, and in the decade following the publication of *The Uncommitted* the term "alienation" was bandied about so freely that it became all but meaningless. Probably because it represented such a convenient variation on the time-honored theme of storm and stress, "alienation" was transformed into a new catchword for characterizing the youth of the 1960s and early 1970s. Adolescents were portrayed as turning against the "system" in droves, "dropping out" like Keniston's ivy league undergraduates, taking up residence in the hippie paradise of Haight-Ashbury, blowing their minds on drugs and acid rock, living together in sin, staging protests, and generally raising cain. All this behavior was viewed as a massive reaction against the core values of American society and even heralded by some as a revolution.

We do not deny that there was an unprecedented amount of "political activism" and "campus unrest" during this period nor that there were striking changes in dress and grooming. But what the social critics (and prophets of doom) failed to recognize was that any actual violence involved a small and highly visible fraction of the nation's adolescents. As Adelson *(1970)* has suggested, many commentators did not pay sufficient attention to the context and political climate in which such violence took place. Sure enough, as the turbulence has died down and conservatism come into vogue once more, the young have begun to regain something of the image which prevailed during the more placid 1950s. The current crop of college students—somewhat ironically, we think—is being described as serious, studious, and hard-working.

Unfortunately, the public "overkill" may have obscured an important point. It is unlikely that this decade's generation of adolescents is radically different from those of the previous one. While they may not receive much publicity, there are probably still many youngsters who, for one reason or another, cannot find a worthwhile niche in society. The dramatic and affluent young have generally received the most attention and sympathy in this regard, but there are no doubt youngsters at the other end of the scale whose plight, though less romantic, is just as poignant. Indeed, Erikson himself has remarked on the possible resemblance between the two groups: "The reason may be that their own gifts have not found contact with the productive aims of the machine age or that they themselves belong to a social class (here 'upper-upper' is remarkably equal to 'lower-lower') that does not partake of the stream of progress" *(1968, p. 185)*.

The black teenager   One of the most interesting studies in this connection is a piece of research by Hauser *(1972)*. Like Marcia's work *(1966)* on identity status, Hauser's investigation represents an attempt to apply Eriksonian theory directly. But rather than studying identity *status* in late adolescent and somewhat atypical college students, Hauser has attempted to examine identity formation *during* adolescence in a sample of lower-class white and black teenagers. (Since studies of lower-class youngsters *and* of black youngsters— with the exception of delinquents—are both quite rare, this research is all the more noteworthy.)

Hauser observed his subjects—22 black and white high school students, all male—over a period of four years, from the beginning of tenth grade until after graduation from high school. They were given in-depth interviews twice a year, and from these contacts the examiner extracted a number of self-descriptive statements for each subject. In a subsequent session, each was given a "deck" of cards containing all these self-characterizations and asked to rate them on a scale from 0 to 9 according to the following criteria: "How I am now; How I would be if I were a perfect son to my mother; How I will be in 10 years; How I am in the eyes of my friends," and so forth. If the subject thought that a particular statement did not correspond to him at all, he was instructed to score it "0"; if it fit perfectly, it was to be scored "9." At the end of the four year period, the self-ratings of the blacks and whites were compared.

In undertaking this comparison, Hauser had five possible "identity variants" in mind, all of which bear a certain similarity to Marcia's identity statuses *(Marcia, 1966)*. Hauser describes *progressive identity formation* as the "prototype for normal adolescence." A youngster who conforms to this pattern develops a view of himself that is increasingly well integrated and stable as he moves through his teens. *Identity diffusion*, on the other hand, occurs when there is a failure "to achieve the synthesis and continuity so essential to identity development" *(1972, p. 120)*. Instead of becoming increasingly well defined, the adolescent's image of himself becomes more and more fragmented with the passage of time. *Identity foreclosure* resembles progressive identity formation at first glance but actually represents an attempt to "dodge" the critical issues of adolescence by settling upon a particular self-definition prematurely. According to Hauser, foreclosure occurs when a youngster begins to characterize himself in a certain way relatively early in his teens and then simply holds onto this self-image throughout—despite the changes that are presumably taking place in his life. *Negative identity* is described as an especially unfortunate variant of foreclosure. Once again, the adolescent in question selects an identity prematurely, but in this case "he is committed to those roles and values which have always been presented to him as undesirable. His sense of identity is based on the repudiated and the scorned" *(p. 120)*. Finally, Hauser mentions the *psychosocial moratorium*. This variant is the opposite of identity foreclosure in that the youngster refuses for a time to make "any single commitment" or to adopt "any single direction." Preferring to leave matters unresolved for the moment, he tries out and experiments with a wide range of possibilities. The overall impression is one of "openness and change."

Having identified these variants, Hauser concluded that the predominant pattern among his white teenagers was *progressive identity formation*, while the blacks were characterized by *foreclosure* or *negative identity*. Sadly, it was all too easy to perceive the reasons for such a disparity in the actual interviews. The world of the black adolescents, as they described it, contrasted sharply with that of their white classmates:

To begin with, there were those limitations daily imposed upon them. They spoke of racial restrictions placed on part-time jobs, parties and dates, recreation opportunities and housing.

Potential work opportunities were also laden with difficulties. Few positions seemed to exist for the blacks where recognition or advancement were possible. Except for the armed forces, the black adolescent envisioned a future of dull, distasteful work. Someday, if all went well, he imagined becoming "boss" of a neighborhood store.

A third set of determinants involved "heroes," those admired figures so important in adolescence. For the blacks, there were few men who were idealized in any way, few adult figures considered worthy of emulation. Most of the Negroes flatly stated that they had no heroes, no people they wish to resemble either now or in the future. But these same subjects readily listed numerous "antiheroes," men they wished never to resemble. They named bums, drunkards, gangsters, petty thieves, and often their father. Together or taken separately, these aspects of the environment generate individual constraints and devaluations. The thrust of these degrading experiences is toward self-limitation and ever-diminishing self-esteem, two issues frequently discussed by the black adolescents in their twice-yearly interviews. *(Hauser, 1972, pp. 124–125)*

Hauser is careful not to generalize his findings to *all* black adolescents (it should be noted in addition that his sample was extremely small), but his research does suggest the constriction and limitation of identity that can occur in youngsters who are forced out of the mainstream of their culture—for whatever reason. No doubt these black teenagers felt just as thwarted in their attempts to achieve a healthy sense of individuality as did Keniston's "alienated" undergraduates.

Overview

Indeed, all the research on adolescent problems that has been viewed thus far might be said to converge on a single point. In this chapter, the darker side of the identity crisis has become evident. We have seen that in some youngsters the heightened sense of individuality and the awareness of approaching adulthood prove too burdensome. What they perceive in the mirror of this new consciousness is too unattractive or too confused to form the basis for a secure identity. Whatever the reason—a severely deprived childhood, a long history of academic failure, a chaotic family situation that offers little hope of any future love or comfort, a crushing lack of opportunity, or a background that has offered them everything but a genuine set of values—they cannot look forward to adulthood. And when the past and present cannot be integrated with the future or when the future promises to be only a dreary extension of the past, some teenagers break down into mental illness and others "drop out," some seek escape in drugs and others become what they would least like to be, some refuse to make any choices at all and others choose simply not to be. We doubt that they constitute a majority, but they are a troubling and tragic minority.

REFERENCES

ADELSON, J. What Generation Gap? *New York Times Magazine*, January 18, 1970, pp. 10ff.

ANNESLEY, P. T. Psychiatric Illness in Adolescence: Presentation and Prognosis. *Journal of Mental Science*, 1961, **107**, 268–278.

BALL, J. C., ROSS, A., & SIMPSON, A. Incidence and Estimated Prevalence of Recorded Delinquency in a Metropolitan Area. *American Sociological Review*, 1964, **29**, 90–93.

BALSER, B. H., & MASTERSON, J. F. Suicide in Adolescents. *American Journal of Psychiatry*, 1959, **166**, 400–404.

BANDURA, A., & WALTERS, R. H. *Adolescent Aggression*. New York: Ronald, 1959.

BAYER, A. E. Early Dating and Early Marriage. *Journal of Marriage and the Family*, 1968, **30**, 628–632.

BENDER, L. Drug Addiction in Adolescence. *Comprehensive Psychiatry*, 1963, **4**, 131–134.

BLEDSOE, J. C. An Investigation of Six Correlates of Student Withdrawal from High School. *Journal of Educational Research*, 1959, **53**, 3–6.

BLUMENTHAL, M., & GLICKMAN, L. Ten Months Experience with LSD Users Admitted to a County Psychiatric Receiving Hospital. *New York State Journal of Medicine*, 1967, **67**, 1849–1855.

BOGG, R. A., SMITH, R. G., & RUSSELL, S. D. Some Sociological and Social-Psychological Correlates of Marijuana and Alcohol by Michigan High School Students. Paper presented at the Ohio Valley Sociological Society and the Midwest Sociological Society Joint Meeting, Indianapolis, Indiana, May 2, 1969.

BRAUCHT, G. N., BRAKARSH, D., FOLLINGSTAD, D., & BERRY, K. Deviant Drug Use in Adolescence. *Psychological Bulletin*, 1973, **79**, 92–106.

BRECHER, E. (Ed.). *Licit and Illicit Drugs: The Consumers Union Report.* Mount Vernon: Consumers' Union, 1972.

CARTER, A. B. Prognostic Factors of Adolescent Psychoses. *Journal of Mental Science*, 1942, **88**, 31–81.

CARTWRIGHT, D. S. Psychological Test Differences between Gang Boys and Others: Summary Prepared for Advisory Group Meeting, 1962. (Dittoed)

CERVANTES, L. F. Family Background, Primary Relationships, and the High School Drop-Out. *Journal of Marriage and the Family*, 1965, **27**, 218–223.

CHEIN, I. The Status of Sociological and Social Psychological Knowledge Concerning Narcotics. In *Narcotic Drug Addiction Problems.* Washington, D.C.: U.S. Department of Health, Education and Welfare, 1959.

CLOWARD, R. A., & OHLIN, L. E. *Delinquency and Opportunity: A Theory of Delinquent Gangs.* New York: Free Press, 1960.

COHEN, A. K. *Delinquent Boys: The Culture of the Gang.* New York: Free Press, 1955.

COLEMAN, J. *Abnormal Psychology and Modern Life.* (4th ed.) Glenview, Ill.: Scott, Foresman, 1972.

COMBS, J., & COOLEY, W. Dropouts: In High School and After School. *American Educational Research Journal,* 1968, **5**, 343–363.

DAVIS, G. Prevalence Figures, Adjustment, Personal Characteristics, and Parental Antecedents with the Illicit Use of Drugs. Unpublished master's thesis, University of Connecticut, 1970.

DEGREES AWARDED IN VARIOUS FIELDS. *Chronicle of Higher Education,* 1973, **8**, 8.

DOUVAN, E., & ADELSON, J. *The Adolescent Experience.* New York: Wiley, 1966.

EISENBERG, L. Introduction. In J. Money (Ed.), *Reading Disability: Progress and Research Needs in Dyslexia.* Baltimore: Johns Hopkins Press, 1962. Pp. 3–8.

EMPEY, L. T. Delinquency Theory and Recent Research. *Journal of Research in Crime and Delinquency,* 1967, **4**, 28–42.

ERIKSON, E. Identity and the Life Cycle. *Psychological Issues,* 1959, **1**, 1–171.

ERIKSON, E. *Identity: Youth and Crisis.* New York: Norton, 1968.

FEDERAL BUREAU OF INVESTIGATION. *Crime in the United States: Uniform Crime Reports—1964.* Washington, D.C.: U.S. Department of Justice, 1965.

FREEDMAN, J., & RIVERA, R. Education, Social Class, and Patterns of Delinquency. Paper read at the American Sociological Association, St. Louis, August 1962.

FREEHILL, M. F. The Co-operative English Test in Academic Counseling. *Colleges and Universities,* 1954, **29**, 244–252.

GARRISON, K. C. A Study of the Aspirations and Concerns of Ninth-Grade Pupils from the Pupil Schools of Georgia. *Journal of Social Psychology,* 1966, **69**, 245–252.

GATES, A. I. The Role of Personality Maladjustment in Reading Disability. *Journal of Genetic Psychology*, 1941, **59**, 77–83.

GLASER, D. Social Disorganization and Delinquent Sub-Cultures. In H. C. Quay (Ed.), *Juvenile Delinquency: Research and Theory.* New York: Van Nostrand Reinhold, 1965.

GLUECK, S., & GLUECK, E. *Physique and Delinquency.* New York: Harper & Row, 1956.

GOETHALS, G., & KLOS, D. *Experiencing Youth.* Boston: Little, Brown, 1970.

GOLD, M. *Status Forces in Delinquent Boys.* Ann Arbor: University of Michigan Institute of Social Research, 1963.

GOLD, M., & WILLIAMS, J. R. The Effect of "Getting Caught": Apprehension of the Juvenile Offender as a Cause of Subsequent Delinquencies. *Prospectus: A Journal of Law Reform,* 1969, **3**, 1–38.

GORDON, R. Social Level, Social Disability, and Gang Interaction. (Mimeographed) 1965.

GORDON, R., SHORT, J., CARTWRIGHT, D., & STRODTBECK, F. Values and Gang Delinquency: A Study of Street-Corner Groups. *American Journal of Sociology,* 1963, **69**, 109–128.

GOTTSCHALK, L. A., TITCHENER, J. L., PIKER, H. N., & STEWART, S. S. Psychological Factors Associated with Pregnancy in Adolescent Girls: A Preliminary Report. *Journal of Nervous and Mental Disease,* 1964, **138**, 524–534.

GOULD, R. E. Suicide Problems in Children and Adolescents. *American Journal of Psychotherapy,* 1965, **19**, 228–246.

GRUNEBAUM, M. G., HURWITZ, I., PRENTICE, N. M., & SPERRY, B. M. Fathers of Sons with Primary Neurotic Learning Inhibitions. *American Journal of Orthopsychiatry,* 1962, **32**, 462–472.

GUSFIELD, J. The Structural Context of College Drinking. In G. L. Maddox (Ed.), *The Domesticated Drug: Drinking Among Collegians.* New Haven: College and University Press, 1970.

HANEY, B., & GOLD, M. The Juvenile Delinquent Nobody Knows. *Psychology Today,* 1973, **7**, 48–55.

HATCHER, S. M. The Adolescent Experience of Pregnancy and Abortion: A Developmental Analysis. Unpublished doctoral dissertation, University of Michigan, 1972.

HATHAWAY, S. R., & MONACHESI, E. D. *Adolescent Personality and Behavior.* Minneapolis: University of Minnesota Press, 1963.

HAUSER, S. T. Black and White Identity Formation: Aspects and Perspectives. *Journal of Youth and Adolescence,* 1972, **1**, 113–130.

HEKIMAN, L. J., & GERSHON, S. Characteristics of Drug Abusers Admitted to a Psychiatric Hospital. *Journal of the American Medical Association,* 1968, **205**, 125–130.

THE HEROIN PLAGUE: WHAT CAN BE DONE? *Newsweek,* July 5, 1971, pp. 27–32.

HORNER, M. Sex Differences in Achievement Motivation and Performance in Competitive and Non-Competitive Situations. Unpublished doctoral dissertation, University of Michigan, 1968.

HORNER, M. Toward An Understanding of Achievement-Related Conflicts in Women. *Journal of Social Issues,* 1972, **28**, 157–175.

IFFERT, R. E. Retention and Withdrawal of College Students. *U.S. Department of Health, Education and Welfare Bulletin,* 1958, No. 1.

JACOBINZER, H. Attempted Suicides in Adolescence. *Journal of the American Medical Association,* 1965, **191**, 7–11.

JACOBINZER, H. Attempted Suicides in Children. *Journal of Pediatrics,* 1960, **56**, 519–525.

328   **Adolescence and Individuality**

JACOBS, J. *Adolescent Suicide*. New York: Wiley, 1971.

JACOBS, J., & TEICHER, J. D. Broken Homes and Social Isolation in Attempted Suicides of Adolescents. *International Journal of Social Psychiatry*, 1967, **13**, 139–149.

JENCKS, C. Inequality in Retrospect. *Harvard Educational Review*, 1973, **43**, 138–164.

JESSOR, R., CARMAN, R., & GROSSMAN, P. Expectations of New Satisfaction and Drinking Patterns of College Students. *Quarterly Journal of Studies on Alcohol*, 1968, **29**, 101–116.

JESSOR, R., COLLINS, M. I., & JESSOR, S. L. On Becoming a Drinker: Social-Psychological Aspects of an Adolescent Transition. *Annals of the New York Academy of Sciences*, 1972, **197**, 199–213.

JOHNSON, A. Juvenile Delinquency. In S. Arieti (Ed.), *The American Handbook of Psychiatry*. Vol. I. New York: Basic Books, 1959.

JOHNSTON, L. *Drugs and American Youth*. Ann Arbor: Institute for Social Research, 1973.

JONES, M. C. Personality Antecedents and Correlates of Drinking Patterns in Women. *Journal of Consulting and Clinical Psychology*, 1971, **36**, 61–69.

JONES, M. C. Personality Correlates and Antecedents of Drinking Patterns in Adult Males. *Journal of Consulting and Clinical Psychology*, 1968, **32**, 2–12.

KENISTON, K. *The Uncommitted: Alienated Youth in American Society*. New York: Delta, 1960.

KONOPKA, G. *The Adolescent Girl in Conflict*. Englewood Cliffs, N.J.: Prentice-Hall, 1966.

LICHTER, S. O., RAPIEN, E. B., SIEBERT, F. M., & SLANSKY, M. *The Drop-Outs: A Treatment Study of Intellectually Capable Students Who Drop Out of High School*. New York: Free Press, 1962.

MACCOBY, E. (Ed.). *The Development of Sex Differences*. Stanford: Stanford University Press, 1966.

MACKAY, J. Clinical Observations on Adolescent Problem Drinkers. *Quarterly Journal of Studies on Alcohol*, 1961, **22**, 124–134.

MADDOX, G. L. Drinking Prior to College. In G. Maddox (Ed.), *The Domesticated Drug: Drinking Among Collegians*. New Haven: College and University Press, 1970.

MARCIA, J. E. Development and Validation of Ego Identity Status. *Journal of Personality and Social Psychology*, 1966, **3**, 551–558.

MARCUS, I. M. Family Interaction in Adolescents with Learning Difficulties. *Adolescence*, 1966, **1**, 261–271.

MARWELL, G. Adolescent Powerlessness and Delinquent Behavior. *Social Problems*, 1966, **14**, 35–47.

MASTERSON, J. F. Prognosis in Adolescent Disorders—Schizophrenia. *Journal of Nervous and Mental Disease*, 1956, **124**, 219–232.

MASTERSON, J. F. *The Psychiatric Dilemma of Adolescence*. Boston: Little, Brown, 1967a.

MASTERSON, J. F. The Symptomatic Adolescent Five Years Later: He Didn't Grow Out of It. *American Journal of Psychiatry*, 1967b, **123**, 1338–1345.

MASTERSON, J. F., CORRIGAN, E. M., KOFKIN, M. L., & WALLENSTEIN, H. G. The Symptomatic Adolescent: Comparing Patients with Controls. Paper presented to the American Orthopsychiatric Association, 1966.

MASTERSON, J. F., & WASHBURNE, A. The Symptomatic Adolescent: Psychiatric Illness or Adolescent Turmoil? *American Journal of Psychiatry*, 1966, **122**, 1240–1248.

MERCER, M. Personal Factors in College Adjustment. *Journal of Educational Research*, 1943, **36**, 561–568.

MERTON, R. K. *Social Theory and Social Structure*. (Rev. ed.) New York: Free Press, 1957.

MILLER, W. B. Lower Class Culture as a Generating Milieu of Gang Delinquency. *Journal of Social Issues*, 1958, **14**, 5–19.

MONGE, R. Developmental Trends in Factors of Adolescent Self-Concept. *Developmental Psychology*, 1973, **8**, 382–393.

MORROW, W. R., & WILSON, R. C. Family Relations of Bright High-Achieving and Under-Achieving High School Boys. *Child Development*, 1961, **32**, 501–510.

NYSWANDER, M. *The Drug Addict as a Patient*. New York: Grune & Stratton, 1956.

OFFER, D. *The Psychological World of the Teenager*. New York: Basic Books, 1969.

OFFER, D., SABSHIN, M., & MARCUS, D. Clinical Evaluation of Normal Adolescents. *American Journal of Psychiatry*, 1965, **121**, 846–872.

PEARSALL, P. Personal communication, 1973.

PERRELLA, V. C., & BOGAN, F. A. Out of School Youth—Part 1. In A. E. Winder and D. L. Angus (Eds.), *Adolescence: Contemporary Studies*. New York: American Book, 1968. Pp. 243–254.

PIERCE, J. V., & BOWMAN, P. H. Motivation Patterns of Superior High School Students. The Gifted Student. *U.S. Department of Health, Education and Welfare, Cooperative Research Monograph*, 1960, No. 2.

PLATT, A. M. *The Child Savers: The Invention of Delinquency*. Chicago: University of Chicago Press, 1969.

POPE, H. Unwed Mothers and Their Sex Partners. *Journal of Marriage and the Family*, 1967, **29**, 555–567.

SCHNEER, H. I., & KAY, P. The Suicidal Adolescent. In S. Lorand and H. I. Schneer (Eds.), *Adolescents: Psychoanalytic Approach to Problems and Therapy*. New York: Hoebner, 1961.

SELLIN, T., & WOLFGANG, M. E. *The Measurement of Delinquency*. New York: Wiley, 1964.

SHAW, M. C., & McCUEN, J. T. The Onset of Academic Underachievement in Bright Children. *Journal of Educational Psychology*, 1960, **51**, 103–108.

SHORT, J. F. Gang Delinquency and Anomie. In M. Clinard (Ed.), *Anomie and Deviant Behavior*. New York: Free Press, 1964.

SHORT, J. F. Juvenile Delinquency: The Socio-Cultural Context. In L. W. Hoffman and M. L. Hoffman (Eds.), *Review of Child Developmental Research*. Vol. II. New York: Russell Sage, 1966.

SHORT, J. F., RIVERA, R. J., & MARSHALL, H. Adult-Adolescent Relations and Gang Delinquency. *Pacific Sociology Review*, 1964, **7**, 59–65.

SHORT, J. F., & STRODTBECK, F. L. *Group Process and Gang Delinquency*. Chicago: University of Chicago Press, 1965.

SMART, R. G., & FEIER, D. Illicit Drug Users: Their Social Backgrounds, Drug Use, and Psychopathology. *Journal of Health and Social Behavior*, 1969, **10**, 297–308.

SPERRY, B. M., STAVER, N., REINER, B. S., & ULRICH, D. Renunciation and Denial in Learning Difficulties. *American Journal of Orthopsychiatry*, 1958, **28**, 98–111.

STINCHCOMBE, A. L. *Rebellion in a High School*. Chicago: Quadrangle, 1964.

SUCHMAN, E. A. The "Hang-Loose" Ethic and the Spirit of Drug Use. (1968) In D. Rogers (Ed.), *Issues in Adolescent Psychology*. New York: Appleton, 1970. Pp. 369–379.

SUDDARTH, B. M. Factors Influencing the Successful Graduation of Freshmen Who Enroll at Purdue University. (Mimeographed) Progress Report No. 1, November 1956; Progress Report No. 21, April 1957, Purdue University.

SUMMERSKILL, J. Dropouts from College. In N. Sanford (Ed.), *The American College: A Psychological and Social Interpretation of Higher Learning.* New York: Wiley, 1962.

VAILLANT, G. E. Parent-Child Cultural Disparity and Drug Addiction. *The Journal of Nervous and Mental Disease*, 1966, **142**, 534–539.

VITAL STATISTICS OF THE UNITED STATES, 1965. Vol. II. *Mortality.* Washington, D.C.: U.S. Department of Health, Education and Welfare, 1967.

VOSS, H. L., WENDLING, A., & ELLIOTT, D. S. Some Types of High School Dropouts. *The Journal of Educational Research*, 1966, **49**, 363–368.

WARREN, W. A. A Study of Adolescent Psychiatric In-Patients and the Outcome Six or More Years Later: II. The Follow-Up Study. *Journal of Child Psychology and Psychiatry*, 1965, **6**, 141–160.

WEIL, A. *The Natural Mind.* Boston: Houghton Mifflin, 1973.

WEINER, I. *Psychological Disturbance in Adolescence.* New York: Wiley, 1970.

THE 1974 WORLD ALMANAC. New York: Doubleday, 1974.

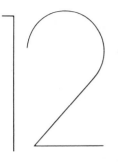

Conclusion: The Recurring Problem of Feminine Identity

In drawing to a conclusion, we may begin (and end) with a few words about the title of this book: *Adolescence and Individuality.* It was chosen because it seems to embody the essentially distinctive feature of adolescence. Only in his teens, as his intellect and body mature and as society entrusts him with greater autonomy, does the youngster truly become aware of himself—of his past and of his future, of his capabilities and of his liabilities, of his responsibilities and of his opportunities. Here is our conception of adolescence, and as is no doubt evident by now, it owes a great deal to Erik Erikson.

Review of Basic Points

In his blending of psychoanalytic and interpersonal themes, Erikson recalls Freud and Sullivan, and in emphasizing the "individualistic" aspects and evolutionary significance of adolescence, his thinking resembles Hall. Indeed, we can now appreciate how very much ahead of his time Hall was when he observed: "In adolescence, individuation is suddenly augmented and begins to sense its limits and its gradual subordination to the race which the Fates prescribe" *(1904, II, 58)* and "for those prophetic souls interested in the future of our race and desirous of advancing it, the field of adolescence is

the quarry in which they must seek to find both goals and means"
(1904, I, 50).

However, we have argued in addition that Erikson furnishes a
much more workable model of adolescent development than any of
these other theorists. By insisting that adolescence was "inevitably"
a period of storm and stress, whatever the specific cause, Hall, Freud,
and Sullivan all led us into an irreconcilable confrontation with the
actual data on the subject. Erikson's concept of "normative crisis"
can accommodate "the facts," (i.e., that though adolescence may
be stressful for *some* teenagers, it is not unusually so for all—or
even for most). And it also seems more reasonable to wish a
"moratorium" on teenagers than to demand that they undergo severe
"adolescent turmoil."

Finally, having dispensed with the broader issues, we have tried
to demonstrate that Erikson's theory can be employed as a "conceptual umbrella" for much of the research on adolescence. His
account of the adolescent identity crisis (exceedingly complex, as
we have seen) pinpoints many of the significant changes that do,
in fact, take place during adolescence—changes in time perspective,
self-concept, vocational orientation, and values. Similarly, although
they may be somewhat ambiguous (see Weiner's criticisms in
Chapter 11), the concepts of "identity confusion," "foreclosure," and
"negative identity" can be used to illuminate the darker side of
adolescence—delinquency, dropping out, drugs, alienation, and
suicide.

Indeed, we have observed attempts to apply the theory directly:
Hauser's work *(1972)* on "identity variants" and Marcia's research
(1966) on "identity status," for example. Hauser's findings indicate
that when a youngster lacks sufficient opportunities in life and
heroes, a "foreclosed" or "negative identity" is likely to result.
Similarly, Marcia has discovered that adolescents who appear to
have undergone a true identity crisis and moratorium also seem to
be better balanced psychologically.

The Recurring Problem of Feminine Identity

But there is a sizable "catch" in all of this, and the research
generated by Erikson's theory has only made it more obvious.
Hauser's study was limited to *male* adolescents, and so were
Marcia's initial efforts. The attempt to extend "identity status" research to *female* adolescents has been less successful *(Josselson,
1972, 1973; Marcia & Friedman, 1970; Schenkel & Marcia, 1972)* or, at
the very least, more confusing. In one study *(Marcia & Friedman,*

1970), girls who had foreclosed on an identity turned out to be the highest in self-esteem. In another study, a group of "Achievements" carried off most of the honors when compared with female "Foreclosures," "Diffusions," and "Moratoriums" *(Schenkel & Marcia, 1972)*. And in yet a third, *(Josselson, 1972, 1973)*, there were *no* notable differences among the four statuses.

These inconsistencies may, of course, be methodological in origin. In psychology it is notoriously difficult to find measurements and tests that will hold up between one study and the next. However, since the research on men has, on the whole, seemed more coherent, we suspect that there may be a more fundamental reason as well. Marcia hints—and we are inclined to agree with him—that Eriksonian theory has its limitations as far as women are concerned *(see Marcia & Friedman, 1970)*. Like the other theorists we have reviewed, Erikson is ultimately tripped up to a degree by the mysteries of feminine development.

The "identity-crisis model" works very nicely for male teenagers. In addition to the research of Marcia *(1966)* and Hauser *(1972)*, we have seen that the male youngster's view of the future typically becomes more differentiated and that his occupational plans become more realistic with increasing age. We have also seen that boys who are most strongly identified with the "masculine" role tend to be the most self-assured. The same, however, cannot be said of girls. On the contrary, we have observed that the girl's orientation to the future remains somewhat vague during adolescence, that her vocational plans often fail to crystallize, and that "highly feminine" girls are not necessarily higher in self-esteem than "nonfeminine" ones. And we could list many other disparities between male and female development that might create difficulties for Eriksonian theory.

Such difficulties arise, in our opinion, because the model itself is a somewhat "masculine" one. With the possible exception of "sexual polarization versus bisexual confusion," almost all the part conflicts of the identity crisis have a decidedly masculine ring to them—"temporal *perspective* versus time confusion," "role *experimentation* versus role fixation," "*apprenticeship* versus work paralysis," "*leadership and followership* versus authority confusion," "ideological *commitment* versus confusion of values," "*self-certainty* versus self-consciousness." What these conflicts all seem to point toward is issues that *men* must confront in adulthood—what plans to formulate, which roles to play, which work to pursue, what niche to occupy in society, and so forth. Although some boys may have greater opportunities than others, the decisions are still, in a sense, theirs to make. However, as all the data on the "double standard" indicate, adulthood is a much more ambiguous proposition for the girl. She will arrive at such decisions "on her own" almost by default if she does not marry. If she does marry, ironically, many of these choices will be made *for* her, or, at the very least, she will always have someone else to take into account.[1]

Erikson's Account of Identity Formation in Women

Erikson himself seems to have recognized that the normative crisis during adolescence that he describes applies somewhat better to males than to females. Indeed, we are already familiar with his attempt to describe two kinds of "initiative" in early childhood (see Chapter 7), and some years after he had proffered his initial thoughts on identity formation *(1950, 1959)*, Erikson composed an essay on women *(1964)*, which is included near the end of his most recent book on adolescence *(1968)*.

In this essay, he appears to be aware of the girl's special problems. Although she may achieve some sense of identity before marrying, he declares, the man whom she manages to attract will most likely impart the finishing touches:

Young women often ask whether they can "have an identity" before they know whom they will marry and for whom they will make a home. Granted that something in the young woman's identity must keep itself open for the peculiarities of the man to be joined and of the children to be brought up, I think that much of a young woman's identity is already defined in her kind of attractiveness and in the selective nature of her search for the man (or men) by whom she wishes to be sought. This, of course, is only the psychosexual aspect of her identity, and she may go far in *postponing its closure* while training herself as a worker and a citizen and while developing as a person within the role possibilities of her time. *(1968, p. 283)*

Yet we detect in this passage a suggestion that it is somehow fitting and proper for a young woman's identity to remain a bit ambiguous and tentative prior to marriage. Marrying and having children, after all, constitute the greater portion of her contribution to society—or at least so Erikson implies in the following series of rhetorical questions:

But how does the identity formation of women differ by dint of the fact that their somatic design harbors an "inner space" destined to bear the offspring of chosen men and, with it, a biological, psychological, and ethical commitment to take care of human infancy? Is not the disposition

---

[1] We do not mean to imply that men never take their wives or sweethearts into account when making occupational plans. However, traditionally even career women have tended to defer to men in this respect.

for this commitment (whether it be combined with a career, and even whether or not it be realized in actual motherhood) the core problem of female fidelity? *(1968, p. 266)*

And much of Erikson's argument ultimately boils down to matters of biology and anatomy. He notes that there is a definite parallel between the "ground plan" of the female body and the personality characteristics women are noted for—and the same, of course, applies to men. In fact, Erikson insists, he was first struck by this correspondence in the course of conducting a study on preadolescent children. He had asked his subjects, a group of normal boys and girls who were participating in a larger, longitudinal research project, to construct an "exciting movie scene." A wide variety of toys—building blocks, trucks, cars, dolls—were furnished for this purpose. Although it had not been his intention originally to study sex differences, Erikson claims that these differences turned out to be so striking that they could not be ignored. For two-thirds of the boys, the play constructions took on a "masculine" configuration; for two-thirds of the girls, the configuration was "feminine." Boys typically built *protruding* structures—towers, cones, cylinders, cannons—and arranged for most of the action to take place *outside.* Any movement that occurred was likely to be vigorous—and even violent—in character. (Automobile accidents were, for instance, a rather commonly fantasied event.) The scenes the girls envisioned were far more placid and peaceful—quiet domestic interiors in which families calmly went about their business. Whatever activity there was tended to take place *inside,* and if anything thrilling happened, it was generally caused by someone (e.g., a dangerous man) or something (e.g., a wild animal) *intruding* upon the sanctity of the home. (Erikson reports that most of these intrusions were greeted with "humor" or "pleasurable excitement.")

In short, the differences between the boys' and girls' scenes were reminiscent of differences in their anatomy. For Erikson, this was not simply an interesting coincidence. Rather, it implied a definite causal relationship between anatomical "ground plan" and "experiential mode." The fact that a boy has a "protruding phallus," he concluded, profoundly influences the way in which he relates to the world—and the same can be said of the girl's "creative inner space."

Erikson hastens to assure us that anatomy is not the sole determinant of destiny:

The emphasis here is on predisposition and predilection, rather than on exclusive ability, for both sexes (if otherwise matched in maturation and intelligence) learn readily to imitate the spatial mode of the other sex.

Nothing in our interpretation, then, is meant to claim that either sex is doomed to one spatial mode or another; rather, it is suggested that in contexts which are not imitative or competitive these modes "come more naturally" for natural reasons which must claim our interest. *(1968, p. 273)*

But he also brushes aside the suggestion that the differences he observed could have been brought about entirely by "cultural conditioning" and sex-role training:

A pure interpretation in terms of social role leaves many questions unanswered. If the boys thought primarily of their present or anticipated roles, why, for example, is the policeman their favorite toy, traffic stopped dead a frequent scene? If vigorous activity outdoors is a determinant of boys' scenes, why did they not arrange any sports fields on the play tables? (One tomboyish girl did.) Why did the girls' love for home life not result in an increase in high walls and closed doors as guarantors of intimacy and security? And could the role of playing the piano in the bosom of their families really be considered representative of what these girls (some of them passionate horseback riders and all future automobile drivers) wanted to do most, or indeed, thought they should pretend they wanted to do most? *(1968, p. 272)*

Thus, all in all, Erikson's account of feminine development retains strong, biological overtones. He claims, in fact, that many of the characteristics that little girls display so early in childhood anticipate the reproductive service they will render to the human species:

It makes sense, then, that the little girl, the future bearer of ova and of maternal powers, tends to survive her birth more surely and turns out to be a tougher creature, to be plagued, to be sure, by many small ailments, but more resistant to man-killing diseases (for example, of the heart) and with a longer life expectancy. It also makes sense that she is able earlier than boys to concentrate on details in immediate time and space and has throughout a finer discrimination for things seen, touched, and heard. More easily touched and touchable, however, she is said also to recover faster, ready to react again and elsewhere. That all of this is essential to the "biological" task of reacting to the differential needs of others, especially weaker ones, is not an unreasonable interpretation; nor should it, in this context, seem a deplorable inequality that in the employment of larger muscles woman shows less vigor, speed, and co-ordination. The little girl learns to be more easily content within a limited circle of activities and shows less resistance to control and less impulsiveness of the kind that later leads boys and men to "delinquency." *(1968, p. 281)*

This theme becomes all the more apparent when Erikson turns his attention to the female adolescent. He admits that she is likely to be engaged in a variety of activities that have nothing in particular to do with her future role as a wife and mother. But he explicitly labels such pastimes "masculine" or "phallic-ambulatory," and the "creative inner space" that she harbors always manages to make its way into the picture:

> . . . woman's life too contains an adolescent stage which I have come to call a psychosocial moratorium, a sanctioned period of delay of adult functioning. The maturing girl and young woman, in contrast to the little girl and the mature woman, can thus be relatively freer of the tyranny of the inner space. In fact, she may venture into "outer space" with a bearing and a curiosity which often appears hermaphroditic if not outright "masculine." A special ambulatory dimension is thus added to the inventory of her spatial behavior, which many societies counteract with special rules of virginal restraint. Where the mores permit, however, the young girl tries out a variety of possible identifications with the phallic-ambulatory male even as she experiments with the experience of being his counterpart and principal attraction—a seeming contradiction which will eventually be transformed into a polarity and a sexual and personal style. *In all this, the inner space remains central to subjective experience but is overtly manifested only in persistent and selective attractiveness, for whether the young woman draws others to herself with magnetic inwardness, with challenging outwardness, or with a dramatic alternation of both, she selectively invites what seeks her.* (1968, pp. 282–283, italics added)

And Erikson seems to believe that even this sort of experimentation must eventually cease if a woman is to become a truly fulfilled adult: "A true moratorium must have a term and a conclusion: womanhood arrives when attractiveness and experience have succeeded in selecting what is to be admitted to the welcome of the inner space 'for keeps' " (1968, p. 283).

It should be noted that Erikson does not intend to limit women to the domestic *Kinder, Küche, Kirche* role they have played from time immemorial. On the contrary, he admits that technology—ostensibly the product of "phallic" and "aggressive" men—has brought the world to the very brink of disaster. Once they begin to participate in this technology more fully, women could succeed in easing some of the inevitable strains that men incur as they struggle to compete:

> It is as yet unpredictable what the tasks and roles, opportunities and job specifications will be once women are not merely adapted to male jobs in economics and politics but learn to adapt jobs to themselves. Such a revolutionary reappraisal may even lead to the insight that jobs now called masculine force men, too, into inhuman adjustments. (1968, p. 290)

Such participation, Erikson suggests, may even be necessary to avert catastrophe. But his blueprint for a changing female identity remains curiously shadowy, and his concluding remarks on the subject retain an air of uncertainty. Women should have a direct share in planning for the future, but it is by no means clear *what* share:

> My main point is that where confinements are broken, women may yet be expected to cultivate the implications of what is biologically and anatomically given. She may, in new areas of activity, balance man's indiscriminate endeavor to perfect his dominion over the outer spaces of national and technological expansion (at the cost of hazarding the annihilation of the species) with the determination to emphasize such varieties of caring and caretaking as would take responsibility for each individual child born in a planned humanity. There will be many difficulties in a new joint adjustment of the sexes to changing conditions, but they do not justify prejudices which keep half of mankind from participating in planning and decision making, especially at a time when the other half, by its competitive escalation and acceleration of technological progress, has brought us and our children to the gigantic brink on which we live, with all our affluence. . . .
>
> We may well hope, therefore, that there is something in women's creativity which has waited only for a clarification of her relationship to masculinity (including her own) in order to assume her share of leadership in those fateful human affairs which so far have been left entirely in the hands of gifted and driven men, and often of men whose genius of leadership has eventually yielded to ruthless self-aggrandizement. *(1968, pp. 292–293)*

And there is, throughout Erikson's essay, the assumption that "competition" is fundamentally (and even biologically) "masculine," whereas "care and nurturance" are basically "feminine." Women have nothing to gain, he implies, from openly challenging men:

> . . . since a woman is never not-a-woman, she can see her long-range goals only in those modes of activity which include and integrate her natural dispositions. A truly emancipated woman, I should think, would refuse to accept comparisons with more "active" male proclivities as a measure of her equivalence, even when, or precisely when, it has become quite clear that she can match man's performance and competence in most spheres of achievement. True equality can only mean the right to be uniquely creative. *(1968, pp. 290–291)*

A Critique of Erikson's Account

We cannot help but be struck by the extraordinary similarity between Erikson's views on womanhood and those of G. Stanley Hall.

Hall, too, as may be recalled, attributed the feminine capacity for mothering to biology:

. . . woman's body and soul are made for maternity and she can never find true repose without it. The more we know of the contents of the young woman's mind the more clearly we see that everything conscious or unconscious in it points to this as the true goal of the way of life. Even if she does not realize it, her whole nature demands first of all children to love, who depend on her for care, and perhaps a little less, a man whom she heartily respects and trusts to strengthen and perhaps protect her in discharging this function. *(1904, II, 610)*

And he was also rather optimistic, though vague, about the position women would eventually assume in society:

Now that woman has by general consent attained the right to the best that man has, she must seek a training that fits her own nature as well or better. So long as she strives to be manlike she will be inferior and a pinchbeck imitation, but she must develop a new sphere that shall be like the rich field of cloth of gold for the best instincts of her nature. *(1904, II, 617)*

We do not mean to imply that Erikson's efforts to fathom feminine development should be dismissed as outmoded or "sexist." Much of the data on sex differences are, as a matter of fact, entirely consistent with his account. Research already suggests that adolescent girls are more enthralled with the prospect of marriage than boys are—and that they thus permit their future plans to remain more "nebulous" and "tentative" than boys do. We have also observed that girls are, on the whole, more "sympathetic" and "socially oriented" than boys—as well as being more "dependent" and "passive."

There is, besides, an awesome array of data to suggest that boys and girls do organize and categorize experience somewhat differently. In their extensive reviews of the literature, Maccoby *(1966)* and Garai and Scheinfeld *(1968)* cite a host of studies that have shown boys to be more "analytic" and girls to be more "verbal." The old saw that boys perform better in mathematics and science and girls in languages and literature is definitely substantiated by research. Even more compelling is the fact that such differences begin to appear rather early in life. Female infants begin to speak, on the average, earlier than male infants, and later on in childhood girls learn to read more readily than boys *(Garai & Scheinfeld, 1968; Maccoby, 1966)*. On the other hand, even in nursery school, boys are likely to persist longer than girls in trying to solve difficult problems and to be less "rattled" by failure *(Crandall & Rabson, 1960; Moriarty, 1961)*. But almost all sex differences—even those involving size and strength—are relative rather than absolute. There are individual girls who excel in math and auto mechanics; there are individual boys who are fluent in languages and proficient at typing.

Furthermore, what actually *causes* the differences that exist (other than the strictly anatomical ones, of course) remains very much at issue. Although he admits that they may be reinforced by experience, Erikson seems to assume that such differences are biological in origin, and he is joined in this opinion by a number of eminent researchers *(Garai & Scheinfeld, 1968; Sherman, 1971)*. On the other hand, there are equally eminent psychologists *(Hoffman, 1972; Lynn, 1962; Maccoby, 1966)* who appear to believe that learning and experience may be the principal factors. At the very least, Hoffman insists, in our present state of knowledge it is impossible to determine how much is "learned" and how much is "innate." Boys are, she concedes, more "active" than girls almost from birth, but there is evidence that they are treated differently almost from birth as well. There are studies that indicate that parents talk more to female infants *(Goldberg & Lewis, 1969; Kagan, 1969; Moss, 1967)* and that they roughhouse more with male infants *(Moss, 1967)*. There are numerous others *(Block, 1973; Collard, 1964; Kagan & Moss, 1962; Komarovsky, 1950)* that suggest that boys are specifically *encouraged* to become more "aggressive and autonomous" and girls more "passive and dependent."

It is even possible to take a middle-of-the-road position on the entire issue. Bardwick *(1971)* has argued, for example, that boys are probably innately more aggressive and active than girls. However, she adds, societies very likely capitalize on such differences, tolerating and reinforcing aggression, with all its accouterments, in boys and discouraging and suppressing it in girls.

Obviously the controversy over sex differences cannot be settled here once and for all—and it is possible that the question will never be settled. It may be that the little girl's genes are largely responsible for her image of "sugar and spice." It is also feasible that experience rather than biology constitutes the more critical influence. The recipe for femininity (and masculinity) may even require equal parts "nature" and "nurture."

In our opinion, however, Erikson's strongly biological orientation on this particular issue creates a problem for his theory as a whole. In the final analysis, his stand appears somewhat inconsistent. Adolescence is envisioned as the period during which a "conscious sense of individual uniqueness" emerges, and hence it is also a period in which a number of significant choices are supposed to be made. But Erikson implies that a girl's "creative inner space" exercises a certain "tyranny" over her in this regard, simply because she is never not a girl. No matter what her individual talents may be, the more or less standardized role of wife and mother always intrudes its way into the picture. Thus she may have to defer many of the decisions that boys typically confront and resolve—life goals, occupation, ideological commitments—or at least to approach them in a gingerly and tentative manner.

It would follow that the girl's "psychosocial moratorium" is likely to be less adventurous and free-wheeling than that of the boy. (Actually, the statistics on delinquency already attest to this difference.) But since Erikson declares that the freedom to experiment during adolescence contributes very substantially to a firm sense of identity, it would also follow that her sense of individuality is not as highly developed. The necessity of "pulling her punches" and remaining "ladylike" in her pursuits may restrict her opportunities for self-discovery.

Certainly, the data we have reviewed provide some support for this hypothesis. In addition to being less "achievement-oriented" and more uncertain about their future plans, adolescent girls are, as we have seen, generally less sure of themselves than boys, more anxious, and more convinced of. their own incompetence. They are also considerably less likely to be afforded the advantages of a college education—despite their rather creditable performance in high school. These differences are, of course, relative, and it would be hazardous to push the point too far. Nonetheless, there is an aura of "negative identity"—or at the very least "foreclosure" or "diffusion"—that hovers over the research on feminine development.

Furthermore, when we recall Erikson's pronouncement that the growing child's sense of security is intimately bound up with his mother's own sense of self-worth, such findings give us pause. We seriously wonder if girls who believe themselves to be "inferior" to boys, who have less opportunity to become educated and perhaps less opportunity as well to experiment and "find themselves," are actually the best candidates for bringing up children. Is this really the sort of training to wish upon the "future mothers of America"?

In addition, Erikson's essay on womanhood appears to gloss over the fact that a substantial number of women (in this country at any rate) are *already* active participants in the economy. According to the *1974 World Almanac*, women constitute almost 40 percent of the total work force in the United States. There is, in fact, an entire class of occupations—teacher, nurse, secretary, filing clerk—that have come to be defined as "feminine." So, whether or not they plan or are prepared for it, a large number of adolescent girls will eventually enter the work force. Economic necessity (in the form of divorce, death, or an inadequate standard of living) may even compel them to. (Besides, we shudder to think what would happen to our "masculine" and technologically sophisticated society if all the occupants of so-called "feminine" jobs were suddenly to tender their resignations.)

Erikson could (and probably would) argue that the vocations we have cited are all yet another manifestation of the woman's capacity for nurturance and care, but even here objections may be raised. It has been suggested, ironically enough, that female teachers are to blame for the boy's relatively poor performance in elementary and junior high school. Critics argue that women, who are, of course, more numerous in the lower grades, are less tolerant of aggression and more prone to shower rewards on their "well-behaved" female pupils. There are also complaints that they fail to provide the "appropriate masculine models" for learning *(Garai & Scheinfeld, 1968)*. And Silberman *(1970)* contends that American teachers have traditionally received poor training precisely because their profession has been dismissed as "women's work."

Finally, what becomes of the "creative inner space" of women who have devoted themselves solely to raising their families? How are they to meet the Eriksonian crisis of "generativity versus stagnation" once their children are grown? And as a closely related problem, what about the increasing clamor for population control? Although societies are notoriously unpredictable in this regard, the falling birth rate in industrialized countries suggests that procreation is currently becoming a less popular pastime for many young adults. If the trend continues (and there are those who insist it must if the world is not to become fatally overcrowded), what implications will it have for feminine development? No doubt a certain proportion of women will always have to concern themselves with childbearing, but what if large numbers decide or are encouraged to make limited use of their reproductive capacities?

Indeed, we might ask about the implications for *masculine* development as well, implications that Erikson acknowledges only in passing. Although adolescent boys may have more opportunities to "test out" and more vocational options than girls, there are those who argue that sex-role stereotypes create special burdens for men as well *(Brenton, 1966)*. Men, they suggest, might benefit if they could be relieved of the "machismo" image—and feel less pressured to compete, succeed, and contain their emotions, not to mention assuming the responsibility for several "dependents." (Possibly they might live longer too.)

A Plea for Equality

In a recent article on sex-role conceptions, Block *(1973)* sums up the issues we have raised with admirable clarity. When it was necessary for men to go out foraging for food and women to stay home suckling children, the present dichotomy of "aggressive and active" versus "passive and nurturant" might have made eminent good sense:

The question for our times, however, is to what extent past socialization requirements must or should control current socialization emphases in our complex, technological, affluent society where, for example, physical strength is no longer especially important and where procreation is under some control. Under present conditions, and for the future, we might ask: What is necessary? What is "natural" in regard to sex typing? *(Block, 1973, p. 519)*

Furthermore, after reviewing the data on sex-role stereotypes, Block concludes, as we do, that adolescents of both sexes might find themselves enhanced if there were some degree of redefinition:

Extant socialization patterns appear to attenuate the human possibilities residing in the individual, whether male or female, and both a redefinition of conventional sex role and a revamping of socialization practices are required if our societal goal is to encourage individuation and personal maturity for our young. *(1973, p. 526)*

However, interestingly enough, Block also acknowledges a certain debt to Erikson. She declares: "I reject Freud's dictum that 'anatomy is destiny' and am in accord with Erikson *(1968)* that anatomy, history, and personality combine to form one's destiny" *(1973, p. 513)*. That is precisely what Erikson *does* proclaim, and in the very essay we have criticized *(Erikson, 1968, p. 285)*, but as is apparent, Block has drawn somewhat different conclusions from this formulation than Erikson himself has. Block recognizes that anatomy, history, and personality can be combined in some highly individualistic ways, and she advocates that young people be given more leeway to do so. Erikson (at least in our opinion) appears to be more reticent. He seems reluctant, in the final analysis, to grant the female adolescent the sort of free-wheeling psychosocial moratorium he has recommended for adolescents in general. Judging from his account, the girl must always carry out her transition from childhood to adulthood more circumspectly than the boy—and always mindful of her "creative inner space."

However it is *history* that may be more at issue here than anatomy. The moratorium is, after all, something of an ideal, and as far as adolescents are concerned, it is a relatively new one. Indeed, at the beginning of this book we argued that the concept of adolescence as a period of experimentation and self-exploration has won wide acceptance only in the twentieth century, that is, that this ideal is, in part, an invention of industrialized society, with its vast wealth and its mass educational systems. Even today, in areas where the young are forced to work at an early age and left largely untutored, the notion of an adolescent moratorium is no doubt much less meaningful. Self-knowledge of the sort that Erikson describes depends to a degree on leisure and opportunity.

We may also surmise that adolescents in our own country differ considerably in this respect. Although talent and intelligence play a part, the affluent youngster probably approaches the ideal of the moratorium more readily than the deprived one, the white adolescent more readily than the black adolescent, the male teenager more readily than the female teenager. Block's argument is especially germane here. Her conclusions seem to echo those of present-day civil rights and Women's Liberation spokesmen: that, insofar as *historical* conditions are responsible for restricting one class, race, or sex, such barriers should be removed and that, as much as possible, "equality of opportunity" ought to prevail. We can only concur, for our review of research on adolescence has indicated— particularly with regard to delinquents, blacks, and girls—that it does not prevail as yet. And this observation brings us to our final point.

Suggestions for Future Research

Almost every book, article, and doctoral dissertation in psychology ends with a call for "further research." If the truly definitive study were ever to be done in a particular area, it would, of course, put a large number of psychologists out of work. But in the field of adolescent development, the cliché has the ring of authenticity. To understand teenagers more fully, to comprehend their special capacities and problems, a great many studies will have to be carried out. We feel confident (and we believe we have demonstrated) that Erikson's comprehensive and intricate model of adolescence can provide a workable frame of reference for much of this research. Indeed, Hauser's work *(1972)* and that of Marcia and his associates

(1966) constitute important and interesting first steps. But there is much, much more to be done.

We have also referred frequently to the Douvan and Adelson survey *(1966)* and to Offer's longitudinal study *(1969)*. Both have proved to be extremely valuable pieces of research, but they are unfortunately somewhat out of date. Douvan and Adelson collected their data in the early 1950s; Offer interviewed his subjects in the early 1960s. Particularly in view of the changing historical conditions identified here, more research of this type is required. Indeed, what we would most like to see in the near future is a series of studies that *combine* the more clinical approach of Offer and Douvan and Adelson with the more stylized techniques of Hauser and Marcia.

In order to do justice to adolescent individuality, we have to do more intensive research, we have to study more aspects of identity formation, we have to find new ways of measuring phenomena like "self-certainty," "ideological commitment," and "sexual polarization." Finally, and most of all, we have to examine a broad spectrum of the nation's young: affluent youngsters, deprived youngsters, early adolescents, late adolescents, members of ethnic minorities, and, it goes without saying, female adolescents. Only in this way can we begin to grasp the full range of the adolescent experience and find a basis for further verifying or revising various aspects of the Eriksonian model.

Epilogue

In his short story, "Luca," Alberto Moravia describes an adolescent who could be cited as an almost classical case history of "identity confusion." The son of well-to-do and rather manipulative Italian parents, Luca finds himself in his sixteenth year almost overwhelmed by the many demands of adolescence. He has grown suddenly and feels exhausted, he is mysteriously troubled by sexual urges and begins an ill-fated flirtation with his cousins' governess, he finds his schoolwork a bore and realizes that his classmates consider him something of an outcast. But most of all, he despairs at the thought of becoming what his parents, and indeed the rest of the world, expect him to become: a hard-working and successful lawyer who will take over his father's practice and marry a girl from a "good family." And in his despair, he begins to rebel secretly against his parents, to fail in school, to starve himself, and ultimately to long for death. In his weakened condition, Luca almost succeeds in annihilating himself. He contracts pneumonia, develops a high fever, falls into a delirium, and is saved only by the ministrations of an affectionate and skillful nurse. But the crisis of his illness, Luca discovers, has somehow brought him face to face with himself. And as he regains his strength, he is able to establish the first truly intimate relationship of his life with his nurse.

Luca's tribulations are fictional, of course, and an exaggeration of the more normative adolescent crisis. We would not wish his suffering on any youngster, but we would retain as our "impossible dream" the hope that all adolescents might someday look forward to the future with the same degree of optimism and insight:

Luca closed his eyes. At that same moment the train, with a long and mournful whistle, plunged into a tunnel. When he opened his eyes again he saw nothing but darkness, while a damp wind blew in his face from the dark walls of the tunnel, mixed with a faint drizzle of water and puffs of steam. Echoing from the vault of the tunnel, the beat of the wheels sounded to him like a monotonous, exultant voice repeating the same words over and over again. He seemed to be able to distinguish these words—the same words, full of hope, that had borne him company ever since his awakening from the delirium, day by day during his slow recovery; and he knew that, from now onward, not only the clatter of a train in a tunnel or the whiteness of snow on a mountain peak, but all things would have a meaning for him and would speak to him in their own mute language. Then the train, with another whistle, came out into the light of day.

REFERENCES

BARDWICK, J. *The Psychology of Women.* New York: Harper & Row, 1971.

BLOCK, J. Conceptions of Sex-Role: Some Cross-Cultural and Longitudinal Perspectives. *American Psychologist*, 1973, **28**, 512–526.

BRENTON, M. *The American Male.* Greenwich, Conn.: Fawcett, 1966.

COLLARD, E. D. The Achievement Motive in the Four-Year-Old Child and Its Relationship to Achievement Expectancies of the Mother. Unpublished doctoral dissertation, University of Michigan, 1964.

CRANDALL, V. J., & RABSON, A. Children's Repetition Choices in an Intellectual Achievement Situation Following Success and Failure. *Journal of Genetic Psychology*, 1960, **97**, 161–168.

DOUVAN, E., & ADELSON, J. *The Adolescent Experience.* New York: Wiley, 1966.

ERIKSON, E. *Childhood and Society.* New York: Norton, 1950.

ERIKSON, E. Identity and the Life Cycle. *Psychological Issues*, 1959, **1**, 1–171.

ERIKSON, E. *Identity: Youth and Crisis.* New York: Norton, 1968.

ERIKSON, E. Inner and Outer Space: Reflections on Womanhood. In R. J. Lifton (Ed.), *The Woman in America.* Boston: Beacon, 1964.

GARAI, J. E., & SCHEINFELD, A. Sex Differences in Mental and Behavioral Traits. *Genetic Psychology Monographs*, 1968, **77**, 169–299.

GOLDBERG, S., & LEWIS, M. Play Behavior in the Year Old Infant: Early Sex Differences. *Child Development*, 1969, **40**, 21–31.

HALL, G. S. *Adolescence*. Vols. I–II. New York: Appleton, 1904.

HAUSER, S. Black and White Identity Development: Aspects and Perspectives. *Journal of Youth and Adolescence*, 1972, **1**, 113–130.

HOFFMAN, L. Early Childhood Experiences and Women's Achievement Motives. *Journal of Social Issues*, 1972, **28**, 129–155.

JOSSELSON, R. Identity Formation in College Women. Unpublished doctoral dissertation, University of Michigan, 1972.

JOSSELSON, R. Psychodynamic Aspects of Identity Formation in College Women. *Journal of Youth and Adolescence*, 1973, **1**, 3–52.

KAGAN, J. On the Meaning of Behavior: Illustrations from the Infant. *Child Development*, 1969, **40**, 1121–1134.

KAGAN, J., & MOSS, H. A. *Birth to Maturity*. New York: Wiley, 1962.

KOMAROVSKY, M. Functional Analysis of Sex Roles. *American Sociological Review*, 1950, **4**, 508–516.

LYNN, D. Sex Role and Parental Identification. *Child Development*, 1962, **33**, 555–564.

MACCOBY, E. (Ed.). *The Development of Sex Differences*. Stanford: Stanford University Press, 1966.

MARCIA, J. E. Development and Validation of Ego-Identity Status. *Journal of Personality and Social Psychology*, 1966, **3**, 551–558.

MARCIA, J. E., & FRIEDMAN, M. L. Ego Identity in College Women. *Journal of Personality*, 1970, **38**, 249–263.

MORAVIA, A. Luca. In *Two Adolescents*. New York: Bantam, 1950.

MORIARTY, A. Coping Patterns of Preschool Children in Response to Intelligence Test Demands. *Genetic Psychology Monographs*, 1961, **64**, 3–127.

MOSS, H. A. Sex, Age, and State as Determinants of Mother-Infant Interaction. *Merrill-Palmer Quarterly*, 1967, **13**, 19–36.

OFFER, D. *The Psychological World of the Teenager*. New York: Basic Books, 1969.

SCHENKEL, S., & MARCIA, J. E. Attitudes Toward Premarital Intercourse in Determining Ego Identity Status in College Women. *Journal of Personality*, 1972, **40**, 472–482.

SHERMAN, J. *On the Psychology of Women*. Springfield, Ill.: C. C Thomas, 1971.

SILBERMAN, C. *Crisis in the Classroom*. New York: Random House, 1970.

THE 1974 WORLD ALMANAC. New York: Doubleday, 1974.

Index